The Art of Theatrical Design

[*The Art of Theatrical Design*]… is one of the best, most comprehensive looks at theatrical design that I have come across. It is a perfect book for a beginning designer; chock full of new terms, information, exercises, examples, and illustrations.

-Craig Choma, Associate Professor of Theatre, Knox College

The Art of Theatrical Design: Elements of Visual Composition, Methods, and Practice addresses the core principles that develop the student designer into a true artist, providing a foundation that ensures success with each production design. This text concentrates on the skills necessary to create effective, evocative, and engaging theatrical designs that support the play contextually, thematically, and visually. It gives students the grounding in core design principles they need to approach design challenges and make design decisions in both assigned class projects and realized productions. This book features:

- In-depth discussions of design elements and principles for costume, set, lighting, sound, and projection designs
- Coverage of key concepts such as content, context, genre, style, play structure and format, and the demands and limitations of various theatrical spaces
- Essential principles, including collaboration, inspiration, conceptualization, script analysis, conducting effective research, building a visual library, developing an individual design process, and the role of the critique in collaboration
- Information on recent digital drawing tool technology, such as the Wacom® Inkling pen, Wacom® Intuos digitizing tablets and digital sketching, and rendering programs such as Autodesk® Sketchbook Pro and Adobe® Photoshop®
- Chapter exercises and key terms designed to provide an engaging experience with the material and to facilitate student understanding

Kaoime E. Malloy is an Associate Professor of Costume Design for the University of Wisconsin Green Bay Department of Theatre and Dance, where she teaches Costume Design, Stage Makeup, Costume Technology, Introduction to Theatre Design, Understanding the Arts, Fashion History, Costume Crafts, and special topics in design and technology. A member of United Scenic Artists Local 829 and IATSE, she freelances as a theatre designer, makeup artist, and technician throughout the United States.

The Art of Theatrical Design

Elements of Visual Composition, Methods, and Practice

Kaoime E. Malloy

Focal Press
Taylor & Francis Group

NEW YORK AND LONDON

First published 2015
by Focal Press
70 Blanchard Road, Suite 402, Burlington, MA 01803

and by Focal Press
2 Park Square, Milton Park, Abingdon, Oxon OX14 4RN

Focal Press is an imprint of the Taylor & Francis Group, an informa business

© 2015 Taylor & Francis

Library of Congress Cataloging in Publication Data application submitted.

ISBN: 978-1-138-02150-1 (pbk)
ISBN: 978-1-138-02149-5 (hbk)
ISBN: 978-1-315-77770-2 (ebk)

Typeset in GillSansStd-Light
By diacriTech, Chennai

Printed and bound in India by Replika Press Pvt. Ltd.

To my husband Patrick, who has always believed I could do anything, no matter what.

CONTENTS

PREFACE

When I was in graduate school, one of my professors—Dan Nemteanu, a visiting scene and costume designer from Sweden—told me something that made a big impression on me. In Europe, he said, all artists, regardless of the medium they will eventually choose to work in, receive the same basic training. Potential theatre designers and visual artists alike take the same classes, working side-by-side learning the same fundamental building blocks and essential visual concepts of design and the visual arts. Budding painters, sculptors, and theatrical designers work together, learning to draw, master perspective, render three-dimensional form in two-dimensional space, and to work in different media for their first two years of education. It is only after this fundamental instruction has taken place, when the elements and principles of design are understood and mastered, when basic drawing skills have been learned, that young artists begin to study the particulars of their intended fields and media. This had been the foundation of his education growing up in Europe, and it showed in every aspect of his work. Dan is more than a designer; he is an artist whose medium is theatre, a thing I think all of us who have been fortunate enough to study with him hope to be.

This method of training made perfect sense to me, because the basic building blocks of art are the same, regardless of media. Theatre designers use the elements and principles of design with every project, just as other visual artists do. Even sound designers use them. So I had to wonder why these concepts are so often pushed to the side in theatrical design education, or relegated to a relatively low status in terms of importance. It underscored a fundamental difference in my mind with regards to how theatre designers can be perceived in the larger artistic community. In Europe, we are *artists*. In the United States, we are *designers*. And our training reflects this elementary, yet important difference.

Like most student designers of my particular educational generation, my introduction to the elements and principles of design took place in a kind of "catch-all" class, one intended to serve several purposes at once, and to meet multiple educational goals. Although part of a conservatory program, my basic design course spent only a small portion of the allotted class time in one semester on exploring the elements and principles of design, in order to include instruction in several other topics such as hand drafting. In this class, the elements and principles came fast and furious, with little time to explore any of them in more than passing detail, and there was no time spent on teaching us how to draw. Looking back, this seems incredibly odd to me, given that drawing is the main language of communication between a designer, the director, and the rest of the production team. This was, of course, before computers became part of our daily lives and work practices as visual artists. But even though computers and drawing programs have changed the speed and sophistication levels at which ideas can be created and rendered visually, not to mention how quickly they can be shared over long distances, they have not changed this basic fact. Drawing is a necessary skill, but one that often seems to be neglected in beginning theatre design training.

In many university theatre programs, there are certain assumptions that are made about beginning design students—ones that might ultimately serve them as they make their way through our programs, doing their best to navigate through the challenges and pitfalls—and those that do not serve them as well in terms of their education. In fact, these assumptions might do them a fair amount of disservice when it comes to meeting educational goals. We often expect beginning design students to be able to engage in a costume, scene, makeup, or lighting design class (usually at an upper level) without ever having taken a substantive foundational course in design. We expect them to come to these classes ready and, more importantly, able to get down to the business of learning design right away without previous experience. But more often than not, beginning design students have no idea what that means. And, to further complicate the issue, students often immediately want "to do their own work" and start creating realized designs rather than the task at hand, without knowing what that really entails or having the tools to go about it. Or, they expect that the director will "tell them what they want," and then they will go off and somehow make that happen without truly engaging with them to create a collaborative design. Or worse, they look at the increasingly sophisticated—and admittedly *awesome*—equipment in our various inventories and immediately want to play with all the cool toys before they ever have any concept of how to use them to do what we as designers truly hope to do with our work: create a visual interpretation of the play that makes a connection with the audience and draws them into the experience of the performance.

Beginning designers need a firm understanding and control of the vocabulary of design in order to both design and communicate effectively. Often we as educators are forced to combine this material into an all-encompassing class that attempts to cover both design vocabulary and basic technical practices into one. At best, we may elect to send our students over to the Art Department "if they're interested in the elements and principles of design," where they will indeed gain experience in these fundamental building blocks of all design disciplines—but it will not be in a theatrical *context*, where these core elements and principles are continually related back to theatrical design. At the worst, we have to try and cover these concepts within another design class, losing precious time to basic principles when we want to give the students a deeper experience in a specific design area. The end result is an unsatisfactory experience for both the student and the instructor.

As an additional challenge, we may also put our students into a collaborative working situation on our productions without ever teaching them how to participate fully in this unique environment as an engaged and informed member of the design team who brings their own ideas and responses to the play to the discussion. Too often, beginning designers expect that the director will have all the answers; that they will

present a clear and firm idea of the direction the production should take, when in fact they may want to discover that path with the design team and the acting company. That is what collaboration is all about, and theatre is a collaborative art form. How can you collaborate if you don't know how?

This book grew out of necessity. When I began it several years ago, there were no introductory theatre design texts. Instead, I used foundational books written for art students rather than theatre students because only in art texts could I find the coverage and exploration of the design elements that mirrored the depth that I employed in my class. But I longed for a book that would include *all* the information that I covered, one that bridged the gap between art and theatre and served the needs of theatre students just as well as the art students were being served. Preferably, given the rising cost of textbooks, one that would be useful throughout their entire design education. And then, on a chance discussion about my desire for this nonexistent book, the book now in your hands began to take shape.

In graduate school at the University of Iowa, my peers and I used to refer to the way we were taught to approach plays, our art, our creative process, design, and the performance itself as "The Iowa Way." There, a unique group of exceptionally talented professors who were experts in the various aspects of our art form instilled us with a unique artistic aesthetic and method that we all carry with us to this day. This method still informs my creative process and continues to evolve and change as I grow as an artist. I now share that method with my students, and in this book, I now share it with you.

Kaoime E. Malloy
2014

ACKNOWLEDGMENTS

This book would not exist and I would not be able to write it without the support of many people who have helped me become the artist and person I am today and who have supported this book in one way or another.

I have wonderful colleagues at the University of Wisconsin Green Bay who supported this project by generously allowing me to use their work in the pages of this book. My thanks go out to my design colleagues, Jeffery P. Entwistle and R. Michael Ingraham and the directing colleagues that guide us in our creative endeavors, Laura Riddle and John Mariano. Your work is always inspiring in so many ways. A special thanks to Donna Entwistle who works tirelessly to help me bring my designs to life. Without you there would be no costumes on the stage.

To my Iowa colleagues who graciously donated images of their work to be used in the pages of this book, I cannot thank you enough. Pip Gordon, whose ability and creativity with light is unrivaled—no one paints with light like you do and I treasure every time we've worked together. Frank Ludwig, an amazingly talented set designer whose ability to sculpt space is exquisite. I am incredibly grateful for the depth of your generosity in contributing to this project.

I offer a great deal of thanks to Alison Ford. Not only is Alison an incredibly talented designer who donated images of her work to this book, she is also the first person that hired me to teach elements of design. Without her unwavering confidence and support I would never have found my way to teaching or written this book. Thank you for giving me a chance when I walked into your office.

Without the professors that taught and mentored me through my development as designer I would not be the theatre artist I am today. I am indebted to Linda Roethke, Dan Nemteanu, and David Thayer for sharing their knowledge with me, for shaping my design aesthetic, nurturing my creative process and teaching me the essential skills I needed to be an artist. Most of all, for the knowledge that the perceived division between art and theatre is an illusion. I am grateful to Eric Forsythe, who knows more about acting and performance than anyone I know and who continues to be one of my favorite directors. What I learned from you continues to inspire me and collaboration with you is always a pleasure.

My students are a continual source of inspiration that frequently amaze me with their creativity, ability and enthusiasm. Thank you for spending a little time in my classes. I hope you get as much from me as I get from all of you.

A special thanks to Stacy Walker, Meagan White, Victoria Chow, and the wonderful staff at Focal Press, who have been incredibly supportive of this book from the beginning. I couldn't wish for a better publisher.

To you, dear reader, I hope you find something within these pages to inspire you, to challenge you and make you hunger for more.

PART ONE

BEGINNINGS

CHAPTER 1

WHAT IS THEATRICAL DESIGN?

WHAT IS THEATRICAL DESIGN?

Theatrical design is the art of creating and composing the visual and aural elements that shape a performance space. It encompasses the development of scenery, costumes, lighting, sound, and multimedia effects to create pictures onstage. These elements combine to create an environment in which the action of the play can take place and where the audience can experience the performance. Design brings the world of the play to life.

Theatrical design is different from many other art forms in that it is a collaborative art. Design does not exist in a vacuum. No one theatre artist works independently to create a performance. Instead, a production is brought into existence through the combined efforts of many skilled and specialized artists working together, sharing a common conceptual approach. Unlike a novel, a play does not exist solely to be read; it is meant to be performed and its greatness and wonder can only truly be accessed in this manner. A play requires actors to embody each of the characters, to take on their personalities and behaviors and make them real for the audience as the story is told. Through the characters, the audience is able to make an emotional connection with the events, ideas, and themes of the play. The design anchors them in the world of the play, communicating information about that world to the audience that supports the dramatic action and draws them in, engaging them with the performance on a sensory level.

WHAT DO DESIGNERS DO?

A **theatrical designer** is an artist who creates and organizes one or more aspects of the aural and visual components of a theatrical production. Some designers specialize in one area of design—scenery, costumes, lighting, sound, multimedia/ projections, or hair and makeup—while others work in multiple areas. Regardless of their area of specialization, each designer is working towards the same goal: the successful realization of the playwright's vision on the stage. In order to do this work a designer needs to possess a wide range of skills. They need to be able to read and analyze a script effectively, not only to note the details that are relevant to their individual design area, but also to understand the story, identify key themes, plot details, and important actions, and to follow character development. They must be familiar with theatre history and literature and understand how they inform both the performance and visual style of a play. They must be familiar with the history of dress, art, and décor and be able to do appropriate research to inform and inspire their work. They must be imaginative and inventive, able to find inspiration and use it to develop creative conceptual approaches to the visual interpretation of the playwright's work. They have to be resourceful, innovative, and problem-solvers. Designers choose the visual and audio elements that go into the stage picture carefully, in order to shape, influence, and guide the audience's impression of the world of the play

Because theatre is a collaborative endeavor, designers must be good communicators in order to express their ideas and to work effectively with their colleagues. They must be organized and able to manage their time efficiently so that they can meet work deadlines. In order to communicate their design ideas to the director they must be able to draw and render with sufficient skill, whether through traditional or digital methods. Increasingly, designers are being asked to have a working knowledge of various computer software programs that are applicable to their design specialty, as design and technology become more closely linked. They need to have an understanding of the human form in three-dimensional space as well as the advantages and challenges inherent in different theatrical configurations. Drafting, painting, construction, sewing, patternmaking and draping, and mathematics are also skills that are needed to varying degrees.

Above all, designers need to be observers of the world. Like all artists, designers take in information from the world around them and use it to inspire and inform their work. They respond to and take note of the way other artists have used the visual elements of composition in their practice. Designers are avid visitors of museums, connoisseurs of the arts in all forms: fashion, painting, furniture, architecture, textiles, photography, literature, music, dance, theatre, and more. They are students of history and culture, curious about the influences that have shaped us as people, as individuals, and in communities the world over. Paying attention to both function and aesthetics, designers look to the world around them for the information and vision that inspires them to reveal and understand the action of a play in a visual form, making it accessible to an audience.

THE DESIGN AREAS

The **scenic designer** is responsible for the composition of the stage environment that the actors inhabit and for selecting all of the elements that make up the set, including platforms, levels, walls, and all structures whether they appear organic or manmade. Furniture, light fixtures, curtains, pillows, and interior décor are also part of their responsibility. Their work encompasses the design and selection all of the properties for the show, from items carried by the actors—such as letters, books, dishes, and luggage—to large articles like chests of gold, food, blackboards, or any other item required to facilitate the action. The set may be as simple as a bare stage or a complicated extravaganza with multiple locations, automated scene changes, and spectacular special effects. Both spaces require careful thought, design, planning, and creative choices.

The space that is created by the scene designer is more than a representation of the playwright's imagination. It is more than a house or a room, a palace or a park; more than the literal place it represents. It is a space that will shape and is in turned shaped by the actions of the actors that will inhabit it. It is responsive to the needs of the action in a way that an ordinary location is not. In short, it is designed to serve the needs of the play. It will help to establish location, time period, time of day, the tone and stylistic approach to the production, and communicate information about the characters that live in the space. It will present an overall design concept, image, or metaphor that supports the content of the play. The set must also be unified with the other design elements and address all the practical considerations involved with how the space will be used by the actors.

The **costume designer** is responsible for the visual realization of the characters. They interpret the playwright's words, using them to analyze each character and transpose that understanding into clothing that reveals their identity to the audience. Costume is an important tool that enriches and supports the actor's performance. Using the language of clothing to create a visual narrative, the costume designer seeks to produce evocative costumes that evolve over the course of the play to mirror the progression of the character. The choices made by the costume designer also reflect the overall conceptual approach to the production and, like the scenery, contribute to the mood and atmosphere of the performance. Color, pattern, texture, and weight of fabrics can all contribute to the director's approach.

Clothing reveals important information about each character. Social status, occupation, location, and time of year can easily be communicated through what an individual chooses to wear. Careful selection of fabrics, accessories, color, and level of wear and cleanliness can give insight into a character's mood, health, age, state of mind, and personality. How a garment is worn gives as much insight into character as what is being worn. A well-fitted dress made of light and diaphanous fabrics might speak to the vibrancy and happiness of a young ingénue falling in love for the first time, while an ill-fitting one made of dark, heavy fabrics might weave the tale of a widow mourning her husband's death and losing weight from the burden of her grief. A handsomely tailored suit can speak volumes about the man who wears it; but spill a few drops of blood on the lapels and his tie, or let a straight razor peek out from his pocket and the outfit takes on an entirely different meaning. Costumes can also be used to show the relationships between characters, subtly underscoring the connection between families, lovers, coworkers, classmates, or members of the same community. Choosing similar colors, textures, or silhouettes can create a sense of group identity, unifying a chorus of dancers or a crowd of bystanders, ensuring they are a part of the world of the play and that the audience can understand who they are.

The **lighting designer** is responsible for illuminating the stage space so that the actors and the environment may be seen. They are in charge of all forms of light on the stage. They select the number of instruments and their types. They set their intensity, location and angle, determining how the light that is being cast will strike the stage. They choose how to alter the appearance of the light cast on the stage, changing the color, the texture, and the pattern. They ensure that practical light fixtures that are part of the set will turn on and off as needed. The lighting designer composes the cues and determines how long each will last, setting the duration of light on the stage picture.

Part of this task is choosing what to reveal with light and what to conceal. Light focuses the audience's attention, drawing it to the important parts of the action and upping their emotional investment. Light has an incredible potential to create a sense of mood and atmosphere through the use of color, value, and selective lighting. By using all of the tools at their disposal, a lighting designer is able to paint the stage with light, modeling the scenery and the actors to enhance their three-dimensional form for greater visibility and to create compelling pictures that pull all the visual design elements together into a unified picture.

The **sound designer** is responsible for the design of all of the audio components for a production. Their work is varied, ranging from simple reinforcement of sound, allowing the actors and any musicians to be heard more clearly and succinctly, with a balanced composition of sound to the creation of a complete sound design that complements and enhances the production. Sound design can include the careful selection of preshow, intermission, and post-show music, to help set the mood and atmosphere, introducing the audience to the world of the play and maintaining continuity throughout their experience of the performance. It may also include any incidental music or underscoring to support the dramatic action. Sometimes, a sound designer might even compose all of the music for a production, tailoring it specifically for that play.

A sound designer is also responsible for all of the sound effects the script requires, whether they occur offstage or onstage or from motivated sources. Ringing telephones, doorbells, lightning, breaking glass, or elaborate sound compositions containing multiple effects may be used to create the desired result. Ambient sound may be incorporated as part of the design to help establish the location, time of day, the season, and to support the style and conceptual approach of the production. Although the sound designer is a relatively recent addition to the design team, more and more directors are realizing the potential of sound design and what it can contribute to a production in the hands of a creative designer.

The **projections designer** (also known as the multimedia designer) is an even more recent position in theatrical design. The projection designer is responsible for the design and creation of all images, moving and still, that will be projected onto the stage or into the theatrical space. There are multiple uses for projections in a production. They can be used for simple purposes, such as adding narrative announcements at the beginning of scenes to act as title cards or to add uncomplicated images to various scenes, complementing the action and illustrating it in a lively and engaging way. Or projections can be used to enhance the stage picture, providing high-resolution digital images that can be projected onto the surface of the scenery to alter its shape, change locations quickly, or even to take the place of scenery entirely. They can be projected throughout the auditorium to immerse the audience in the production environment or focused onto small surfaces carried by an actor as they move across the stage. Cameras placed strategically throughout the playing space can present multiple views of the action, projecting them onto the set to become part of the performance that actors can interact with. Projections have the potential to establish location and style, enhance the mood and atmosphere, reveal important story elements, aid the dramatic action, add in a new performance element, and support the overall design concept of the production. It is a new and exciting area of design.

THEATRICAL SPACES AND THEIR IMPACT ON DESIGN

One of the most important factors designers need to keep in mind when doing their work is the type of theatre being used for the production. The configuration of the theatrical space has a significant impact on all aspects of the production, shaping the performance. Costume details that can easily be seen in an intimate arena theatre will be lost in a large proscenium space. Light instrument positions that serve a proscenium theatre well may shine the light directly in the audience's eyes in a thrust space. Scenery designed for a proscenium theatre will block the sightlines of the audience in an arena theatre. A found space requires careful consideration regarding the placement of the audience and the acting space, whereas the audience location in most other theatre spaces is usually preset.

The type of space is important because a theatre is not just a place to view a performance. It is a place that supports the exchange of emotion between the actor and the audience and facilitates the communal experience of the performance between the audience members. There is no ideal shape or size for a performance space and no one configuration is better than another. Each type of theatre has advantages that can be used to the designers' benefit and limitations which might require that adjustments be made as part of the production process.

Proscenium Theatre

A **proscenium theatre** is the type of theatre we are most familiar with because it was the most common type of stage space in the eighteenth through the twentieth centuries in the Western world. In this configuration, the stage is situated at one end of the building, separated from the audience by the proscenium wall, a large rectangular opening that frames the stage. This type of theatre was developed to focus the attention of the audience through the opening of the proscenium, accentuating the perspective effects created by the painted scenery of the period. The playing space behind the proscenium may be deep or relatively shallow and is framed on either side by a set of wings that provide offstage space. Some of these theatres also have an apron or forestage situated in front of the arch, offering another playing area, and scenery may extend into this space from the main part of the stage. In modern proscenium theatres the apron may also be capable of lowering to the auditorium floor or beyond, doubling as an orchestra pit for musicals and concerts. This type of theatre usually has a fly loft above the stage, which allows for scenic elements to be flown in and out of the stage space. The seating area may be set up in any one of a number of configurations, often with orchestra seating on the auditorium floor, seating galleries on both sides and one or more floors of audience seating. The combination of the fly space and wings allows for a wide variety of scenic and lighting effects in a proscenium theatre and the stage itself might also offer additional options such as trapdoors and hydraulic systems that can be used to raise and lower the stage floor to add special dramatic effects and facilitate elaborate scene changes. Proscenium theatres often seat a large number of people, putting a fair amount of distance between the actors and the audience. Costumes, scenery, and makeup need to be bolder and broader in order to carry over the distance to communicate effectively to the audience. However, there is an obvious advantage created by the proscenium arch, which serves to focus the audience's attention on the action it frames.

Arena Theatre

An **arena theatre**, also referred to as theatre in the round, is a theatre where the audience entirely surrounds the

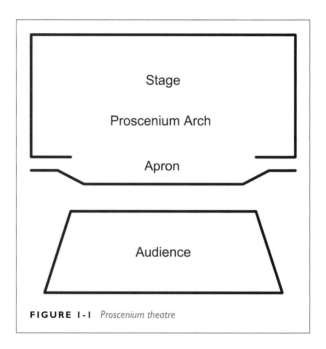

FIGURE 1-1 *Proscenium theatre*

performance space or acting area. Like a thrust space, actors enter and exit through a series of aisles or **vomitories** that are situated off the playing space. An arena theatre offers several advantages, including an increased intimacy between the actors and the audience and a wide range of entrances and exits. But it also offers challenges related to blocking, lighting, scenery, and sightlines. Because the audience is seated around the entire playing space, scenery cannot substantially block their view of the action and lights must be carefully focused so that they do not shine in their eyes or light the seating area, inadvertently drawing focus. Hanging scenic elements above the stage may be important to establish the environment, but might also add additional challenges to the lighting designer. Blocking must take into account the fact that the audience becomes part of the composition. Costumes in intimate theatres can require more detail and realism, especially with historical garments, because the audience is very close to the actors. Makeup can be especially challenging, as any ageing or special effects require film-level quality to be believable. As with a thrust space, the sound designer has multiple locations for sound sources and can create an entire environment with their design, but must carefully balance the sound output to ensure quality.

Thrust Theatre

In a **thrust theatre**, or three-quarter round, the stage extends out into the audience and the seating surrounds the playing area on three sides. Sometimes the thrust may be enclosed by a proscenium arch at the back of the stage, but this space is often shallow and the audience's view into the space is limited. Actors can enter and exit from behind the proscenium or through

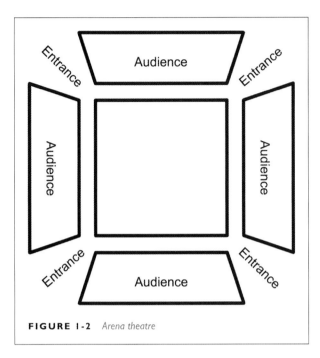

FIGURE 1-2   *Arena theatre*

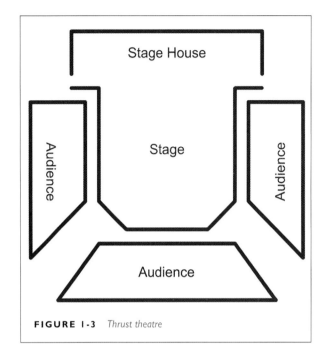

FIGURE 1-3   *Thrust theatre*

aisles or vomitories that are situated off the playing space and extend out through the audience.

A thrust theatre essentially offers a combination of a proscenium stage and an arena stage. This configuration allows for increased intimacy with the audience, giving them the opportunity to focus on greater details in costumes and the set. However, the playing space only provides one wall for vertical scenic elements along with the stage floor. All scenery in the stage space itself needs to maintain clear sightlines for the audience and must be designed carefully. Blocking is more difficult than on a proscenium stage, as the playing space offers multiple views that the director has to take into consideration and the spectators can be seen as well as the actors. Consequently, focus can become an issue. Lighting designers face the challenge of maintaining focus on the acting area without spilling light onto the audience, drawing attention away from the action or inadvertently shining light into their eyes. Sound designers have the potential to surround the audience with sound from multiple directions, but careful balance is required to ensure that everyone can hear equally.

End Stage

An **end stage** is a theatre in which the audience and the acting area occupy the same architectural space. Generally, the audience is seated in front of the playing space, but it is also possible to arrange the seating in other configurations to allow for a different stage space, such as thrust. The back wall of the stage may be framed with a proscenium arch allowing for a curtain and access to a small backstage area.

This type of theatre allows for flexible scenic elements that can take advantage of flexible stage configurations. Theatres in this format are usually small, allowing for a close connection between the actors and the audience, but may prove challenging for lighting positions and actor entrances and exits.

Black Box Theatre

A **black box theatre** is a flexible space made to provide multiple stage configurations. The space may not always be black, but it is shaped like a large, unembellished cube, hence

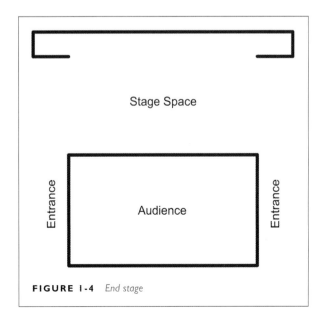

FIGURE 1-4   *End stage*

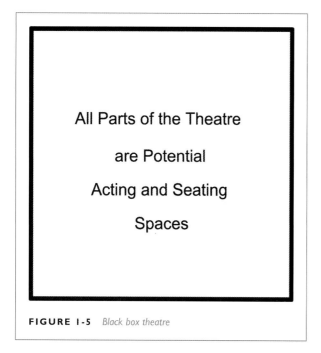

FIGURE 1-5 *Black box theatre*

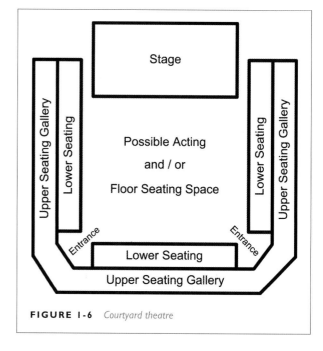

FIGURE 1-6 *Courtyard theatre*

the name. Seating in a black box theatre is by necessity moveable and unfixed, allowing the director and designers to set up any stage arrangement they desire, adjusting the seating as required. The possibilities are almost limitless. Technical galleries may also be provided in the stage architecture, offering additional lighting positions. The main advantage of a black box space is its flexibility and it offers few limitations.

Courtyard Theatre

A **courtyard theatre** combines the qualities of several different theatre types, and is modeled after a traditional Elizabethan stage. Seating is provided in elevated galleries that surround a central area, which may or may not have fixed seating. The entire audience area faces a proscenium stage. The central space is often flexible, allowing it to be used in a variety of configurations, including thrust, flat floor, and end stage. Courtyard theatres are not always rectangular. The Hall Two stage at the Gateshead is a ten-sided courtyard theatre. The flexibility of this type of theatre provides designers and directors with multiple options when it comes to the layout of the space and the elevated seating ensures that sightlines in the central playing area are less problematic. Entrances and exits can be made through the proscenium arch or vomitories in the audience space. Lighting positions are varied and malleable and the level of intimacy can be adjusted by reconfiguring the space. Use of the proscenium as the main acting area creates more distance between the audience and the actors and sightlines on the extreme side seating on the

galleries may be challenging for the scenic designer. All in all, a courtyard theatre is an interesting theatrical space that offers lots of possibilities.

Found Space

A **found space** is a nontheatrical building or location that is adapted and used for a performance. A found space can literally be anywhere, indoors or out. Some possibilities of found spaces include the foyer of an office building, an old grocery store, a park, churches, a warehouse, a street corner, or the steps outside a museum. Found spaces may sometimes be altered to suit the needs of a particular production, adding specific architectural elements to meet the needs of the individual production. Designers working in these types of theatrical spaces can face all the challenges of traditional theatres as well as others, including creating scenery around static building features, lighting around structural elements, and impaired sightlines created by unusual spaces. But a found space may offer unique advantages not available in a traditional theatre, such as unusual backgrounds and textures, interesting atmosphere, environmental sounds, and other elements that are complementary to the production.

Environmental Theatre

An **environmental theatre** is a theatrical space that has been completely transformed to create a unique environment for the performance. Often, the architecture of the space is a key element in the production. In an environmental theatre, the acting and audience spaces may be intermixed, sometimes with no provided seating. Performances are immersive, with shifting or multiple focuses and the physical space is an important production element, blurring the line between audience, performer, and space. Many productions are site specific. A good example of this is Punchdrunk's *Sleep No More*, a film noir, interactive retelling of *Macbeth* performed in three abandoned New York City warehouses, where the audience is asked to don Venetian carnival masks and move from room to room, following the characters they choose and exploring the environment as the play progresses. Environmental theatres serve up the opportunity to create complete, lush environments that completely immerse the audience in the world of the play, challenging the boundaries of theatre and redefining them within the context of the performance.

Like all art forms, theatre contains content. In the case of theatre, content takes the form of a dramatic script. Dramatic literature contains structure and format and can be divided into different genres and styles. Our understanding of plays, as with all art forms, is based on the content of the work and the context, both of the play itself and the personal context we bring to it. The following chapters will examine these important concepts and their importance for design.

THE LANGUAGE OF DESIGN AND THEATRICAL SPACE

Arena theatre: A theatre where the audience entirely surrounds the performance space. Also known as theatre in the round.

Black box theatre: A flexible theatre space made to provide multiple stage configurations.

Costume designer: The artist that is responsible for the visual realization of the characters through clothing.

Courtyard theatre: A theatre space that combines the qualities of several different theatre types, modeled after a traditional Elizabethan stage.

End stage: A theatre in which the audience and the acting area occupy the same architectural space.

Environmental theatre: A theatrical space that has been completely transformed to create a unique environment for the performance.

Found space: A nontheatrical building or location that is adapted and used for a performance.

Lighting designer: The artist that is responsible for illuminating the stage space so that the actors and the environment may be seen.

Projections designer: The artist that is responsible for the design and creation of all images, moving and still, that will be projected onto the stage or into the theatrical space. Also known as the multimedia designer.

Proscenium theatre: A theatre space whose main feature is an arch that frames the stage near the front.

Scenic designer: The artist that is responsible for the design of the stage environment that the actors inhabit.

Sound designer: The artist that is responsible for the design of all of the audio components for a production.

Theatrical design: The art of creating and composing the visual and aural elements that shape a performance space.

Theatrical designer: An artist who creates and organizes one or more aspects of the aural and visual components of a theatrical production.

Thrust theatre: A theatre space where the stage extends out into the audience and the seating surrounds the playing area on three sides.

Vomitories: Aisles that extend from the stage through the seating area of a theatre that can be used as entrances and exits.

CHAPTER 2

FORM, CONTENT, AND CONTEXT

WHAT IS FORM?

Form has several meanings in art and design. It can refer to the materials used to create a set, prop, or costume—the wood, fabric, and other things used to build the item. Form can also be used to refer to the shape, appearance, and the arrangement of those materials, in other words, the entirety of the visual elements used and the way they are assembled. In design and the visual arts, form is a synthesis of all the visual aspects of a work and, through it, we are able to perceive that work.

In terms of a performing art, such as music, the definition of form encompasses the whole of the musical elements and how they are composed and played, in other words, the form the music takes. In theatre, form refers to the play, the actors, and all the design elements that contribute to the production taken together as one type of performing art; but it can also be used to identify the style and genre of the play or of the visual and acting approaches that are applied to a production. The dialogue of a play may be written in verse or prose, taking on the form of poetry, or it could be written in an easy vernacular that reads and sounds like average, normal, or everyday speech. The visual approach may be highly stylized or abstracted, taking on the aesthetics of a particular stylistic form, such as cubism or classicism. The acting may be based on the behavioral characteristics of a particular time period, complete with appropriate manners of speech and movement, or it may be natural and realistic. For our purposes, we will also use the word to describe the nature of our design approach to the play, the form that our design will take.

As in the visual arts, theatrical designers select the materials that are used to realize their designs carefully, considering how they will inform, support, or even contradict the content of the play and the work as a whole. Clay has a different visual appeal than wood. Flutes have a different sound than trumpets. Jazz dance has a different aesthetic than ballet. A sculpture is not the same as a painting. Tragedy has a different thematic tone and style than farce. A brick wall has a different visual feel and impression than one made of natural stone. A costume made of light silk moves differently than one made of heavy wool. Varying materials and artistic styles engage the viewer in different ways, creating divergent impressions and invoking varying responses, and designers must keep this in mind when developing their conceptual approach to their work.

Analysis and evaluation that relies on the visual elements of the artwork exclusively to provide understanding is called **formalism**. In this type of evaluation, the subject matter of the piece becomes secondary. All other considerations are pared away in order to focus on the form and materials of the piece. In many ways, it is a sensual way to approach art and design, as the viewer responds to the visual appeal of the work, how it looks and whether or not the arrangement of elements is pleasing to the eye over all other considerations, such as genre, theme, and story. Some theatrical productions may require this kind of approach in order to effectively communicate their key ideas or to draw the audience into the performance. Others may rely on visual spectacle to reinforce the heightened nature of the performance or literary style. There are certainly entire genres of performance that employ spectacle as a primary tool, both visually and thematically. Visually stimulating and compelling design choices can enhance a production and help the audience connect to the performance, but they can also overwhelm a production and potentially be distracting. Consequently, the designer must be sure that their visual interpretation of the world of the play complements the style of the script as well as the style and goals of the performance.

CONTENT

Content refers to the meaning of the artwork, its substance or message, and can include several important aspects that a designer must consider. A play tells a story, and the circumstances, characters, and other details of that story make up the **subject matter**. Subject matter includes the **plot** of the play, the action that takes place on the stage in front of the audience, and the **story**, those actions and important events that have occurred before the action of the plot takes place. It contains the emotions of the characters and the ideas, themes, symbols, stories, or spiritual connotations the play examines, suggests, or communicates. Content can be textual, visual, aural, or thematic. In its quest to create or explain meaning, it might present ideas in an objective, interpretive, or subjective manner. It may engage the viewer emotionally and intellectually and draw them closer to the action, or push them away, creating emotional distance and tension. Content can explain points of view, present values, create symbols, illustrate beliefs, tell stories, or provide emotional catharsis, both for the artist that created the work, by purging an emotion or an emotional experience, and for the viewer who connects to that content. Content is one way of beginning to understand a play, by reading it, analyzing it, and seeing it in performance. Although content is distinct from form, it is very often tied to it, particularly in theatre, where the work of the designers seeks to interpret content and present it in a way that makes it available to an audience.

Content is not a fixed entity. It is shifting and personal. It changes depending on who is viewing the play and what experiences, values, cultural differences, and emotions they may bring to the act of viewing. These influences are referred to as **context**. The viewers' emotions and experiences are deeply influenced by context, and it can have an equally profound impact on the artist that may in turn affect and be a part of their work. Context in all its aspects is an important design consideration. The intended audience may dictate the choice of play to be presented in the first place, and will affect all choices that follow.

Context can be influenced by a variety of factors, and is a critical component of every play and production. A work of art is never created in a vacuum. There are always external and environmental factors that come into play. The events of the playwright's life and the time period in which they lived will influence not only what they choose to write but how they write it. Their social status will affect their views on different aspects of their world and the series of events that take place in the script, whether historical or imagined. The values of the culture they live or lived in may play out within their writing, which can include artistic conventions and aesthetics. Their own personal standards and principles, including morality and religious leanings, may be reflected in the overall tone of the play or be found in the personality and opinions of one or more of the characters, and these values can often be quite different from those of the time we live in. This can sometimes make plays or other art forms from previous time periods seem simple or anachronistic. Considering their historical context is an important tool to understanding, responding to and interpreting them effectively.

It is also important to recognize all of these aspects of context with regards to both the audience and yourself as a designer. The very things the playwright brought to their creation of the script in terms of their individual circumstances and point of view we also bring to our perception and experience of the play. Our upbringing, morals, values, experiences, culture, and beliefs color our response to everything around us and to the script. This is referred to as **personal context**.

For example, reactions to the depiction of a scantily clad female figure will differ profoundly between cultures where women are expected to be heavily clothed and those where this manner of dress is considered socially acceptable. Likewise, reactions to the depiction of Christian religious images will differ greatly between predominantly Christian and non-Christian cultures. Using context as a basis for approaching, evaluating and ultimately understanding a work of art in any genre is called **contextualism**. It considers the "big picture," and expands understanding by taking environmental factors and the world around the play and the author into account. It offers many ways of looking at and giving meaning to a play beyond its form and genre. Very often in theatre, we refer to researching and understanding the context of a script as "immersing ourselves in the world of the play." This process can be an effective way for a designer to see the play as a whole, rather than simply focusing on their particular design area.

In theatre, the play is the primary source of content and context. A play is the playwright's telling of a story, a series of actions that embody a truth from their point of view. This story is presented in a dramatic form. It is written to be performed rather than read and only when performed can we have true access to its full potential, complexity, and—ultimately—its greatness. The text is presented in dialogue rather than a narrative, which is meant to be spoken by actors playing the characters as they move through the story, following the plot as invented by the author. Actions may be suggested by stage directions, but they serve primarily as a framework, a suggestion of staging. The script itself is a blueprint for the vision of the playwright, which must be interpreted by the director, designers, and actors in order to create a living performance. In order to accomplish this effectively, the script must be studied and analyzed to identify its various dramatic components. These individual parts are essential to our understanding of the play and will guide us through the process of visual realization. The play contains all of the basic information required for designers to begin the investigation that will inform their design choices: time period, location, season, time of day, characters, style, and genre.

The playwright has a complete understanding of the play's context and content. Writing a play requires a lot of effort, study, and research and all of the relevant information gathered in the process is incorporated into the final manuscript. Because of this, and because designers seek to interpret the playwright's ideas and vision, the play is the place to begin your investigation into the world of the play. It will guide you in your extended examination inside and outside of the script and in your research into the individual components that contribute to it as a whole.

THE LANGUAGE OF FORM, CONTENT, AND CONTEXT

Content: The meaning of the artwork.

Context: The external, cultural, and environmental factors that influence the creation of an artwork.

Contextualism: The practice of using context as a basis for analyzing and understanding art.

Form: A synthesis of all the visual aspects of a design.

Formalism: seeking meaning through the visual appearance of an artwork alone.

Personal context: The individual context that we bring to our viewing of art.

Plot: The action that takes place on the stage in front of the audience.

Story: Those actions and important events that have occurred before the action of the plot takes place.

Subject matter: The plot, story, circumstances, characters, and other details of a play.

CHAPTER 3

GENRE

WHAT IS GENRE?

Genre answers the question, "what is the form of the play?" Genre is a literary term that is applied to many forms of artistic expression. Its definitions apply to any form of art, literature, or discourse, based on the application of a set of stylistic criteria that allows for the recognition of common attributes. Genre is an ostensive definition, one that permits us to group plays under a set of shared literary or visual characteristics, making it possible to discuss them as a whole. It takes time and dedication to reading scripts in order to understand and appreciate the various genres of dramatic form, each with its own characteristics and structure, some more heightened and artificial, with others being more realistic. But by looking at these forms, it is possible to perceive that genre is less a limitation or an absolute of specific types of drama, but rather a simple way of looking at plays that is fluid and changing, offering endless variations and combinations of form. Doing so also allows us as designers to identify and understand the characteristics and particular needs of different literary styles and how they will inform and guide our visual choices.

TRAGEDY

Tragedy is a type of drama that deals with serious or somber themes. Often, the story is focused on a great person or hero who, through a fatal flaw or the application of overpowering outside forces that are beyond their control—such as the will of the gods or the laws of society—is destined to suffer a downfall. In tragedy, their fate is predetermined; the hero cannot escape, and any attempt to do so leads inevitably to their destruction. Tragedies treat the sorrowful events that the heroic protagonist encounters with great dignity and seriousness, and often examines quintessential philosophical themes, such as the role of human beings in the universe and whether or not life has meaning. In the West, tragedy has its origins in ancient Greek theatre, where the depiction of ancient myths and stories, pitting man against the forces of the gods, was commonplace. According to Aristotle, whose *Poetics* is considered to present the classic discussion of the form of **Greek tragedy**, the playwright seeks to elicit both pity and fear from the audience, presenting a story that shows a reversal of fortune of people known for their superior accomplishments, which ultimately provides a catharsis for the feelings it provokes in the audience. According to Aristotle, in order to arouse these feelings from the audience, a tragic protagonist cannot be completely good or completely evil; they must instead be someone that the audience can identify with—they must be true to life. The disastrous consequences that come to pass at the end of the play are the result of erroneous or misguided actions on the part of the **protagonist**, the main character of the play. These actions are destined to occur because of a fatal flaw in their character or a horrendous error in judgment. The suffering of the protagonist is often out of proportion with his or her offense and the causes of suffering are diverse. It may be ignorance or deceit, the doing of evil acts, or simply living in a cruel and unjust universe. Through their suffering, we as viewers can see ourselves reflected in their behavior.

Shakespearean tragedy has its roots in Greek tragedy and as such, shares several characteristics with that classical dramatic form. More often than not, these are the stories of one remarkable, outstanding individual of high status, one dynamic hero (or, on occasion, a heroine), and their journey. Their downfall is as inescapable as that of a Greek protagonist, but in Shakespearean tragedy the cause is always the actions of men rather than the application of outside forces. The misfortunes that occur to the protagonist are not the result of the intercessions of the gods—they do not simply happen. The hero always contributes to their own downfall, and the story inevitably leads to their death. Shakespearean tragedy is a tale of suffering and disaster of exceptional proportions. Hamlet does not merely lose his life in the pursuit of revenge for his father's death, he also loses the woman he loves. His actions drive Ophelia to madness and, ultimately, to her death. He alienates his mother, drives away his friends, and takes the life of an innocent man. In feigning madness, he ultimately succumbs to the power of his own suggestion, and by the time death claims him, his sanity is in doubt. His losses are staggering in their totality and diversity.

In Shakespeare's tragedies, there is often the inclusion of abnormal mental states. Characters suffer from insanity, hallucinations, and sleepwalking. Although these states are included, they are never the inciting incident that sets events in motion. Rather, they are the byproduct of circumstances and the stresses on the characters. The supernatural is also sometimes included. Witches and ghosts interact with the protagonist, often to impart critical information that could otherwise not be known. These instances are always related to character, and lead to the hero taking actions that they might otherwise not have sought out for themselves. Without the knowledge gained from the ghost of his father, Hamlet would not know of his uncle's treachery, nor seek to right it. Without the intercession of the witches, Macbeth would not seek to become king by murdering Duncan. The influence of chance is also included in these plays, as this is an important factor of life and contributes to the overall effect of the story. The fact that human beings may start a chain of events that they cannot control is true, believable, and tragic.

Modern tragedy is focused on the ordinary man in extraordinary, tragic circumstances. It rejects Aristotle's idea that tragedy can only happen to those in high places and embraces the idea of depicting ordinary people in everyday surroundings. In modern tragedy, the hero is a person who is willing to lay down their life in order to maintain, as Arthur Miller described, their sense of personal dignity. This character refuses to stand by and do nothing in the face of a challenge to his or her individual self-respect, or of his image, or what he perceives to be his rightful place in the world. Instead, they choose to resist the seemingly constant world around them, to struggle against and to question their circumstances and the immutability of their environment. Through this examination of their existence, the emotions of fear and pity that are associated with the genre of tragedy are revealed. Rather than a fall precipitated on a fatal flaw, the protagonist's downfall is the result of causes that are within the character itself and how the character struggles with the forces of the world around them and the accepted order of things. From this struggle, the events and the characters are brought to a state of catharsis and we as an audience learn from the experience.

Miller's *Death of a Salesman* is a clear example of a modern tragedy. In it, the character of Willy Loman is unable to reach a state of self-realization, despite his examination of his past. He cannot accept the miserable state of his life, nor is he able to recognize and receive the love of his family. Although he does eventually come to recognize that what he is truly selling is himself, this is only a partial insight into the carefully fabricated web of lies and self-delusion that is his life. In the end, his only solution to maintaining the hold he has on whom and what he believes himself to be is to take his own life, in order to leave his son a tangible inheritance which he can use to fulfill the American Dream.

DRAMA

In contrast to tragedy, the characters in **drama** represent themselves as ordinary human beings. This allows the reader and audience to analyze the events of the play for themselves and to make their own judgments, a key feature in drama as genre. Dramas can be found in theatre throughout history and in many cultures around the world, and encompass a wide variety of stories and locales. Most of us are probably more familiar with the modern drama of the West. **Modern drama** ceased to deal with events, themes, and characters taking place in far removed locations but instead focused on ideas, actual life, and emotions. It is realistic rather than heightened, dealing with issues of morality, social institutions, and contemporary social problems. Henrik Ibsen is considered to be the father of modern drama and his plays, such as *Hedda Gabler*, examine social problems as well as characters that are emotionally driven individuals and their participation in self-destructive relationships. In his plays, Ibsen focuses on the inner lives of his characters and is often critical of traditional society and the moralities they represent. His work set a standard for modern dramas that continues to inform dramatic plays, films and television.

Drama can encompass several different subgenres. **Historical dramas** seek to examine a particular time in history or a specific group of people. Some may attempt to portray historical events accurately, while others may only be loosely based on these events and the people that contributed to them and still others may simply use the time period as a backdrop for the events that take place. *Miss Evers' Boys* by David Feldshuh is an example of a play that attempts to portray the historical events surrounding the Tuskegee syphilis experiment realistically and truthfully. In contrast, Brian Friel's *Translations* is an illustration of a historical play that presents the events of the forced English translation of Irish Gaelic place names in Ireland in the early nineteenth century in a more romantic and emotional manner through the lives of the characters and how this enforced colonialism affects them. **Biographical dramas** differ from historical ones in that they focus on the life of one individual or group, and attempt to present truthful or compelling pictures of the subject and the events surrounding their lives. Shakespeare's *Henry V* and Peter Shaffer's *Amadeus* are examples of these types of dramas.

Courtroom dramas use the setting of the justice system as a main component to explore thematic ideas, with all the associated elements present. Examples of this subgenre include *Twelve Angry Men* by Reginald Rose, *Nuts* by Tom Topor, and *To Kill a Mockingbird* adapted by Christopher Sergel. **Political dramas** focus on characters, themes, and plots that relate to political issues in the world. *The Balkan Women* by Jules Tasca, Václav Havel's *The Memorandum*, and *In the Heart of America* by Naomi Wallace are examples of plays where the protagonist confronts the harsh realities of bureaucracy, conflicts, and governmental corruption.

COMEDY

The plots of comedic plays emphasize triumph over adversity, a light and humorous tone, ridiculous events or actions, and happy endings to thematic conflict. Very often, the triumph is one of love in the face of trouble, which can be seen in the romantic comedic works of Shakespeare and Sheridan. **Comedy** also depends on the ability to provoke laughter. It leaves the audience with a sense of enjoyment and the idea that life is basically good. Laughter results not only from comic situations in these plays but also from witty dialogue. Characters are often ordinary people and, subsequently, plots may revolve around relevant situations and the kinds of problems these characters face. **High comedy** may take the form of satire, employing irony, sarcasm, and ridicule to expose and denounce the failings of genteel society, whereas **low comedy** emphasizes the use of slapstick and physical humor to elicit laughter. No matter the form, comedy often centers on the elevation of fortune of a central and sympathetic character. Comic heroes are often charming and sympathetic underdogs, able to easily win the support of the audience through their intelligence and skill. Lowborn, they are able to prove their worth as their character is tested throughout the course of the play. Often, the most ridiculous characters are ones that are pompous and self-absorbed despite their noble birth.

FARCE

Farce is a subgenre of comedy containing exaggerated characters, extremely improbable plots and situations, mistaken identity or disguises, and elements of slapstick and physical comedy to generate a humorous effect. In farce, the humor is broad, often involving elaborate wordplay, the deliberate use of nonsense, confusion, misdirection, and absurdity. A correspondingly broad style of performance is required to match the action. The plot is fast paced, increasing in speed and momentum as the play progresses, like a snowball rolling down a hill. Pressure must be maintained at all times on the events; complications and roadblocks must be introduced constantly to provide obstacles that serve to tighten the noose around the characters as they move through the play.

In a farce, the characters are often in some kind of peril. They need something and they have to go to great lengths to get it, with hilarious results. The greater the threat, the more ridiculous the action can become, and the crazier the characters can behave. Although the situation is often completely ridiculous to the audience, the characters themselves and the predicaments they experience in their situation may be very real. Often, the plot is built on a lie. One character lies and then in order to keep from being caught, they must continue to lie. The lies build on each other, and other characters may be forced to lie as well in order to perpetuate the previous lies of the other characters. Lies may contradict one another, and the various holes the characters dig for themselves get deeper and deeper until they finally collapse. Prime examples of farce are *Noises Off* by Michael Frayn, *Rumors* by Neil Simon and *Unnecessary Farce* by Paul Slade Smith.

SATIRE

In **satire** gallows humor, irony, sarcasm, and ridicule are used to expose and denounce folly and vice. It may target an individual, a group, or even an institution in order to point out weaknesses, hypocrisy, or other characteristics to the audience.

Although it is a subgenre of comedy, satirical elements can also be found in more serious drama. Closely linked to parody, satire can be used to make fun of political or other public figures and thereby affect their perceived public worth or value. Political satire is a highly popular form of entertainment and has often been used subversively to draw attention to and advance political arguments where criticism and political dissent are forbidden. Television shows like *The Daily Show* and *The Colbert Report* continue to demonstrate the popularity of this form of satire, using humor to direct the audience's attention to various social and political issues at the expense of their subjects.

Many of theatre's greatest playwrights have employed satire to one degree or another. Oscar Wilde is famously known for his satirical plays. *The Importance of Being Earnest* uses ridicule, dramatic irony, and parody to satirize and mock the ridiculous behavior and superficiality of the upper class. Joan Littlewood's *Oh, What a Lovely War!* uses irony and satire to bring attention to the tragic losses endured for little gain in World War I by taking lively popular songs from the period and juxtaposing them with the realities of trench warfare.

TRAGICOMEDY

Tragicomedy combines traditional elements of both comedy and tragedy into one play. When the term was originally coined by the Roman playwright Plautus in the second century BCE, it was used to describe a play in which the roles of gods and men, masters and slaves were reversed. Gods and heroes acted in comedy and burlesque, while slaves adopted the dignity seen in tragedy. Later, in the Renaissance, the term came to denote a genre of play that was largely comic, but contained tragic elements, extending to any work where some characters came close to death. Averted catastrophes, sudden reversals of fortune, and happy endings were all common characteristics of the genre. Elizabethan versions of the genre often included some element of the grotesque to the mix. Shakespeare's *Merchant of Venice* is an example of this variation.

After the classical age of drama there is no clear definition of the genre. Since the nineteenth century, the term tragicomedy has been used to describe a wide variety of dramatic forms, and therefore the term as currently used can be difficult to define. Modern tragicomedy is sometimes used interchangeably with absurdist drama, possibly suggesting that laughter is the only legitimate response when characters are faced with the fact of a meaningless existence. **Dark comedy** and satire are also similar in tone to tragicomedy. All three of these forms of drama use irony, ridicule, sarcasm, and gallows humor to expose and condemn folly and vice in society.

MELODRAMA

In **melodrama**, plot and characters are exaggerated in order to appeal to the emotions of the audience. This emotional resonance is very basic: the audience should connect with and like the good characters and despise the ones who oppress them. Characters are often exaggerated stereotypes that do not change morally or psychologically throughout the play, who engage in heightened actions and exciting events where good is always rewarded and evil is always punished in the end. The plot is simple, so as not to distract from the moral distinctions between the characters, centering on heroes and heroines who undergo superhuman trials at the hands of unscrupulous villains. The emphasis of melodrama is on extremes of reversals—poverty to wealth, certain death to rescue and life, disgrace to redemption, and so on. There is also an endless supply of plot twists to move the action forward, including narrow escapes, violent conflict, miraculous discoveries, and disguises, all of which lead to a resolution of the situation, based on sound moral principles. Does this sound like modern television? It should. Melodramatic elements are common in blockbuster films, daytime dramas, and reality shows.

MUSICAL THEATRE

Musical theatre is a dramatic genre that combines music and songs with spoken dialogue and dance. In these plays, the emotions and story are communicated through words, music, and movement in a stylized form that differs from purely spoken dialogue. Heightened emotion leads to song, which reveals the character's goals and feelings as well as plot. Emerging during the nineteenth century in the West, the genre culminated notably in the work of Gilbert and Sullivan in Britain and in that of Edward Harrigan and Tony Hart in the United States.

In America, modern musicals can be divided into subgenres of **musical plays** and **musical comedies**, each of which has their own artistic purpose. Musical plays focus on the play itself; everything is subservient to the script. Music, dialogue, and production numbers are completely united to create a single artistic event with believable characters, a credible plot, and authentic atmosphere. Design elements are used to support the merging of those individual components. *Show Boat* by Oscar Hammerstein II and Jerome Kern was the first of these plays in America, and set the standard for all that came after. *West Side Story* by Arthur Laurents, Stephen Sondheim, and Leonard Bernstein, Sondheim's *Sweeney Todd* and *The Phantom of the Opera* by Andrew Lloyd Webber are all examples of musical plays.

Musical comedy developed in the early twentieth century by borrowing elements of several different types of musical theatre that came before it. Satire, parody, and chorus girls came from burlesque. Attractive settings, costumes, and spectacle were taken from musical extravaganzas as well as large scale production numbers. Musical revues donated the idea of set routines for featured performers, and from operetta came light plots, romance, glamour, and the idea that the boy always gets the girl and good always triumphs over evil. Add to that the kinds of characters and locales that American audiences were familiar with either personally or through magazines and newspapers, lively music, jaunty lyrics, and recognizably colloquial dialogue, and musical comedy became a uniquely American style that continues to thrive to this day. Musical comedies dominate Broadway with their infectious and memorable music, engaging plots and technical excellence.

OPERA AND OPERETTA

The main component of **opera** is music. In opera, a script, in the form of a libretto, is combined with a musical score that is performed by musicians and singers in a theatrical setting. While there may be spoken dialogue in opera, it is usually underscored throughout with music. Often the entire libretto is sung by the performers. The plot of an opera may be serious or comedic with the emotions of the characters communicated to the audience through solos, duets, trios, quartets, and choral sections that display the talents of the principal singers. It encompasses the same technical aspects of spoken theatre, such as costumes, sets, lights, and sound, and may also include dance and ballet. Opera is part of the Western classical musical tradition that began in the sixteenth century in Florence, Italy, which later spread to the whole of Europe with national traditions being established in Germany, France, Italy, and England. It has a reputation of seriousness and grandeur both in musical style and overall appearance, with lavish sets and costumes that support larger than life characters.

Operetta means "little opera," initially because operettas were only one act long. Sometimes it is also referred to as "light opera," a term used in reference to the lighter style of the chosen subject matter. This does not mean that the genre lacks musical thought, complexity, or preparation, only that it often seeks to promote feelings of happiness and joy over the heavier, darker themes of grand opera and serious dramas. Operettas are often romantic, comic, and sentimental rather than tragic, and commonly unpretentious. However, this does not always guarantee a happy ending or that every song is upbeat. This lack of pretentiousness extends to the musical score, which is intended to be played by a theatre orchestra rather than a full symphonic/operatic one, with music that is memorable and, often, very popular.

Operetta developed out of the works of the *opera comique* in France in the later nineteenth century. The word *comique* by this time had come to mean something more true

to life that pure comedy, focusing on humanity and portraying it in a realistic way, setting comedy and tragedy side-by-side in the same piece. Generally, operettas are shorter in length than operas, and are often less serious, with plots that are lighter or more comedic in nature. Topical satire is a common component in operetta, although that is not to say satire is never found in a full length opera. In contrast to its cousin, there is often a fair amount of dialogue in between the musical components, such as arias, choral, and recitative, etc. Usually this dialogue does not have musical underscoring, as it does in opera, although at times a musical theme may be played underneath spoken words.

Operettas and musicals share characteristics that can sometimes blur the lines between the two genres. As operetta is the historical predecessor of the modern musical, this is understandable. Musicals and operettas both originally focused on romantic plots, offering escapism from everyday life. Several modern musicals contain complex polyphonic ensembles that are more commonly associated with operetta. *Rent* and *Spring Awakening* both use recitative and through composition, a term used to describe music that is non-repetitive, uninterrupted by dialogue, relatively continuous and which has only forward, linear motion. One way to describe the differences between them would be to say that musicals are plays that contain singing and dancing, while an operetta is a light opera with acting.

CHILDREN'S THEATRE

Children's theatre is a blanket term used to describe several dramatic genres specifically aimed at younger audiences, including theatre for children, theatre for youth, and theatre for young audiences, each relating to a specific age group. In children's theatre, the performers are usually adults, using a script that has been created or adapted for a specific age group. Theatre for young audiences also includes participation theatre, where the performance is structured around a script and specific opportunities for active audience involvement have been included, as well as theatre by children and youth, where the performers are teenagers and children rather than adults. Although plots may be less complicated to be understood by the target audience, universal themes are common and the acting and technical elements are approached with the same level of expertise and seriousness. Plays in this genre may be full-length stories or a series of episodes used to engage the audience and communicate emotion. Some productions will use a full range of design elements to an extensive degree, while others may only use them minimally. These plays can contain a wide range of subject matter, from realistic stories to fairy tales and fantasy.

TABLE 3-1 *Genres and their associated qualities.*

Genre	Qualities That May Inform the Visual Presentation
Tragedy	Serious, Weighty, Big, Heavy, Over the top, Larger than life, Heightened, Grand, Stylized, Depressing, Heroic, Dark, Inevitable, Intense, Classical, Emotional, Tragic, Serious, Sad, Simplicity, Missing information, There is an accepted order of things, Suffering, Fate, inescapability, Cathartic, Life is binary – bad/good, just/unjust, ugly/beautiful, Supernatural elements, Hierarchical, Vengeance, Militarism, Duty, Honor, Unhappy endings, Death, Universality, Hubris, Magnitude.
Comedy	Light, Funny, Fast paced, Entertaining, Topical, Incongruity, Illogical, Surprise, Contradictions, Suspension of Natural Laws, Foolishness, Complications, Romance, Struggles of love, Complexity, Imaginative, Playful, Randomness, Improvised, Colorful, The body is funny, Forgiveness, Equality of the sexes, Happy endings, Puns, Malapropisms, Contrast between social order and individual characters.
Farce	Exaggerated, Fast paced, Stock Characters, Slapstick, Physical, ridiculous, nonsensical, Over the top, Relentless, Exaggeration, Mistaken Identity, Exaggeration, Stylized, Buffoonery, Outrageous, Colorful, Silly, Oversized, The body is funny, Happy endings.
Satire	Witty, Smart, Engaging, Ironic, Parody, Complexity, Language is important, Aristocratic, Political, Irreverent.
Tragicomedy	Dark, Humorous, Black comedy, Ironic, Complexity, Raises important life issues, Serious subjects, Misinformation, Conflicting messages, Sarcastic.
Drama	Accessible, Realistic, Easy to understand dialogue, Universal themes, Experiential, Universal appeal.
Modern Drama	Realistic, Character driven.
Melodrama	Stock Characters, Caricature, Good triumphs over evil, Exaggeration, Episodic form.
Musical Comedy	Lighthearted, Fun, Uplifting, Catchy.
Opera	Heightened, Grand, Big, Over the top, Elaborate, Ornate, Serious, Classical, Expensive, Dark, Heavy, Larger than life characters, Extraordinary events, Supernatural elements, Theatricality, Emotional.
Operetta	Light, Fun, Comedic, Detailed, Romantic.
Children's Theatre	Lively, Fantastical, Bright, Colorful.

THE LANGUAGE OF GENRE

Biographical dramas: Dramas that focus on the life of one individual or group, and attempt to present truthful or compelling pictures of the subject and the events surrounding their lives.

Children's theatre: A blanket term used to describe several dramatic genres specifically aimed at younger audiences, including theatre for children, theatre for youth, and theatre for young audiences, each relating to a specific age group.

Comedy: A genre that emphasizes triumph over adversity, a light and humorous tone, ridiculous events or actions and happy endings to thematic conflict.

Courtroom dramas: Dramas that use the setting of the justice system as a main component to explore thematic ideas, with all the associated elements present.

Drama: A genre where the characters represent themselves as ordinary human beings, allowing the audience to analyze the events of the play for themselves and to make their own judgments.

Farce: A subgenre of comedy containing exaggerated characters, extremely improbable plots and situations, mistaken identity or disguises, and elements of slapstick and physical comedy.

Genre: The literary form of the play.

Greek tragedy: The form of tragedy that was developed in ancient Greece, where the disastrous consequences that come to pass at the end of the play are the result of erroneous or misguided actions on the part of the protagonist and the interference of outside sources.

High comedy: A subgenre of comedy that relies on intellectual humor, satire, irony, sarcasm, and ridicule to expose and denounce the failings of genteel society.

Historical dramas: Dramatic plays that seek to examine a particular time in history or a specific group of people.

Low comedy: A subgenre of comedy that emphasizes the use of slapstick and physical humor to elicit laughter.

Melodrama: A genre where plot and characters are exaggerated in order to appeal to the emotions of the audience.

Modern drama: Realistic drama that focuses on ideas, actual life, emotions, issues of morality, social institutions, and contemporary social problems.

Modern tragedy: Focuses on the ordinary man in extraordinary, tragic circumstances.

Musical comedy: A subgenre of musical theatre characterized by songs, dialogue, and dancing, connected by a light or romantic plot.

Musical plays: A subgenre of musical theatre that focuses on the play itself and everything is subservient to the script.

Musical theatre: A dramatic genre that combines music and songs with spoken dialogue and dance.

Opera: A genre where a script, in the form of a libretto, is combined with a musical score that is performed by musicians and singers in a theatrical setting.

Operetta: A short opera, usually with light, romantic or humorous plot and typically containing some spoken dialogue.

Protagonist: The main character in a play.

Satire: A subgenre of comedy where gallows humor, irony, sarcasm, and ridicule are used to expose and denounce folly and vice.

Shakespearean tragedy: The form of tragedy developed in sixteenth/seventeenth-century theatre, where the protagonist cannot escape their downfall, but the cause is always the actions of men rather than the application of outside forces.

Tragedy: A type of drama that deals with serious or somber themes.

Tragicomedy: A genre that combines traditional elements of both comedy and tragedy into one play.

CHAPTER 4

STYLE

WHAT IS STYLE?

The concept of **style** is an important one in theatre, yet it can be very confusing because the word style has so many meanings. In all art forms, when we talk about style we can be referring to several different things. We might be referring to a **historical style**, the aesthetic conventions of a particular historical time period, such as the Renaissance. Or we might use the word style to refer to the artistic traditions of a particular location, culture, or nation, such as Japanese or African style. The word can also be used to describe the individual artistic look or feel of a particular artist. We can say a piece is Rubenesque or Picasso-esque when discussing a work that contains some of the visual characteristics that are inherent in the artist's personal style. Style can also be used to identify a particular artistic technique, such as pointillism, abstraction, or photorealism, or be used to associate a group of artists whose style shares common characteristics, such as the impressionists, pre-Raphaelites, cubists, or expressionists.

By definition, style is the arrangement of a variety of objects into a group of categories that make them easier to recognize, understand, and talk about. As with genre, identifying style makes further analysis and study possible. Style identifies a family of resemblances or shared characteristics among individual works that allows us to group them together under one descriptive heading, and then break those resemblances down even further, into smaller and smaller groups. Just as families may resemble each other, works of art may be similar in appearance, and styles of stage design may look like each other as well. They may have differences too, but they often share enough characteristics that make classification possible. The

common recognizable element may be in the use of color, line, shape, or subject, but it may simply be felt in a qualitative sense. An overall, *pervasive quality* is often the basis for classifications of style: some stylistic terms such as "classical" or "romantic" seem to rely on the viewer's feelings about a piece as much as they do on the artist's technique or approach.

In theatre, style is used to classify the manner in which the play is written, acted, and produced. It includes the design approach, method of acting, and delivery of the dialogue as well as the literary modalities of the script.

REALISM

In the style of **realism**, the intent is to create a truthful representation of real life onstage. Characters bring to mind real people, and dialogue is presented in a way resembling normal speech, following the conventions of language and the manner of speaking within the time period the play was written. The various visual elements—sets, costumes, lights, props, and makeup—are chosen to create a realistic location and show a slice of life onstage.

When realism first emerged as a theatrical style in the mid-nineteenth century, it was partially a reaction to the extreme characters and situations presented in traditional melodrama, comedies, and vaudeville acts that had spectacle as a focus. As social, economic, and political events became more volatile and people worked towards social reforms, artists—including those in the theatre—began to realize that art of all kinds could be used as a powerful agent for education and change. Technological advances also suggested that science could solve the problems of humanity, and both of these ideas became themes in realist plays. Rather than using subjects of grandeur and myth, or stock characters, these works focused attention on the ordinary person, along with the psychological and social problems they faced. The style flourished, along with the acting techniques of Konstantin Stanislavsky, which emphasized motivated portrayals of character, and was embraced by Ibsen, Chekov, and other realist authors. Now the term is often used to refer to any play or production where a faithful slice of life presented to the audience is the primary goal, with ordinary people going about the routines of their daily lives. The standard of realism tends to dominate many forms of literature and has been applied to diverse theatrical art forms, including television and film. Even daily comic strips now often reflect the activities of the everyday lives of their characters.

NATURALISM

Naturalism is an extreme form of realism and shares many characteristics with it as a dramatic style. The production values of naturalism are very close to those of realism; however, they may be carried to an extreme. Settings are highly detailed and often meticulously researched. In a naturalistic production, a kitchen sink or individual lamps maybe be practical, meaning that the sink actually possesses running water and each lamp can be turned on directly by the actors onstage. Costumes are faithful historical reproductions of the applicable time period.

Historically, the main difference between the two styles, as espoused by the founder of naturalism, author Émile Zola, is the application of the scientific method to the creation of characters. His plays and novels place high emphasis on the influences of environment and heredity in the development of character. Zola abhorred the idea of creating sympathy for a character through psychological means. Instead, he insisted the playwright should serve as an objectively accurate observer, faithfully recording and stating the facts he sees. Zola wanted to rid the stage of fictitious characters, instead presenting real characters taken from life, scientifically analyzed, and presented with no embellishment or artifice. The ultimate goal of naturalistic theatre was famously described by Jean Jullien: "A play is a slice of life put onstage with art" (*The Living Theatre*, 1892). Characters, in his opinion, should act independently of the playwright to follow their own destiny and be driven by their own internal motivations. Jullien also felt that the story of the play did not end with the conclusion of the performance, and instead believed that audience members should be free to consider what might happen next.

Any production that relies on immaculate detail, completely functional scenic elements, historically accurate costumes, and realistically motivated light sources with working onstage fixtures is, if not following the exact philosophy of naturalism, at least borrowing from its design and production aesthetic.

CLASSICISM

Classicism has, as its aesthetic ideal, the return to the formal order that characterized the art and theatrical forms of ancient Greece. In the theatre, this style grew out of the appreciation of French playwrights such as Jean Racine, Pierre Corneille, and Molière for the rules and structure of classical Greek plays, namely the **three unities** of time, place, and action. Unity of time refers to the idea that the entire action of the play should take place within one fictional 24-hour period. Unity of place dictates that the play should take place in one single location and unity of action refers to the concept that the play itself should be constructed around a single plot line, with few or no subplots. This could be a conflict between honor and duty, a tragic love affair, the desire for revenge or some other subject that served to unite the action of the play. Although mentioned in Aristotle's *Poetics*, the unities were codified in the neoclassic period, and still continue to influence the structure of plays today. An example of a modern play that utilizes the three unities is *Twelve Angry Men*. In this play, 12 jurors debate the fate of a boy on trial for murder in real time, within the small jury room of a courthouse, a place they cannot leave until the verdict is reached.

Other aspects of classicism involve the idea that the truth is found in archetypes or "norms," which can be discovered through the application of reasoned thought and the investigation of phenomena. Norms are also found in human behavior, and the playwright should write about these universal aspects. Neoclassicists saw purity in form, and therefore preferred plays to fall into either the category of comedy or tragedy. Any play that contained mixed dramatic content was seen to be inferior. Plays should teach moral lessons; evil must be punished and good must be rewarded. Characters must receive the poetic justice they have earned and, in doing so, the play imparts morality and right from wrong. Tragedies must show the terrible consequences of evil actions, and comedies must ridicule immoral behavior. However, this must be presented in a pleasing format or else the audience will not pay attention. Finally, the playwright should focus on things that occur in real life and not include any aspect of the supernatural unless it was already part of the story, such as elements derived from the Bible or Greek myth, and even then they should not be the main focus of the play. Plays in this style tend to be very realistic within their historical context and require design elements that support this fact.

ROMANTICISM

Despite its title, the term **romanticism** has very little to do with the subject of romance, though there are several plays within this style that deal with romantic themes. Romanticism grew out of neoclassical trends in drama, literature, and art where intellect, reason and rational thought were seen as supreme ideals. In direct contrast, romanticism has at its heart the idea that imagination is supreme to reason. Imagination is seen as the ultimate creative power, akin to that found in nature, or assigned to the gods, and is seen as the most significant ability of the mind. It can be used to unite feeling and reason, as imagination is the ultimate factor in creating art of all kinds, and is inextricably linked to two other aspects of the style: the reverence for nature and the interpretation of myth and symbols. Imagination is also linked to the importance of emotions, intuition, instinct, and poetic narrative and the idea that the source of all of these qualities is the individual artist themselves. Romantic plays serve to reflect the world within, rather than the world around us.

Although nature is often used as a subject in romanticism, the preoccupation with nature goes beyond this simple use. Nature is used as a metaphor for describing the universe. Abandoning the idea of the world and everything in it as a well-oiled machine, the romanticists instead turned to the idea of the universe as an organic, living thing, whole and unified. This plays out in the sensuous description of natural phenomena, intent on capturing every detail and in the view that the natural world is a refuge from artificial civilization and a source of healing. As a source of inspiration for romanticists, nature also reflects the volatility of human emotions, as well as the uncertainty of life.

Symbols and myth are very important in the style of romanticism for two reasons. First, they are seen as an aesthetic human parallel to the representative language found in nature. Second, symbols are capable of communicating many ideas at once and can have personal as well as cultural meaning. Nature can, in romantic works, be infused with a symbolic language tied to the expression of emotion.

The heroes of romantic plays are individuals, from the hero-artist to the antihero to the outcast. Rather than follow any set rules of religion or philosophy, they follow the idea that each person must find their own path. Romantic plays are full of poetic dialogue and theatricality, from Tony Kushner's adaptation of *The Illusion*, to *Faust*. They focus on the spiritual, emotion over rationality, and often feature characters struggling with the universe, where the artist is celebrated as a mad genius that must rise above the physical world to discover their individualism in the quest for the truth.

STYLIZATION

Stylization is a departure from absolute realism that emphasizes design over exact representation. In theatre, it is the process of taking a play beyond reality through distortion, exaggeration, or some other stretch of convention, in terms of both performance and design. The degree to which something is realistic or stylized is one of the fundamental characteristics of visual design. To give a very simple example of the differences between the two visual styles, the less a design resembles something that can be found in the physical world, the more stylized it is. A design that is composed of recognizable images, however distorted or stylized, is referred to as **representational**. If a design is composed entirely of things that are not found in the physical or natural world or are not recognizable, then the design is considered to be abstracted. **Abstraction** relies on the visual language of line, form, color, and so on to create a design that may have no references to the world around us. Abstraction is often referred to as nonfigurative, nonrepresentational or nonobjective design and exists along a continuum. The abstraction can be complete, partial, or even simply a slight departure from reality. It is also possible to distinguish design that tells a story, which is called **narrative**, from a design that does not and is purely **decorative**. While it is possible for a decorative design to be either representational or stylized, a narrative work is almost always representational, at least to some degree.

Stylization can be created in a number of different ways. In ancient Greece, for example, human figures were **idealized** based on the idea of perfect mathematical proportion, and several models would be used in order to create a perfect, "ideal" figure based on composite idealizations. The Greeks believed the proportions of the human body were beautiful because they reflected the fundamental order of the universe. It was the task of the artist to apply this order to architecture, music, and the making of images of all kinds. Artistic creation became the search for perfection: the right shape, correct proportion, right balance, and the complete finish.

Stylization can also occur when the shapes, forms, and subject matter in a design are simplified or distorted. Detail can be eliminated or simplified in order to focus the viewer's attention where it is desired or for artistic effect. This can be seen in theatrical design when a complicated, realistic set is pared down to the minimal scenic elements that are required to facilitate the play's action. A fully furnished room with walls, windows, and doors may be reduced to a rug on the floor and the furniture needed for the action. A replica of a period garment may be simplified into a costume design that maintains the basic look and silhouette of the given time period, while eliminating extraneous details that are not needed to support the character.

Stylization can also be effectively created by applying an **artistic style** to a design. A designer may choose to apply the aesthetic characteristics of a particular artist or artistic trend to their designs for a distinctive look. In this way, a design could be "Picasso-esque," or "Banksy-eque," or executed in a "comic book style." There are several different types of stylization in theatre, most of which are defined by adding the suffix "-ism" to an established term.

TABLE 4-1 *Theatrical styles and their key characteristics.*

Theatrical Style	Key Characteristics
Expressionism	The action of the play is presented through the subjective eyes and emotions of the playwright. The experience of theatre should be emotional, powerful, and forceful. The use of nightmares and dreams as a source of distortion is common.
Symbolism	Theatre seeks the profound mysteries of life and is dominated by a poetic, dreamlike quality. The creation of atmosphere and mood is far more important than action and plot. Recognizable symbols may not necessarily be present. Instead, motifs are symbolic of the playwright's consciousness.
Absurdism	Life is irrational and nonsensical and theatre should reflect that fact. The truth can never been known and understanding is impossible. Action becomes cyclical, unproductive, and repetitive to reflect that everything is meaningless.
Classicism	The return to the formal order that characterized the art and theatrical forms of ancient Greece.
Impressionism	As in the art movement of the same name, theatre seeks to capture the impression of a particular moment in time using mood, atmosphere, and feeling.
Futurism	Theatre is totally integrated and the actor is a subjugated machine. Progress is all, the success of the past is repeated, and a glorious industrial future is anticipated by all.
Dadaism	A revolutionary approach towards both drama and art, where nothing is sacred and expectations are contradicted at every turn.
Constructivism	Plays that build a story through the action they present, rather than telling a story. A type of bare bones theatre, where theatrical illusion is stripped away, with no sentimentality or individual emotions.
Postmodernism	Presenting events of the past without any nostalgia or sentimentality. Theatre should present the new with the old, juxtaposing one against the other.
Feminism	Theatre that is by, for, and about women, presenting their voice, attitudes, beliefs, hopes, and desires.
Romanticism	An idealized type of theatre that explores destiny, history, success against all odds, all while idealizing nature and emotions.
Realism	Theatre that presents the truth, in the hope that things can be changed for the better.
Naturalism	Be true to life and reveal everything in exacting detail and in real time. Life is not expected to change.
Didacticism	A narrative form of theatre focused on rousing the intellect rather than emotions, forcing the audience to be a spectator rather than an observer in order to arouse the capacity for action.

EXPRESSIONISM

Expressionism is an artistic style developed in the early twentieth century that is concerned with the communication of emotion, rather than focusing entirely on artistic technique. Its goal is to evoke the subjective response that an artist, poet, or playwright has to their subject and communicate it to an audience. There is no attempt to develop a realistic impression of the world. Instead, expressionism focuses on capturing the extreme and distorted emotions of the sensitive individual to their environment, events, and individuals. In expressionism, truth lies in the soul, spirit, and vision of the artist. The response of the artist to their environment is so intense that it affects the stylistic form of art and literature. Subjective distortion and exaggeration of shape and form is common in expressionism as the external reality is molded to match that of the interior life of the artist, partially in reaction to dealing with an increasingly mechanized world. This distortion is meant to relay a personal view of reality, rather than an objective one.

An expressionistic play will often be nonlinear in structure, focusing instead on an idea, theme, or motif to unify the action. Cyclical or circular structure is not uncommon, with events repeating over and over and circling back on each other. Characters are often based on types rather than individuals, and may have no names beyond their occupation or position, such as the Husband, the Student, or the Teacher. The action of the play may take the characters on a quest, where the protagonist looks for an elusive prize or goal, stopping at various locations as they move towards their objective. Dialogue is often short and simple, requiring stylized movement to assist in the communication of emotion. Design for expressionistic plays needs to reflect the emotional intensity of the script as well as support the aesthetic of distortion and exaggeration inherent in the style itself. The expressionist movement had a great deal of influence on modern drama. Locating a contemporary play without some element of expressionism can be difficult. Whenever we see a performance where it seems as if what we experience with our mind is more important than what we see with our eyes, its influence can be felt.

SYMBOLISM

Symbolism is a style of theatre that originated in France in the late nineteenth century that focused on and explored the mysteries of life through the rejection of objective reality. Instead, it relied on subjective experience, intuition, dreams, and poetry to create a form of theatre that focused more on the creation of atmosphere than it did on plot and action. The characters in symbolist plays always reflect the personality and inner life of their authors rather than being unique individuals with their own temperament and nature. Language is the primary tool for communication in symbolism, and consequently the visual elements, characters, and action are subordinated to the words spoken. The symbolists believed that art had a degree of autonomy, divorcing it from social concerns and political problems and thereby allowing it to move beyond reality and into the higher realms of Truth with a capital T.

The "symbols" presented in this genre may not be actual, recognizable symbols, but are rather a reflection of the consciousness of the playwright. In symbolism, suggestion is considered to be a more effective method of communication than obvious, realistic representation. Many of the common symbols used in these plays have an origin in nature, such as the moon or water, dark forests, even castles that are cold and uninviting, which never become warm and hospitable. Adolphe Appia and Max Reinhardt, two powerhouses of the theatre in the nineteenth and early twentieth centuries did their best to bring the visual and thematic concepts of the genre to life on the stage through set and lighting designs. Projections of light were combined with music to create mood. Stage spaces were undefined, often filled with shadows and haze to create a dreamlike state. Dialogue was mysterious, often delivered with rhythmic cadence, and utilized variations in intensity to create emotion through vocal technique. Movements of the actors were exaggerated and distorted, sometimes relying on static poses and even puppets to portray a simplified quality or characteristic. Costumes were often reflections of the dream state; gauzy, draped and ethereal. Ultimately, symbolist performances are characterized by distortion and exaggeration, which were used for effect. Much modern dance, particularly the work of Isadora Duncan, reflects and relates to the symbolist ideals.

Symbolism had a considerable influence on writers in Europe and the United States, as well as visual artists such as Henri Rousseau and Toulouse-Lautrec. Although Maurice Maeterlinck is considered to be the preeminent symbolist playwright, the style also affected the writings of James Joyce, Edgar Allan Poe, and Eugene O'Neill, among others. Because the symbolists directly confronted the ideals of the realists, they had little commercial success; but their work both inspired and made it possible for other playwrights to create works that were nonrealistic but accessible. Elements of symbolism appear in *Ubu Roi* by Alfred Jarry, *Salomé* by Oscar Wilde, *Pelleas and Mélisande* by Maurice Maeterlinck, and *Spring Awakening* by Frank Wedekind.

FUTURISM

At the beginning, **futurism** was strictly a literary movement. It began in 1909 when Italian poet Filippo Tommaso Marinetti wrote and published a manifesto outlining the tenants of futurism in a prominent Parisian newspaper. It was a short-lived movement running only 1910 to 1930 and later absorbed by the propaganda wing of the Fascist Party in Italy. Some of the techniques were used by playwright Eugène Ionesco in his work, and the influence of futurism can still be seen in modern performance art.

In futurism the past is rejected and progress is glorified. Technology is embraced as the harbinger of a new and great industrial future. In his manifesto Marinetti praised fast cars as a new idealistic standard of beauty, and called for the destruction of libraries and museums that, in his eyes, only valued the old, the dead, and the dying. No one in this movement was over the age of 40. The ideal futurist man was young, aggressive, and a warrior who hated the past and leapt towards the future, embracing technology as a way to rescue theatre from the logical and outdated basis of literature. In this movement war was not seen as something to avoid, machines were not the tools of dictators and tyrants. Both were, in fact, seen as a source of great beauty, and war was seen as a way to cleanse society of its ties to the past. Futurism did not produce any great plays or playwrights, but it did influence future anti-realistic art and artists and promoted modern technology. Modern multimedia performances share in the legacy of this theatrical style.

Futurist plays are characterized by simultaneous events and actions that take place in multiple areas of the performance space as well as the propensity for actors to move among the audience. There may be confrontation between the audience and the actors. The playing space may be filled with utilitarian objects. Multimedia techniques may be used as part of the performance. The language employed is simple, blunt, and direct, often with masculine or militaristic overtones. The script may include political ideologies, manifestoes, shouting, and even mechanical noises. In any case, design for plays in this style is often called upon to reflect the underlying values of this particular aesthetic movement.

THEATRE OF THE ABSURD

Stylistically, **absurdism** is based on the philosophy of existentialism, which calls for the use of the will rather than reason in order to deal with the problems that arise in an increasingly antagonistic world. When absurdism came into being, continental Europe had just experienced great devastation in the form of economic, agricultural, architectural, and human loss after the events of World War II. Memories of suffering dominated the minds of artists and non-artists alike. In this fertile ground of common misery, the roots of absurdism took hold and grew.

In absurdist plays life has no meaning and existence is useless. There is no conventional sense of time, place, or structure. Plays are often organized in a circular format with actions and events repeating over and over. The play often ends exactly where it began. Characters often experience deep emotional anguish and pain, and the only coping mechanism they possess is laughter and the exercise of their mental capacities. Characters can be deeply complex and realistic, or highly caricatured and stereotypical. Miscommunication between characters is common as dialogue is often vague, rambling, or nonsensical. Physical action may be highly stylized and it is not uncommon to see elements of acrobatics, dance, and circus techniques used in a performance. After all, absurdist qualities are highly evident in the work of silent film comics, such as Buster Keaton, Charlie Chaplin, and the Keystone Kops.

Design for an absurdist play or production can go in a variety of directions. Realism may be called for in order to draw a sharp contrast to the absurdity of the action, plot, or characters, or to set up false expectations for the audience. The visual world could also be presented in a heightened, cartoon-like manner, emphasizing the illogical nature of the script itself. In many cases, multiple approaches are suitable for any given play and can be equally effective.

EPIC THEATRE: DIDACTICISM AND BRECHTIAN THEATRE

Based on Erwin Piscator's idea of a "working-class theatre," by and for the people, **didacticism** seeks to provide both entertainment and education. Its goal was to make the audience think and act. Bertolt Brecht perfected this style of theatre, developing Piscator's ideas into a form by working with his own company, the Berliner Ensemble. Although his theories have been debated by countless theatre professionals since their inception, they continue to inspire and stimulate directors around the world.

Epic theatre is largely presentational in its aesthetics. At the heart of this style is the desire to remind the audience that they are viewing a performance. There is no desire to invite the audience to lose themselves in the lives of the characters onstage. Instead, there is an attempt to create a sense of distance and alienation by frequently interrupting the action, destroying the theatrical illusion so that audience will engage with the story on an intellectual rather than an emotional level. Locations change frequently and abruptly.

Rather than playing a character, an actor *presents* them to audience. Actors are often required to be able to step in and out of character, so that they can comment on their character, acting simultaneously as both character and narrator. Instead of embodying dramatic action, the play narrates it. Its presentational nature demands decisions that lead to action from the audience rather than eliciting their feelings. Arguments are presented that appeal to our reason and intellect and communicate knowledge. All of this serves to create an active state of watching that discourages passivity and, since Brechtian drama often deals with characters that are caught in the middle of political or social upheaval, the audience should leave the performance knowing that they have the ability to enact real change in the world.

In terms of design, didactic theatre is often minimal. A proscenium space may be desired because its very presence reminds the audience that they are outside the action of the play. Trappings of the theatrical space maybe exposed. Lighting instruments, racks of costumes, or any other item that serves as constant reminder of the performance *as* a performance are common. This can include cameras, projections, and other theatrical elements that remind the audience that what they are seeing is not real. Brecht frequently used a curtain on a clothesline, drawing it across the length of the stage to reveal changes in location behind it as an element of alienation. Movement can be highly stylized, realistic, or anything in between. Strict naturalism, however, is usually rejected as it does not fully encompass the scope of humanity within the whole of their society.

POSTMODERNISM

Postmodernism is a term that applies to a theatrical style that emerged in the mid-twentieth century as part of the artistic reaction to modernism. Postmodernism denies the existence of an absolute truth, calling its veracity into doubt and instead asks the audience to interpret events for themselves, eventually reaching their own understanding. There can be many possible truths in postmodernist theatre; no single one is correct. Consequently, postmodernist plays tend to raise questions rather than supply answers and invite the audience to begin their own investigation of the events and ideas they present. Postmodernist theatre discards the idea that theatre is a representation of life, and requires the audience to reexamine the boundaries between reality and art. The idea of make-believe is rejected. Instead, the performance is seen as a real-life event where the audience must participate. The theatrical performance can be largely experimental, developed through improvisation and experimentation rather than through a scripted narrative, and each performance is intended to be

a unique spectacle. There is no intention to repeat the play in the same way each time it is performed. The narrative itself is often nonlinear, presenting scenes in a seemingly random order, out of sequence or time. Flashbacks are a common device. Scenes may appear broken or be incomplete, and plays may have an unresolved conclusion that can be different with each performance. Characters are often presented as fragmented pieces combining an idea, a theme, or parts of a traditional character rather than as a realistic person, and character development is minimized. In terms of design, postmodernist performances are often technologically enhanced, combining different forms of media and multiple art forms simultaneously to create a spectacular, experimental, and representational environment.

THE INFLUENCE OF STYLE ON DESIGN

As you can see, there is a wide variety in theatrical styles. In order for a designer to be able to create a design that is appropriate for the play, they need to be familiar with the characteristics of the style in which it was written. Each of the styles discussed here all have unique qualities that have the potential to influence the visual choices made by the designer, regardless of their design area. This does not mean that a designer has to be a slave to the aesthetics of a particular style, only that an awareness of the intention of the playwright and the conventions of the script's style can be very useful when developing your conceptual approach. Even when the director decides to alter the style of the script, or to adapt the play and apply a different style to the production, it can be extremely useful for the designer to have an understanding of the play's original style as well as the new style that is being applied.

One of the things the designer must keep in mind with regards to style is the element of consistency. Once a visual characteristic or stylistic convention has been established, particularly in a realistic style, any deviation from that convention has the potential to be disruptive for the audience, unless a comic effect is desired. For example, in a realistic world, we expect that there will be a logical and understandable connection between objects and the sounds they make. We do not expect a telephone to look like a fish, or to bray like a donkey when it rings. But in an abstract world, it may make perfect sense for a telephone to do those very things. In fact, a braying fish telephone may be *exactly* what the play calls for, and it may communicate important details to the audience in a way that a regular telephone could never hope to in that context. Of course, a designer may choose to break the stylistic convention on purpose for a specific effect, to create focus, to underscore a specific moment, or to heighten the dramatic action. Doing this tends to have a rather abstract effect, but when used carefully and with purpose it can create a dynamic and engaging moment.

Unity of the design elements is also an important consideration when discussing style. In modern theatre, it is definitely possible for there to be a bit of variation in style between the design areas. A director may want the set design to be minimally realistic, with only the suggestion of walls to define the space, relying on real furniture and props to anchor the action within the acting areas, but ask for the costumes to be completely realistic in order to define the characters in a full and engaging way. They may then ask the sound designer to provide realistic sounds, such as doorbells, television programs that the characters watch as part of the action, or the sound of a realistic, motivated busy cityscape outside an apartment window—and yet have no window, television, or doorbell for the actors to interact with directly onstage. The director might ask the lighting designer for realistic, motivated lighting that suggests time of day, location, and season, but without any practical light sources. On the surface, these requests might seem to be at odds with each other stylistically. But when taken together, we can see that the desired focus is on the actors and the human story that is being told rather than the external environment. What the director is asking for is a degree of reality that allows the audience to identify with the characters and the situation they find themselves in, without being caught up in extraneous details that are not needed to tell the story. It is up to the designers to make sure that their designs work together while fulfilling this request. While there is some disparity in the level of realism in each area, unity can be created through other visual means, such as the use of similar lines in all of the designs, or common colors throughout. The point is that the styles have not strayed so far from each other that they *cannot* be unified. The design team has to work together to ensure that the design elements complement each other and that the final picture presented on the stage makes sense within the context of the play and the particular production.

THE LANGUAGE OF STYLE

Abstraction: Design that relies on the visual language of line, form, color and so on to create a design that may have no references to the world around us.

Absurdism: Based on the philosophy of existentialism, which calls for the use of the will rather than reason in order to deal with the problems that arise in an increasingly antagonistic world. In absurdist plays life has no meaning and existence is useless. There is no conventional sense of time, place, or structure.

Artistic style: A design style based on the aesthetic conventions of an individual artist.

Classicism: A style characterized by a return to the formal order that was found in the art and theatrical forms of ancient Greece.

Constructivism: Plays that build a story through the action they present, rather than telling a story.

Dadaism: A revolutionary approach towards both drama and art, where nothing is sacred and expectations are contradicted at every turn.

Decorative style: Design that is meant to be purely beautiful from an aesthetic or formalist point of view.

Didacticism/epic theatre: A working-class style of theatre characterized by an attempt to create a sense of distance and alienation by frequently interrupting the action, destroying the theatrical illusion so that the audience will engage with the story on an intellectual rather than an emotional level.

Expressionism: An artistic style developed in the early twentieth century that is concerned with the communication of emotion, rather than focusing entirely on artistic technique.

Feminist theatre: Theatre that is by, for and about women, presenting their voice, attitudes, beliefs, hopes, and desires.

Futurism: A style where the past is rejected, progress is glorified, and technology is embraced as the harbinger of a new and great industrial future.

Historical style: The aesthetic conventions of a particular time period in history.

Idealized: Creating a composite version of an object, model, or form based on the idea of perfect mathematical proportions.

Impressionism: As in the art movement of the same name, theatre seeks to capture the impression of a particular moment in time using mood, atmosphere, and feeling.

Narrative style: Design that tells a story.

Naturalism: An extreme form of realism that shares many characteristics with it as a dramatic style.

Postmodernism: A style of theatre that removes the idea of make-believe from performance and rejects the idea that universal truths can be accessed or achieved through an artistic representation of life.

Realism: The style that seeks to present a truthful representation of real life onstage.

Representational: A design that is composed of recognizable images, however distorted or stylized.

Romanticism: A style characterized by the idea that imagination is supreme to reason.

Style: An overall pervasive quality of an artwork that makes it possible to identify its aesthetic characteristics and discuss them.

Stylization: A departure from absolute realism that emphasizes design over exact representation. In theatre, it is the process of taking a play beyond reality through distortion, exaggeration, or some other stretch of convention, in terms of both performance and design.

Symbolism: A style of theatre that focuses on and explores the mysteries of life through the rejection of objective reality. It relies on subjective experience, intuition, dreams, and poetry to create a form of theatre that focuses more on the creation of atmosphere than it does on plot and action.

Three unities: Time, place, and action.

CHAPTER 5

DRAMATIC STRUCTURE

WHAT IS DRAMATIC STRUCTURE?

A playscript is a unique form of literature. Unlike narrative forms, such as a short story or novel where action, dialogue, reflection, and description are used to tell the story and give the reader a complete picture of what is happening, a play essentially contains only **dialogue**. Although a script might also include directions that indicate a certain action should take place, such as the entrance or exit of a character or a special effect, these directions are not spoken aloud and are therefore not communicated to the audience. Instead, these stage directions are incorporated into the performance and become part of the experience of the theatrical event. While a book is meant to be read, a script is meant to be performed, with actors taking on the roles of the individual characters. The story is told through the performance and via the interaction of the actors with the audience. Reading a play requires a designer to synthesize all the information provided via dialogue, stage directions, character interaction, and unspoken subtext in order to visualize the action.

Like other genres and forms of literature, dramas need to have structure in order to be effective. Much like the foundation of a building, dramatic structure supports the play and gives it form. It is said that form follows function. This is also true with the structure of a play. However, it is also possible for the form of a play to dictate its function, meaning that the content and style of a script often determines how the action and story will be presented. Understanding the structure of drama and being able to identify its elements is an essential step in the process of script analysis, which is one of the first steps a designer must take in the design process.

THE ELEMENTS OF DRAMATIC STRUCTURE

The Greek philosopher Aristotle was the first person to consider the idea of what made a play good or bad. In his famous literary work *Poetics* he examined the play *Oedipus* by Sophocles in depth and identified six elements that he believed were required in order for a drama to be successful. They are, in order of importance:

1. Plot

2. Character

3. Thought

4. Dialogue

5. Music

6. Spectacle.

In Aristotle's opinion, all of these elements had to be present, but he considered plot to be the most important of the six, as it both motivated and contained all of the other elements of dramatic structure. These six components make up the foundation of classical play construction. Now, the essential components of dramatic structure are described differently:

1. Story

2. Plot

3. Dramatic action

4. Conflict

5. Character

6. Theme and meaning

7. Balance.

Story

A **story** is a complete retelling or recounting of an event or a series of events from which the plot of a play is derived. It contains all the history and events leading up to the actions within the play, with all the little details. It is everything that happens before the play starts, but it may also contain what comes after the events in the play. Often, but not always, a story is arranged in chronological order with a beginning, a middle, and an end.

A play presents a section or sections of a complete story in order to achieve dramatic effect. In theatre, the story influences the action of the play as well as the characters, driving both forward. In traditional storytelling, the narrative is conveyed in a singular voice. One person tells the story to an audience; but in theatre, the narrative is plural, told through multiple characters and voices that create a multifaceted picture.

Plot

The **plot** of a play is a selection and arrangement of scenes from the story to be presented in a theatrical format. It is what actually occurs onstage in front of the audience. A plot is carefully designed and constructed in order to reveal the exact parts of the story that the playwright wishes to convey. Characters, events, and individual moments are carefully linked together and manipulated in order to reveal the story to the audience in the manner that the playwright wishes. A well-constructed plot divulges information layer by layer and moment by moment, keeping the audience engaged and informed just enough to make them want to find out what happens next.

Attributes of Plot

A story has a beginning, a middle, and an end and the same is true of plots. In **traditional** or linear dramatic structure, the plot follows a cause and effect pattern, moving in a linear fashion from one point to another, from beginning through to the end. Each step in the development of this type of dramatic action has a name and a purpose associated with it and it can be represented by the Freytag Pyramid. Gustav Freytag was a nineteenth-century dramatist and novelist who was the first to visualize the path of dramatic structure. His method

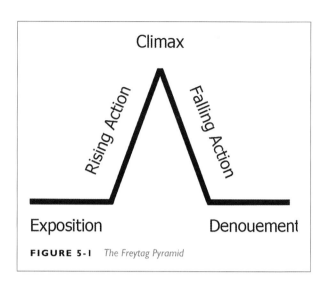

FIGURE 5-1   *The Freytag Pyramid*

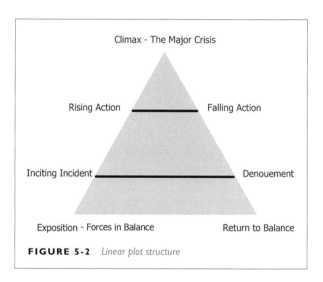

FIGURE 5-2   *Linear plot structure*

of explaining the progression of climatic dramatic structure is displayed in the Freytag Pyramid.

The Freytag Pyramid can be a useful place to start when describing the traditional, linear structure of a plot.

Exposition

Exposition is our introduction to the plot and often to important aspects of the story as well. Exposition provides background and information about location, backstory, characters, occasion, time period, and underlying themes of the play. Earlier events that are crucial to our understanding of the plot are revealed, relationships between characters are described, and initial mood is established. Traditionally, exposition occurs at the beginning of a play and the plot begins late in the story, requiring exposition to bring the audience up to speed.

Forces in Balance

When the play begins the forces at work in the world it presents are usually in **balance**. The status quo is established so that the audience will be aware of the shifting of dynamics as tension begins to escalate. At the beginning of a play, balance can be a deceptive thing; it may not reveal the true nature of the situation. There may be something wrong that the characters are unaware of or that has yet to be revealed.

Inciting Incident

Sometimes called the point of attack, the **inciting incident** is the first increase in tension or the point at which the story is taken up. With the arrival of the inciting incident the exposition officially ends. If this occurs early in the play, then less exposition is needed. If it happens later, then more exposition will be required. This event sets the rest of the play in motion, leading to the rising action.

Rising Action

After the inciting incident, during the **rising action** of a plot, tension and conflict increase as secondary obstacles are introduced to further complicate the main internal conflict of the play. These obstacles get in the way of the protagonist as they try to reach their goals. Secondary conflicts can take several forms, including the introduction of new information or actions, or foes of lesser importance than the antagonist, or characters that work for that person. Such characters can also have their own motivations or act for unknown reasons. **Subplots** may be introduced, setting up secondary events, actions, and storylines with minor characters that serve to support and develop the main action of the play or that come back later as key elements at key moments.

At this point in the play, the protagonist will encounter a crisis that propels the action forward. When all seems lost, when nothing the protagonist has done has helped their cause and the desired goal seems unreachable, they must stop and think in order to develop a new approach to the problem. Only when they step back and take the time to tap their inner resources will the protagonist be able to come up with an effective strategy. This process inevitably leads to the play's climax.

Climax

The **climax** is the culmination of all the events and action that came before and has led up to that moment. It is a turning point in the play and marks a change in the state of the protagonist, for better or worse. This is the moment that the audience has been waiting for, when the big questions of the play will be answered. Who killed the king? Will the boy get the girl? Will good triumph over evil? Will the main character succeed in gaining revenge? If the play is a tragedy, then all the good fortune that the protagonist has experienced previously will be reversed and things will start to go badly. In a comedy, the misfortunes and pitfalls that the protagonist has endured will lift and things will begin to go their way. Sometimes, the climax consists of a showdown between the protagonist and the antagonist, with the winner of the encounter being determined by the genre of the play. Regardless, here the levels of suspense and tension are at their highest.

Falling Action

After the climax, the action begins to fall as the conflict between the protagonist and the antagonist starts to unravel. One or the other of them succeeds and achieves their goal. **Falling action** encompasses a moment of reversal, where the course of the plot changes and may include a final moment of suspense, where the final outcome of the play's main conflict is uncertain. During the falling action, the various strands of the plot begin to wind down and the action moves to tie up the remaining loose ends in the story.

Denouement

The **denouement** is the **resolution** or conclusion of the plot. Here, all the remaining threads of the plot are tied up and the audience may be left with a glimpse of the characters' futures. The good characters are rewarded; the evil ones are punished or redeemed. Lovers and families are reunited. The dead are laid to rest. The protagonist of a comedy usually ends up in a better place than when they started, while the protagonist in a tragedy is worse off or dead as the result of a catastrophe.

The denouement is the point in the play where a device called a *deus ex machina* may be introduced. This term derives from the tradition in Greek drama of the timely arrival of the gods in a "god machine," or *deus ex machina*, to interfere in the protagonist's life. When this plot attribute is employed, someone or something arrives or intercedes in the action to save the day, against all odds. The king pardons the protagonist; a letter arrives that explains the truth of what was going on; a disguised character reveals their true identity or a pretender is unmasked; the lost treasure miraculously appears. Although this plot device is still used, it is often considered to be a poor substitute to a fully resolved play.

Return to Balance

At the end of the play there is a return to a state of balance. The status quo may not be the same as it was at the beginning of the play, but the balance of power has been restored. Comedies often end with feasts or weddings or other types of celebrations. Evil-doers are sent to jail, heroes are rewarded. Tragedies see the protagonist removed from his or her normal life. Often, they are dead and a funeral or final scene provides a sense of closure. In any case, there is a complete ending to the story.

In some plays there is a deliberate cutting off of the falling action to create an ending without a definite conclusion. The playwright may choose to do this in order to leave the audience unsettled, or to generate questions about the play's subject or theme, or even to leave an opening for the characters to return in another play. It is also worth noting that not all climactic plots will occur in chronological order. Some may occur in the form of flashbacks, or even begin in the middle of the action, with little or no exposition.

Dramatic Action

Dramatic action is a term used to describe several things within a play. At the most basic level, dramatic action refers to the events that occur in the play and how they are revealed, including all the dialogue, movement, action, and the development of the plot. A play is, after all, essentially a series of events that are organized to reveal a message or for a specific purpose, and it accomplishes this through the representation of characters in action. In this case, action encompasses not only what the characters *do*, but *why* they do it as well. Dramatic action is also a living, evolving thing that builds throughout the course of the play in three ways. Through a sense of purpose, both the characters and the audience become aware of a goal and the desire to achieve it. We see the dramatic action increase because of the strength of the characters' passion or their suffering as they work towards this goal and the dramatic action continues to progress as their own perception and understanding of their situation develops over the course of their struggle throughout the play. In essence, dramatic action provides a solid framework for character interactions and dialogue to follow.

In order to be effective, dramatic action should possess several key qualities. There should be a sense of completeness, allowing the action to be entirely self-contained and to possess an internal consistency. There should be a beginning, a middle, and an end that carry the audience through the play, sustaining interest and moving the plot forward. These not only provide a sense of unity, they allow the audience to be actively engaged with the play. Dramatic action must be organized and shaped towards a goal. Without an objective and action that leads

towards it, the play will flounder and struggle to maintain the attention of the audience. Finally, dramatic action should be engaging and maintain interest. One of the easiest ways to accomplish this is through variety. However, variety without a solid structure can become predictable and simply repetitious. When this happens the audience's interest can be lost as their enjoyment of the play fades away.

There are several different ways to organize dramatic action and to create the sense of unity that is required to provide internal consistency. Unity can be created by linking scenes together through a common theme or idea, or by the logical progression of events and actions that result from cause and effect. Using one character as the central focus of the play can shape the action and tie it together. Unity can also be provided through the use of distinctive language, by a predominant visual style or a dominant mood throughout the play.

Conflict

Conflict is another crucial element of dramatic structure. It occurs when a character is prevented from getting what he or she wants. Action is the direct result of conflict and a play, by its very nature, follows the path of the central conflicts of the plot towards their final resolution. A central conflict is usually composed of the contradictory desires of two or more characters, or by the obstacles preventing the major character from achieving their goal. What one character wants or needs prevents the other from getting what they want. Their struggle to remove the obstacles to their goals provides the action. Usually, once the conflict is resolved, the play is over. Conflict also provides interest and moves the plot forward. We generally don't see the characters on a normal day, let alone their best day; instead, we watch them as they navigate through what is probably the most challenging experience of their lives.

Conflict is usually presented in one of three ways. *Physical conflict* refers to the struggle of man versus man. This type of conflict tends to be very powerful, emotional, and raw, and usually has a lot of appeal for the audience. Conflict between individuals is easy to relate to, because we as audience members have all experienced this type of encounter in varying degrees, so we are able to respond on a basic, human level. *Psychological conflict* shows the struggle between man and himself. This type of conflict—where the audience witnesses the characters struggling with or trapped by their own actions, psyche, mind, and inner demons—is also very engaging. By witnessing the struggles of others, we are able to see them in ourselves. Spiritual or *metaphysical conflict* represents the struggles between man and forces outside himself. This type of conflict is often seen in Greek, Roman, or Shakespearean plays. Whether these outside influences represent the will of the gods, or of fate, or nature, in the end they show the struggle of the characters against inevitable or insurmountable odds. And of course, it is always possible to have all three of these types of conflict within a script.

Strongly Opposing Forces

Conflict arises from the struggle between forces of equal power working against each other—i.e. **strongly opposed forces**. Drama seeks to present this conflict to the audience. Each side must want to achieve their goal so badly that they are willing to do whatever it takes to manifest it, even if it means the complete and utter destruction of their foes. The intensity and strength of this desire in turn makes the conflict found within the script that much stronger. No one wants to see or cheer for a character or group of characters that are apathetic about achieving their goals. We want to watch a driven set of individuals strive with all they have to get what they want.

Character

The **characters** in a play are crucial to our experience of drama. It is through the characters in a script that we as audience members are able to find our way into the world of the play. Characters engage our emotions. They provide opportunities to empathize with the plot, actions, and story of the play. There are several different types of characters in drama. Each of these character types serve different functions within a play, helping to create a fuller and richer world as well as moving the story forward. Some are principal characters, taking on major roles within the play and others are supporting, perhaps taking less stage time but often providing crucial information or playing a vital role within the plot.

Of key importance in any play is the **protagonist**. This is the main character that drives the action of the play forward. In essence, the play is the protagonist's story and one of the ways to identify this individual is to determine which character changes the most over the course of the play. Doing this makes it possible to decide whose story is being told. While it is more common for there to be only one main character in a script, it is definitely possible to have more than one protagonist in a story.

The **antagonist** is the character that directly opposes the protagonist and attempts to keep him or her from reaching their goals. It is not necessary for the antagonist to be a human character. The obstacles that prevent the protagonist from getting what they want can be an individual, a group, society, or even nature. In some plays the role of the antagonist is represented in the will of the gods or the actions of fate, against which the protagonist must struggle throughout the course of the play. In addition to these two roles that characters fulfill there are number of different character types.

- *Representative*: Rather than an individual these characters represent entire groups, fulfilling a sort of "everyman" role. They are quintessential in their identity and provide reference to and an illustration of the social norm.

- *Extraordinary*: These characters are larger than life. They are the heroes, the kings, the queens, the miracle workers. They are generally removed from everyday life and the people that inhabit it.

- *Supernatural*: These characters are either nonhuman or possess supernatural powers. They include angels, demons, monsters, and animals.

- *Stock*: These are stereotypical characters that are two-dimensional and easily recognizable. They display characteristics that are common to a particular type of character, for example the maid, the young lovers, the miser, and so on. Long a part of traditional theatre styles such as *commedia dell'arte*, stock characters are still crucial components in comedies and melodrama.

- *Major*: These are characters of primary importance to the plot and story. This will certainly include both the protagonist and the antagonist, but is not limited to these characters alone.

- *Minor*: Another word for secondary characters, this is a broad term used to describe characters in supporting roles.

- *Narrator and chorus*: A narrator is an outside observer who guides us through the story. These characters may be integrated into the action of the play or stand completely outside of it, watching it along with the audience as it unfolds. The chorus is a group of characters, large or small, that act as one. They may be used to represent a group of people like the residents of the town, or they may be used to show the thoughts and conscience of another character. Both of these types of characters may address the audience directly, providing commentary on the actions and the characters within the play.

Theme and Meaning

If Aristotle believed that **thought** was a key component of drama, where does thought fit into modern dramatic structure? The idea of thought lives on in the thematic components of the play, in the arguments presented by a script and in the overall meaning of the action. Meaning is suggested and revealed through the relationships between characters, the conflicts that are presented in the resolutions that are reached, by the ideas that are presented by the script, the empathy created between the audience and the characters, and through theatrical devices such as **song**, **music**, and **spectacle**. Theme is developed by the repetition of ideas, points of view, character, and dramatic action.

Meaning is usually implied rather than stated outright in drama, although it can be clearer in some plays than in others. Regardless of whether meaning is clear or implied, this does not mean that there is only one of meaning for each script. Each audience member brings their own personal context to their experience of a performance. This will naturally affect their response and understanding. Generally, place provides an open opportunity for multiple interpretations of meaning, all of which should be supported by evidence taken directly from the script itself.

Balance

In drama, balance is less of a continually existing element than a desired outcome. Many plays thrive on a lack of balance, maintaining inequality between forces or characters and even crafting a final ending that leaves the play feeling unresolved. A reasonable amount of balance within the script might be a more traditional expectation of dramatic structure, but balance is also one thing that offers the audience a way into and a way out of the narrative. Balance at the beginning can provide a recognizable world for the audience. As the action progresses and the balance shifts, conflict and tension are created in a dynamic fashion and the audience is carried along with the action. By returning to a more balanced state at the end we are allowed to feel a sense of completion and satisfaction with the outcome. However, many playwrights will choose to take the audience outside of their comfort zone and leave them with a resolution to the action that is distasteful or harder to accept in order to present something that is more real or truthful, regardless of our collective preference for a neat and clean or happy ending.

NONTRADITIONAL STRUCTURE

Although linear, climactic structure has been an important component in theatre for thousands of years, it is by no means the only form of plot structure in drama. Because structure is a key component that offers the audience a way to connect with the play, it is a natural area of experimentation for playwrights.

Altering play structure is a simple way to create something new and unique, presenting new possibilities for both performance and interpretation.

One of the first alternate forms of structure to be accepted as a legitimate form was **episodic structure**. Developed and refined by twentieth-century German playwright and dramatic theorist Bertolt Brecht, episodic structure sought to focus on the intellectual reasons behind behavior instead of eliciting an emotional response to drama and spectacle. Brecht sought to push the audience away from their emotions and created many theatrical devices to alienate the audience. The epic style of theatre he created used multiple perspectives to tell the story rather than focusing on the experience of one character alone, allowing the audience to experience the truth from more than one point of view.

In episodic structure, the plot begins early in the story, making extensive exposition unnecessary. The plot may be epic and far-reaching in nature, covering many locations and events and spanning extensive periods of time, even years. Multiple characters allow for the presentation of different points of view and perspectives, and parallel plots exist, often to reinforce the primary plot. Juxtaposition and contrast are also common. Scenes may alternate in length or style from serious to comedic or public to private, or they may move back and forth between one group of characters to another. The overall effect of an episodic plot is cumulative as the individual stories come together to create a complete theatrical experience. This type of plot is common in film and television, where episodic techniques are used to cover stories that are far-reaching in scope. When television shows with year-long plots and huge story arcs are examined, their episodic nature becomes clear. These techniques compel the audience to tune in and keep watching in order to find out what happens to the characters they have come to care about.

It is also possible to create structure through experimentation. **Experimental** theatre is a catch-all term that encompasses a variety of structural styles that do not fit into the traditional, climatic arrangement of plot structure. The inspiration for this type of dramatic structure and narrative style can be found in many places, including ritual, patterns, avant-garde art and literature, serial structure or completely experimental forms. As more and more theatrical artists try out different ways of working to create performances, the library of dramatic structure becomes more and more diverse.

THE LANGUAGE OF DRAMATIC STRUCTURE

Antagonist: The character that directly opposes the protagonist and attempts to keep him or her from reaching their goals.

Balance: An even distribution of power between forces in the play. The status quo.

Characters: The individuals in the play.

Climax: The culmination of the all the events and action that came before and has led up to that moment. The highest levels of suspense and tension in the plot.

Conflict: When a character is prevented from getting what he or she wants.

Denouement: The resolution or conclusion of the plot.

Dialogue: Conversation between characters or between characters and the audience. The primary component of a play.

Dramatic action: The events that occur in the play and how they are revealed, including all the dialogue, movement, action, and the development of the plot.

Episodic structure: A plot that focuses on multiple scenes, characters, and viewpoints.

Experimental structure: Nontraditional play structure; any plot that does not fit into the classification of traditional structure.

Exposition: The introduction to the plot of the play that gives important aspects of the story.

Falling action: The point in the play after the climax where the levels of stress and tension begin to dissipate as conflicts begin to be resolved.

Inciting incident: The first increase in tension or the point at which the story is taken up.

Music: Songs or underscoring in a musical format.

Plot: A selection and arrangement of scenes from the story to be presented in a theatrical format.

Protagonist: the primary character in a play.

Resolution: Another term for denouement.

Rising action: The point of a play where plot, tension, and conflict increase as secondary obstacles are introduced to further complicate the main internal conflict.

Spectacle: Lights, costumes, scenic elements, and other special effects.

Story: A complete retelling or recounting of an event or a series of events from which the plot of a play is derived.

Strongly opposed forces: Forces of equal power working against each other.

Subplot: Secondary events, actions, and storylines with minor characters that serve to support and develop the main action of the play.

Thought: Thematic content and ideas.

Traditional structure: A linear plot that focuses on a climax, with a clear beginning, middle, and end.

PART TWO

ELEMENTS OF DESIGN

CHAPTER 6

LINE

WHAT IS A LINE?

Strictly defined, a **line** is a path traced by a moving point. A point is the smallest mark you can make on a surface with a tool or implement. When you place your pencil on a piece of paper and then *move* the point along the surface, you create a line. A point is said to have no dimension. It has neither height nor width. Line creates the first dimension: length. Although line is considered to have only one dimension, in terms of artistic expression, line possesses many additional qualities that can be exploited by the artist for visual effect. There are a number of ways to alter line beyond its length in order to communicate emotion or ideas. Line is in fact, one of the most expressive and versatile design elements because of the amount of variety that be created by using it.

Of all the elements of design, line is the most familiar to us. We all use line every day. Line is the basis of letters, which form our alphabet. We work with line when taking notes, reading street signs, signing our names, or doodling. Line is a basic and highly effective tool of communication. It can show us which direction to go, guide car and foot traffic, define locations, deliver important messages, and warn us of danger. It is part of our everyday experience and how we relate to the world around us, and we are all familiar with line as an outline through our early experiences as children with coloring books.

But, line is far more than a tool for creating an outline or boundary. There are many different types of lines and, as a design element, line possesses a number of qualities that can be used to create dynamic visual effects. Line also serves several important functions in a composition.

LINE QUALITIES

In terms of appearance, lines can have an almost infinite number of variations. There are many types of lines, and they can vary in the following ways.

- *Weight* refers to the actual thickness of the line, as well as the amount of pressure used to create the line itself, resulting in a dark or light mark on the paper. Thick, thin, light, dark, and heavy are some of the words to describe line weight.

- *Texture* describes the perceived feel or surface characteristics of the line. It may also refer to the overall character of the line in question. Smooth, jagged, soft, hard, bold, timid, curvilinear, rectilinear, curvy, rough, angled, solid, and broken are some of the words used to describe this line quality.

- Lines also vary in *speed*. Lines will have different visual appearances based on how fast or how slowly they were made as well as different emotional connotations generated by the speed in which they were made. Fast lines have a sense of urgency and sharpness, and slower lines can create a softer, more tranquil feel. In addition, it is almost impossible to create the visual qualities of a fast line by making the mark slowly, and vice versa. Consequently, the speed with which the line is made has a direct relationship to the overall look and feel of the resulting mark or image.

FIGURE 6-1 *Line qualities*

• Lines also possess *direction*, which creates movement within a composition. Depending on their direction, lines will lend various qualities and suggest different feelings in a composition, contributing to the overall effect of the design and intent of the designer. Lines may be vertical, horizontal, diagonal, radial, or even ambiguous, covering several directions, all of which can be employed within a design for maximum effect.

TYPES OF LINE

There are several different types of lines, all of which can be employed for different effect within a composition. The lines you use, and how you use them will be based on what you want to accomplish both visually and conceptually.

Outline is a type of line with no variations in width that is used to delineate a two-dimensional shape from the surrounding background by defining the edges of that shape.

Although it defines shape, outline communicates no real information about depth, mass, or volume and is therefore strictly two-dimensional.

As stage designers, we often discuss outline using another term, **silhouette**. Silhouette can be used to refer to the overall shape of a costume or the outline of a piece of furniture, or may be used to refer to the way an object or actor is lit onstage.

A **contour line** is one that follows the edges of a form and possesses variations of line weight. Using contour line creates the suggestion of a three-dimensional quality in an image. Contours are the boundaries we perceive of three-dimensional objects. When contour line is used exclusively to create a drawing, it is called a *contour drawing*.

Descriptive line is a type of contour line that communicates mood and feelings through variations in **line quality**. It is evocative and expressive. When descriptive line is used in a drawing where defining shape is less important than capturing the feeling and dynamics of movement or a pose, the resulting drawing is called a *gesture drawing*. Gesture drawings

FIGURE 6-2   *Outline and silhouette*

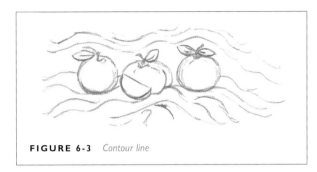

FIGURE 6-3   *Contour line*

FIGURE 6-4   *Descriptive line and gesture drawing. Tartuffe by Molière. Conceptual sketch, scenic design by Kaoime E. Malloy*

Actual lines are those that are real, complete, and unbroken rather than implied or psychic. They trace a clear path within an image or close around an area to form a shape. **Open lines** are ones that do not connect in any way, but instead function as a kind of visual texture. Although they do not serve to enclose a shape or delineate it from the background, open lines can often be used to create linear

FIGURE 6-5   *Implied line*

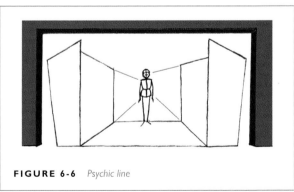

FIGURE 6-6   *Psychic line*

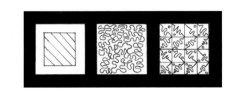

FIGURE 6-7   *Actual, open, and closed lines*

are often very dynamic and fluid, conveying more information about mood and movement then they do about the specifics of form. Initial sketches of rough design ideas might be rather **gestural** in nature as well, capturing the feeling of a character or environment while omitting final details. In addition, the use of line is often very personal and unique, and it is frequently possible to identify a particular artist simply through their specific use of line qualities and treatments.

An **implied line** is a broken line or series of broken lines, dots, or dashes that suggest movement, guiding the viewer's eye around an object without depicting it clearly or totally, allowing the eye to complete the entire shape of the object automatically as it follows the implied line. Implied lines rely on the eye's natural tendency to fill in patterns to create the impression of a shape and it can therefore create a dynamic sense of movement and energy in a composition.

A **psychic line** is an imaginary line that occurs when there is an implied connection between two objects in a composition. Usually, there is no actual line connecting the objects, only a perceived directional clue that guides the viewer's eye from one point to the next. Psychic lines can also be used to create emphasis within a composition, focusing the viewer's attention on specific areas.

compositions that are shapes in and of themselves and can be used to create pattern, value, texture, and suggest mass and volume. **Closed lines** are ones that enclose an area to create a shape. Closed lines can be said to meet each other as they travel around the paper to define the edges of an object.

THE FUNCTIONS OF LINE

Lines Define Shape

Lines are important to the visual artist because they can be used to describe and define shapes and, by doing so, the viewer can recognize objects. Artists will often delineate the form of an object by using line to create shapes and reveal the edges of an object, or its outline. Line carves out the shape of a form from the surrounding area and defines it for the viewer. When line is the main element used to create an image, the resulting work is usually referred to as a *drawing*, regardless of the chosen medium.

For example, the object in Figure 6.8 is immediately understood to be a flower, even though it lacks some of the qualities of the actual object, such as dimension or color. It is not the same size as an actual flower, but we still recognize the flower through the use of different line qualities and types of line that define the shape of the individual petals and the flower as a whole. The lines used to create the image identify its edges, and form a boundary between the flower and the space around it.

Line Creates Value and Emphasis

Line can be used to create areas of *value*, or light and dark, within a composition. Value is the presence or absence of light. Through changes in value, as light moves around a three-dimensional form, we as viewers can perceive not only its shape, but also its three-dimensional qualities: weight, depth, mass, and volume. We are able to see how it carves out and

occupies space. Value can also be used to suggest the illusion of light moving across an image on a flat surface, transforming it and producing the appearance of three dimensions. One of the easiest ways to accomplish this is by building up successive layers of lines that overlap and thereby create darker areas in a composition. Hatching, crosshatching, contour hatching, and pointillism are all techniques that can be employed to suggest value, depth and mass using only line.

Hatching is a technique that utilizes a series of closely placed parallel lines to create darker areas in a work of art. The lines used to create hatching can be thick or thin, dark or light, broken or unbroken. If these lines of hatching follow the implied shape of the object, and therefore contribute to the sense of three dimensions as they move across it, they are referred to as **contour hatching**, because they are reinforcing the contours of the object. Lines of hatching that overlap, crossing over one another in different directions, usually at perpendicular angles, are called **crosshatching**. Crosshatching makes it possible to build up very dark areas without losing the distinct linear quality of the individual lines.

Pointillism is a technique used to create a range of value by building up layers of dots, points or dashes. They can be placed side-by-side, in clusters or overlapped for effect, until the desired level of darkness is reached. Pointillism is also a painting technique where dots of color are combined, overlapped and layered to form a complete image. This technique was used extensively by the French painter Georges Seurat and can also be seen in the work of Vincent van Gogh.

It is also possible to build up areas of value with line through other line techniques such as *scribbling*, which can utilize both linear and circular strokes to create a range of values. As with crosshatching, marks can be layered to build up darker areas.

Line can be used to create emphasis by developing more visual weight in areas of the composition, drawing our attention to that part of the image. This can be accomplished by varying line weight, direction, speed, and texture, or by building up successive layers of lines that create darker areas that draw focus and grab the viewer's attention.

Line Can Communicate Feelings and Mood

Because line possesses so many evocative qualities, artists can easily manipulate it as a design element to convey mood and emotion. Variations in speed evoke a different response. Quick, sketchy lines may establish a sense of hurry, anticipation, acceleration, or even fear, desperation, or the feeling of being hunted. In a costume design sketch, quick lines may suggest lighter, thinner, and more transparent fabrics or show how the costume will move on the actor. Slow, thick, heavy lines may suggest a state of ease, relaxation, safety, weight, stability,

FIGURE 6-8 *Line defines shape*

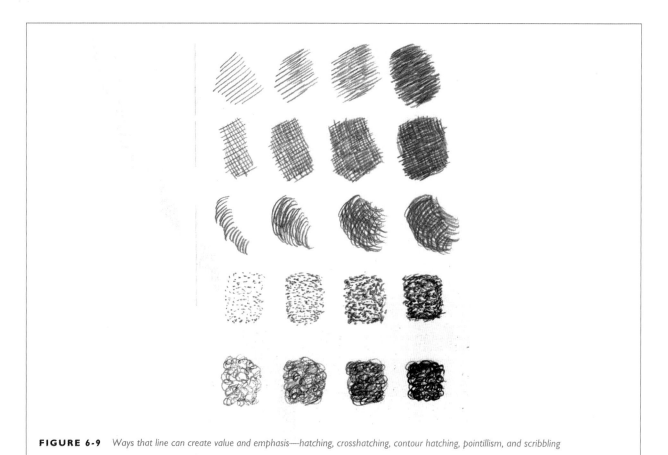

FIGURE 6-9 *Ways that line can create value and emphasis—hatching, crosshatching, contour hatching, pointillism, and scribbling*

FIGURE 6-10 *Ways that line can create emphasis*

stagnation, or the slow passage of time. Extensive vertical lines in a set design that reach out of sight might create a feeling of being overwhelmed by the environment, of being small in a large world, or of an omnipresent force that is watching the action of the play at all times. Vertical lines in a costume may make an actor look taller, or establish a sense of rigidity or stiffness of moral fiber. Radial lines in a set may establish a sense of excitement, or narrow the audience's focus, pulling their attention to a specific area or actor that is crucial to the story of a production.

FIGURE 6-11   Chicago, *University of Wisconsin Green Bay, set design by Jeff Entwistle, lighting design by R. Michael Ingraham, costume design by Kaoime E. Malloy*

Line Can Create Direction and Movement

Our eyes tend to follow lines to see where they are going—like trains on a track or the dividing line in the center of a highway. Lines start in one location and end in another; the paths they trace guide the viewer's eye through an image. Artists can use this natural tendency to direct the viewer's eyes around an image and to suggest movement within a composition. Different directions convey different emotional qualities, moods, or ideas. How we perceive these directions is often related to our experience of gravity.

Horizontal lines are the most placid and the most calming. They suggest natural phenomena with peaceful connotations, such as the horizon line, a still body of water, or a body in repose. A horizontal line can also suggest forward movement, but the mood and speed of that movement will depend on the speed of the line itself. In contrast, vertical lines have an assertive quality and, depending on their direction, can suggest upward or downward movement. Diagonal lines are the most dramatic. They always imply action, vigorous movement or speed, perhaps related to our experiences of sledding down a snowy hill at an angle or riding up and down on a roller coaster. Radial lines are active and explosive, suggesting outward movement and energy, like the excitement of fireworks shooting out in all directions or rays of light emanating from the sun. Lines in sets, costumes, and lighting can have the same dramatic effects and can be used to create focus or guide the audience's eyes for the same purpose, or to evoke a sense of emotion in the audience.

FIGURE 6-12   *Line movement*

THE LANGUAGE OF LINE

Actual line: A line that is real, complete, and unbroken.

Closed line: A line that connects to form a shape or joins with other lines for visual effect.

Contour hatching/cross contour: Lines of hatching or crosshatching that follow the shape of an object, moving around it, thereby creating the illusion of three dimensions along with value.

Contour line: A line that defines the shape of an object, but which varies in weight and thickness, contributing to the illusion of mass and volume.

Crosshatching: Layers of hatched lines that move in different directions, resulting in darker values.

Descriptive line: A type of contour line that communicates mood and feelings through variations in line quality.

Gestural line: Quick, freely drawn lines that imply past, present, or future movement or the gesture of a subject. With gesture line, delineating shape is less important than capturing the dynamics of movement.

Hatching: Closely spaced, usually parallel lines that are used to create value.

Implied line: A line that fades, diminishes, or is otherwise deliberately broken as it moves across a composition, positioned in such a way that the viewer's eye automatically connects the individual marks to form a line.

Line: The path of a moving point traced by an instrument, medium or tool.

Line quality: The physical characteristics of a line.

Open line: A line or lines that are not connected.

Outline: The edge of a two-dimensional object or shape defined by a line of even thickness and weight, which separates it from the surrounding area. Outline does not imply volume or mass, it simply defines shape.

Pointillism: A technique used to create a range of value by building up layers of dots, points, or dashes.

Psychic line: An imaginary line that connects two or more objects in an image and suggests a connection between them, real or implied.

Silhouette: The overall shape or outline of an object.

Value: The amount of light and dark present in a work, independent of color.

LINE EXERCISES

Exercise #1: Exploring Expressive Line

Materials:

- 9 × 12 drawing pad

- Pencils of varying hardness and softness

Method

The purpose of this exercise is to explore line as a tool for expression, experimenting with the relationships between lines as they come together, touch, and move apart, varying their width, direction, speed, pressure, and other descriptive qualities as you fill in the paper.

1. Begin with your paper in a landscape orientation, with the longest side facing you. Starting at one edge, draw a line with your pencil from one side of the paper to the other, creating a meandering path, a winding road, a convoluted trail, or a precise road. The only constraint is that it cannot cross back over itself. This first line will guide and influence all the other lines that come after it, so consider it carefully.

2. The next steps are to draw in more lines on either side of this first line, varying the line quality and expression while still relating the new lines to the one that precedes them. Let each new line build on the one that came before it and serve to offer up new changes and potential to the one that comes after it. Lines may touch other lines, moving close and then moving away to create open areas. You may then choose to fill in these spaces or leave them empty. You can go over lines to make them thicker; sketch them quickly to alter their feeling; draw them slowly to make them heavy; experiment with pressure to make your marks pale or dark. Use a soft pencil to make dark lines or a hard pencil for light lines. The only restriction is that lines may not cross over one another and they may not meet at 90-degree angles. How they move across the page and how they relate to one another as they do so is up to you. The only requirement is to fill in the paper completely.

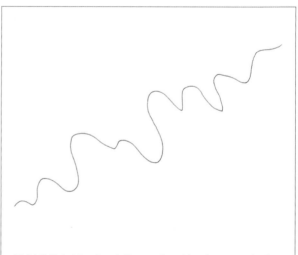

FIGURE 6-13   *Step 1: Draw a shaped line from one side of the paper to the other*

FIGURE 6-14   *Add more lines relating to the first line to create a final composition*

Exercise #2: Telling a Story with Line

Materials:

- Paper 9 × 12
- Pencils
- Ruler

Method

The purpose of this exercise is to explore the expressive qualities of line as a design element by using it to tell a story across a series of panels or storyboards. Storyboards are a very useful conceptual tool for set and lighting designers to sketch out their ideas for individual scenes or looks just as a film director might use them to plan individual camera shots. Here they are used in much the same way as a comic book artist would to tell a story panel by panel.

1. Begin by dividing your paper into a three-inch grid, three across and four tall. This will give you 12 panels total.

2. In each panel, you are allowed three lines or points total. Your line begins when you touch your pencil to the paper and ends when you either lift the pencil or you reach one side of the square. As long as you keep your pencil connected to the paper and the line you make is unbroken, it counts as one line. Remember that one of the functions of line is to define shape, so line can be used in this manner in these panels.

3. Decide what story you want to tell in your 12 images. It could be as simple and representational as the sun setting over a lake or as complex and nonrepresentational as the progression between one emotion and the other, using line as an analog representation of each feeling.

4. Following the guidelines and with your story in mind, begin in the upper left-hand panel and tell your story using three lines per panel, traveling across the top squares. It is up to you if you want to begin the second row with the left square so that your story reads like sentences, or move from right to left to connect the images between the two rows visually. How the images relate to one another is an important consideration in the overall composition.

5. Explore variations in line quality throughout each panel. Vary thickness, speed, pressure, direction and so on to help communicate your narrative.

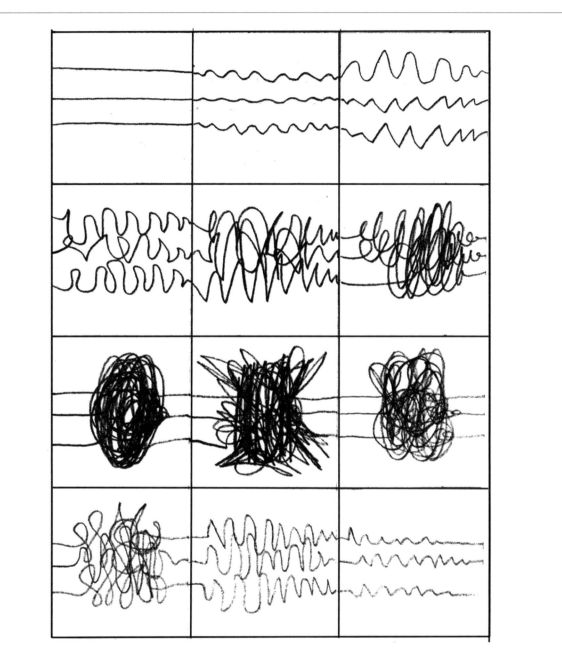

FIGURE 6-15 *Telling a story with line example*

CHAPTER 7

SHAPE, FORM, MASS, VOLUME, AND SPACE

WHAT IS SHAPE?

A **shape** is a two-dimensional, recognizable object or **form**. It occupies an area with identifiable boundaries or **edges**, which can be created in a number of ways. A shape can be formed by a line or lines that define its outer edges, for example, a square outlined on paper. The series of lines separates the area inside the **boundary** they create, defining it as a "square" and everything outside of it as "not a square." The line that frames the shape also forms a series of edges that are shared by both the shape itself and the surrounding background. A shape can be defined by a shift in texture or pattern, such as a square of unmowed grass in the middle of a mowed lawn, or a small square filled with lines inside another, blank square. A shape can also be produced by a shift in color, such as yellow polka dots on a blue background or by two differently colored areas sitting side by side.

The terms *shape* and *form* are often used interchangeably in design and the visual arts, but form can have secondary meanings. In addition to being a reference to the shape of an object, it may also refer to the genre, medium, or overall effect of the work, in other words, an art form. Form is also used to refer to a three-dimensional object, or one that appears three-dimensional.

TYPES OF SHAPES

There are two main categories of shapes: geometric and organic. **Geometric shapes** are the standard shapes that we can find in geometry: squares, circles, triangles, ellipses, parallelograms, stars, and so on. Because geometric shapes

often define a **plane**, a surface that possesses only height and width, they can also be referred to as **planar shapes**. A cube, for example, is comprised of six geometric shapes—squares—that fit together to create a three-dimensional form. Each of these squares is one plane of the cube. **Organic shapes** are those that are irregular in shape, and resemble living things found in nature. Another term for this style of shape is **biomorphic**. Organic shapes are often irregular and can be highly **subjective**. They may exist solely in the imagination of the artist. But both organic and geometric shapes can also be highly representational, very realistic, and be accurate and faithful depictions of recognizable objects. Both types of shapes can be used in a composition, or a design might focus on or be dominated by one type of shape over the other.

Shapes that are characterized by curved lines are called **curvilinear**. Their edges are smooth and flowing, gently guiding the viewer's eye around the object. They have a more natural feel and flavor. In contrast, shapes dominated by right angles and planes are called **rectilinear**. These shapes have hard, precise edges that lend a sharp, ordered feeling to a composition. They appear to be more structured, artificial, or manmade. Compositions can certainly be created principally with just one of these styles of shapes, but most designs combine both to produce the desired visual and conceptual effect.

COMPOSITION

Composition is essentially the arrangement of shapes and other design elements within a **format**. Format is the size and shape of an artwork, which establishes a set of boundaries and restrictions on its appearance, organization and presentation.

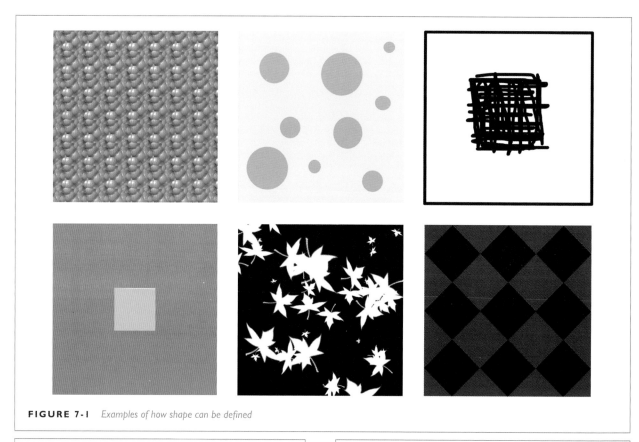

FIGURE 7-1   *Examples of how shape can be defined*

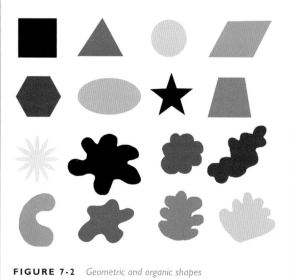

FIGURE 7-2   *Geometric and organic shapes*

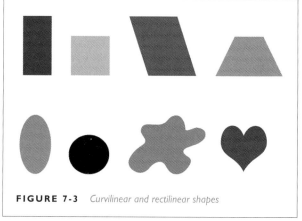

FIGURE 7-3   *Curvilinear and rectilinear shapes*

A more inclusive term for composition is **design**, which refers to both the selection of visual elements and their subsequent arrangement in a composition. A composition is created not only by the shapes that are selected by the designer and how they are subsequently arranged, forming complex patterns and structures, but also by how they relate to and interact with one another, carving out new shapes and forms from the space that exists between and around the objects. This is a very important consideration in theatrical design, where we are constantly dealing not only with shape, but also with the mass, volume, and space of a theatrical stage, inhabited by actors.

MASS, VOLUME, AND SPACE

We cannot talk about shape without discussing the related concepts of mass, volume, and space. A shape is a form that occupies a defined, flat area. It is two-dimensional. In contrast, a **mass** is a three-dimensional form that occupies a measurable **volume** of **space**. A square drawn on a piece of paper is a shape; a cube is a three-dimensional object with several sides that possesses mass and volume. Because we see the world in images we may also talk about the *shape* of a three-dimensional form. In this case, we are emphasizing our awareness of the outline of the object against a background, in other words, its silhouette, such as the shape of a mountain against the sky, an actor against a set, or a chair against a wall. Images in representational art can also occupy this interesting middle ground.

Space in our technological world often is interpreted as a **void**, as nothingness. We think of space as a huge emptiness devoid of life and perhaps, by implication, of meaning. It is just there. It seems to do nothing. We even use the word "space" to suggest a negative condition. When we say someone is "spaced out," we mean that they are blank, unfocused, and not really present in the here and now. However, the space around a shape or work of three-dimensional art is not a void. It is very much there and as such, must be considered when planning a composition or design, particularly when the end result will be a three-dimensional object or arrangement of objects such as a costume or set design.

Space is a dynamic visual element that interacts with the lines, shapes, colors, and textures of a work to give them definition. In dance or theatre, it can separate individuals and create tension. It can be a dynamic obstacle to overcome.

How can there be a line without space on either side to mark its edges? How can there be a shape without the space around it to define it? How can there be relationships between objects or actors without space to both separate them and bring them closer together?

All art forms with mass exist in three-dimensional space, such as sculpture, architecture, jewelry, dance, and theatre, to name a few. They are defined by and take their character from the ways in which they carve out volumes of space within and around them. Because of this fact, space is an important consideration when creating these forms of art.

FIGURE 7-4   *Shape versus mass and silhouette (Shaiith/ Shutterstock.com)*

When we view a three-dimensional work, we inhabit the same space that it does, and we need to walk through it or around it in order to experience it completely, rather than just looking *at* it. In the case of theatre, the stage space may be arranged in such a way that the audience sits in front of the stage, on three sides of the playing area, or all around it. Each of these different configurations changes the ways in which the audience perceives the space and responds to it.

This way of actively participating with a work of art by being part *of* it is called *immersion*, and many artists are using it as an additional design element when creating work, even with forms of art that do not intrinsically possess immersion as a key component. Instead of simply walking around a sculpture to experience it, viewers might now find themselves walking *through* a sculpture that occupies an entire room or gallery space, with their movement through the work contributing to their perception of the piece. Theatre is immersive by nature, and is also interactive, meaning that the audience participates in the performance to a degree by reacting to the events depicted onstage. A theatre performance may also be heavily dependent on audience interaction, such as *The 25th Annual Putnam County Spelling Bee*, where audience volunteers become contestants in the competition along with the actors. With any theatre production, because theatre is live and every audience is different, no two performances will ever be the same. This relationship between the actors and the audience is at the heart of the theatrical experience.

POSITIVE AND NEGATIVE SPACE

Shape and space work together to form a finished design. They create a sense of balance and unity, of the individual elements working together to produce a coherent and evocative whole. Space can be divided into two distinct types: positive and negative. **Positive spaces** are those occupied by the main subjects of the work. The subject is sometimes referred to as the **figure**, most likely due to the traditional use of the human figure as a subject for fine art. Positive spaces often inhabit the **foreground** of a composition. The foreground is the part of an image or design that is nearest to the viewer. The spaces around, within and behind the positive spaces are called **negative space**. Negative space can also be referred to as the **background**. The background is the part of a composition that is farthest away from the observer. Onstage, in a proscenium theatre, the area downstage is the foreground and the area upstage is the background. Between the foreground and the background is an area referred to as the **middle ground**. The middle ground may also contain important design elements or be used for impact, especially onstage. Other stage spaces such as thrust or arena staging will alter the relationships and locations of the background, middle, and foreground.

Both positive and negative spaces are dynamic compositional elements. The area occupied by positive space has a shape, and the negative space around it also has a shape. It is possible to reveal the form of the subject in a design by concentrating on the negative space, showing everything around the subject but not the subject itself. Eliminating all the other elements around a figure will create a silhouette of the figure. Doing so will also reveal the shape of the negative space. Positive and negative spaces are interdependent; they share boundaries and edges and each helps to determine the shape of the other. Placement and arrangement of the subjects in a composition can dramatically alter the way negative shape interacts within any format. Consequently, a designer must consider negative space equally when developing their ideas. It can be easier to see this relationship between positive and negative space in a black and white image.

In Figure 7.6, built entirely with line and geometric shapes, the relationship between the positive and negative space is relatively easy to see. The way in which the black squares share edges and are defined by the white triangles in the border of the image is clear. It is easy to observe how the positive space of the black squares on the perimeter of the composition interact with the negative space inside it, creating a large, multi-armed cross in the center of the image. What makes the configuration interesting is not simply the positive space, creating a bold pattern, but the way it plays off the negative space, creating a dynamic composition that is balanced and engaging.

Sometimes, the relationship between positive and negative space can appear confusing. If the contrast in the image is high and the ratio between the two is close enough for the eye to be able to shift between them to see one or the other dominantly, the result is called a **figure/ground reversal**. This is an optical effect, requiring conscious effort on the part of the viewer to shift their focus and see one part of the composition as the foreground and the other as the background. In Figure 7.7, both the high contrast between the black and white shapes and the balance of the placement of the forms in the composition contribute to the ability of the viewer's eye to switch back and forth between seeing black forms on a white background, and white forms on a black background.

Shape and all its related components are important elements in theatrical design. We are working within a three-dimensional stage space, dressing people who possess mass and who will move about in the volume of the environment that is

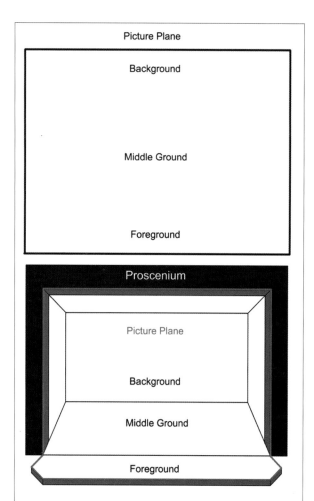

FIGURE 7-5   *Foreground, middle ground, and background on the picture plane and onstage*

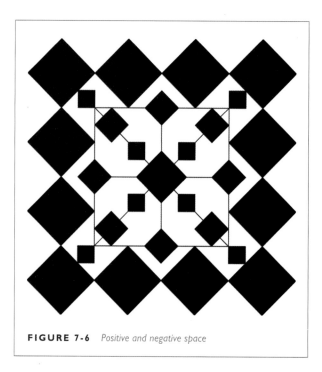

FIGURE 7-6   *Positive and negative space*

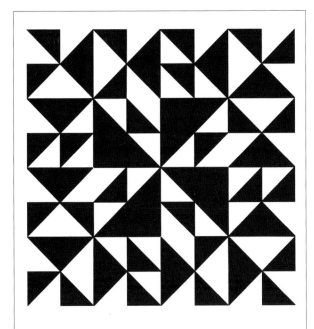

FIGURE 7-7   *Figure ground reversal*

specifically composed and selected for them and then revealed and shaped by light, sound, and multimedia. Even the director uses shape to arrange the actors in groups that are influenced by the stage environment.

THE LANGUAGE OF SHAPE, FORM, MASS, VOLUME, AND SPACE

Background: The area of a composition that surrounds the subject.

Biomorphic shape: Abstract shapes that resemble living forms.

Boundary: The perceived border or edge of a shape, which indicates its limits.

Composition: The arrangement of shapes.

Curvilinear shape: Shapes that are dominated by curved edges and lines.

Design: Another word for composition.

Edges: The perceived outline or boundary of a shape.

Figure: The positive space in a composition. It can also be used to refer to the main subject in an image.

Figure/ground reversal: A two-dimensional composition where the foreground and the background appear to reverse positions.

Foreground: The area of a composition occupied by the subject.

Form: A synonymous term for shape. Form may also be used to refer to the type of artwork, i.e., sculpture, painting, or be used to describe a three-dimensional object.

Format: The size and shape of the work surface.

Geometric shape: Shapes that are derived from mathematics and geometry, such as circles, triangles, and squares.

Mass: In three-dimensional artwork, an object that occupies a volume of space. In two-dimensional artwork, mass refers to an object that appears to be three-dimensional, creating the illusion of volume with various techniques.

Middle ground: The area of a composition between the subject and the background.

Negative space: The space that surrounds the subject in a work and/or the shapes that are defined by the spaces between objects.

Organic shape: Shapes that appear as if they were derived from a living process or organism. Also referred to as biomorphic.

Picture plane: The flat surface of a two-dimensional work of art.

Planar shape: A two-dimensional shape that possesses the qualities of a plane.

Plane: A defined area that is two dimensional, possessing only height and width. Also a compositional format that can be used to create the illusion of three dimensions with advancing and receding elements or techniques.

Positive space: The space occupied by the subject in a composition.

Rectilinear shape: Shapes that are defined by hard edges, lines, or boundaries that form angles, suggesting the idea of a rectangle.

Shape: A two-dimensional, recognizable form defined by line, a shift in color, value, or texture that allows it to stand out from the surrounding area.

Space: The areas around, between, or within the visual elements in a composition. The areas occupied by shapes in a two-dimensional work.

Subjective shape: Shapes created by the artist's imagination.

Void: A large, open space within a composition that serves as a dynamic design element.

Volume: A defined, measurable amount of three-dimensional space.

SHAPE EXERCISE

Positive and Negative Space
Materials

- Color or black and white photograph/image no smaller than 8½ × 11

- Pencils

- Black felt pen

- Tracing paper the same size as your image

Method

The object of this exercise is to identify the main shapes in the image you choose, to become aware of how these shapes share edges and boundaries, and to understand the relationship between positive and negative space.

1. Select a color or black-and-white photograph to use for this exercise. It should be an image that has objects in both the foreground and the background, preferably with some space between and around the objects.

2. Lay a sheet of tracing paper over the image and carefully outline the main shapes in the image with pencil. The idea is to synthesize details in order to minimize the number of shapes.

3. Once you have all of the shapes outlined, duplicate the outlined composition on another piece of tracing paper by laying it over the first and tracing the lines.

4. On both sheets, go over the lines with the black marker.

5. On one sheet, using your original image as reference, color in the main objects in the image with black, identifying them as positive space. The uncolored parts now become negative space. Observe how the shapes share edges in the composition.

6. On the second sheet fill in the negative space from the first image with the marker, turning it into positive space. The positive space of the previous drawing now becomes negative space. Has your perception of the boundaries of the shapes changed with the reversal of the coloring?

CHAPTER 8

VALUE

WHAT IS VALUE?

We rely primarily on our eyes to understand form, and form is revealed to us by light. When you pick up a three-dimensional object with your eyes closed, feeling it with your hands, you can learn some general information about the form, but no real detail. If you open your eyes, the form is instantly much clearer because of the way light is reflected from the object, revealing its shape. If you then rotate the object, you soon have a complete grasp of its mass and volume, because you are able to perceive it from all sides.

Looking at a three-dimensional artwork you can easily see its dimensions. It is right in front of you. You can walk around it and perceive its form. In a two-dimensional piece, mass and volume have to be created in other ways. One of the most effective tools to visually define and model the three-dimensional qualities of a form on a two-dimensional surface is **value**.

In the visual arts, value is the term used to describe the level of light and dark in any piece. Plainly speaking, value is the absence or presence of light. In two-dimensional artworks, such as a drawing or rendering, the use of value provides visual clues about three-dimensional forms through the creation of implied and reflected light, which illustrate the way light moves around an object. By duplicating this pattern of light, mass and volume can be reproduced convincingly on a flat surface. Creating the illusion of three-dimensional form is called **modeling** and this is the same principle a lighting designer will use to model the figure on stage. This type of value is considered to be **plastic**, meaning that it is malleable and can be manipulated as needed in order to create the desired effect.

Several things occur when light strikes the surface of a three-dimensional object. Light will reach the part of the object that is closest to the light source first. This area will consequently have the brightest value. This area is called a **highlight**. Light will then move around the object in patterns that are determined by its form. Rounded surfaces will allow light to change gradually from highlight to **shadow**, whereas angular, planar surfaces will dictate a **hard edge** between highlight and shadow where edges meet. Shadows are created on surfaces of a three-dimensional object where light cannot reach or is blocked. In between highlight and shadow there are usually a series of **halftone** values as the light moves from light to dark. Halftones are tonal values halfway between the highlights and shadows and reveal the transition of light as it moves around the object. Although objects have their own **local value**, lightness and darkness that is inherent to their appearance, modeling with highlights and shadows from one or more light sources in an image reveals the form in a more realistic and convincing way. Highlight, shadow, and halftones are all relative. The brightest highlight in a design can actually be a comparatively low value and it is possible for the deepest shadow to be fairly light. The remaining values are usually dictated by the amount of **contrast** between the darkest shadow and the brightest highlight. In other words, how much difference there is between the brightest bright and the darkest dark. So, all value is relative because it is dependent on the range of tones present in any particular composition. Understanding value is obviously critical in order to create an effective lighting design for the theatre, where light is the main element of the design, but it is equally important for all designers, as value has a strong effect on the perception of form, color, and the creation of mood. Value is a key component in theatrical drawings and renderings, where shape, form, and mass must be accurately depicted not only for the purpose of aesthetics, but to communicate ideas and key information about real three-dimensional spaces that will be inhabited by actors in actual garments all revealed by light that shapes and models their forms.

THE VALUE SCALE

Value is measured in terms of a **value scale**, where white is the lightest value and black is the darkest, with several **neutral values** in between in percentages of ten for a total of 11 values. In reality, there is an infinite range of values between black and white and the human eye is able to perceive around 40 individual tones. Combining white and black to produce a series of grays that are devoid of color creates *neutral values*. These grays are also referred to as *achromatic*, because they possess no color, or chroma.

VALUE AND COLOR

Value is also one of the intrinsic properties of color. The value of every color can be altered through the addition of white or black in order to make it lighter or darker. Doing so affects the amount of light that the pigment is able to reflect back to the eye. It is also possible to compare colors to the value scale in order to determine the **relative value** of each color. Relative value is the lightness or darkness of a color. For example, yellow is a bright color that has a lighter relative value than purple, which has a deeper, darker value. Knowing the relative value of color is important when making decisions about the overall look of a design or composition because value has a large influence on the mood of an image.

Both colors and monochrome grays can be classified as or grouped into **high key** or **low key** values. High key values are those from the middle range of the value scale to white, including all the gradients in between. Low key values span the range from the middle tone to black, and all the gradients in between. Careful use of each group of values can produce a variety of effects and both allow for a sophisticated definition of shape, form, and mass; but they do have different visual effects and elicit different responses from the viewer. High key values have a brighter, lighter feel and may therefore suggest a happier mood, whereas low key values have a darker, heavier feel and may give the impression of sadness, brooding, or melancholy. Lighter values may give the impression of more light within a composition, or suggest a specific time of day. Darker values may be used to indicate a night scene, or may be used to create a dynamic sense of tension or lend an air of mystery.

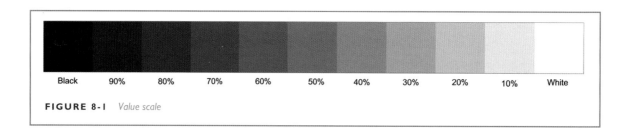

FIGURE 8-1 *Value scale*

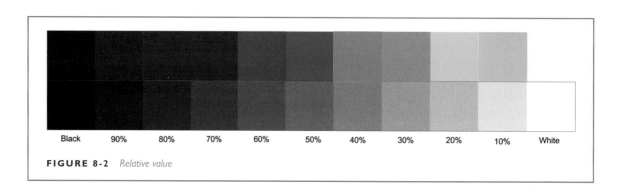

FIGURE 8-2 *Relative value*

Consequently, when selecting the range of values to be used in any composition, the desired emotional effect of the final piece must be taken into account. Of all the design elements, value is second only to color in its potential for creating mood and emotional impact. It is one of the most compelling visual elements.

Relative value is also useful for determining the **value pattern** of a composition. A value pattern describes the organization of light and dark within a work of art. In a black-and-white image, the value pattern can be determined in a straightforward manner. It may be more difficult to see in a color rendering. One way to easily perceive the value pattern of a color image is to make a black-and-white photocopy, or to set the color definitions of a digital image to grayscale on a computer with an image editing program. The copy machine or the computer program will instantly translate the colors in the image into their relative values and reveal their pattern in the process. Changes in value are necessary in a composition in order to provide visual interest and to create an enjoyable arrangement for the eye to follow. It also provides structure and creates unity, a sense that all the elements in a design are working together in an effective manner.

When the value pattern is contained within the shapes that make up a composition, the values are said to be **closed**. Often, there is a distinct border or edge that surrounds each shape or the boundaries of each form and the value it contains is clean and clearly defined. When there is no clear delineation between tones and the values bleed over into the areas that surround them the composition is said to be **open**. It is also possible for value to be purely **decorative**, where the range of lights and darks serves

to emphasize the flat nature of a two-dimensional format rather than modeling three-dimensional forms. Used in this manner, value becomes a purely ornamental design element that can create pattern, texture, and visual interest.

WAYS THAT VALUE CAN BE CREATED

Value can be created on a flat surface in several ways. Various linear techniques can be effectively employed to create a range of tonal values. Making several parallel lines close together in order to build up a darker tone is called hatching. Crosshatching is created by hatching over existing lines in another direction, building up multiple layers of parallel lines and thereby creating a darker value. Contour hatching is a type of hatching that follows the contour of a shape, reinforcing its three-dimensional form and mass. Repeating tiny dots or dashes over and over to build up darker areas is called **stippling**. With any of these techniques, using more lines or dots, tightly packed together, creates darker values and lighter values are created with fewer marks. When viewed up close, these linear techniques may seem a little coarse, but at a distance, they blend together to effectively create areas of light and dark.

It is also possible, and often desirable, to create shifts in value through more subtle methods, where the change between the lightest lights and the darkest darks are gradual and subtle. **Blending** occurs when the transition of value from light to dark happens progressively, little by little, and the change between values is soft and flowing. Two of the most versatile and expressive blending techniques are chiaroscuro and sfumato.

Chiaroscuro literally means "light and dark," and is a blending technique perfected during the Italian Renaissance to model three-dimensional forms in a highly realistic manner on a flat surface. Chiaroscuro considers how light travels across the surface of a three-dimensional object, using highlight, halftones, shadows, reflected and implied light to suggest the illusion of mass and volume. The Italian painter Giotto is credited with inventing the technique and was the first artist to use highlights and shadows to suggest dimension, but it is Leonardo da Vinci who is considered to have perfected the technique. In da Vinci's drawings and paintings, light is a dynamic element that gently caresses the subject of his compositions, revealing three-dimensional form through the delicate and effortless transitions of light to dark. **Implied light** appears to travel around the subjects, completing them and anchoring them in their format while subtle halftones are echoed back onto the surface of the objects as **reflected highlights** to enhance the perception of three dimensions.

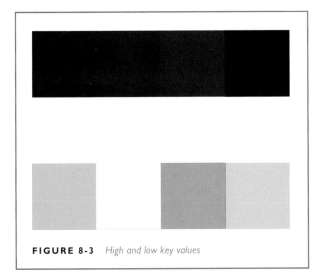

FIGURE 8-3   *High and low key values*

FIGURE 8-4 *Value pattern in a color rendering—*The Mountain Giants *by Luigi Piradello, costume design by Kaoime E. Malloy*

FIGURE 8-5 *Open value—Edgar Degas,* Danseuse debout, le bras droit levé (Standing dancer, right arm raised) *ca. 1891. Closed value— Edwin Austin Abbey,* Richard, Duke of Gloucester, and the Lady Anne. *Decorative value—John La Farge,* Cherry Blossoms Against Spring Freshet, *1882–1883 (Images © Yale University Art Gallery).*

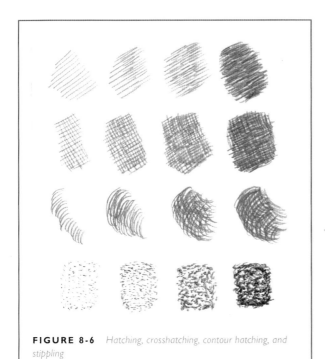

FIGURE 8-6   *Hatching, crosshatching, contour hatching, and stippling*

Sfumato is a fine type of shading where the transitions from light to dark are very soft and so subtle that there is no discernable outline or hard edge around an object. The meaning of the word itself is 'to tone down' or to 'evaporate like smoke.' Paintings and drawings that employ this blending technique often appear hazy and soft, as if the subject were being viewed through a thin veil of smoke. By using it, darker values are brightened and lighter values are slightly dulled, creating a delicate, soft shift between tones. Da Vinci was the most well-known master of this technique, and the advantages of this blending style can easily be seen throughout his work; but the technique can also be clearly seen in the drawings of Georges Seurat.

Given the importance of value in revealing form and the need for designers to create representational drawings and renderings of their designs that accurately present their ideas for directors and their design colleagues, the need for a clear understanding of value is clear. A certain degree of skill is required to use value to create realistic three-dimensional form on a flat surface and these techniques will be explored in greater detail in Chapter 11 and Chapter 22.

FIGURE 8-7   *Chiaroscuro*

FIGURE 8-8   *Georges Seurat,* L'Écho, *study for* Une Baignade, Asnières (Bathing Place, Asnières) *(Image © Yale University Art Gallery)*

THE LANGUAGE OF VALUE

Blending: The technique of moving from one degree of value to another in a smooth fashion.

Chiaroscuro: "Light and dark." The technique of blending values to show the bending of light around a form in order to represent the illusion of three dimensions on a two-dimensional surface.

Closed value compositions: An image where the values are confined within shapes.

Contrast: The differences between light and dark in a composition.

Decorative value: Value that emphasizes the two-dimensional nature and flatness of a composition and uses dark and light tones for ornamental effect.

Halftone: A value halfway between the highlight and shadow.

Hard edge: A crisp line between a bright highlight and a deep shadow.

High key: The range of values from middle gray to white.

Highlight: The area of an object or composition that receives the greatest amount of direct light, or the brightest area of an image related to shadow.

Implied light: The perception of light as it moves around an object.

Local value: The relative lightness or darkness of a surface without light falling on it.

Low key: The range of values from middle gray to black.

Modeling: Creating the illusion of three dimensional form through the use of light. In drawing and rendering, modeling means to duplicate these light patterns on a flat surface.

Neutral values: Lights and darks created with black and white only, without color. These are also called achromatic values.

Open value compositions: An image where the values bleed over the boundaries of shapes into surrounding areas.

Plastic value: Value used to create the illusion of mass, space. and volume.

Reflected highlight: Highlights that are reflected back onto an object from the surface underneath it.

Relative value: The comparative lightness and darkness of any color. Also referred to as chromatic value.

Sfumato: A subtle and gradual blending from light to dark values.

Shadow: The area of an object or composition that receives the least amount of direct light or a surface where light is blocked. The absence of light.

Stippling: Creating texture with very fine drops of paint with a sponge, airbrush, by spattering, or through other means.

Value: The amount of light and dark present in a work, independent of color.

Value pattern: Organized areas of light and dark within an image.

Value scale: A visual tool that shows the graduated tonal values between black and white, usually containing nine to 12 steps between them.

VALUE EXERCISE

Value in Color

Materials

- Tracing paper

- White illustration board or foam core

- Pencils

- Tortillions

- Fixative

- Double-sided tape or spray adhesive

Method

The objectives of this assignment are to learn to see the subtle values of light in a color picture, and to translate them into monochrome—black and white.

1. Find a high-resolution color picture of a famous painting, preferably in a book rather than on the Internet. The picture should really be no smaller than roughly 6" × 8" so that you have a good-sized image to work with.

2. Place a sheet of tracing paper over the image and gently outline the shapes in the composition. Then translate the color values into shades of gray and black using the value scale as reference. You will have to look at the color image carefully to determine which the darkest value is and which is the lightest, as well as the ranges of value in between. Use tonal, blended shading to fill in each area rather than hatching or crosshatching. The goal is to create a smooth, even monochrome value pattern of the original color image.

3. Be very careful so you do not damage the print or the book in any way.

4. Mount your finished value study on white illustration board or foam core. Use a cover sheet if the graphite on your tracing is very heavy in order to keep it from smudging—or use spray fixative. Even though this is a tracing it should be presentation-quality work. Be sure the edges of your board are straight and even and that the border around your study is even as well.

On the bottom right-hand corner of your mounting board, write the name of the artist, the title of the painting, the title of the book, and the page number for reference.

CHAPTER 9

COLOR

WHAT IS COLOR?

Color is the element of light that is reflected back from an object to our eyes. The color of the light reflected back to us is dependent on the color of the **pigment** inherent in the object itself. No other element of design gives us as much pleasure or is more symbolic of mood and emotion than color. Color is a very evocative component in art and design and it can have a profound effect upon the viewer. Our reactions to it are more than biological; they are both very personal and often culturally influenced. For example, in the West, black clothing is traditionally worn at a funeral and the color itself is associated with somber occasions, unpleasant emotions, even evil. In contrast, brides in the West wear white, a color associated with innocence in most Western cultures. However, in Japan, black is worn by grooms at weddings and is considered an auspicious color, and white is reserved for funerals where it is perceived as the color of mourning and of rebirth.

In addition, color is likely to be subject to an array of intensely personal interpretations. If you ask ten people what their favorite color is, you're likely to get ten different answers. If you ask them to respond to a specific color, how it makes them feel, what correlations they make between the color and their emotions, you're also likely to get ten different replies, especially if the group is culturally diverse. Consequently, a theatre designer must think carefully about their color choices.

Each color selected will have influence on the audience on both conscious and unconscious levels.

THE PHYSICS OF COLOR

Our ability to perceive color is dependent on light. Nothing possesses color intrinsically. We see color because objects absorb some of the white light from the sun or synthetic sources and reflect a limited range of light rays back to our eyes. A green apple appears green because it absorbs all other light wave frequencies and reflects only a narrow range from yellow to turquoise. If we were to shine a red light on the apple, it would appear black, because red light contains no light waves in the frequency required for our eyes to perceive the color green.

Even though light and its color frequencies exist on a linear scale between the ultraviolet and infrared spectrums rather than a circle, looking at a **color wheel** can be a useful visual tool to understand the relationships between colors. The most common color wheel is based on the theories of Louis Prang developed in 1876, and is referred to as the Prang's or artist's color wheel. This representation of color is familiar to most people. A basic color wheel generally displays only the true hues or colors as they appear in the visible spectrum. If value is included, the color wheel is usually presented as a sphere.

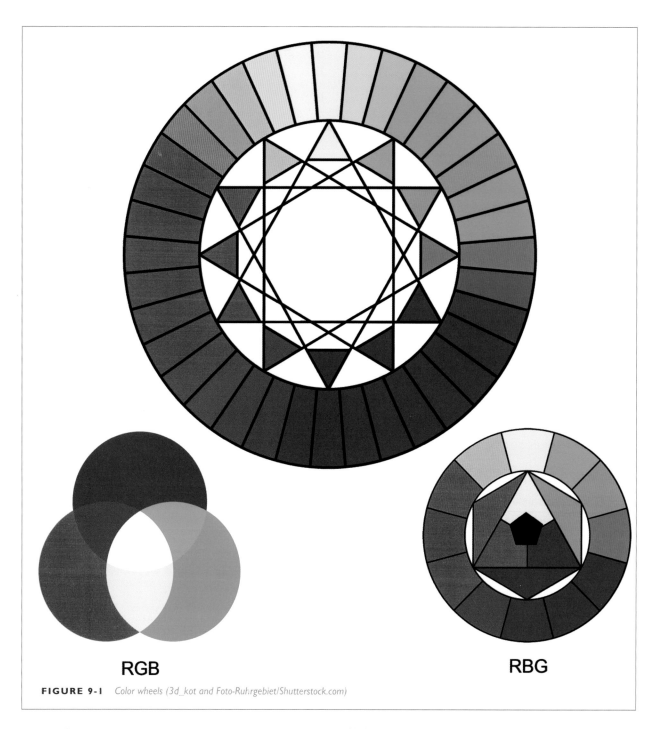

RGB   RBG

FIGURE 9-1   *Color wheels (3d_kot and Foto-Ruhrgebiet/Shutterstock.com)*

THE COLOR WHEEL AND COLOR THEORY

The color wheel visually represents several important relationships between colors. It is a convenient and easy way to see how colors relate to and interact with each other. Three colors on the color wheel are called **primaries**, because they cannot be made from other colors. They are therefore considered to be pure hues. In paint pigments, these colors are red, blue, and yellow. Primary colors sit at even distances around the color wheel, where the differences between their optical characteristics and ability to reflect light rays are evenly spaced

and balanced. The precise names of the primary colors may vary slightly between types of paints, manufacturers, and between paints and dyes. If the three primary colors are mixed together in equal amounts, the result is a dull black because all the light rays are absorbed and none can be reflected back.

Secondary colors are created by mixing equal parts of two primaries together. In pigment, these colors are green, orange, and purple. Each of them sits equidistant between their two primaries on the color wheel, and like the primaries, is positioned for their optical and light reflective qualities.

FIGURE 9-2 *Semi-neutral colors*

Tertiary colors are created by mixing a primary color and its adjacent secondary color together. In pigment, these colors are yellow-orange, red-orange, magenta, violet, teal or blue-green, and yellow-green. Although there are an infinite number of colors that can be mixed between primaries, these are the main color relationships that are identified on a color wheel.

Colors that sit directly across from each other on the color wheel are called **complements**. When complementary colors are mixed together, the result is some variety of gray, with the exception of red and green, which create brown when mixed. Rather than creating a new hue, the gray color occurs because complementary colors **neutralize** each other and cancel each other out, meaning that they reduce the light rays that can be reflected back to the viewer and dull the colors down to a neutral. This process can be exploited to create a variety of brilliant **semi-neutral** colors that liven up a composition by harmonizing with the dominant colors in a design.

Mixing colors with pigment is referred as **subtractive mixing**, because the amount of possible reflected light diminishes, or is subtracted, with each additional combination of colors. When all the colors are mixed together, the result is a dull black, where all light is absorbed, and little to none is reflected back to the viewer.

There is another type of color mixing called **additive mixing**, which is based on how light rays combine to create color. You might be familiar with this color wheel from the display settings on your computer monitor. The primaries in additive mixing are red, green, and blue, or RGB. Magenta, yellow, and cyan are the secondary colors in additive mixing. When red, blue, and green light rays are combined the result is a white light. The mixing process is called additive because the addition of each color increases the range of perceived light.

COLOR PROPERTIES

Color possesses several important physical properties that are important to the artist and designer.

Hue is the name of the color itself. Crimson, turquoise, viridian, and purple are all examples of hues. Often, hue refers to the pigment used to create the color, but it can also be used to refer to a color that resembles a recognizable pigment. For example, several pigments used in artist's paints are potentially toxic or are very expensive, so other, usually synthetic pigments are substituted to duplicate the appearance of a well-known color. Cadmium red traditionally gets it brilliant red color from cadmium, a toxic mineral. In order to make the paint safer to use, another pigment is used to

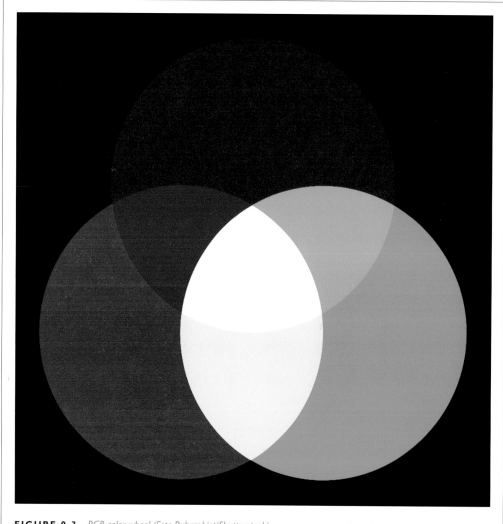

FIGURE 9-3 *RGB color wheel (Foto-Ruhrgebiet/Shutterstock)*

create what is called *cadmium red hue*. This color produces a red with similar optical properties to the traditional cadmium reds, but with less toxicity and a reduced cost.

Value is the amount of light or dark present in the color. **Tints** are created by adding white to a color, creating a lighter value. **Shades** are created by adding black, creating a darker value. Most colors are recognizable in a full range of value, meaning that red is still identifiable as being derived from red even when lightened with white to make pink. However, there are colors that are radically transformed through the addition of black, and no longer resemble their original hue in the darker values. Yellow is a primary example of this effect. If the hue is already a mix of two or more colors, the addition of black can result in very flat, dull shades that have little or no ability to reflect light.

Relative value refers to the comparison of light and dark between colors. Usually, colors are compared to the value scale in order to determine their relative value. Purple is darker than red, which is darker than yellow, and so on. Because colors with a darker intensity have more visual weight in a composition, relative value and the subsequent balance between colors can be an important design consideration.

Chroma, also called **saturation**, addresses the purity of the color, meaning the amount of pigment present. The purest colors are said to have high saturation. The palest colors, a lower saturation. You can alter chroma by adding water or any appropriate dilutents to paint to adulterate the pigment.

Tones are created by neutralizing a hue, either by adding gray or its complementary color, which alters the **intensity** of the color. Intensity refers to the dullness or brightness of a color. Grays created in this manner are called **chromatic grays**, while those created by simply mixing black with white are called **neutral grays**. A pure hue is said to have high intensity, while a dulled hue possesses a low intensity. When mixing color, it

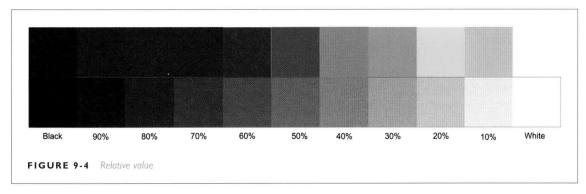

FIGURE 9-4 *Relative value*

| Black | 90% | 80% | 70% | 60% | 50% | 40% | 30% | 20% | 10% | White |

is important to remember that complementary hues already contain amounts of all three primary colors, so their ability to neutralize or dull color without the addition of black is very effective. When colors are dulled by adding their complements rather than black, the result is vibrant tones that reflect light and add depth to a composition by preserving hints of their original hues.

Ultimately, the effective use of color in design is about relationships, in understanding how hues interact with and affect each other. The intensity and consequently the visual weight of any color increases as the background approaches its complement, because of simultaneous contrast. Careful selection of the hues surrounding any color can intensify or diminish its visual impact, making it appear brighter or darker, or even altering the perception of the size of an object. Because of this fact, a designer might choose to follow certain sets of organizational principles when selecting colors.

COLOR SCHEMES AND HARMONIES

When selecting colors for a composition, an artist may choose to use related hues, ones that have certain resonances or that appear to naturally work well together. These are called **color schemes** or harmonies. Color schemes can provide a sense of visual organization in a composition, establish mood, and create areas of interest, emphasis, and balance.

When one color is used exclusively in a composition, along with all its tints, shades, and tones, the color scheme is called **monochromatic**. *Mono* meaning one, and *chroma* meaning color.

If an artist chooses to use complementary colors, those hues directly across from each other on the color wheel, along with their tints, shades and tones, the color scheme is called **complementary**. These colors react dramatically to each other, setting up visual tension—a dynamic bond of opposites— that intensify each other. A color scheme can also employ a **double complement**, using two sets of complementary colors as the basis of the composition. A related color scheme is called a **split complement**, using two complementary colors,

and the two colors directly adjacent to one of them. The three images in Figure 9.7 show the same composition using three sets of complementary colors: orange and blue; red and green; and purple and yellow. Notice how the complements intensify each other and add visual tension to the composition.

If the colors used in a composition are adjacent to each other on the color wheel and share a primary color between them, using their tints, shades, and tones, the resulting color scheme is called **analogous**. An analogous color scheme potentially offers a wide variety of color choices, which can be very subtle and closely related. The four designs in Figure 9.8 show four different analogous color schemes applied to the same image and the variety and vibrancy that are possible using this color harmony.

When an artist chooses to limit themselves to a small range of colors in a piece, they are said to be using a **closed** or **restricted palette**. The word "palette" refers to the artist's tool used to hold paint, and is commonly used as a metaphor for the range of colors employed in a design. If the artist uses all or a large number of the colors available to them, they are said to be using an **open palette**.

If an artist restricts their palette to those colors between the ranges of red and yellow on the color wheel, with all their tints, shades and tones, the color scheme is referred to as **warm**, because these colors often remind us of the sun, fire, daytime, and heat. By contrast, if an artist restricts their palette to those colors between blue and green, the color scheme is considered to be **cool**, because these colors remind the viewer of water, rain, darkness, and a cooler temperature.

There are two more color phenomena worth discussing, which artists often use to communicate feeling and create engaging images. The first is called **simultaneous contrast**. Simultaneous contrast occurs when two colors of equal intensity, usually complements, are set side-by-side. This positioning makes the two colors appear more vibrant because of the contrast between them. In the case of red and green, as seen in Figure 9.11, the colors almost appear to vibrate. Simultaneous contrast is such a powerful tool that it can cause images of the same size to actually appear to be different sizes.

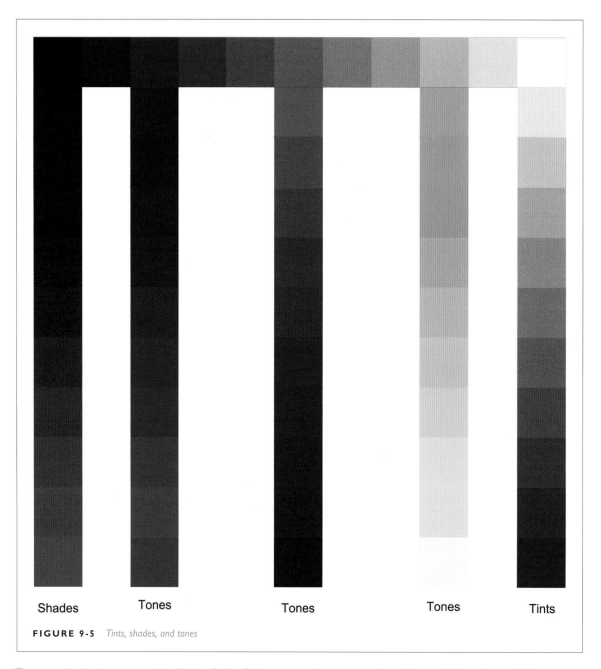

Shades	Tones	Tones	Tones	Tints

FIGURE 9-5   *Tints, shades, and tones*

The second color phenomenon is called **optical mixing**. Optical mixing takes advantage of the eye's ability to combine flecks of closely spaced individual colors, blending them into other colors as if the pigments were actually mixed. Artists have exploited this attribute to create complex pieces, using techniques such as pointillism, using tiny dots of color to create objects. Like hatching and crosshatching, up close, the technique might appear crude; but with distance, the eye is able to translate the individual points of color into complex and detailed images.

COLOR SYMBOLISM

Although color is a primary influence in our lives and despite a great deal of scientific inquiry into the role that color plays in our perception of the world there is very little agreement on the meaning of individual colors by experts and laypersons alike. Color is such an intensely personal experience that it can be extremely difficult to pin down any one meaning or group of meanings that everyone can assign to specific colors. Our response to color is influenced by many factors, including our culture, personal preference, individual experiences, and even the opinions of those around us. Despite the ambiguity and subjective nature of the interpretations of the meaning of color, it can't be denied that it plays an important part in our lives, however subjective that role may be.

Color attracts our attention. In nature, color is a key component in attracting a mate and in reproduction, as well as in camouflage for both plants and animals. It elicits emotional

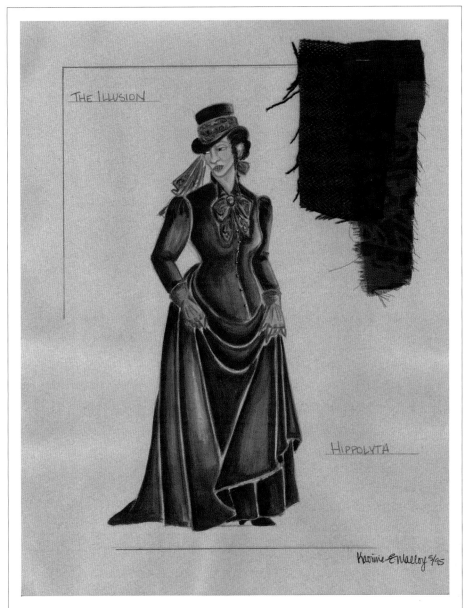

FIGURE 9-6   *Monochromatic color scheme—The Illusion by Tony Kushner, costume design by Kaoime E. Malloy*

responses. Wearing specific colors can help communicate our mood to others, support how we feel, or even be used to counter or disguise our emotional state and make us feel better. Some colors draw us in, while others repel us. Colors are used to warn us of danger, to direct traffic patterns, and are associated with specific holidays and religious ideas and concepts. It is a key component in advertising because of its potential to create focus and influence our buying patterns as consumers. It influences our eating habits. Who doesn't want to dig into a plate full of bright, vibrant and colorful foods? In short, it permeates our daily existence in ways that cannot be avoided.

Given that color is such a subjective design element, Table 9.1 provides qualities that are often associated with a short list of colors. It is by no means inclusive of all meanings assigned to these colors in all cultures, but is intended as a starting point in understanding the influence of color as a metaphorical tool that can be exploited to great effect by a designer. In general, bright colors are indicative of strong, powerful emotions, and lighter colors are associated with less intense feelings. Dark colors appear more somber and have more visual weight, and light colors have less visual weight and have happier connotations. Remember that tints, shades and tones are all different colors, and the addition of one color to another can alter the meaning significantly.

FIGURE 9-7 *Complementary color schemes*

FIGURE 9-8   *Open and closed palette—*Cabaret *by John Kander and Fred Ebb, costume design by Kaoime E. Malloy, University of Wisconsin Green Bay*

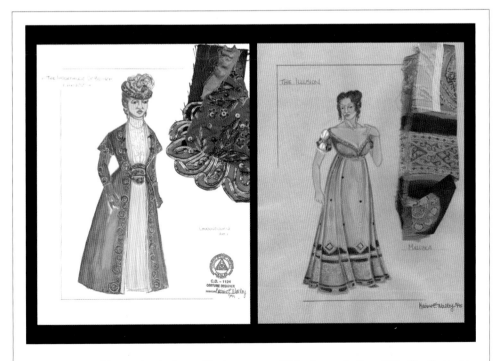

FIGURE 9-9   *Warm and cool palettes—*The Importance of Being Earnest *by Oscar Wilde,* The Illusion *by Tony Kushner, costume design by Kaoime E. Malloy, Iowa Summer Repertory*

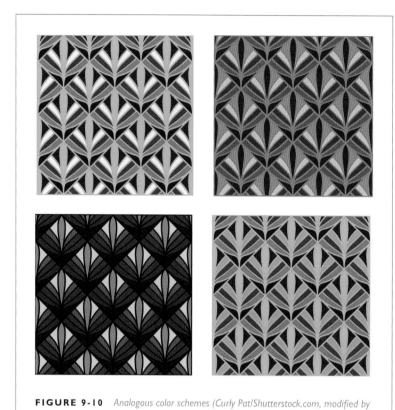

FIGURE 9-10   *Analogous color schemes (Curly Pat/Shutterstock.com, modified by Kaoime Malloy)*

FIGURE 9-11   *Simultaneous contrast*

FIGURE 9-12   *Optical mixing—Assassins by Stephen Sondheim, costume design by Kaoime E. Malloy, Coe College*

TABLE 9-1 *Color meanings and qualities.*

Color	Associated Meanings and Qualities
Red	A warm and powerful color, red is intense and energetic, often associated with fire, heat, love, passion, sexuality, action, speed, excitement, and strength. It is the color of blood, and therefore connected to life, but it also has been used to represent anger, danger, violence, aggression, and other extreme emotions. In several non-Western cultures, red is a sacred color that also represents good luck and is traditionally worn by brides in both China and Japan. In the West, it is often associated with the devil.
Blue	Blue is a soothing, peaceful color that often represents tranquility, stability, and calm, possibly because of its association with water and the sky. It has been used to suggest order, trust, security, confidence, and loyalty. In the West, blue is the color of the Madonna and is consequently sometimes associated with motherhood, virginity, and faith. Since the beginning of the twentieth century in the West, it has been the traditional color for boys. It is also used as a metaphor for cold, technology, sadness, and depression. "Having the blues," is a common part of our vernacular.
Yellow	Yellow is a bright, uplifting color that is a symbol for happiness, optimism, the sun and sunlight, hope, royalty, wealth, idealism, intellect, and enlightenment. It also has been used to represent jealousy, deceit, cowardice, illness, dishonesty, and a warning. In Dynastic China, only the emperor was allowed to wear yellow. In Islam, it represents wisdom. In the Christian tradition, Judas wore yellow.
Green	Because of the large amount of green in the natural world, the color is connected to nature, new life, growing things, balance, harmony, spring, renewal, life, growth, fertility, youth, good luck, and health and balance. However, it is also associated with envy, jealousy, inexperience, and illness.
Purple	Purple is a regal color that has long been associated with royalty, nobility, power, dignity, transformation, mystery, wisdom, and spirituality in several cultures. Murex, a rich purple dye made from shellfish, is so costly to produce that once it was only worn by royalty. Purple has also been used to represent arrogance, cruelty, and mourning and is associated with deep feelings.
Orange	Orange is a vibrant, energetic color that can represent energy, flamboyance, warmth, enthusiasm, and fire, although with less intensity than red and a reduced sense of danger.
Black	In Western cultures, black usually represents mourning, death, unhappiness, and evil. Black is also associated with sophistication (the little black dress), elegance, wealth, mystery, introspection, power, sexuality, depth, and style. It can also represent unhappiness, anger, evil, remorse, depression, and loneliness.
White	In the West, white is strongly connected to purity, innocence, cleanliness, birth, simplicity, goodness, humility, spirituality, angels, and marriage. In Eastern cultures, it is the color of mourning and death. White can also represent sterility, cold, detachment, inexperience, and snow.
Brown	Because of its connection to the color of the earth, brown is often connected to the outdoors, the hearth and home, comfort, stability, endurance, nature, and growing things. Brown may also be viewed as a mundane, dreary color that indicates stubbornness, rigidity, immovability, and a lack of focus or an inability to concentrate.
Gray	Gray is an ambiguous color that can represent maturity, dignity, modesty, conservatives, practicality, security, and reliability. But it can also be associated with indecision, confusion, a lack of excitement, ambiguity, feeling lost, uncertainty, old age, uncertainty, exhaustion, disuse, and sadness.

THE LANGUAGE OF COLOR

Additive mixing: A model that explains the mixing of colors using light. Each color of light is added together to create white light, which contains all colors.

Analogous: A color scheme that uses only colors that share a primary hue, including all of their tints, shades, and tones.

Chroma: The Greek word for color, which is used to refer to the saturation or purity of a hue.

Chromatic gray: A gray created by mixing two complementary colors, or by mixing a neutral gray with a color, thereby producing a hue that possesses some aspects of color.

Closed/restricted palette: A color scheme that limits the number of hues used in a work.

Color scheme: The selection of colors used in a composition.

Color wheel: A diagram that shows the relationships between colors laid out in the format of a circle.

Complementary: A color scheme that uses complementary colors, including all of their tints, shades, and tones.

Complements: Colors that sit directly opposite each other on the color wheel.

Cool colors: Hues that are perceived to be cool in temperature.

Double complementary: A color scheme that uses two main colors and their complements, including all of their tints, shades and tones.

Hue: The actual name of the color, usually referring to the name of the pigment that is used to create it.

Intensity: The dullness or brightness of a color. Intensity is decreased through neutralizing the color by adding its complement or a neutral gray.

Monochromatic: A color scheme that is based on one color alone, including the hue and all of its tints, shades, and tones. A monochromatic color scheme may also utilize the color's complement to create vibrant neutral tones.

Neutral gray: A gray with no chroma, created by mixing only black and white pigments.

Neutralize: Reducing the intensity of a hue by adding gray or its complement, to dull out or cancel the color.

Open palette: A color scheme that uses a large range of colors, often the full range of hues available without restriction.

Optical mixing: A visual effect that takes advantage of the eye's ability to combine flecks of closely spaced individual colors, blending them into other colors as if the pigments were actually mixed together.

Pigment: The material that provides the color in paint. Pigments can be made of natural or synthetic materials.

Primaries: Colors that are true hues, created from single pigments that have no other colors in them. There are three primary colors in both pigment and light, although they are different.

Relative value: The lightness or darkness of a color in relation to other colors, compared to the value scale.

Saturation: The amount of pigment present in a color. Saturation is altered by diluting the color in some manner, thereby reducing the purity of a hue.

Secondary: Colors that are mixed from equal parts of two primary colors. There are three secondary colors.

Semi-neutral: Colors created by mixing complementary colors together in varying degrees to produce hues between the original color and a neutralized, chromatic gray.

Shade: A color mixed with any amount of black, to darken its value.

Simultaneous contrast: An optical phenomena that occurs when two colors of equal intensity, usually complements, are set side by side in a composition. This positioning makes the two colors appear more vibrant, because of the visual contrast between them.

Split complement: An analogous color scheme with two additional contrasting colors, directly adjacent to the true complementary color.

Subtractive mixing: A model that explains the mixing of pigments. Each additional color reduces the amount of light that can be reflected back to the viewer.

Tertiary: Colors that are created by mixing a secondary color with its adjacent primary color. Tertiary colors are also referred to as intermediate colors.

Tint: A color mixed with any amount of white, to lighten its value.

Tone: A color mixed with a neutral gray or its complement, in order to neutralize the color.

Value: The lightness or darkness of a color.

Warm colors: Hues that are perceived to be warm in temperature.

COLOR EXERCISE

Color Copy/Enlargement

The objective of this exercise is to accurately reproduce both the drawing of image, the colors from the image and the style in which they were applied in the original work. On a piece of illustration board, you will reproduce the image you choose, enlarging it in the process to twice its original size. This will give you more area to work with as you attempt to recreate the method and style of the paint application. The copy will be executed in acrylic paint. You may select a set, costume or light rendering, a fashion illustration or a painting for this exercise. Suggested artists include Léon Bakst, Erté, Franz Marc and Picasso.

Materials

- Color image no larger than 9" × 12"

- Illustration board (size determined by your original image), color to match the background of your selected image

- Acrylic paints

- Brushes

- Ruler

- Pencils

Method

1. The best way to enlarge your swatch is to use a grid for reference to register the image (see the example in Figure 9.13). Make a black and white copy of your image and then draw a grid onto the paper in ½-inch increments.

2. On the illustration board, draw a grid *very lightly* with a pencil in one inch increments. Make sure that your marks are light so that you not put creases into the board or create marks that cannot be covered with the paint later.

3. Using the grid to register the image, transfer the cartoon of the image to the illustration board. Outline the shapes as much as you need to be able to paint them, but do not feel as if you have to transfer absolutely everything now. Some details can be transferred later, once you have a layer of paint on the surface, when they might otherwise be lost underneath it.

4. Erase all your grid lines, outside the cartoon and inside as best you can. Even light pencil will show through light paint

colors, especially when the paint layer is thin. Graphite can also blur and smudge when paint is applied to it, making your light colors appear muddy. It is best to remove it beforehand.

5. Spend some time matching the colors, writing down the "recipe" for each, noting how much of each color in your kit was needed to mix the color for each section of the image. If your illustration board is colored, remember that the underlying color will affect the final look of your paint. If your board is dark, you may want to lay down a thin underpainting of white before you begin.

6. Practice painting on a scrap piece of board before you begin to paint in your color copy. Once the acrylic is on your board, only more paint can cover it. A little time spent practicing on another piece of board can go a long way towards a successful finished piece.

7. Paint in the image on your board. You may find it useful to paint in all areas that are one color at a time, or you may decide to paint the image in sections. Either way, mixing up enough of the colors you need before you start and then storing it in an airtight container between painting sessions can ensure that your colors match from one session to the next, and saves time on mixing paint.

8. Use a bag eraser to clean up the board once you are finished.

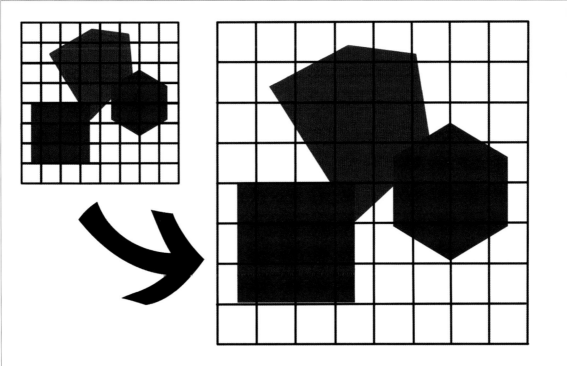

FIGURE 9-13 *Grid examples for enlargement*

FIGURE 9-14   *Franz Marc,* Yellow Cow, *color copy project, Introduction to Theatre Design Class, University of Wisconsin Green Bay*

CHAPTER 10

TEXTURE

WHAT IS TEXTURE?

Texture is a familiar phenomenon that each of us experiences every day. All of the objects around us possess **texture**, which refers to both the tactile and the visual quality of a surface. When we run our hands over an object, such as our clothing, our sense of touch is engaged allowing us to perceive the physical qualities of the surface we are touching. Texture that can be perceived through our sense of touch is called **actual texture** or real texture. It is three-dimensional, and the changes in the object's surface are palpable and concrete. In contrast, **implied texture** or visual texture is created through changes in surface qualities that are simulated and two-dimensional, creating a convincing visual copy of an actual texture. Visual texture engages our sense of sight, drawing us into an image through variations in all the design elements that create the illusion of a tactile surface or that create a **pattern**. A pattern is an arrangement of decorative elements such as shapes that are repeated over and over on a surface, whether that surface is paper, fabric, flooring, wallpaper, or another object. Our eyes follow pattern and therefore it is another way to make a connection between the viewer and the image in front of them.

Actual texture can be created in a number of ways. One of the simplest ways to create texture is through **collage**. A collage is a composition created by applying three-dimensional objects to a two-dimensional surface. **Paper collé** is an artistic forerunner of collage, utilizing papers with different surfaces that are glued onto a flat format to create different textures. Collage, however, can employ any number of three-dimensional items and elements to produce

the final textured composition. Paper collé and collage are very effective tools in theatrical rendering, where they can be used to insert areas of complex detail into a design that would otherwise need to be drawn out by hand. They can also be used as the primary compositional tool when doing renderings. Although collage utilizes three-dimensional elements when creating a composition, it differs from an **assemblage**, where the intent is to use three-dimensional objects to create a final sculptural form.

Real textures are an essential component of costume design, where the variations of surface qualities between fabrics are crucial to the overall look, effect, movement, and function of individual costumes. In fabric, patterns and implied and real textures merge on a flexible, flowing surface that will communicate volumes about a character through the fabric's look and feel, and the costume's construction. Some costumes will mold to the body, revealing the natural shape of the actor; others will serve to conceal the body or encase it as surely as a suit of armor. The fabric's appearance and tactile feel will determine how the actor responds to the garment, as well as dictate how they will move when they are wearing it. These factors can be influenced by the conventions of a time period, by a particular location, or by the designer's stylistic choices. All of these qualities will influence us as audience members, drawing us into the characters, or setting us apart from them and creating distance, depending on the objectives of the costume designer.

Paint quality is another important aspect of real texture. Paint quality refers to the visual and tactile impression of the surface of paint in a work of art and includes both real and implied textures. Different art mediums from pencils

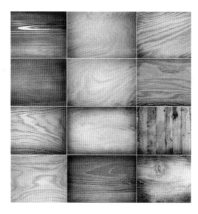

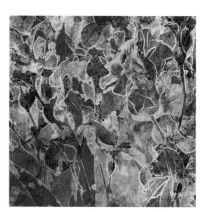

FIGURE 10-1   *Actual and implied textures (kak2s and Irina_QQQ/Shutterstock.com)*

FIGURE 10-2   *Collage rendering—Shakespeare—Titus Andronicus—set design by Kaoime E. Malloy*

and markers to paints and collage all have different textural qualities in terms of both their actual feel and their visual look. These differences can be employed, exploited, and manipulated to create the final desired result in any design. Some paints—such as oil, acrylic, and encaustic—are inherently thicker and opaque and consequently lend themselves more readily to three-dimensional techniques. Others, such as watercolor, have transparency and thinness as their main outstanding feature, and therefore are more suitable for creating implied and simulated textures. There are also a number of paint additives for oils and acrylics that can enhance the three-dimensional qualities of the paint or add additional surface textures during the application process. Other specialty texture paint products are used extensively in scene painting, where they can be used to create a variety of real textures on the flat surfaces of a wide range of scenic elements. They can also be used on scenic models

to show a realistic facsimile of what the final set design will look like onstage. Some artists even choose to add sand or other materials to their paint in order to produce interesting textural elements. Media that are thinner or transparent, that do not lend themselves readily to three-dimensional texture techniques, can still be used to create realistic implied textures through skillful manipulation during application to a surface, and all media have the potential to produce simulated textures.

Paint quality also refers to the visual look of a medium. This can include such qualities as sheen, gloss, or matte finishes, transparency or opacity, powdery or solid, waxy or oily, plastic or brittle, wet or dry, linear or fluid, and other characteristics. Each of these traits should be considered when planning a design, as they will all contribute a unique appearance to the final look.

One of the most recognizable actual surface painting techniques is **impasto**. In impasto, very thick layers of paint are applied to the surface of the work and the individual brushstrokes or marks of the painting knives can be seen in the final picture. When dry, impasto marks rise above the actual surface of the painting, as if they are coming out of the image itself. Impasto is a technique employed to great effect by several artists, including Vincent van Gogh. Impasto marks change the way light is reflected from the composition, which affords the artist a certain degree of control over how light interacts with the other design elements. This can change both the overall appearance and the mood of an artwork. Impasto can also simulate the actual texture of the objects represented in the work, albeit in a highly stylized way. The raised marks can make the viewer experience the memory of the tactile surface of the object being represented. It also allows the viewer to see the hand of the artist in the final image. It can be easier to determine the speed, direction, pressure, and weight of an individual mark in thick, heavy paint. By seeing these things, we can become more connected to the artist, their emotions, and their intentions. Impasto techniques can accomplish the same thing onstage, whether part of the scenery treatment or on other items such as masks or properties.

Another common actual texture technique is **sgraffito**. In this method, the artist scratches into the top layer of wet paint in order to reveal the layers of dried paint underneath. The final result may seem similar to impasto, but the resulting marks are usually shallower and may be more linear in nature, depending on the tool used to remove the paint. In theatrical design, sgraffito may be employed in other ways—such as carving lines into Styrofoam to create wood grain before painting or incising marks into planks of wood to produce a distressed surface—but the technique itself is the same.

TYPES OF TEXTURE

As discussed previously, texture falls into two broad categories: real and implied. But within these two main classifications there are several variations of texture, or ways in which texture can be created.

Simulated texture seeks to create the illusion of real, three-dimensional surfaces in a two-dimensional format. Simulated textures can be highly realistic or even stylized and symbolic, but are generally trying to replicate a recognizable surface, such as wood grain, marble, velvet, fur, and so on. There are several different techniques that can be employed to create simulated texture, but one of the most recognizable and convincing is *trompe l'oeil*.

Trompe l'oeil is a French term that means "to fool the eye," and it is a highly realistic painting technique extensively employed in Renaissance and Baroque art, where the term has its origins in perspective illusionism. In reality, the technique dates back to Greek and Roman mural painting, which sought to represent scenes of real life in a highly realistic manner. The murals discovered in Pompeii provide some of the finest examples of this technique. *Trompe l'oeil* creates the illusion of three-dimensional forms in the manner of photographic realism. It employs value, chiaroscuro, and linear and atmospheric perspective to render objects with a level of accuracy that fools the eye.

Trompe l'oeil is an important technique for the theatrical designer. It has long been employed in scenic design to create the illusion of reality onstage. In the Baroque period, traditional wing and drop sets consisting of a succession of receding flats were painted in this manner to produce the illusion of highly realistic interior and exterior scenes. *Trompe l'oeil* is still a highly utilized scene painting technique, used to create the illusion of three-dimensional pieces or textures on two-dimensional surfaces, such as trim details on crown molding or a wooden parquet or tile design on the stage floor, or to depict a realistic scene in a backdrop.

Simulated textures are very important to the theatrical lighting designer, who may seek to create the impression of realistic elements, such as leaves, stars, or the shape of a window purely through light in the stage space. Adding texture to light in the form of patterned **gobos** in individual instruments is an easy way to introduce texture to the overall picture created by the lighting. A gobo, derived from the term "go between" or "goes before optics," is a metal circle incised with a pattern that can be slipped inside a lighting instrument to alter the shape of its beam. In some instances, the patterns required may be specific in order to achieve a particular effect; but in others the goal may simply be to break up the light as it travels through the stage space. It is

FIGURE 10-3 Trompe l'oeil *painted concert backdrop (Lakeview Images/Shutterstock.com)*

FIGURE 10-4 Trompe l'oeil *painted scenic curtain (Maryna Pleshkun/Shutterstock.com)*

FIGURE 10-5   *Abstracted texture (Irina_QQQ/Shutterstock
.com)*

also possible to add texture to light through the use of fog
machines or other chemicals that produce haze in the air.
Both of these techniques add a three-dimensional quality
to the beams of light from the instruments, delineating their
shape and allowing the audience to perceive light in a unique
and different way, as an additional compositional element in
the overall picture.

Another important type of texture is **abstracted
texture.** This is real or implied texture that has been simplified,
rearranged, stylized, or distorted in order to fulfill the visual
needs of a design. Abstracted texture may be highly symbolic,
such as wavy lines for water, created either two- or three-
dimensionally, or it can be a two-dimensional representation
of a three-dimensional surface. For theatre, abstract textures
are often used to design unique surface treatments on fabrics,
props, costume items such as jewelry and hats, or to generate
patterns in light in various ways, such as through the use of
gobos.

Invented texture comes from the artist's imagination.
Invented textures are changes in implied or tactile surfaces
that are created by an individual artist that usually have no
relation to a recognizable or real textured surface. They may
be highly abstract or distorted, or produced in unusual ways
or with unconventional materials. These types of textures
can be a dynamic and exciting compositional element
because they are new, original, and often highly innovative.
In theatre, where we as designers are often creating new
and previously unknown worlds, invented texture is a very
useful component in making evocative and compelling visual
choices.

TABLE 10-1   *Real and implied texture techniques*

Real Texture Techniques	Implied Texture Techniques
Impasto	*Tromp l'oeil*
Sgraffito	Frottage
Texture gels	Rubbings
Splattering	Pouncing
Dripping	Scumbling
Paint additives	Dry brushing
Brushstrokes	Monoprint
Painting knives	Printing
Combing	Stamping
Foils	Resists
Embossing powder	Sponging
Gesso	Glazing
Foil and gesso	Airbushing
Collage	Hatching
Paper collé	Cross hatching
Tissue paper and paint	Stippling
Modeling paste	Spattering
Engraving	Stenciling
Bronzing powder	Interference colors
Assemblage	Burnishing
Paint skinning	Plastic wrap wash
Intarsia	Wet in wet

THE VOCABULARY OF TEXTURE

Abstract texture: Actual or implied texture that has
been simplified, rearranged, or distorted in order to
fulfill the visual needs of a design.

Actual texture: Changes in surfaces that are real and
three-dimensional. Also known as real texture.

Airbushing: Applying paint with an airbrush, which
atomizes the paint and produces a fine mist.

Assemblage: An artwork created by joining three-
dimensional objects together to form a three-dimensional
shape.

Bronzing powder: A metallic powder that can be
mixed with a paint medium to create a metallic paint or
placed on top of paint to add texture.

Burnishing: Polishing the surface of the paint or other media to a shine.

Collage: A composition created by gluing three-dimensional objects on a flat surface to alter the visual and tactile quality of the work.

Combing: Drawing combs of various sizes and shapes through wet paint on a surface to create pattern and texture.

Dripping: Allowing paint to fall on a surface in drops, strings, and ropes to create texture.

Dry brushing: Applying paint with a dry brush and allowing the bristles to separate with each stroke to create a textured effect.

Embossing powders: A fine powder available in a variety of colors that is placed over a stamped image and then heated to create a raised impression.

Foil and gesso: Imbedding aluminum foil in gesso to create a heavy textured painting surface.

Foils: Synthetic and precious metal metallic foils that can be applied with adhesives to painted surfaces to create texture.

Frottage: Capturing the texture of a surface by placing a piece of paper over it and rubbing a pencil or other drawing medium against the surface to transfer the texture.

Gesso: An acrylic paint mixture consisting of emulsion mixed with gypsum, chalk, pigment, or any combination of the three, usually used for preparing a ground prior to painting.

Glazing: Using layers of thin, transparent washes of paint on top of a painted surface to enhance the underlying color.

Gobo: A metal frame cut with a pattern that is inserted into the lighting instrument that filters the beam as it is cast, changing its shape.

Impasto: A very thick, highly textured application of paint to a surface where the marks of the brushes, individual strokes, or painting knives remain visible.

Implied texture: Changes in surface textures that are simulated and two-dimensional, which create a convincing visual copy of an actual surface. Also known as visual texture.

Intarsia: A form of inlaid marquetry that allows for the creation of intricate patterns and textures in wood.

Interference colors: Paint that possesses components that refract lighting, allowing them to appear differently on various surfaces.

Invented texture: Changes in implied or tactile texture that are created by an individual artist that usually have no relation to a recognizable, real textured surface.

Modeling paste: A heavy paste that can be used to create a textured ground for a painting, add texture to a model, as glue for collage, or to create a sculpture.

Monoprint: A printing technique that allows for only one print of the created image by transferring a wet painted image from a smooth surface to a piece of paper.

Paint additives: Textural elements that can be added to paint to change its quality, such as sand, glass beads, and gravel.

Paint quality: The visual and tactile impression of the surface of paint in a work of art. Paint quality includes both real and implied textures.

Paint skinning: Creating a flexible "skin" of paint that can be cut up and used as a design element by applying a layer of paint to a smooth surface, allowing it to dry, and then peeling it off in one piece.

Painting knives: Metal and plastic hand held knives in various sizes and shapes that can be used in place of brushes to apply paint to a surface.

Paper collé: A technique whereby papers with different textures are glued on a composition to change the visual and tactile surface quality. It is an artistic precursor of collage.

Pattern: A decorative design often created through repetition.

Plastic wrap wash: Using plastic wrap over a wet wash of paint, letting it dry, and then peeling it off to alter the surface texture.

Pouncing: Using a balled up cloth or paper to apply paint to the painting surface by pressing it against the paper over and over to create texture.

Printing: Creating multiple copies of the same image on the painting surface through various means.

Resists: Materials that prevent paint from penetrating the painting surface.

Rubbings: Capturing the texture of a surface by placing a piece of paper over it and rubbing a pencil or other drawing medium against the surface to transfer the texture.

Scumbling: Applying a very thin coat of opaque paint over a painted surface to produce a soft or dull effect.

Sgraffito: Scratching into paint while wet to reveal the surface underneath.

Spattering: Loading a brush with highly diluted paint and quickly running a finger or palette knife across the bristles to disperse a fine spray of color across the surface of your painting surface, producing speckles of color.

Sponging: Applying paint with a sponge to created texture.

Stamping: Printing multiple images on the painting surface through the use of a premade stamp cut into shapes or patterns.

Stenciling: Applying paint through a precut template to create an image or texture.

Stippling: Creating texture with very fine drops of paint with a sponge, airbrush, by spattering or through other means.

Tactile: Something that can be perceived through the sense of touch, or invokes the sense of touch.

Texture: The tactical and visual quality of a surface.

Tissue paper and paint: An assemblage technique that combines paint and light paper, embedding it in the paint to create texture.

Tromp l'oeil: A technique that uses realistic imagery to convincingly paint the illusion of three-dimensional space; where objects are depicted in a highly realistic manner, as if they were photographed.

Wet in wet: Applying paint to a wet surface.

TEXTURE EXERCISES

In the first column, an item that possesses real or actual texture is listed. In the next column, create an implied or simulated version of that item's surface quality using a two-dimensional technique. In the third, create an abstract version of the same texture, using either two or three dimensions, or a combination of the two. Pencils and colored pencils can be used for this exercise.

TABLE 10-2 *Texture exercise grid*

Item	Implied/Simulated Texture	Abstract Texture
Popcorn		
Grass		
Water		
Leaves		
Fur		
Pebbles		
Plaid		

CHAPTER 11

CREATING THE ILLUSION OF DEPTH ON A FLAT SURFACE

WHY IS IT IMPORTANT TO CREATE THE ILLUSION OF DEPTH ON A FLAT SURFACE?

Designs for the theatre, sets, lights, and costumes, exist in three dimensions. Like sculpture, which is also a three-dimensional art form, theatrical design elements are often meant to be experienced from several different sides, or vantage points. Even if the stage space is not arranged so that the audience sits on more than one side, able to see the set from different viewpoints, the actors have to move through the space and will experience it as a real, navigable environment. Costumes will be seen from all sides as they move through the set and lighting

FIGURE 11-1 *Blithe Spirit by Noel Coward, scenic design by Frank Ludwig, Viterbo University*

will not only carve out volume as it travels from the instruments to the stage floor, it will reveal the form, mass, and volume of all the other elements that it strikes. When designers go into a design meeting, however, it is not always possible or even practical to show our designs in the final, three-dimensional form, even on a smaller scale. Very often, we will be required to present two-dimensional images that accurately and effectively present the illusion of the three-dimensional qualities of our work on a flat surface. This requires the careful creation of implied space within a composition in order to create the illusion of depth on the flat surface of paper, in sketches, drawings, and renderings.

IMPLIED SPACE

Implied space means to suggest three-dimensional space on a two-dimensional surface. In two-dimensional art forms, the actual surface is the flat surface of the work itself, and we tend to view it all at once. On this surface, called the **picture plane**, other quantities, qualities, and dimensions of space and the objects presented within that space can be suggested and represented. Another way to think of this concept is when elements and objects are not explicitly present in a composition, but they are visible and identifiable, and the illusion of mass, volume, and form can be perceived, they are said to be implied. It is the difference between space that is *suggested* and space that is *constructed*. Both define and determine the relationships between objects, but only one is truly three-dimensional.

FORMAT AND DEPTH

One of the ways to easily define space in a flat image is to consider how the subject relates to the boundary created by the **format** of the piece. Changing the size of your subject will radically alter the perception of the format itself. For example, if you draw a very small person in the center of your page, the page suddenly becomes a large space—a field for the person to roam about in. If you draw a large figure that takes up the entire page, then the space has become small and the person looks confined. If you draw two people on the page and another object within the space, such as a tree, and you want to show where all three things are in relation to one another, you could chose to place one person behind the tree, and the other person very close to the bottom of the page. The person behind the tree will appear to be the farthest away, because the tree is in front of them, obscuring part of the figure from view. The person near the edge of the page will seem to be close to the viewer, because it is both in front of the tree (and consequently the other person) and close to the boundary presented by the format. These relationships take place in the third dimension, **depth**, and are not dependent on the perception of either the people or the tree as a realistic, three-dimensional object. Although depth can be established in several different ways, there are two simple visual clues that help to create the illusion of depth in any composition.

CREATING THE ILLUSION OF DEPTH IN A TWO-DIMENSIONAL COMPOSITION

The first visual clue when creating depth is **overlap**. As demonstrated in the previous example, when two forms overlap we perceive the one in front as complete and the one behind as partial. We also see the one in front as being closer, and the one behind as being further away. Using this basic idea, depth can easily be implied on a two-dimensional surface by arranging the

subjects in a set order. Altering the **focus** of the objects placed in the background can also imply depth. By making the background images less distinct or less detailed, they will appear to be further away and objects in the foreground will draw more focus.

The second visual clue is **position**. Position relies on the relationship between objects relative to our bodies. When seated at a desk, for example, we look down to see the objects closest to us, and up to see the objects that are further away. Consequently, if an object is placed at the bottom of the picture plane, causing us to look down, we perceive it as being closer to us, and objects near the top, requiring us to look up to see them appear to be further away. Throughout history, many cultures have relied almost entirely on these two basic clues to imply depth in two-dimensional artworks. Certainly for set designs, items placed further upstage appear farther away than those that are downstage, closer to the audience.

FIGURE 11-3 *Focus and detail for creating depth, (Jitka Volfova / shutterstock.com)*

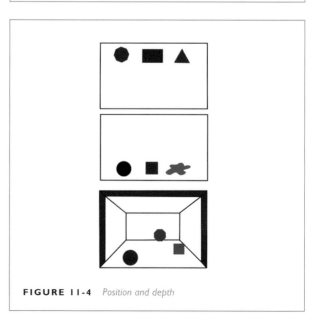

FIGURE 11-4 *Position and depth*

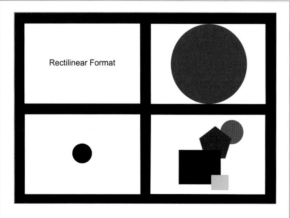

FIGURE 11-2 *Format, overlap, and depth*

THE RENAISSANCE SYSTEM FOR CREATING THE ILLUSION OF DEPTH

The chapter on value presented the idea of modeling with light, particularly through the use of **chiaroscuro** and **sfumato**, developed by the Italian Renaissance artists of the fifteenth century. These techniques are a part of a larger visual system created and exploited by artists of the Quattrocento for depicting the world around them in a highly realistic and convincing manner. By employing this system, they were able to create the illusion of depth and three-dimensional form on a flat surface in ways that had previously been unknown. Just as Renaissance artists took note of the optical evidence of light and shadow to model rounded forms, they also developed techniques for constructing an optically convincing space in which to set these forms. These techniques are: linear perspective, foreshortening, and atmospheric perspective. In order to create dynamic renderings that accurately reflect the illusion of space, theatrical designers need to know how to use all three of these techniques along with modeling techniques such as chiaroscuro.

LINEAR PERSPECTIVE

Linear perspective is a way to convey the illusion of three dimensions and depth on a two-dimensional surface. The techniques involved in this type of perspective allow an artist to render an object *as it is perceived by the eye*. This is different than using **isometric perspective**, where the goal is to show all measurements of an object to scale no matter how far or close they are to the viewer. Linear perspective is also called *true perspective*, because the image created with it will be true to what the eye sees when we look at an object.

Linear perspective is based on two observations. The first is that forms appear to diminish in size as they recede from the viewer. Because of this, an object that is smaller will naturally give the impression of being farther away in a composition. The second observation is that parallel lines that are moving away from the viewer seem to converge, until they meet at a point on the **horizon line**, where they disappear. The horizon line is the place where the earth and the sky appear to meet in the distance, generally considered to be at eye level. This point where the parallel lines converge is called the **vanishing point**. We have all experienced the visual phenomenon of parallel lines converging firsthand as we drive down a road that appears to get narrower the further away it is from us, until it finally disappears on the horizon.

When there is only one vanishing point in a composition and all parallel horizontal lines within it converge at a central point on the horizon line, it is called *single point perspective*. Although one vanishing point may at first seem to be limiting, it is possible to create very realistic scenes in this manner. Beginning in the Italian Renaissance and lasting through the early nineteenth century, theatrical scenery often employed a wing and drop system for creating sets, where flat panels would be moved in from either side of the stage or flown in from above. These flats would be painted using masterful forced perspective and **tromp l'oeil** painting techniques to create highly detailed and realistic settings, including interiors, exteriors, gardens, and other locations.

Two point perspective utilizes two vanishing points and all the parallel horizontal lines in an image come together at one or the other of these points on the horizon line. Using two vanishing points allows the artist to create a more realistic image and more complex views than when using one vanishing point alone. In reality, most set designs will require more than two vanishing

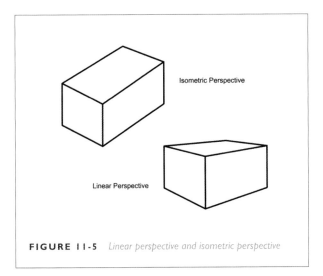

FIGURE 11-5 *Linear perspective and isometric perspective*

FIGURE 11-6 *Single point perspective, (MarinaSM / Shutterstock.com)*

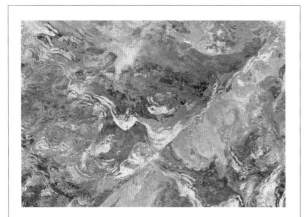

FIGURE 11-7 *Tromp l'oeil faux marble scenic painting,* *(Kompaniets Taras / shutterstock.com)*

FIGURE 11-8 *Two point perspective, (Denis Kuvaev / shutterstock.com)*

points to render an accurate representation of the scenery. In this case, a designer will employ *multi-point perspective*, where the vanishing points of each object in the design are determined individually. This allows each item to be drawn in a very realistic manner, true to how they are perceived by the eye.

The development of linear perspective was a revolutionary change for how artists viewed the picture plane. For artists prior to those in the Quattrocento, a painting was a flat surface covered with shapes and color. There was no attempt to create an optically convincing representation of what the artist actually saw. For Renaissance artists, including theatrical designers, it became a *window onto a scene.* They took up linear perspective with as much delight as a child takes up a new toy and they employed it in new and exciting ways to create highly realistic works of art.

In order for pictorial space to be consistent, the logic of linear perspective must apply to every form in the picture, be it inanimate, human, or animal. When an object is subjected to linear perspective, it appears compressed when seen from the main line of sight, which causes distortion in the dimensions of the form on both the horizontal and vertical axes. This effect is called **foreshortening**. You can experience it directly by

placing your hand in front of your face, and then tipping it backwards at the wrist away from you. The size of your hand has not changed, but because your fingers are further away from your eyes, your hand now looks as if it has become shorter. It now appears to be receding into the distance.

Foreshortening presents some difficulties and challenges for an artist, because the rounded curves of organic forms do not lend themselves easily to the principles of linear perspective. In other words, it can be hard to find the vanishing points for rounded forms. In addition, our mind tends to fight our eyes when drawing a foreshortened object, making it more difficult to capture what we are actually perceiving rather than what we think "should" be there. Mastering foreshortening is essential to create an optically convincing theatrical rendering.

One of the simplest ways to incorporate foreshortening into a theatrical drawing or rendering is to use a **perspective grid**. A grid is a simple visual tool where horizontal and vertical lines bisect at equal distances across the picture plane. A perspective grid consists of a network of vanishing lines drawn on a floorplan in order to approximate the location of planes and vanishing points that will be needed on a drawing. The initial grid is set up using the principles of single point perspective. A perspective grid is based on the required vanishing points for the design. Once a basic, one point perspective grid is established, it can be used over and over for multiple designs, although it is likely that each design will require its own grid because its vanishing points will be unique. Many image editing programs also have perspective grid utilities incorporated into their tools, making it easy to adjust the grid for each object or composition. By imposing the grid over the object you want to foreshorten, the vanishing points for rounded and organic objects can easily be estimated and then drawn in a fairly accurate manner.

The third and final element of the optically based system developed during the Renaissance is called **atmospheric perspective**. If you have ever stared off into a series of hills or mountains, you may have noticed that each succeeding range

FIGURE 11-9 *Foreshortening, (Nella / Shutterstock.com)*

appears paler, bluer in color, and less distinct. This is an optical effect caused by the atmosphere. Particles of dust and moisture in the air scatter light between us and the objects we look at, making them more diffuse. Of all the colors in the visible spectrum, blue scatters the most, which is why the sky appears blue, and objects tend to take on a bluish tinge the further they are away from us. Leonardo da Vinci was the first artist to employ atmospheric perspective systematically to his work, but it can be an important and effective visual tool for a theatrical designer as well. The careful application of atmospheric perspective allows a designer to convincingly represent the depth of the stage, create emphasis and to accurately show the dimensions of three-dimensional forms on a flat surface.

Taken as a whole, the system of chiaroscuro, modeling with light, linear and atmospheric perspective, and foreshortening allow the designer to create realistic drawings and renderings that will accurately represent and communicate what the final designs will look like onstage, which is an important part of the collaborative process. Ideally, drawings and renderings should accurately represent the design, so there is no discrepancy in the appearance of the work between the page and the stage.

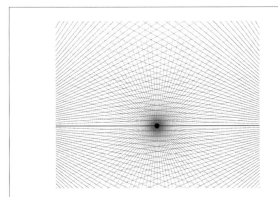

FIGURE 11-10 *Perspective grid created with Adobe Photoshop*

FIGURE 11-11 *Atmospheric perspective—Mt. Ktaadn, Frederic Edwin Church, 1853 © Yale University Art Gallery*

THE LANGUAGE OF CREATING DEPTH ON A FLAT SURFACE

Atmospheric perspective: A method of conveying depth based on the observation that objects become bluer and less distinct as they move into the distance.

Chiaroscuro: "Light and dark." The technique of blending values to show the bending of light around a form in order to represent the illusion of three dimensions on a two-dimensional surface.

Depth: A measurement of dimension, inward, downward, or backward.

Focus: The sharpness of an image.

Foreshortening: The distortion that occurs in the dimensions of forms in linear perspective on both the horizontal and vertical axes.

Format: The physical qualities of an artwork; the size and form it takes.

Horizon line: The point in the distance where the sky and the ground appear to meet.

Implied space: Suggesting three-dimensional space on a two-dimensional surface.

Isometric perspective: A method of drawing where the goal is to show all measurements of an object to scale no matter how far or close they are to the viewer.

Linear perspective: A drawing method of rendering objects as perceived by the human eye, based on the observations that objects appear to get smaller as they move farther away, and that parallel lines appear to converge in the distance.

Overlap: Laying one object over another. Overlap provides a visual clue for perceiving depth.

Perspective grid: A network of horizontal and vertical lines drawn on a floorplan in order to approximate the location of planes and points on a drawing.

Picture plane: The flat surface of a two-dimensional work of art.

Position: Where an object is located within a composition. Position provides a visual clue for perceiving depth.

Sfumato: A subtle and gradual blending from light to dark values.

Tromp l'oeil: A technique that uses realistic imagery to convincingly paint the illusion of three-dimensional space; where objects are depicted in a highly realistic manner, as if they were photographed.

Vanishing point: The point where parallel lines appear to converge on the horizon line.

PERSPECTIVE EXERCISE

Creating a Perspective Grid Quickly with Adobe® Photoshop®

There are several ways to create a perspective grid in Photoshop®. This method uses the polygon tool and vanishing points to drop them into a file quickly and easily.

1. **Begin by creating a new 8" × 10" file at 300dpi resolution**. Rotate the canvas to the landscape orientation by selecting image → image rotation → 90° CW.

2. **The next step is to establish the horizon line**. To help ensure that the line is straight you can make the grid visible on the canvas by selecting view → show → grid. Choose the paintbrush tool from the tool menu and set the pixel size to 8 px. Left click your cursor on one side of the canvas either at the midpoint or just below. Holding down the shift key, left click on the other side of the canvas where you want the horizon line to end. The program will draw the line in between the two points.

3. **Choose the polygon tool from the tool menu**. Once you do this, there are a few settings in the toolbar at the top of the screen that you will have to change. By default, the number of sides of the polygon tool is set to a low number. Change that number to 100. To the left of the sides dialogue box is the custom shape icon. Click the small arrow next to it to open its dialogue box. Set "indent sides by" to 99% and be sure the "star" box is checked.

4. **To create a one point perspective grid you will use one vanishing point.** You can set the vanishing point in the center or on in any other location on the horizon line. For the purpose of this demonstration, it has been set in the center. Left-click on the horizon line and holding the mouse button down, drag the cursor out beyond the boundaries of the canvas until you reach the grid spacing you desire. The polygon tool will create a wheel of evenly spaced, radial spokes. Notice that you are able to rotate the radial lines as long as you keep the mouse button depressed. Rotate them into the position you desire, release the cursor, and then hit enter to set the vector shape path on the background. The program will create a new layer containing this vector path for you, which you can see in the layer panel in the lower right-hand corner of the screen.

5. **If the spacing of the lines is sufficient for you, go ahead and merge the layers by selecting layer → flatten.** If you want more grid lines, repeat step 4, being careful to click on the same vanishing point to start and then rotate the radial spokes, centering them between the lines of the previous polygon.

6. **To create a two point perspective grid you will be selecting two vanishing points.** In order to get the perspective correct, they may be on or off the canvas. The polygon tool will let you select a starting point for the radial spokes off the canvas. Left-click on the horizon line to one side, on or off the canvas, (do your best to maintain the horizon line if you do move off the canvas) and then drag the radial lines across the canvas until you cover the entire image and achieve the grid you desire for the first vanishing point.

7. **If the spacing is sufficient, hit enter to move the vector shape to the canvas. If you need more lines and your vanishing point is off of the canvas, *do not hit enter.*** Once you hit enter, the center point of the spokes disappears. This is not a problem if the vanishing point is on the visible horizon line, because you can easily find it again. But if it is off the canvas, you will not be able to find it and your new grid lines will not be parallel. Instead, click on the vanishing point again and drag the spokes out, rotating them as needed to center them between the previous ones. Then hit enter to move both vector shapes to the background. You can also add a center vanishing point grid to the image if desired.

8. **Repeat steps 6 and 7 for the second vanishing point.**

9. **Flatten all layers.**

You now have a perspective grid ready to use as a guide for drawing.

MODELING EXERCISES

Chapter 23 contains detailed instructions on how to draw and model the four basic shapes that make up all compositions—spheres, cubes, cylinders, and cones. Drawing these shapes and practicing how to model them effectively under various lighting conditions will build your technical skills and inform all of your drawings and renderings, making them more realistic.

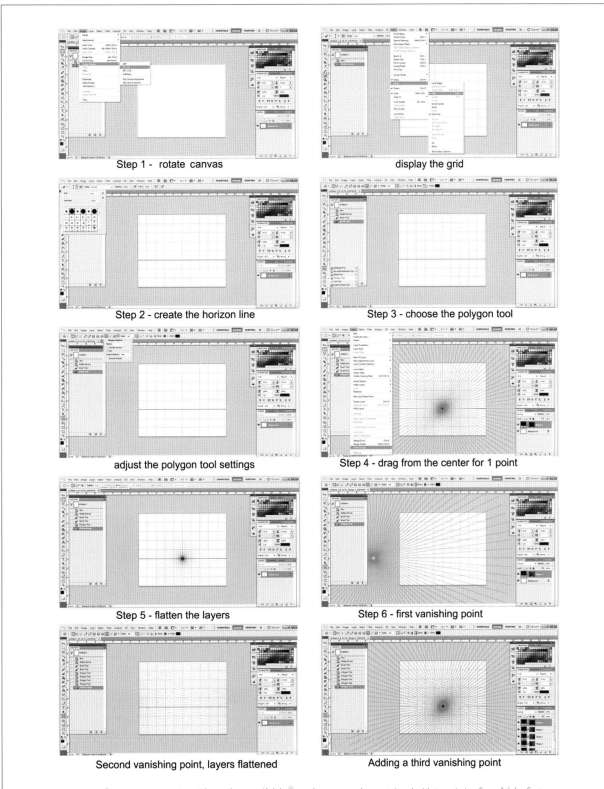

Step 1 - rotate canvas

display the grid

Step 2 - create the horizon line

Step 3 - choose the polygon tool

adjust the polygon tool settings

Step 4 - drag from the center for 1 point

Step 5 - flatten the layers

Step 6 - first vanishing point

Second vanishing point, layers flattened

Adding a third vanishing point

FIGURE 11-12   *Creating a perspective grid, step by step (Adobe® product screen shots reprinted with permission from Adobe Systems Incorporated.)*

PART THREE

PRINCIPLES OF DESIGN

CHAPTER 12

UNITY AND VARIETY

In the previous chapters, we discussed the *elements of design*, along with the need for a vocabulary that allows us to explore, work with, and talk about the foundational visual components that are inherent in all visual art. Without this vocabulary, and an understanding of the elements of design, it can be challenging to create and evaluate artwork of various kinds in an effective and compelling manner. The elements of design are the building blocks of art. They are the basic components and materials the artist works with. You can think of them as the wood, paint, paper, and other supplies that are at the artist's disposal when creating a work of art. The *principles of design* are the tools that the artist uses to manipulate these materials. They are the hammers, saws, paintbrushes, and rulers with which a designer shapes the elements into an evocative form. In the following chapters, we will examine the principles of design, and how they are used to shape the elements to create a design.

When an artist decides to make a work of art, they are faced with an infinite number of choices:

- How big or small should the work be?

- What kinds of lines should be used and where should they go?

- What kinds of shapes should be used? How many?

- How much space should there between shapes?

- What colors should be used and how much of each one?

- What amounts of light and dark values?

- Should there be texture? If so, how much?

- What style should the artwork take? Realistic? Abstract? Stylized?

- What is my intent with this piece? What do I want to communicate to the viewer?

Somehow, the elements of design must be organized in such a way as to satisfy the artist's expressive intent while creating an effective composition that the viewer can respond to. As we've said before, this organization of design elements is called *composition*. The more inclusive term is *design*. The task of making decisions can be overwhelming without some guidelines to follow. These guidelines are called the principles of design.

WHAT ARE UNITY AND VARIETY?

Unity is a sense of oneness, of things belonging and working together to create an integrated and coherent whole. Unity means that there is some sort of organizing relationship that is holding the elements in a design together. Another word for this quality is **harmony**. Harmony is defined as a pleasing, orderly, or consistent arrangement of parts. Unity is by far the most important principle in composition and may be the closest thing to a rule that can be found in art. When an image is unified, all the parts seem to work together to form a composition and to communicate an idea. Without unity, a sense that more than mere chance has put all the visual elements together, or the impression that the elements in the piece are separate and disjointed, a design falls apart.

Variety is difference, which provides visual interest. We discuss unity and variety together because they always coexist in a work of art. A solid wall painted white has unity—but it is static and boring. There is nothing to engage our attention or relieve the monotony of the wall's surface. It becomes predictable and we as viewers turn away. If you ask 50 people to make a mark on the wall without giving them any guidelines you will get plenty of variety, but no unity whatsoever. In fact, there will be too much variety. The marks will be chaotic and separate. It will not engage the viewer because they will not be able to identify anything that organizes the visual elements. Ask each individual to sign their name rather than simply making a random mark and you will gain unity in the form of subject matter—their signature. However, you still might not achieve visual unity unless guidance is provided with regards to the location of each signature.

Unity and variety exist on a spectrum that ranges from total blandness to total disorder. For most works of art, the artist strives to find just the right point on that spectrum—a point at which there is sufficient visual unity enlivened by enough visual variety to maintain visual and intellectual interest. Unity and variety can affect all of the visual elements. Although there are specific ways to create unity, a piece can have unity and variety of line, shape, color, value, or texture.

VISUAL UNITY VERSUS CONCEPTUAL UNITY

A work of art can have **visual unity** and variety or **conceptual unity** and variety, meaning that these two principles can affect both the way a piece looks and the subject matter in equal measure. It is possible for a design to have visual unity without having conceptual unity and conceptual unity without visual unity. It is also possible for a design to have both.

Conceptual unity refers to images that are related and unified by ideas and subject matter rather than by similarity in visual elements. Another term for this type of unity is **thematic unity**. Individual elements are tied together by an underlying theme or concept that is part of what the designer is trying to convey to the viewer. Conceptual unity requires the viewer to interpret the work of art in order to understand how the elements fit together. For instance, a hydrogen bomb cloud, piles of bones, and a Japanese temple building may all relate to the idea of nuclear war. Although their forms are different, they all have something in common.

Visual unity affects the visual appearance of a composition. In order to create visual unity, there must be some similarity or other complementary relationships between the visual elements, the shapes, lines, colors, values, and textures.

The visual elements must appear organized, as if they belong together and agree with one another, creating focal points and drawing the attention of the viewer to specific parts of the composition. We unconsciously search for order and coherency in both nature and things made by human hands. When present in a composition, it makes us feel more comfortable and we therefore give more attention to the image. When order is missing, it makes us feel uneasy and we may not be willing to invest the time and effort into appreciating a composition that needs to be understood. This is important to a designer, because you don't want to lose the audience's attention because of unrelated elements.

HOW UNITY IS CREATED

One of the simplest ways to create unity in any composition is through **repetition**. Repetition is created by repeating something over and over again and can be applied to any of the design elements. Repetition serves to relate the various visual elements in an image to each other. Unity can be created through repetition of color or of value. It can be established by repetition of shape, line, or texture. The use of recurring elements establishes pattern and provides **visual rhythm**, a sense of movement within an image—and, since we as viewers look for similarities that help tie a work of art together, these two qualities help to generate unity.

When looking at a work of art, be it a painting, a sculpture, or a stage design, it is natural for the human eye and mind to look for ways to organize the different visual elements within it into groups in order to analyze and understand what they are seeing. We look for pattern and shape to help us see relationships between the individual elements in a composition. This tendency is called **reification**, which is part of **gestalt theory**. Reification is the process of identifying complex spatial relationships based on limited visual information. Gestalt is a German term that means "shape," "form," or "whole." Gestalt theory is a method of describing visual perception and the psychology of art and is concerned with the relationships between an entire work of art and the individual parts that make it up. One phrase that is commonly used to describe gestalt theory is "the whole is more than the sum of its parts." This way of understanding visual perception was developed by German psychologists in the early 1920s and is defined by several important concepts that have a strong effect on visual unity. These principles are similarity, uniform connectedness, proximity, alignment, continuation, closure, common fate, the law of prägnanz, and the relationship between figure and ground.

SIMILARITY

Similarity refers to how elements in an image are alike. Elements can resemble each other visually and they can also resemble each other thematically. Remember that it is possible for a design to be unified conceptually, but not unified visually and vice versa.

A composition can contain a great deal of information, however, the mind can only process so much input at a time. When this happens, the mind naturally looks for the similarities between elements in a quest for organization and understanding. Categorizing similar objects into groups simplifies the visual information being presented, and makes it possible to process more of it at one time. Similarity is a powerful unifying concept, and the more the various elements resemble each other, the easier it for our eyes to organize them into groupings. Conversely, the less alike the elements are, the more difficult it is to organize them visually. Consequently, dissimilarity is an equally effective tool in creating variety. All of the gestalt concepts can be used either way, to create unity or variety, depending on the goals of the designer.

There are three main types of similarity: size, shape, and color or value.

In Figure 12.1, size is the dominant visual factor. Our eyes naturally tend to notice the larger shapes first and then organize them into a group because of their similarity. Although there is also a connection between all of the objects because of their similar shapes, size is the most influential organizing feature in this example. If the difference between the larger and the smaller circles and squares had been less, then the effect of size as a unifying principle would not have been so pronounced. Because there is more variation possible with size than shape, size is usually a more dominant factor in similarity.

The composition in Figure 12.2 is dominated and unified by the exclusive use of one shape. Although there are variations in the size of the circles, they are still all circles, which provides both visual and thematic unity. Even if the circles were different colors, their shape would still link them together. Fabric patterns often rely on this principle to create pleasing and harmonious designs.

The image in Figure 12.3 relies on value to unify the design. Despite the fact that each shape is different and the sizes vary greatly, they still all look as if they are part of a group because the value of each form is the same. Using the same color throughout a composition can create the same effect. Consider the effect of dressing several actors in the same color. When they appear onstage, the audience will easily perceive a connection between them as well as the lack of connection between any actors not dressed in that color. This can be very effective for establishing the relationships between couples, members of a chorus, an army, or citizens of a town or country. The same principle can be used to unify areas of a set together to create locales, residences, districts or neighborhoods.

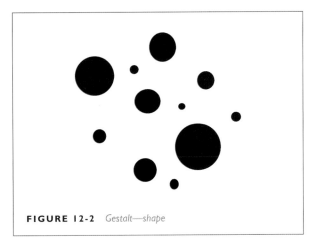

FIGURE 12-2 *Gestalt—shape*

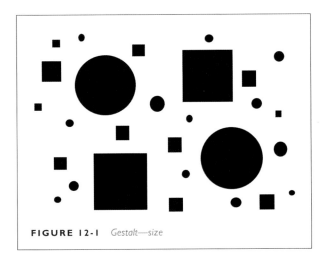

FIGURE 12-1 *Gestalt—size*

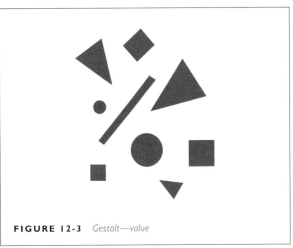

FIGURE 12-3 *Gestalt—value*

UNIFORM CONNECTEDNESS

Related to the idea of similarity is the concept of **uniform connectedness**. This means that elements in a composition that share uniform visual characteristics will appear to be more connected or related than elements that share no common visual characteristics. These shared visual qualities could be texture, pattern, value, size, or other unifying feature used on all elements throughout a composition.

In Figure 12.4, uniform connectedness is created by the application of a uniform texture to all the visual elements, both the shapes in the foreground as well as the background. This unifies the image by creating a standardized, homogenous surface.

PROXIMITY

Proximity addresses where objects are placed in relation to one another. It deals with how close visual elements are to one another, how much space exists between them, and the effect those relationships have on both the individual objects and the composition as a whole. It is one of the simplest ways to create unity in a composition.

In the image on the left in Figure 12.5, the four shapes seem unrelated because of their arrangement within the format. Although balanced through their placement in the four corners, the shapes have no real connection to one another. In the image on the right, the shapes appear to be a group, simply based on their close proximity to one another. Blocking frequently takes advantage of this principle to create relationships between people onstage.

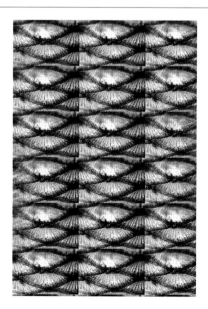

FIGURE 12-4 *Uniform connectedness*

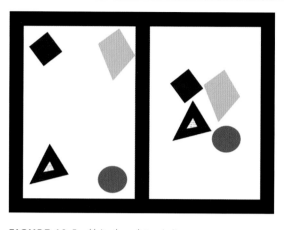

FIGURE 12-5 *Unity through proximity*

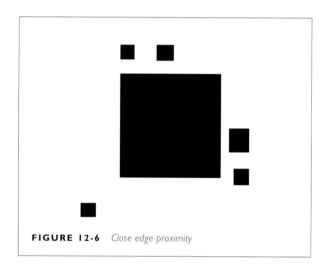

FIGURE 12-6 *Close edge proximity*

Proximity is an important factor in typography. Placing letters close together is what allows us to read. If you alter the proximity of letters to a large degree, it becomes almost impossible to join them together into words. Instead, we see them as individual letters. Proximity is such a strong principle that the visual relationships generated by it will generally be stronger than those created through similarity. There are several types of proximity.

Close edge is the simplest form of proximity, so called because the edges of the elements in a composition are close together. Basically, the closer elements are placed to one another, the easier it is to see them as a group. In this case, the amount of negative space between objects will be relative to the goal of the composition.

In Figure 12.6, the small squares above and to the right of the larger square seem to be related to it because they are close to its edges. In contrast, the small square at the lower left is not as connected to the grouping, because the space between it and the large square is greater than the spaces between the rest of the elements. The relative distance between them ties the four small squares to the large central object, but distance separates the last square from the group that is created by their closer proximity.

Touch is created when elements in a composition are in contact with each other. This contact establishes an immediate and close connection between the parts of a composition. Although they are still separate and unique elements, they appear to be one. This creates a more intimate and stronger relationship than close edge proximity because of the visual link between elements.

In Figure 12.7, changes in size and value have been eliminated to focus on the relationships between the objects in the composition. Notice that the shapes that are touching have more visual weight and are more connected than the ones that are separate.

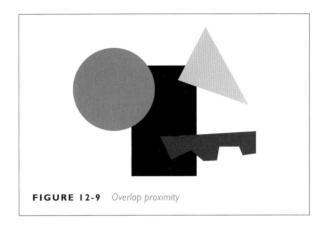

FIGURE 12-9   *Overlap proximity*

In the composition in Figure 12.8, although the elements have more variety in size, shape and value, it is still easy to see how the shapes that are touching have a stronger visual relationship. Although they are individual elements, they can also be perceived as a group or as one compositional unit, which draws focus and ties the entire image together.

When visual elements *overlap*, a strong sense of unity is created. Two items of the same color or value can combine into a new shape, while those of differing visual characteristics will help to establish the illusion of depth; but all overlapping elements will establish a strong grouping within a design.

The example in Figure 12.9 is based on a strong central shape that draws the viewer's eye through both placement and value. The three other shapes that make up the composition are strongly connected to the central rectangle through overlap, unifying the elements and creating a visually appealing group. Their placement also makes them appear to be hovering in front of the central element, suggesting the illusion of depth and three-dimensional space.

It is also possible to combine these aspects of proximity to create a strongly unified design. Often, an additional visual element will be introduced in order to combine the other aspects of proximity together. This can be as simple as using a single colored background to unify the design elements, placing a box around a series of objects to join them together, or even underlining words in a sentence. Each of these actions will create a relationship between visual elements.

The image in Figure 12.10 uses all the aspects of proximity, close edge, touch, and overlap along with similarity of shape, size, and value to create unity. In addition, a background value has been added to aid in tying the individual visual elements together. Although the image is complex, the objects can easily be grouped into three main compositional units that can also be understood as a whole.

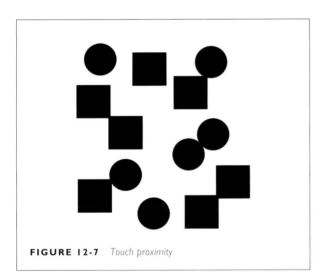

FIGURE 12-7   *Touch proximity*

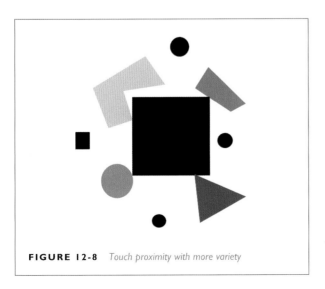

FIGURE 12-8   *Touch proximity with more variety*

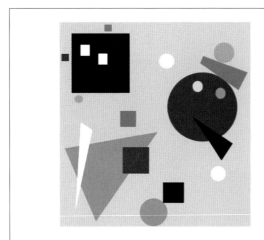

FIGURE 12-10   *Close edge, touch, and overlap proximity*

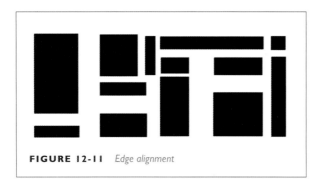

FIGURE 12-11   *Edge alignment*

ALIGNMENT

Alignment is the arrangement of objects along a straight line or lines. These lines may be horizontal, vertical or even

angular. Objects can be aligned along their edges, following an established grid, or on a central axis. Alignment not only organizes visual elements, it creates movement and carries the viewer's eye from one element of a composition to the next. Alignment creates organizational relationships between both the positive and negative spaces.

Any object with a flat edge or edges can easily be aligned with other objects possessing flat edges. Rectangles and squares, as in Figure 12.11, are simple to align because they have more than one flat edge to use. The repetition of right angles also set up a feeling of similarity, which contributes to unity within the composition. The more of the edges you align, the more interconnected each of the shapes will be with those around it and therefore the final design will possess a stronger sense of harmony. An obvious *edge* alignment will occur when the outside edges of objects align to form a shape, as they do in this image. The distance between objects also contributes to the overall gestalt effect. Those that are closer together have a stronger connection than those that are further apart.

Figure 12.12 illustrates that it is also possible to line up angular objects that are not square, provided that the edges of the alignment are clearly defined. Although the shapes at the opposite ends of this composition are also aligned, notice that the perception of alignment diminishes the further away the objects are from one another. The configuration may not be obvious to the viewer. This occurs when shapes are dissimilar. In these compositions, the alignment must be strong enough to unify the elements within them.

Items of any shape can be aligned by arranging them along a central axis. This axis can be horizontal, vertical, or diagonal. Simple shapes are easier to align using this method, but they can be used as a preliminary tool for more complex shapes in the

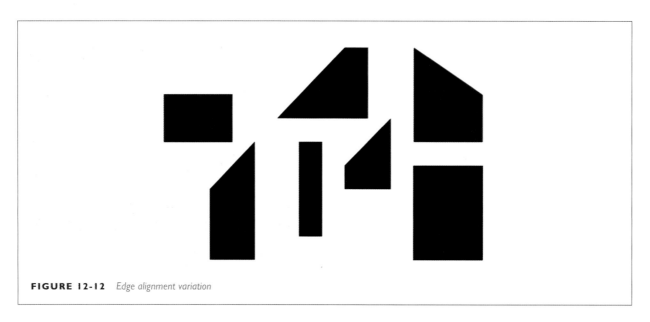

FIGURE 12-12   *Edge alignment variation*

design process. Elements that are parallel also appear to be more connected than those that are not parallel to each other.

In both of the images in Figure 12.13, the parallel elements appear more related. In the image on the left, the three parallel lines can be linked together into a group, even though there are variations in their proximity. In the image on the right, the placement of the four shapes in the middle of the composition along a strong horizontal axis groups them together into one visual unit.

CONTINUATION

Not only do our eyes search for patterns and groups within an image, they also search for movement, elements within a composition that guide us from one part of the design to another. **Continuation** is another way to achieve unity by leading the viewer's eye, causing it to follow the elements that carry on within the design, usually in a line, a direction of movement, or along the edge of an object. Continuation is based on the idea that once the viewer's eye has been engaged, they will continue to follow visual clues until something significant is discovered. There are several different ways to accomplish this.

Perspective lines in a drawing can lead the viewer to a specific visual element. By placing important items at a vanishing point, the viewer's eyes will naturally be lead toward that object by the other elements that point towards it.

Paths can be used to guide the viewer in a specific direction. Paths can take the form of rivers, streams, walkways, tile patterns, roads, sidewalks, cobblestones, telephone lines, rows of gravestones, or any other linear element.

Eye direction can also be used in a composition to create continuation. If the subject of a painting is looking at something within the format, our eyes will follow the path created by their line of sight to see what they are looking at. This can create a

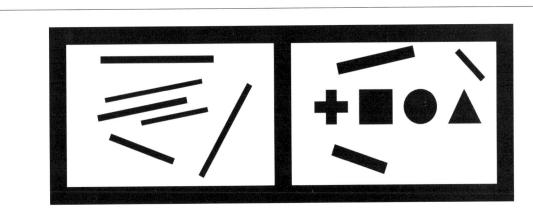

FIGURE 12-13   *Axial alignment*

FIGURE 12-14   *Perspective lines*—The Marriage of Figaro *by Mozart, Krannert Center at the University of Illinois, preliminary sketch for Act 3, set design by Alison Ford*

FIGURE 12-15   *Paths*—Anatomy of Gray *by Jim Leonard, set design by Jeff Enwistle, University of Wisconsin Green Bay Theatre*

psychic line and emphasis within the composition and also serves to connect the two objects together.

Continuation is usually far subtler than alignment or similarity and may take a moment to identify when viewing a composition. But, given that it can be used to join together several elements in one image, or even to join multiple compositions together, it can be a very useful way to create unity within a complete design.

In the first image in Figure 12.16, the composition is unified through similarity, proximity, and value. In the second image, the same elements have been arranged to also provide continuation between one shape and the next. Which of the images possesses a stronger sense of unity? Although the objects in the first image have several things in common and the entire image *is* unified, the second composition creates a stronger relationship between the visual elements because each shape leads the viewer's eye to the next. Objects and visual elements can also continue from one image to another or even one format to another, creating relationships between objects that are seemingly unrelated, as they do in Figure 12.17.

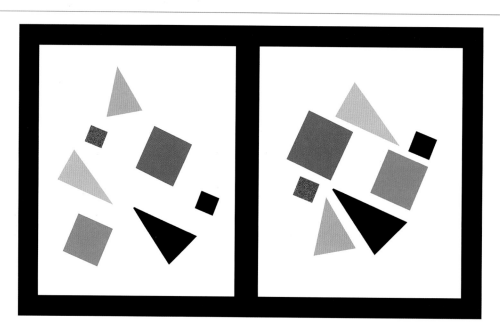

FIGURE 12-16 *Continuation*

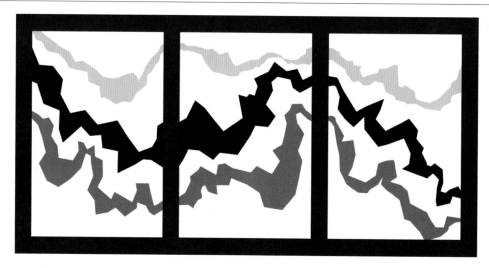

FIGURE 12-17 *Continuation over multiple surfaces*

CLOSURE

At first glance, **closure** is very similar to the concept of implied line. Both rely on the viewer to complete an unfinished image by mentally filling in the missing details. But closure is a little more complicated in its application.

All complex forms are made up of smaller individual elements. For example, a checkerboard is made up of dozens of small squares; a face is made up of individual features—two eyes, a nose, a mouth, and so on. Just as we can generally identify a familiar face when only a handful of the features are visible, so too are we able to fill in the blanks in a composition when enough of the significant details are present. This principle can easily be seen in a simple geometric shape. With enough key information to explain the entire shape, our eyes are able to fill in the missing pieces to "see" the whole figure.

The same technique can be applied to more complex forms, but careful consideration must be given to what is removed and what is allowed to remain. Naturally, some aspects of a visual form will be more critical to its perception and comprehension, while others may be unnecessary and can be eliminated without harm to the understanding of the whole. The quality of the information that is presented is far more important than the quantity.

THE LAW OF PRÄGNANZ

The **law of prägnanz** is a fundamental part of gestalt perception. Basically it states that any complex or ambiguous object will be reduced by the viewer's eye into a simple and complete shape. Artists rely on this principle constantly when beginning a preliminary sketch. A complex arrangement of

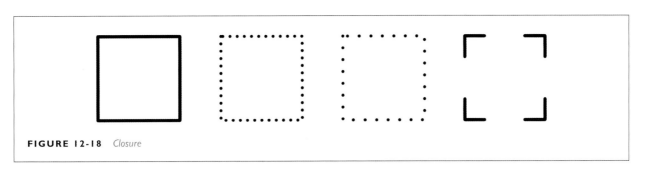

FIGURE 12-18   *Closure*

FIGURE 12-19   *Closure applied to a costume rendering—Fences by August Wilson, costume design by Kaoime E. Malloy, Iowa Summer Repertory*

items can be lumped together into one simple shape in order to determine the boundaries of the physical arrangement. Each object can then be broken down into smaller shapes and placed within the boundaries of the larger outline to accurately draw the details of every item.

In the image on the right of Figure 12.20, a complex arrangement of shapes has been reduced and simplified to its basic outline, allowing the shapes to be seen as one complete unit. Although it is possible to see that the composition is created by using three individual shapes, they are not easily defined until they have each been given a distinct value.

FIGURE AND GROUND

In any design, the visual elements will be perceived as either the figure or the ground. The figure is considered

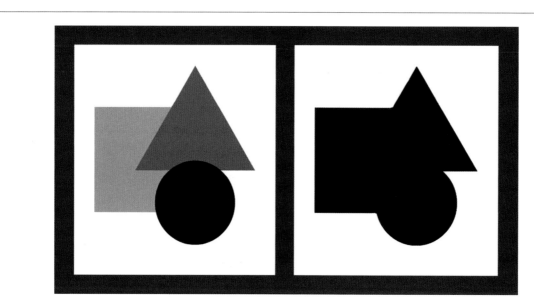

FIGURE 12-20 *Law of prägnanz*

FIGURE 12-21 *Law of prägnanz applied to a design sketch—*Twelfth Night, *costume design by Kaoime E. Malloy, University of Wisconsin Green Bay*

to be the subject of the composition and occupies the foreground. The background or ground is the area on which the figure resides. When we look at a composition, one of the first things we do as viewers is attempt to determine what is the figure and what is the ground. This is usually done quite quickly and often occurs on a subconscious level. The relationship between the figure and ground can communicate what can effectively be ignored without sacrificing comprehension. The figure requires our immediate attention as we begin to approach a design, while the background does not, though it provides context. Generally, the object that occupies the smaller area will be perceived as the figure and the larger area around it will be perceived as the ground.

In the two images in Figure 12.22, the smaller squares are usually perceived to be the figure and the larger squares serve as the ground. However, by altering your perception of the figure/ground relationship, it is possible to see the larger black square as a figure with a hole in the middle, through which you can see a lighter background.

Figure 12.23 is one of the most famous ways of illustrating the **figure/ground** relationship. Initially developed by Danish psychologist Edgar Rubin, it is called Rubin's Vase. When looking at the image, do you see a white vase on a black background? Or do you see two black faces on a white background? When shapes share a common border, as they do in this famous optical illusion, it is possible to shift your perception to see one first one variation of the composition, and then the other, an example of a figure ground reversal. This relationship can be exploited to create unity and variety in any composition.

Although the principles of gestalt theory have been presented individually, more often than not they are used in combination with each other within a design to create an evocative visual image. Each one can be used to create unity and enhance variety, contributing to a dynamic composition.

FIGURE 12-23   *Rubin's Vase*

THE LANGUAGE OF UNITY AND VARIETY

Alignment: The arrangement of objects along a straight line or lines.

Closure: The effect that occurs when enough visual information is presented to allow the viewer to complete an unfinished image by mentally filling in the missing details.

Conceptual unity: A design whose elements are related and unified by ideas and subject matter rather than by similarity in visual elements.

Continuation: The effect of each object in a design leading to the next, creating a sense of movement and leading the viewer's eye.

Figure/ground: The relationship between the subject of a composition (the figure) and the area it occupies (the background).

Gestalt theory: A psychological theory of visual perception that deals with both the whole artistic image and its individual parts and their relationship to one another.

Harmony: A pleasing, orderly, or consistent arrangement of parts.

Law of prägnanz: A fundamental part of gestalt perception that states that any complex or ambiguous object will be reduced by the viewer's eye into a simple and complete shape.

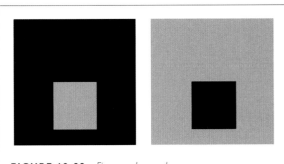

FIGURE 12-22   *Figure and ground*

Proximity: Where objects are placed in relation to one another.

Reification: The human tendency to look for pattern and shape to help us see relationships between the individual elements in a composition.

Repetition: Repeating a visual element or elements multiple times for effect.

Similarity: How the visual elements in a composition resemble each other.

Thematic unity: Another term for conceptual unity.

Uniform connectedness: When objects in a design share uniform visual characteristics.

Unity: A sense of oneness or organization that holds a composition together and makes all the elements work together.

Variety: Visual difference and diversity, which creates interest.

Visual rhythm: The movement created by the repetition of objects in an image.

Visual unity: Unity that is created by a harmonious arrangement of the visual elements of a composition.

CHAPTER 13

BALANCE

WHAT IS BALANCE?

Balance is defined as the equal distribution of visual weight to either side of a perceived or implied **center of gravity**. It is, essentially, the idea of visual equilibrium and suggests the quality of stability in a work of art. Opposing forces are reconciled and brought together in an image. Visual weight is equalized and visual tension may be soothed or heightened. **Visual weight** refers to the apparent heaviness or lightness of the forms arranged in a composition, based on how insistently they draw our eyes. In a three-dimensional artwork, balance is obvious and easy to understand. Even when the perception of imbalance is desired in order to create a specific effect or generate visual tension, the piece itself will fall over if it is not physically balanced. In a two-dimensional work, balance may be more difficult to perceive and comprehend due to the fact that actual physical balance is not required and therefore visual balance can be greatly manipulated for effect. Consequently, it can be useful to bring the analogy of a three-dimensional form toppling over to our evaluations of two-dimensional work. Sometimes, seeing the balance in a two-dimensional form requires a bit of imagination on the part of the viewer.

There are five main types of balance: symmetrical, asymmetrical, radial, occult, and crystallographic. In each, balance is created in different and unique ways that lend different qualities to the final composition. There is no one method for establishing equilibrium in a design. Instead, consideration must be given to the final effect a designer wishes to present within their work.

SYMMETRICAL BALANCE

In **symmetrical balance**, the implied center of gravity is located on a set of two bisecting axes—imaginary lines drawn through the center of the work both vertically and horizontally. Forms on either side of the **axis** correspond to one another in terms of shape, size, and placement. In other words, they have an equal sense of visual weight. Sometimes the symmetry is so perfect that the two sides of the composition are literally mirror images of each other. This is called **bilateral symmetry**. More often the correspondence is close but not exact, which is sometimes called **relieved symmetry**. Forms on either side of the vertical axis are not exact, but balance the composition informally.

In Figure 13.2, symmetrical balance is evident in the set design in this image from *Love's Labour's Lost*. One large, central structure dominates the set marked by two sets of three arches,

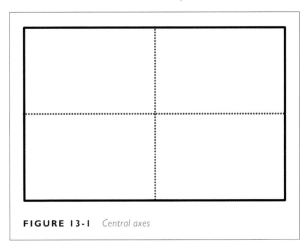

FIGURE 13-1 *Central axes*

FIGURE 13-2 Love's Labour's Lost, *set design by Jeff Entwistle, costume design by Kaoime E. Malloy, lighting design by R. Michael Ingraham, photo by R. Michael Ingraham*

FIGURE 13-3 *Jason Robert Brown, Songs for a New World, set design by Jeff Entwistle, lighting design by R. Michael Ingraham, photo by R. Michael Ingraham*

one above and one below. Each set of arches is identical in shape and style within its unit and has roughly the same visual weight. Two identical stair units connect the upper level to the main floor, winding around the stage space and leading the eye from one level to the other. Aside from one small, moveable wicker bench situated on stage left, each side of the set is a mirror image of the other, providing exact symmetry.

In Figure 13.3, the symmetry is less exact. Although the main playing space and the two sides of the set are mirror images in terms of shape, surface dimension, and height, centered around the large circular set piece that opens up to reveal the cyclorama, the two towers on either side of the stage and the staircases leading up to them are not exactly the same. However, they are roughly the same height and occupy a similar amount of space, so while they are not mirror images of one another, they are close enough to provide relieved symmetry.

Symmetry lends a sense of stability, permanence and formality to a composition; therefore it is sometimes referred to as **formal balance**. This visual quality is especially important in architecture, where the impression of stability, formality, and importance might be especially desired, as in the design of a government building, for example. Symmetrical structures convey a sense of power, strength, and durability to the viewer, supporting the authority of the government, which the building itself represents. It is no accident that many government buildings in the West use the clean, classic aesthetics of ancient Greco-Roman architectural style to suggest power, authority, and endurance. This not only reflects the origins of democracy, it also speaks to the permanence of the art form and by extension, government.

Even though humans are bilateral in nature, seeking out symmetry as an instinctive part of what we are, perfect symmetry can be quiet and sometimes boring. Although an unbalanced composition can be unsettling and might make us feel uncomfortable, there are ways to create equilibrium within a design without relying on absolute, unrelieved symmetry and that often creates more visual interest.

ASYMMETRICAL BALANCE

An **asymmetrical** composition has two sides that do not match, but the composition appears to be balanced because the visual weights in the two sides are very similar. One example of asymmetry can be found in *contrapposto*. Meaning "counterpose," *contrapposto* is an Italian term used to describe the qualities of the human figure when standing with most of its weight on one foot. This forces the hips and the shoulders off the central axis in order to create balance and remain upright. *Contrapposto* poses can suggest movement or imply relaxation, which adds to the overall dynamics and tension of the figure. *Contrapposto* can easily be experienced in your own body in order to understand asymmetry. If you stand with your feet evenly planted and your arms at your sides, you are balanced. Both sides of your body are symmetrical and your body is stable. Stick one arm out to the side and you no longer are symmetrical. Instead, your body will appear and may also feel somehow off-balance. If you then extend the opposite leg out to the side in juxtaposition to your arm, a sense of balance will be created. Your balance is not symmetrical or exact; instead it is informal.

In order to understand how asymmetrical balance is accomplished, we need to look at some general principles of **informal balance** that are used to create it, employing the various elements of design.

FIGURE 13-4   *Asymmetry—Twelfth Night, scene design by Frank Ludwig*

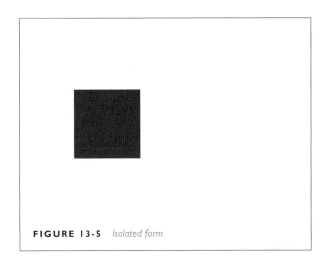

FIGURE 13-5   *Isolated form*

GENERAL PRINCIPLES OF INFORMAL BALANCE

An isolated form has more visual weight. Elements that exist by themselves in any part of the design will draw the viewer's attention because they are more visually engaging than an empty space.

A large form is visually heavier than small one. Size plays an important role in balance because larger forms draw the viewer's focus.

A dark value form is visually heavier than a light form of same size. Just as a dark form draws light, it also draws our attention.

A textured form is visually heavier than a smooth form of the same size. Texture provides visual interest and also carries more visual weight, which engages the viewer.

A form placed close to the central axis is visually heavier than one placed further away, near the outer edge of the composition. If an object is placed in the middle of the format, it will naturally appear to be more important and relevant to the viewer. It will draw focus because our eyes are naturally drawn to the center of an image.

A form gathers visual weight as it moves to the edge of the composition. Using this aspect of informal balance, forms placed near the edges of a composition can balance large open spaces and smaller forms near the edge can also balance large forms placed near the center.

A complex form is visually heavier than a simple form. Whether an object is more intricate due to color, value, texture, or pattern, it will have more visual weight than a form that is less complicated.

A small dark form can balance a larger light form. The smaller, dark form is more visually complex, and therefore has more visual weight.

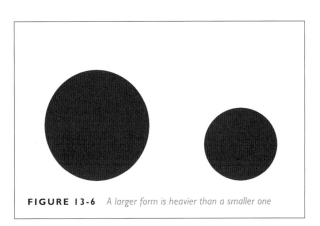

FIGURE 13-6   *A larger form is heavier than a smaller one*

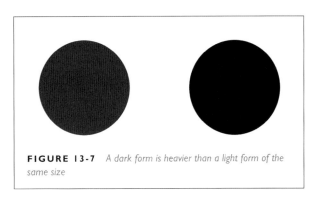

FIGURE 13-7   *A dark form is heavier than a light form of the same size*

Two or more small forms can balance a large form. Whether simple or complex, multiple smaller shapes can provide enough visual weight to balance a larger object.

A diagonal orientation in the composition carries more visual weight than a horizontal or vertical one. Diagonal lines always imply movement and are more dynamic than horizontal or vertical lines. Consequently, diagonal movement of forms in a design will also possess the same qualities.

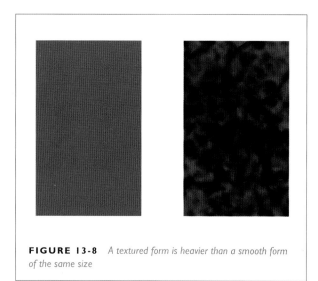

FIGURE 13-8   *A textured form is heavier than a smooth form of the same size*

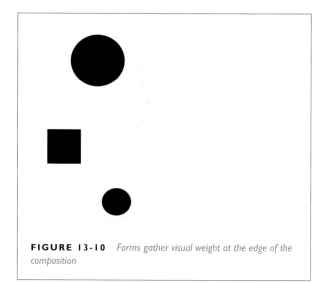

FIGURE 13-10   *Forms gather visual weight at the edge of the composition*

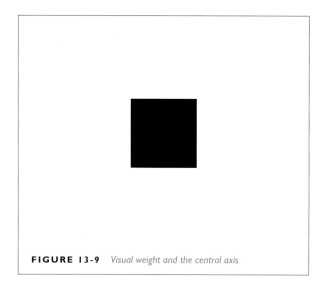

FIGURE 13-9   *Visual weight and the central axis*

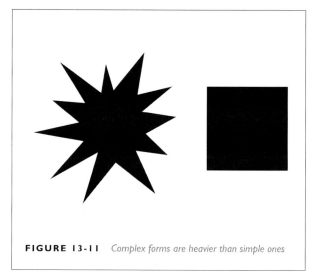

FIGURE 13-11   *Complex forms are heavier than simple ones*

Warm colors are visually heavier than cool colors. Because warm colors tend to be brighter and more vibrant, they usually carry more visual weight.

Intense colors are visually heavier than pale ones. Saturated colors have more visual weight than pastels, and therefore will draw more attention in an image. Consequently, they can be used to balance larger forms.

The intensity and the visual weight of any color increases as the background approaches its complement, because of simultaneous contrast. In Figure 13.18, the two green squares are the same color, but the green of the square is intensified when placed next to its complementary color, red.

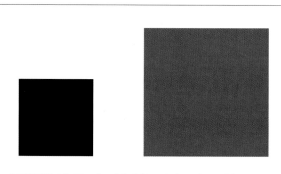

FIGURE 13-12   *Small dark forms balance larger light ones*

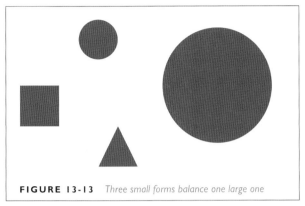

FIGURE 13-13 *Three small forms balance one large one*

FIGURE 13-14 *Multiple small shapes balance larger ones*

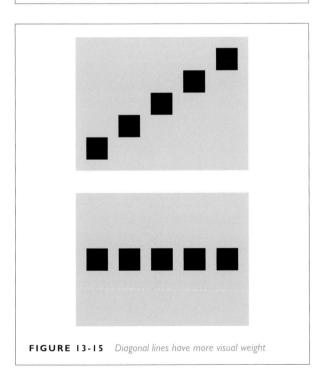

FIGURE 13-15 *Diagonal lines have more visual weight*

FIGURE 13-16 *Warm colors are heavier than cool*

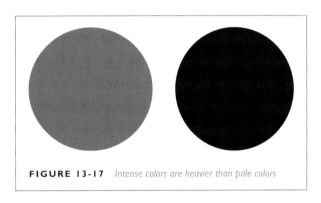

FIGURE 13-17 *Intense colors are heavier than pale colors*

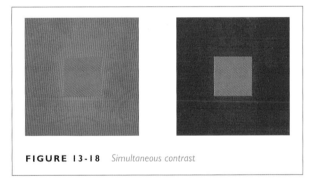

FIGURE 13-18 *Simultaneous contrast*

RADIAL SYMMETRY

When a composition is focused around a central point and the components of the form radiate out from a central axis, like spokes on a wheel, the balance is described as *radial*. **Radial balance** creates a strong focal point in the center of the image, or in a series of components contained within a composition. Clock faces, many flowers, various seashells, and snowflakes are all dominated by this type of balance. Radial balance might be as formal and complex as the ornamental designs in Figure 13.19, which could easily be used for a fabric or tile design, or as simple as a circular fountain centered in the middle of a set.

FIGURE 13-19   *Radial symmetry, (Blackspring / shutterstock.com)*

OCCULT BALANCE

Rather than using a central axis as the basis for visual organization and arrangement, **occult balance** employs several informal principles to create a sense of equilibrium. Works that make use of occult balance possess a strong variety of sizes to show distance. They also display movement in an angular or curved direction in order to move the eye around the composition and, most predominantly, the background dominates the composition more than any other design element. This is different from other compositional styles where the subject is the main focus of the image. In Figure 13.20 there is a variety of sizes of shapes. The movement is circular, and the background is as important to the composition as the shapes within it.

Given the commonplace use of minimalist and environmental sets in theatrical design, where set pieces are limited and carefully chosen for how they affect the playing space, occult balance can be a very useful principle to employ when creating an evocative and compelling scenic design.

CRYSTALLOGRAPHIC BALANCE

Crystallographic balance is created by repeating design elements with equal visual weight throughout the entire surface of a composition. Another name for this type of balance is **all-over pattern**. In this type of balance there is no strong focal point; the visual weight is even and uniform. Some art forms that rely heavily on crystallographic balance include mandalas, quilt-making, and fabric design. A chessboard is also an example of all-over pattern. Theatrical designers often deal with crystallographic balance through designs for flooring, fabrics and lighting gobo patterns.

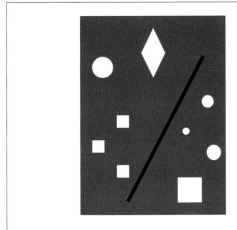

FIGURE 13-20   *Occult balance*

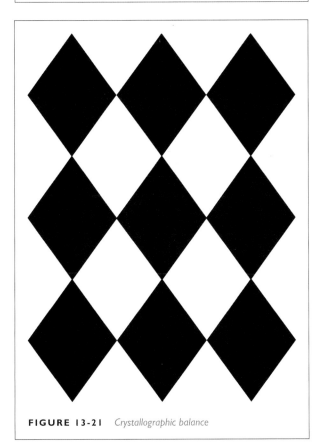

FIGURE 13-21   *Crystallographic balance*

THE LANGUAGE OF BALANCE

All-over pattern: Another name for crystallographic balance.

Asymmetrical balance: A composition that has two sides that do not match; but the composition appears to be balanced because the visual weights in the two sides are very similar.

Axis: A line that divides an object into two equal halves.

Balance: The equal distribution of visual weight to either side of a perceived or implied center of gravity.

Bilateral symmetry: Symmetry where both halves of a design are exactly identical.

Center of gravity: The average center of the weight of an object. In design, this usually refers to the center of the composition, both horizontally and vertically.

Crystallographic balance: Balance that is created by repeating design elements with equal visual weight throughout the entire surface of a composition.

Formal balance: Another name for symmetry.

Informal balance: Another name for asymmetry.

Occult balance: Balance that is created by allowing the background to dominate an image, using a variety of sizes and shapes and creating circular or diagonal movement.

Radial balance: A type of balance that is focused around a central point in an image where the components of the design radiate out from a central axis.

Relieved symmetry: Balance where the correspondence and visual weight between the two sides of a composition are close but not identical.

Symmetrical balance: A form of balance where the two halves of a composition on either side of an implied center of gravity are identical or nearly exact.

Visual weight: The apparent heaviness or lightness of the forms arranged in a composition, based on how insistently they draw our eyes.

CHAPTER 14

REPETITION, RHYTHM, AND PATTERN

WHAT IS REPETITION?

Repetition is the process of repeating one or more of any of the visual elements in a design. Repetition can provide unity in a composition, create pattern, produce a feeling of tension or dissonance, communicate mood and emotion, or establish a sense of rhythm and movement. It can help to show scale, distance, and proportion and often provides information about the relationships between parts of an image. Repetition can be used to place emphasis on the whole of an artwork, or it can be used to emphasize individual parts over the whole. It can also serve to underscore conceptual and thematic elements in a design.

TYPES OF REPETITION

When elements of a composition are repeated, a designer must decide how precise the repetition will be. Will it be a faithful replica, or will the **duplication** or copy be imprecise? Objects that are replicated exactly, with no variations in line, shape, size, color, value, or texture are **exact duplications**. They are faithful reproductions of the original object in every detail. There is no variation. In contrast, when an item is duplicated but details are altered slightly the result is **near duplication**. Near duplication can be as simple as making a shift in color, value, texture, or size or it can involve a minimal change in the overall shape of an object. Although some aspects of the original form have been altered, in near duplication there will still be a

sufficient resemblance that the relationship between the two objects can easily be perceived.

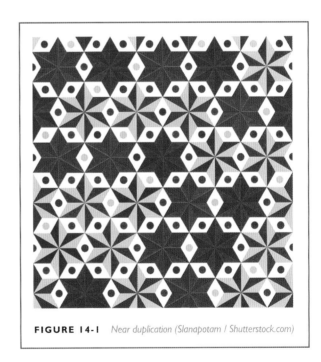

FIGURE 14-1 *Near duplication (Slanapotam / Shutterstock.com)*

Another term for duplication is **simple repetition**, when one visual element is repeated without changes or variation. Although this type of repetition can provide the most unity, it can also be static and boring if not handled carefully. Repeating one element can be very useful when a designer wants to make a specific point and the visual underscoring of repeated elements is necessary to support it. Simple repetition may not always be concerned with the spacing between objects, instead focusing on replication of elements placed wherever they are desired in a composition. In other words, the repetition may appear to be random.

When duplicated objects of the same size or regular variation are arranged in an order with equal spacing this is said to be **regular repetition**. Regular repetition draws the eye along with it, creating a sense of rhythm in a design. A piece with this type of repetition often feels measured and even, with a visual beat or cadence. Objects repeated at regular intervals create movement that can guide the viewer through the composition, helping them to experience the entire design as one unit or direct them to the most important aspects of the image. This type of repetition can be seen in Figure 14.2. It is also possible for repetition to be irregular, where the duplication of elements appears to be random. Because it is a natural tendency for our eyes to seek out pattern and unity,

a designer might choose to use irregular repetition to create tension and dissonance or a sense of unease.

RHYTHM

Rhythm is essentially timed movement. In music, rhythm is a series of notes and beats that lead the listener through the song and melodies. In dance, rhythm is found in the recurring movements of the dancers. In visual art, rhythm is a connected series of objects that guide the viewer through the image or a succession of marks and **motifs** that establish a **pattern**. It is a path for the eyes to follow. In design, a motif is a two- or three-dimensional element or unit, usually decorative, which is repeated over and over. It can also be a dominant thematic element that recurs throughout an image. Pattern is created when the repetition of elements or motifs is predictable. In some art forms, such as mosaic, fabric design, quilt patterns, or parquet and tile flooring, pattern may be the dominant visual element. There may not be a dominant focal point or area of emphasis. This is referred to as **all-over pattern** or crystallographic balance. Instead of

FIGURE 14-2 *Simple repetition*

FIGURE 14-3 *Irregular repetition (topimages, Panom Pensawang, Philip Meyer / shutterstock.com)*

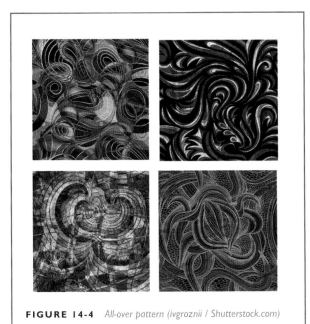

FIGURE 14-4   *All-over pattern (ivgroznii / Shutterstock.com)*

a focal point, emphasis is evenly distributed throughout the entire pattern.

Although all patterns possess rhythm, the difference between rhythm and pattern as individual design principles is the regularity of the repetition that each possesses. In pattern, the individual parts stay the same throughout the composition and therefore have less variety overall. In contrast, rhythm often has a great deal of variety in an individual image. In design, rhythm is created by the interaction between repeated positive shapes that are separated by negative spaces. Using musical notation as a metaphor, the positive shapes are beats and the negative spaces are pauses or rests. Together, they establish rhythm. You experience these visual rhythms with your eyes, much as you understand the rhythm in music with your ears.

Rhythm is based in repetition; without repetition, there is no rhythm. It is also a dynamic part of the world we live in—the world around us is organized by rhythmic events. We see daily rhythms in the seasons, the cycle of the moon, and in waves upon the shore. The sun rises, peaks, and then sets. We are born, we grow, we age, and we die. These natural rhythms measure out the passage of time, organizing our experience of it. To the extent that works of art can take place in time, they too structure our experience of them through rhythm. The performing arts are the most obvious examples—music, dance, film, and theatre. Each of these art forms takes place over a set period and requires an investment of our time in order to experience them. Looking at art takes time as well, and rhythm is one of the means that artists use to give structure to our experience of it. Through repetition, any of the visual elements can take on rhythm in a design.

Rhythm also creates a sense of movement within a composition. Movement can be used to guide the viewer's eye, tell a story, and indicate the passage of time. The terms used to describe movement in art and design are often the same ones that are used to explain the speed or articulated quality of music. Visual rhythms have a beat, a tempo, intervals, and a cadence, just like musical compositions. Some rhythmic visual arrangements are elegant and slow, like a languid *legato* melody in a piece of classical music. They are smooth and soothing, like the calm surface of the ocean broken by the lightest of waves. Looking at them relaxes us. Others are pulsing and fast, with each element punctuated visually like the staccato beat of a brisk Sousa march or the thundering pulse of rock and roll. They are lively and energetic, compelling the viewer's eye to move quickly through the composition. They grab our attention and stimulate our senses, making us feel happy and engaged with the piece. There are several different kinds of rhythm, often associated with the type of emotional response they elicit

FIGURE 14-5   *Linear rhythm*

from the viewer. The type of rhythm used in a design will be dependent on the goals of the designer.

TYPES OF RHYTHM

Visual rhythm can be defined as the movement created by the repetition of objects in an image. Different arrangements of objects will have varying effects on the mood, feel, look, and rhythm of the composition. One of the first things the viewer may notice is the **linear rhythm** of a design. Linear rhythm refers to the movement created by the flow of an individual line or groups of lines in relation to one another. It is often closely related to individual artistic style, making it possible to identify the artist simply through their method of making marks on the paper and the visual qualities of those marks. It is very easy, for example, to recognize the work of Vincent van Gogh, due to his characteristic use of line. All of his work, whether drawings or paintings, share the same thick, closely spaced lines that appear to move with internal energy. The same is true of theatrical designer Desmond Heeley, whose renderings are characterized by lively, bold line work that lends a sense of rhythm, movement, weight, and playfulness to his designs.

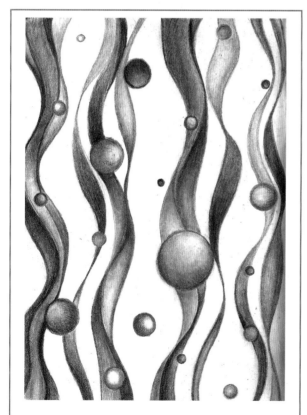

FIGURE 14-6 *Flowing rhythm*

Flowing rhythm is characterized by smooth, gliding movement from one repeated form to another. Flowing rhythm possesses curvilinear qualities that gently lead the eye from one element in a composition to the next. This type of rhythm is often more organic in character, reflecting the movement of water as it flows downstream, rolling hills, or other natural phenomenon.

Visual rhythms are often **regular** in appearance, with evenly spaced intervals and equal repetitions. These types of rhythms are used to organize objects and appear to have a steady beat. These rhythms can be described as **inherent** to an image or a sequence of images and are established by the repetition in the composition. Parking spaces are a good example of regular rhythm, as is a grid or windows on a building. But these types of unrelieved rhythms can appear static and monotonous at times. Variations in rhythm can provide interest and make a design more exciting. When the spacing between repeated elements is varied, or there are variations in the elements themselves, the rhythm they create is irregular or unplanned. In fact, it is possible for irregular rhythms to progress through an entire design without exact duplication. **Irregular rhythm** can be compared to syncopation in music. The uneven beat in a syncopated song gives bounce and energy to the music. Irregular visual rhythm does the same thing for a work of art. The variety within the repetition keeps the rhythms it creates lively, exciting, and compelling.

Alternating rhythm is formed when an element or motif is repeated and the position, spacing, or content is changed in a regular, repetitive sequence. Alternating rhythm is similar to the rests between beats in music. Rests interrupt the pace of the music, but the series of beats and rests set up a rhythmic pattern that is interesting and engaging to the listener. A simple way to create this type of rhythm is to introduce a second motif into the composition. An additional object makes it possible to alternate between the two elements, not only creating a rhythm but a pattern as well. Changing the spacing between repetitions of an element will also set up an alternating rhythm, as will altering the position or content of an object. Even a simple change in value can be enough to set up an alternating rhythm. A checkerboard is a classic example of simple alternation.

When the interchange and variation between one element and the next move in an identifiable sequence, continuing from one motif to the next, it forms a **progressive rhythm**. Gradually transforming one object into another is an example of progressive rhythm, as is a shift from a dark value to a light value in a series of identical shapes. In both, forms are taken through a sequence of progressive steps towards an end result. One of the things that progressive rhythm can introduce very

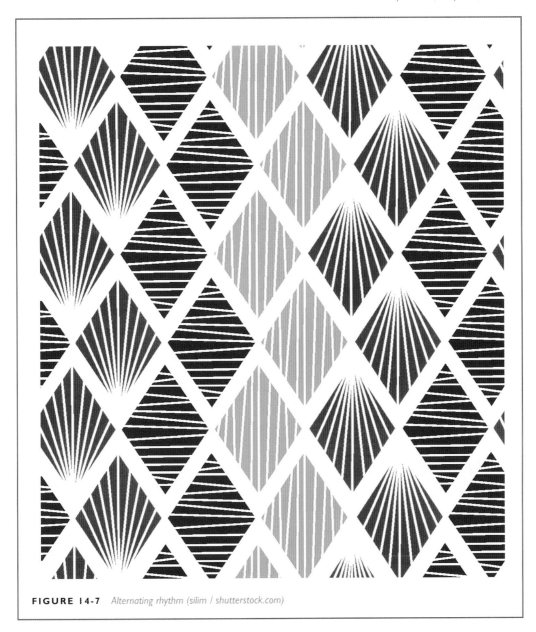

FIGURE 14-7   *Alternating rhythm (silim / shutterstock.com)*

effectively into a composition is the passage of time. Think of the changing shape of the phases of the moon, or the shifting wings of a bird in flight. The succession of these two subjects tracing a path across a format is an expressive metaphor of time moving forward.

PATTERN

Pattern is the result of any repetitive motif or design. Very often in the design arts, pattern is associated with decorative motifs, but in reality repeating any visual element can create pattern. Since pattern is based on repetition, it is no surprise that it will lead the viewer's eye through an image and create movement in a composition. But pattern also serves a decorative purpose. It can be used to embellish an object or

a composition, to add ornamentation and add to the overall aesthetic experience of the viewer. In this case, the function or purpose of pattern is purely to enhance the physical appearance of a design. But pattern can be extremely important in theatrical design. It is important in the overall appearance of any design, regardless of area, where the repetition of shapes can be used to support thematic ideas and concepts, establish location, or reinforce the shape of the body. Pattern is also a key element of the decorative elements of decor, where it is found in wallpaper, parquet and tile flooring, upholstery, and fabrics. Patterns are an essential consideration for costumes, not only because of their importance to fabrics in general but because pattern can be used to manipulate the overall silhouette of a garment. Patterns used in these kinds of items are often strong indicators of time period and are very important when designing

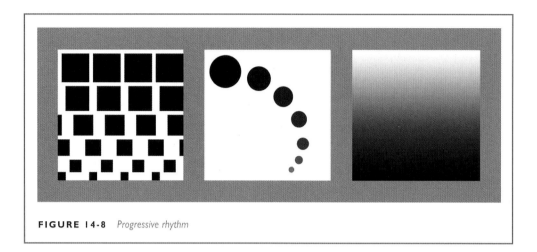

FIGURE 14-8   *Progressive rhythm*

The Marriage of Figaro
Act IV

FIGURE 14-9   *Pattern—* The Marriage of Figaro *by Mozart, Act IV, scene design by Frank Ludwig, Viterbo University (created with Adobe PhotoShop and Vectorworks with Renderworks)*

historical plays. Pattern is also a key way to break up light and an important tool in lighting design to reveal space and paint with light.

TYPES OF PATTERN

There are several different classes of pattern in the physical world. They can be applied to both natural and manmade forms. Any one of these types can be used to create a decorative motif that enhances the look of a design as well as being employed to develop an all-over pattern that dominates one area of a composition. Each can be manipulated using the other principles of design to create interest and variety.

Lattices

Lattice patterns are created by a fixed arrangement of overlapping or intersecting lines (positive space) combined with open areas (negative space) to produce a basket-weave effect. A lattice can be as simple as a grid of horizontal and vertical overlapping lines, or they can be incredibly complicated, with many interlaced lines that create intricate geometric patterns. A lattice pattern may also be created by using a grid as a basic format for arranging motifs or other decorative elements in a composition. In such cases, the grid is usually apparent in the overall design, even if the lines that make it up are implied rather than visible. Some lattices are incredibly formal, with regular intervals between positive and negative spaces and

FIGURE 14-10   *Lattices (Max Krasnov, Curly Pat, Alex Landa / Shutterstock.com)*

others are irregular in nature. Lattice patterns are common in the aesthetic traditions of many cultures around the world and are an important decorative element in architecture, interior design, furniture, fabrics and jewelry.

Spherical

A **sphere** is a three-dimensional round form whose surface consists of a series of points that are all equidistant from the sphere's center. Because the boundary of a sphere is circular, it appears round when viewed from any direction. The term "sphere" refers both to the form itself and the space it contains within it. Spherical patterns are circular in nature, may be irregular in terms of positioning, or can be laid out in a regular formation on a grid and may often possess the visual illusion of three dimensions. A pattern may also be considered spherical if the individual elements that make it up are arranged on an actual sphere, such as the individual square glass tiles laid out on the surface of a mirror ball.

Spirals—Helices and Volutes

A **spiral** is a curve on a plane that winds at a consistently increasing or decreasing distance from and around a fixed, central point. The line that curves around the center creates the pattern. Spirals are very important in Western architecture, where they can often be found as decorative elements in the capitals of the Corinthian, Ionic, and Composite orders of classical Greek columns, but are also common in the aesthetic traditions of many cultures worldwide. They are an integral design element in Celtic and European megalithic art and are also an inherent form found in nature.

Spirals generally fall into one of two categories: volutes and helixes. A **volute** is a two-dimensional spiral whose path exists on one flat planar surface. An example of a volute can be

found in the spiraling arms of a galaxy, or the internal structure of a seashell. There are several different types of volutes, each with their own unique characteristics, based on spacing and the number of arms present. Each is created with a different mathematical formula that describes the spacing and curve that the spiral follows.

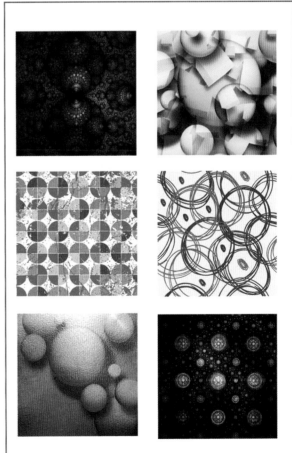

FIGURE 14-11   *Spherical patterns (Andrii Muzyka, Goldenarts, WhiteHaven, sakkmesterke, Silim / Shutterstock.com)*

FIGURE 14-12   *Spirals (anfia focusova, kpatyhka ,gudinny / shutterstock.com)*

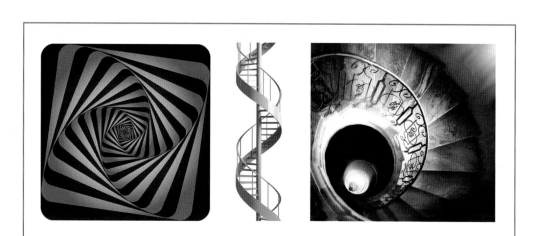

FIGURE 14-13   *Helices (LuckyDesigner, Koksharov Dmitry, arosoft / Shutterstock.com)*

A **helix** is a three-dimensional spiral. Its path lies along the shape of a cone or cylinder. Helices can be right-handed or left-handed, meaning that their rotation either moves away from the viewer, like a screw, or towards the viewer. Helices also have *chirality*, meaning that a right-handed helix cannot be moved, rotated, or flipped to look like a left-handed helix unless it is reflected in a mirror. A right glove and a left glove are different, just as clockwise and counterclockwise are different. Helices also possess *pitch*, the width of one complete turn of the helix as it rotates around its axis.

A *conic helix* traces a path around the dimensions of a cone whose pitch gradually increases from the apex to the base, or decreases from the base to the apex. A corkscrew is an easily recognizable conical helix. In contrast, a *circular helix* has a constant pitch and radius as it traces the surface of a cylinder. This can also be called a *general* or *cylindrical helix*. Helices are important in biology, where they can be seen in the shape of the DNA molecule and in the substructures of certain proteins.

Coiled springs, drill bits, and the framework of spiral staircases are all examples of helices.

Spirals can be used individually and in combinations to create patterns and are important to the theatrical designer because they are significant architectural and aesthetic elements. The pattern of a tile floor may be based entirely on the winding path of a spiral, or spirals may be the basis for period fabric embellishment. Symbolically they are an inclusive motif; no matter where you stand around a spiral, you are part of it. Mazes and other labyrinthine structures have been based on spiral pathways throughout history.

Meanders

A **meander** is a pattern that follows a winding and turning path. It is often curvaceous, serpentine, sinuous, and sensual, like the seemingly random and chaotic pathway of a stream or a labyrinth or the movement of a snake. A meander can be irregular in its repetition, creating completely random patterns or it may be quite regulated, with precisely measured components that repeat at regular intervals to create distinct shapes and decorative motifs. The term meander may also be used to refer to the classic key and fret patterns found in classic Greek art and architecture, and Chinese, Japanese, and Celtic art. Meanders are also a key component of Australian Aboriginal artwork. Because of their significance in various historical and cultural artistic styles, meanders are very important to the scenic and costume designer, as they can help to establish time period, location, and specific design styles.

Waves

There is no uniform definition for what a wave is. In physics, a **wave** is a vibration or disturbance that passes through a medium that is able to conduct the vibration. Mediums can take a variety of forms: liquid, gaseous, solid, and semi-solid. Waves travel through both space and time, transferring energy from one point to another. This movement is called *wave motion*, and often occurs without any permanent shift of the medium's particles. In art and design, we are concerned with the path that is generated by the wave and what form and shape it takes. Wave patterns are found in cultures all over the world and in a variety of different art forms in each. Wave patterns can be seen in fabrics, architecture, interior design elements, hairstyles, fashion, and throughout the natural world. Generally, we tend to think of waves as traveling away from the source of the disturbance that forms them. This assumption of direction is often readily apparent in artistic wave patterns.

FIGURE 14-15   *Waves (Markovka / shutterstock.com)*

FIGURE 14-14   *Meanders (Romaniv Andriiana / Shutterstock.com)*

Branching and Circulation

Branching and **circulation patterns** are so called because they mimic the paths formed by the natural growth of plants or of the system of blood vessels in the body. Connecting a series of forked, three-way joints of lines or linear shapes creates a branching pattern. These patterns usually start with one point that then branches outward in many different directions. Branching patterns may not follow the simple rules of geometry of other types of patterns, but they are easily recognizable and important nonetheless. They are a very efficient type of pattern, able to cover a large surface area by creating the shortest path. Because of this, branching patterns are created and utilized by organisms and structures that need to distribute or collect a large amount of materials or over a long distance. There are many types of natural systems that take advantage of circulatory patterns. Lightning, river systems, and plants are all examples of branching patterns, as are roads and highways. Designers may employ these patterns by recreating the natural forms from which they derive as part of their design, or by using them abstractly.

Polyhedron

In geometry, a **polyhedron** is a three-dimensional object that is made up of **polygons**, which serves as the boundary for an interior volume. A polygon is a flat, enclosed shape that is formed by three or more straight lines. Triangles and squares are examples of polygons. Each side of a polyhedron is referred to as a *face*. Each straight edge of the various polygons meet together to form edges and the corner where three or more edges join together is called a *vertex* (plural *vertices*), which is another term used to describe an *apex*, the point at which angles intersect. Prisms, cubes, and pyramids are all examples of polyhedrons. Generally, polyhedrons are named after the number of faces they possess, such as a tetrahedron (four), cube (six), octahedron (eight), dodecahedron (12), or icosahedron (20). These five polyhedrons are referred to as regular polyhedrons because their faces are identical, regular polygons. There are only five regular polygons possible, and they are often referred to as the *Platonic solids*. There are other mathematical properties that may contribute to the name of a particular polyhedron, such as symmetry, uniformity, or whether the edges, vertices, or faces are all identical.

Stellation and **faceting** may also be applied to a polyhedron to alter its shape. Stellation is the process of lengthening the faces of a polygon or a polyhedron symmetrically to create a new polygon or polyhedron. Polygons and polyhedrons altered in this fashion often take on star-like shapes. For example, a pentagram is a stellation of a pentagon. A hexagram is a stellation of a hexagon. Various mathematical formulas produce different types of stellations. Faceting is created by removing one of more parts of a polygon, which reveals new faces of the polygon or any polyhedron it is a part of. Stellation and faceting are reciprocal or dual processes, meaning that once a polyhedron has been stellated, the resulting dual polyhedron can be faceted. Stellated faces of a polyhedron extend outward from the structure, while faceted faces extend inward.

Polyhedrons have a long history in art and architecture, both as patterns and three-dimensional objects and they continue to be important in design. They have served as the basis for the organization of design elements within an image and as serving as the basis for compositions. The art of intarsia, a mosaic of interlaced wooden pieces that was popular in fifteenth-century Italy, relies heavily on the use of polyhedrons to create patterns and the illusion of three-dimensional forms. In computer-aided design, polyhedrons are crucial in the process of mapping the complex surfaces of three-dimensional forms. In animation and graphics, polyhedrons are used as a kind of mesh where the face of each polyhedron is subdivided over and over in order to create a final, smooth surface.

FIGURE 14-16 *Branching patterns*

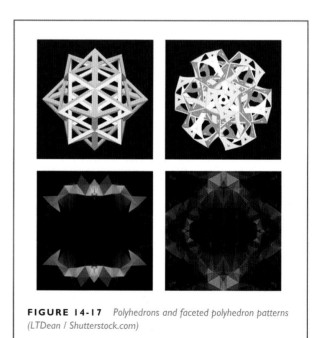

FIGURE 14-17 *Polyhedrons and faceted polyhedron patterns (LTDean / Shutterstock.com)*

Tessellation and Symmetry

A **tessellation** is a repetitive pattern that fills a two-dimensional surface with plane figures, shapes, or motifs

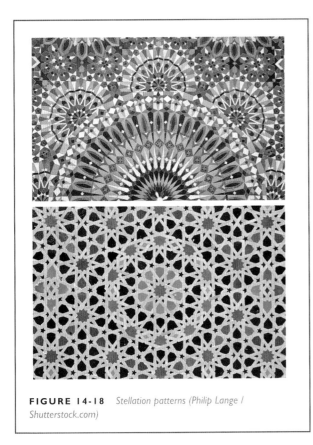

FIGURE 14-18   *Stellation patterns (Philip Lange / Shutterstock.com)*

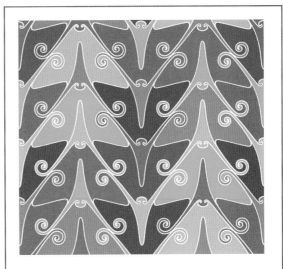

FIGURE 14-19   *Tessellation (antifisa focusova / shutterstock.com)*

that do not overlap and also have no gaps between them. Often, they are created by a regular, repeating geometric pattern. This type of tessellation is called **tiling**. However, a tessellation may also be an irregular assembly of triangles, polygons or other interlocking shapes. A jigsaw puzzle is a simple example of an irregular tessellated surface, but tessellations can be very complex. Tessellations are everywhere in the world around us. Glance at a brick wall, a path made of interlocking paving stones, a checkerboard, a pattern on a quilt, a honeycomb, the skin of a pineapple, fish or snake scales, a soccer ball, or a lace tablecloth and you are witnessing tessellations in action. They are also a common

form of pattern found in wallpaper designs and are an important component in mosaics, tiling, and fabric patterns. The study of tessellation is not limited to art and design. It crosses many disciplines including math, social studies, and languages.

Tessellations can cover surfaces like a square or a page and be affected by the boundaries of those shapes, or the surface can be based on another shape, such as circles, triangles, or polygons. They can cover a flat surface or the surface of a three-dimensional object such as a lampshade, a globe, the surface of a set of stairs, or a box. The shapes used can be geometric or based on natural forms, such as people, plants, and animals. One well-known artist that extensively exploited the process of tessellation to create complex compositions was M.C. Escher.

Tessellation is dominated by repetition, which creates patterns, but it also relies on the various forms of **symmetry** to manipulate shapes. Symmetry generally refers to how the

FIGURE 14-20   *Translation, reflection, and rotation tessellations (Linda Webb, Jennifer Gottschalk, Toni Dal Lago / shutterstock.com)*

individual parts of an image are arranged around an axis and is part of what lends balance to a composition, but in the case of pattern, we are also referring to the quality of similar or exact visual elements that face each other in a design and the manner in which they repeat around or across an axis. There are three basic ways of moving components around an axis: translation, reflection, and rotation.

In **translation**, or *sliding*, elements are moved horizontally along an axis in order to repeat and create a pattern. In **reflection**, or *flipping*, the repeated elements are flipped in orientation as if a mirror had been held up to them either horizontally or vertically. Often, there is also some translation involved in order to build the pattern across a surface. In **rotation**, or *turning*, an image is rotated around a central axis two or more times. The number of times it is repeated is called the *order*. Components can be rotated any number of times, so rotational symmetry can have an order of two, an order of three, or four and so on.

Another important type of symmetry with regards to its effect on pattern is **point symmetry**. In this type of symmetry, every point or part of a design has a matching part and the end result is that a pattern or image looks the same right side up as it does upside down. Playing cards are a primary example of point symmetry, but it can also be found in flooring tiles, fabric patterns, and wallpapers where it is an important component of the overall design.

Fractals

Fractals are a unique form of geometric pattern where the image is repeated at increasingly smaller scales in order to produce unique surfaces and shapes that cannot be represented by classical geometry. Put simply, a fractal is a shape that when divided, consists of parts that are exact replicas of the entire image. This property is called self-similarity. The ability to accurately describe fractals was ultimately achieved in 1975 by Benoît Mandelbrot, a mathematician whose work contributed to the study of chaos theory and was based on the work of several other individuals. Although fractals are mathematical constructs, they are also found abundantly in nature which has led to their inclusion as one of the types of pattern in art. Fractals can be seen in snowflakes and the pattern of frost crystals. There are several different software programs available that allow the user to generate fractals using one of five mathematical processes and fractals have become an art form in and of themselves.

Repetition, rhythm, and pattern are extremely versatile design principles. They allow a designer an infinite amount of

FIGURE 14-21 *Fractals (Fernando Batista / Shutterstock.com)*

flexibility when it comes to manipulating the basic elements of visual composition. They allow you to create multiple variations of your designs in order to fine tune your ideas. How they can influence visual perception, and given their influence on the aesthetic conventions of various cultures and historical time periods, understanding how they influence and affect composition is of key importance to a designer.

THE LANGUAGE OF REPETITION, PATTERN, AND RHYTHM

All-over pattern: Pattern created by repeating design elements with equal visual weight throughout the entire surface of a composition. There is no strong focal point; the visual weight is even and uniform.

Alternating rhythm: Visual rhythm created when an element or motif is repeated and the position, spacing, or content is changed with each repetition.

Branching: A series of forked, three-way joints of lines or linear shapes that mimic the paths formed by the natural growth of plants or of the system of blood vessels in the body.

Circulation: Another name for branching patterns.

Duplication: Creating a replica of an item.

Exact duplication: Objects that are replicated exactly, with no variations.

Faceting: Removing one of more parts of a polygon, which reveals new faces of the polygon or any polyhedron it is a part of.

Flowing rhythm: Smooth, gliding movement from one repeated form to another.

Fractals: A shape that, when divided, consists of parts that are exact replicas of the entire image.

Helix: A three-dimensional spiral whose path lies along the shape of a cone or cylinder.

Inherent rhythm: The visual rhythm set up by pattern in a composition.

Irregular rhythm: Visual rhythms with unevenly spaced intervals and varied repetitions.

Lattice: A pattern created by a fixed arrangement of overlapping or intersecting lines combined with open areas to produce a basket-weave effect.

Linear rhythm: The movement created by the flow of an individual line or groups of lines in relation to one another.

Meander: A pattern that follows a winding and turning path.

Motif: Any recurrent visual element.

Near duplication: When an item is duplicated but details are altered slightly.

Pattern: A decorative design often created through repetition.

Point symmetry: In this type of symmetry, every point or part of a design has a matching part and the end result is that a pattern or image looks the same right side up as it does upside-down.

Polygon: A flat, enclosed shape that is formed by three or more straight lines.

Polyhedron: A three-dimensional object that is made up of polygons, which serves as the boundary for an interior volume.

Progressive rhythm: When the interchange and variation between one element and the next moves in an identifiable sequence, continuing from one motif to the next.

Reflection: When repeated elements are flipped in orientation as if a mirror had been held up to them either horizontally or vertically. Also called flipping.

Regular repetition: When duplicated objects of the same size are arranged in an order with equal spacing.

Regular rhythm: Visual rhythms with evenly spaced intervals and equal repetitions.

Repetition: Repeating one of more of the visual elements in a composition for visual or thematic effect.

Rhythm: A connected series of objects that guide the viewer through the image or a succession of marks and motifs that establish a pattern.

Rotation: Rotating an image around a central axis two or more times. Also called turning or spinning.

Simple repetition: When one visual element is repeated without variation.

Sphere: A three-dimensional, round form whose surface consists of a series of points that are all equidistant from the center.

Spiral: A curve on a plane that winds at a consistently increasing or decreasing distance from and around a fixed, central point.

Stellation: The process of lengthening the faces of a polygon or a polyhedron symmetrically to create a new polygon or polyhedron.

Symmetry: The quality of similar or exact visual elements that face each other in a design and the manner in which they repeat around or across an axis.

Tessellation: A repetitive pattern that fills a two-dimensional surface with plane figures, shapes, or motifs that do not overlap and also have no gaps between them.

Tiling: A tessellation created by a regular, repeating geometric pattern.

Translation: When visual elements are moved horizontally along an axis in order to repeat. Also called sliding.

Visual rhythm: The movement created by the repetition of objects in an image.

Volute: A two-dimensional spiral whose path exists on one flat planar surface.

Wave: In art and design, the path that is generated by a disturbance or vibration through a medium and the form and shape it takes.

CHAPTER 15

SCALE AND PROPORTION

WHAT ARE SCALE AND PROPORTION?

Scale and proportion both have to do with size. **Scale** is size in relation to a standard or "normal" size. For example, a set model is smaller than the actual set onstage. But if it is made accurately, as a faithful replica of the original and **to scale**, then the proportions of the model are the same as the set, only reduced in size by a specific ratio. A set model created in one-quarter scale is only one quarter the size of the actual set, but possesses all of the details of its full-size counterpart. Scale can also be used to refer to the overall size of a work of art. We may use the phrases "small scale," or "large scale" to describe both the size of the work and its scope. Our set model may be grand in scale when examined up close, but next to the actual set, it is small.

    Proportion refers to size relationships between parts of a whole, or between two or more items perceived as a unit. For example, the human body can be divided into approximately eight units that roughly equal the size of the human head. If one feature of the body were doubled in size, it would be out of proportion to the rest of the figure. It would no longer fit in with the established size relationships between the other individual body parts. Throughout history, the "ideal" proportions of the human body in art have changed, particularly the proportions of women, much like changes in fashion. Before the sixteenth century, the ideal female form was more rounded, with full hips and a belly. In the seventeenth century,

the ideal was a small waist, leading to constrictive clothing designed to achieve this goal. Later in that century, a fuller figure was emphasized, influenced by the paintings of Peter Paul Rubens. "Rubenesque" is a term used to describe the rounded proportions of the women depicted in his paintings, which are much fuller than what would be considered ideal today. In the past century, the ideal female figure has undergone dramatic fluctuations. Now the ideal is personified by the slender fashion model, a standard that few women can actually achieve. The standards for the male figure have also changed; setting forth

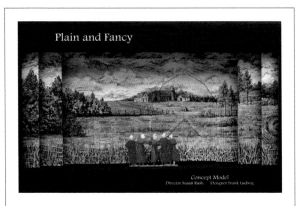

FIGURE 15-1 *Scale set model*—Plain and Fancy *by Stein, Glickman, Horwitt, and Hague, scenic design by Frank Ludwig, Viterbo University, wing and drop set.*

the ideal of an athletic, muscular form highly influenced by the rise in sports activities; again, an ideal that few can realistically achieve. These ideals are reflected in art, advertising, film, and other media.

Aesthetic conventions of different time periods often dictate the proportions of the human form. In ancient Egyptian art, the width of the artist's palm was the unit of measurement applied to the human figure and 20 of these units made up the height of the human body. Artists have also manipulated the proportions of the human body throughout history to achieve their desired affect or to conform to an aesthetic or cultural standard. In the Mannerist period for example, which began in 1520 and lasted until 1580, the human form was often depicted in exaggerated, unrealistic poses and in unnatural settings. The proportions of the body were elongated and distorted in order to reject the realistic focus of Renaissance art in favor of a more emotional approach. This is an example of **exaggerated scale**, which is a very useful tool for creating emphasis onstage. By altering the scale of an object in relation to other objects or the actors onstage, our perception of its importance can be changed. By altering the dimensions of a chair, it can be transformed into a judge's seat or a throne. By changing the scale of a house, it can become a mansion. Modifying the scale of an actor's costume can turn a man into a monster.

THE HUMAN BODY AS REFERENCE

The scale of a work of art is an important element that can be lost in a book or on a website, where everything is reduced to more or less the same size. Size in relation to the viewer is a critical part of the effect an artist considers when they make a work of art. Scale is often perceived in relation to the human figure since we live in our bodies and experience art through them. This is an inherent consideration in architecture. Think about the last time you were inside of a government building or a cathedral. It is likely that the building felt large, tall, and overwhelming. This is because architectural spaces that are designed to impress are often meant to dwarf the size of the people that move through them. This may be done simply to amaze the viewer, but it may also serve to display wealth and to underscore the importance of the activities that take place inside these structures. The sense of scale in relation to the human body can be used to the same effect onstage.

INTERNAL SCALE AND PROPORTION

Another important way to look at artistic use of scale and proportion is to examine the size relationships of elements within a design. In this instance, scale and proportion will always be relevant to the boundaries presented by the format of the composition. A large object in a small format will have a different effect than the same object placed within a large format. When a visual element in an image appears to be out of proportion, it can have a negative or unsettling effect on the viewer. However, this sense of unease may be exactly what the designer is hoping to achieve. Uneven proportion creates visual tension, which can be used to underscore instability and danger in an environment, or support a sense of unpredictability in a character's personality or physical illness in their body.

FIGURE 15-2   *Scale in design, from chair to throne (Adam Fraise, Michael Drager / Shutterstock.com)*

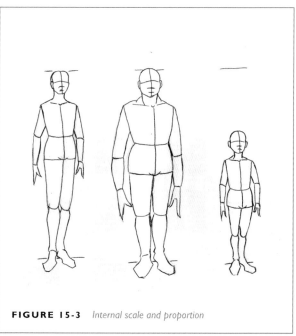

FIGURE 15-3   *Internal scale and proportion*

FIGURE 15-4 *Flyer by Kate Aspengren, scenic design by Darcy White, costume design by Kaoime E. Malloy, lighting design by Zak Viviano, photo by R. Michael Ingraham*

FIGURE 15-5 *Hierarchical scale—Dreamplay by August Stringberg, costumes and heads designed by Kaoime E. Malloy, set design by Jeff Entwistle, lighting design by R. Michael Ingraham, University of Wisconsin Green Bay Theatre*

The three figures in Figure 15.3 all contain the same basic visual elements. However, in each the sizes of the elements have been altered, while the format remains unchanged. This dramatically changes the scale of the composition and alters the proportional relationships within the figures. We could engage in a conversation about which arrangement is more pleasing to the eye, but the choice would ultimately need to be based on the goal of the designer. Unexpected or exaggerated use of scale can create emphasis, support thematic ideas and delight the eye. In Figure 15.4, the scale and proportion of simple cubes have been altered in a set design inspired by the work of Rene Magritte to create an environment that appears to float in the stage space.

THE HIERARCHY OF SCALE

Sometimes the proportion of the human body is varied for symbolic or aesthetic reasons. Often, one or more figures may be made larger for emphasis or to show their importance in the narrative of the work of art, the society that produced it or the culture it borrows from or represents. In a great deal of art, certain individuals are made larger in order to visually underscore their rank, status, political, religious, military, and social significance. Other, less important figures may also be made smaller. In fact, a range of sizes may be applied to an entire group of individuals in order to show their rank and status in descending order. This is called **hierarchical scale**.

IN SEARCH OF IDEAL PROPORTIONS

Throughout history, artists have searched for the perfect proportions in art and architecture. Scale and proportion are intrinsically tied to **ratio**. A ratio is a quantifiable measurement that explains the relationship between two similar things with respect to how many times the first contains the second. For

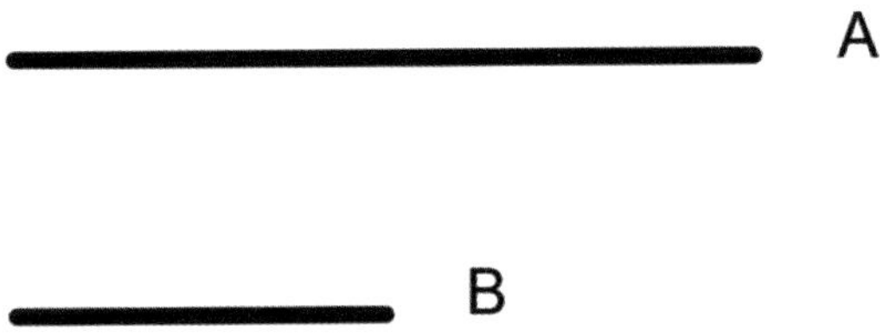

FIGURE 15-6 *Simple 2:1 ratio*

example, in Figure 15.6 there are two lines. Line A is twice as long as line B. Therefore, the ratio between them is 2:1. For every one of A, there are 2 of B.

In ancient Greece, philosophers believed that mathematics was the primary principle that controlled everything in the universe. They said that perfection and divinity could be expressed through ideal form through mathematics. To describe and represent ideal form, they created the **golden mean**, a mathematical ratio that expressed the ideal standards for balance and proportion in both life and in art. It is also referred to as the *golden section*. In art, the golden mean states that smaller parts of an object or an image relate to larger parts as the larger part relates to the whole. This relationship can be represented visually by a line that is divided into two parts: the mean and the extreme ratio. In Figure 15.7, the line AB is divided at point C. When sectioned at this precise point, the ratio of AC to CB is the same as the ratio of AB to AC. Mathematically, this is expressed as AB = CB:AC. The numerical value of this mean and extreme ratio in the golden mean is 1.618. Any new unit or object created based on this division will either be this much smaller or larger than the original object. The Greeks applied this ratio to geometry in order to create the most beautiful and perfectly proportioned rectangle that could possibly be formed from a perfect square. The result is called the **golden rectangle**. The Greeks applied the golden rectangle and the golden mean to art and architecture, even developing an ideal standard for the human form. The concept of creating objects with aesthetically pleasing proportions was part of all aspects of their daily lives.

The golden mean would continue to have an effect on art and architecture for centuries to come. In the thirteenth century, mathematician Leonardo Fibonacci discovered a sequence of related numbers formed by adding two previous numbers together to get a new number: 0, 1, 1, 2, 3, 5, 8, 13, 21, 34, 55, and so on. Called the *Fibonacci sequence* or *numbers*, it demonstrates an ever-increasing ratio of approximately 1.618, the golden mean. This sequence can be created starting with any number and multiplying it by 1.618. Once the second number has been determined, the numbers can simply be added to continue the series. For example, beginning with 10, the sequence would look like this: 10, 16, 26, 42, 68, etc. Scientists now understand that this relationship also occurs throughout nature. The visual representation of this relationship is a spiral. It can be seen in the growth patterns of a pinecone, in the expanding spiral of the nautilus shell, in the spinning of weather patterns and in the spiraling shapes of galaxies. Using this spiral as a tool, it is possible to create larger and larger units based on extensions of the golden rectangle.

Renaissance artists embraced the ideals of mathematical proportions to create visual harmony within scale. The golden rectangle is apparent in some of the most famous Renaissance images, such as da Vinci's *Mona Lisa* and *The Last Supper* and dominates architecture from the period, but modern artists have also embraced the golden rectangle as a visual tool. French painter Georges Seurat was fascinated with the idea of scientific

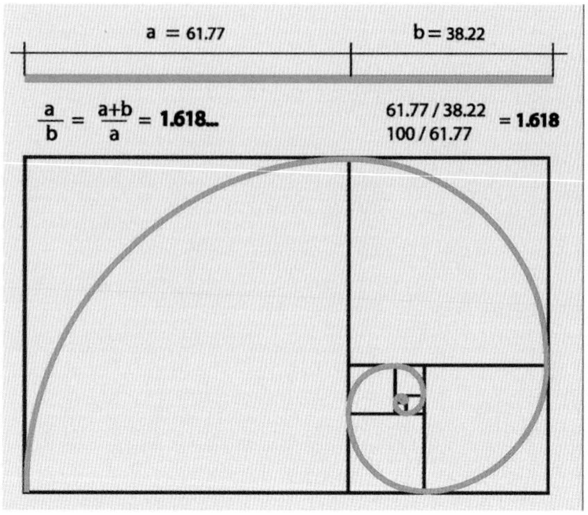

FIGURE 15-8 *Fibonacci spiral (Chuhail / Shutterstock.com)*

measurements and how they affected his pointillism technique. His paintings often employ subtle variations of the golden rectangle to establish ideal proportions and to assist in positioning the visual elements. The golden rectangle is still a useful guiding tool for composition which can be applied to design, particularly when trying to recreate classical proportion and scale onstage.

SCALE IN THEATRICAL DESIGN

Scenery, lights and costumes all interact directly with actors in a theatre production. Since we experience scale and proportion through the reference of the size of our bodies, these principles are incredibly important in stage design. A set that towers over the actors has a very different feel than one that is in proportion to their size. Exaggerated proportions of scenic elements and costumes often contribute to the overall visual style of the play.

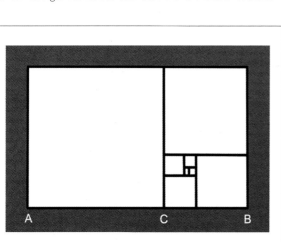

FIGURE 15-7 *The golden rectangle*

FIGURE 15-9 A Funny Thing Happened on the Way to the Forum, *by Sondheim, Shevelove, and Gelbart, set design by Jeff Entwistle, lighting design by R. Michael Ingraham, costume design by Kaoime E. Malloy, photo by R. Michael Ingraham*

In this set design for *A Funny Thing Happened on the Way to the Forum* in Figure 15.9, designer Jeff Entwistle has exaggerated and distorted the proportions and scale of classical Greek architecture in order to support the thematic style of the play. Rather than simply replicate the architectural silhouette of the time period, he has chosen to underscore the farcical nature of the play by allowing the shapes and proportions of the buildings to reflect the humor inherent in the script. Like the action of the play, the set is energetic, exaggerated, and comical with the lighthearted and whimsical feel of a cartoon.

In Figure 15.10, set designer Frank Ludwig has taken an abstract approach to the highly realistic play *The Cherry Orchard* by Anton Chekov. Here, both the exterior and interior elements of the setting have been reduced to the most basic, abstract components. The scale and proportion of the interior is suggested by the size of the two door units without the need for the rest of the house. The vastness of the surrounding countryside is represented by the vertical backdrop which rises out of the floor and extends up into space, carrying our eyes along with it as we are lost in the softly muted landscape painted on its surface. The scale and selection of the pieces serves to underscore the importance of the environment in the dramatic action of the play as well as its effect on the characters who live there.

To further understand the effect of scale and proportion in a theatrical context, consider the role of scenery in a production where all the characters are children. Altering the scale of the scenic elements to reflect the perceived age of the characters rather than the actual age of the actors portraying them can help to create a more convincing visual illusion of children in an adult world. This effect can be further enhanced by the use of costumes that imitate the proportions of the juvenile body versus the adult form. This visual reinforcement also assists the actors to create a more convincing performance by supporting and reinforcing their character choices in a convincing manner.

FIGURE 15-10 The Cherry Orchard *by Anton Chekov, set design by Frank Ludwig, costume design by Mary Wayne-Thomas, lighting design by Jonathan Christman, Wake Forest University, photo by Frank Ludwig*

THE LANGUAGE OF SCALE AND PROPORTION

Exaggerated scale: Manipulating the proportions of an object for visual or thematic effect.

Golden mean: A mathematical ratio developed by the ancient Greeks that expressed the ideal standards for balance and proportion in both life and in art.

Golden rectangle: An ideally proportioned rectangle created from a square through the application of the golden mean.

Hierarchical scale: Making objects or figures in an image larger in order to visually underscore their rank, status, political, religious, military, or social significance.

Proportion: The size relationships between parts of a whole, or between two or more items perceived as a unit.

Ratio: A quantifiable measurement that explains the relationship between two similar things with respect to how many times the first contains the second.

Scale: Size in relation to a standard or "normal" size.

To scale: When an object is created as an exact replica or model of another and the proportions are reduced in size by a specific ratio.

CHAPTER 16

EMPHASIS AND SUBORDINATION

WHAT ARE EMPHASIS AND SUBORDINATION?

Every work of art, whether a stage design or another type of art, is a carefully arranged composition. Visual elements are placed with care and purpose, to achieve the designer's desired effect, to engage the viewer, and to control how they perceive the image. Without the attention of the audience—and the ability to control it—any important details or attempt at communicating ideas and information will be lost. A hierarchy exists between all of the visual components in a composition. Art is rarely uniform, unless we are discussing wallpaper or vinyl flooring. More often than not some elements are more important than others and it is part of the designer's job to clearly identify the most significant parts for the viewer. One way to draw the viewer in and guide them to the elements that are most essential within a piece of artwork is to employ the principles of emphasis and subordination when creating a composition.

Like unity and variety, emphasis and subordination are complementary concepts. We discuss them together, because they occur side by side. Essentially, emphasis and subordination deal with how easy or difficult it is to notice objects in a design. They are tools to direct the perception of the viewer. Creating emphasis is an important skill that a designer must master in order to craft successful and effective designs that will pull the audience in and guide their perception of the performance or artwork. A designer should be able to control which elements are dominant in a design. They should be able to guide the viewer through the image to what should be noticed first and then lead the eye from there.

Emphasis is established when our attention is drawn to one part of the composition more insistently than it is to others. If the emphasis is on a relatively small, clearly defined area, then that area is referred to as a **focal point**. This is where the action of the image begins. When a focal point is used, a designer must be careful to ensure that it harmonizes with all of the visual elements in the composition. Otherwise it will be a distraction that reduces the effect of the entire work. Once the viewer is drawn into the work of art, emphasis can be used to guide their eye around an image, controlling the order in which the various elements of the design are perceived.

Subordination is the process of deliberately making certain areas of the composition visually less interesting. Doing so ensures that the areas of emphasis stand out even more by contrast. The background of a composition is naturally

FIGURE 16-1 *Focal point in a design—Tartuffe by Moliere, scenic design by Frank Ludwig, lighting design by Tony Galaska, Viterbo University*

subordinate to the foreground. Making one part of an image dominant will also result in subordinating the rest of the composition to the area that is emphasized without any additional effort. However, a designer may wish to make the contrast between visual elements more distinct.

Subordination can be employed in varying degrees. Providing less detail in individual parts of the composition will subordinate them to the primary focal point, as will rendering some aspects with less clarity, allowing their edges and details to become blurred and hazy while the primary visual components remain in sharp focus. Using darker values in the less important areas also serves to subordinate them to the main focal point. In fact, many of the ways to create emphasis can also produce subordination.

CREATING EMPHASIS

There are many ways to craft emphasis, all of which focus on ensuring that the important areas of the composition stand out from the rest of the elements around them by making them more visually compelling or by giving them more visual weight. The primary ways to create a focal point in a design include placement, contrast, and isolation.

Placement

In every design, the designer will give careful consideration to the location of the subject and other critical details within the format. Judicious **placement** of key elements is a simple way to create emphasis. If all the visual elements point towards one location in a composition, they will draw our eye in that direction and emphasize that area. This can be seen in Figure 16.3.

FIGURE 16-2 *Subordination—The Balkan Women by Jules Tasca, set design by Jeff Entwistle, lighting design by R. Michael Ingraham, costume design by Kaoime E. Malloy, photo by R. Michael Ingraham*

A **radial design** is a useful tool for understanding this technique. In a radial design the central, emphasized element may be very similar to the other visual components of the composition. Here, the emphasis occurs solely from the placement of the central shape rather than from any visual distinctions between the various parts of the composition. Each of the radial elements leads towards the central shape and the implied movement draws our eyes along with it. This also happens when perspective lines in an image lead to a vanishing point. By placing important compositional elements at their junction, the viewer's eyes will be lead directly towards them. The phenomenon is referred to as **convergence**.

Another way to use placement as a means to create emphasis is by employing the principles of informal balance. Objects that are closer to the center of the format will naturally have more visual weight. Central placement naturally creates emphasis. But remember that objects also gain more visual weight the closer they move to the edge of the format. So, it is not always necessary, or even the most interesting choice visually or conceptually to place the main element in the center of a composition.

Contrast

In a simple composition, it is easy to locate the visual emphasis. In a portrait, for example, the focal point is clear. When a single actor is lit in one light in the middle of the stage, the audience knows where to look. But as a design becomes more complicated, it becomes harder for a viewer to decide where to place their attention. In this case, a strong focal point is not only helpful, but also necessary. Emphasis automatically occurs when an element of a composition differs from the others around it. This is called **contrast**. Anything that disrupts the overall mood or the visual appearance of a design will attract the eye simply

FIGURE 16-3 *Convergence— The Marriage of Figaro by Mozart, Act III, preliminary sketch, set design by Alison Ford, Krannert Center at the University of Illinois*

because it is different. Use of contrast will simultaneously create both emphasis and subordination. The options for creating emphasis through contrasting visual elements are almost limitless. Some examples of contrast include:

- In a complicated pattern composed entirely of regular geometric shapes, an irregular shape will take focus.

- In a grayscale composition, a colored object will create emphasis.

- In an image dominated by dark values, a bright shape will become a focal point.

- A change in the dominant size of objects in a composition will provide contrast and create emphasis. Bigger elements will always be noticed first, but this might not always be the goal of a composition. Sometimes, finding a smaller, hidden element can be a rewarding surprise that provides essential meaning and understanding.

- In a design that is composed primarily of shapes or other simple elements, the placement of text or another graphic component will take focus.

- In a composition organized by a particular color scheme, anything that deviates from that scheme will attract the eye and create emphasis.

In Figure 16.4, elements of geometric pattern and splashes of red provide distinct contrast from the overall color scheme in this production of *The Memorandum* by Vaclav Havel. The bright color and pattern draw the viewer's eye to create focus and emphasis and bring attention to the actors' faces.

Isolation

Emphasis by **isolation** is a variation of emphasis by contrast. When one element in a design is separated from the rest of the visual elements, we cannot help but notice it, especially when the other elements are grouped closely together. Even if the isolated element is identical to the other components in the composition, setting it off by itself will create a focal point and capture the viewer's attention. Isolation is often enhanced through the judicious use of contrast, especially in value or color. Isolation can also be used to create movement, drawing the viewer's attention from one object to the next. Carefully isolated objects, judiciously placed throughout a design, can serve to unite a composition and help to communicate important thematic ideas or tell a story.

Occasionally, in order to meet specific design challenges or to support conceptual ideas a designer will use a variation of the principle of isolation by choosing to use a very specific **single element** within a design. Sometimes this element is not only dominant, but visually overwhelming as well. This is common in advertising and graphic arts, where the goal of a composition is often to sell a product or project a certain image about a company or individual. But it is also used in theatrical design, where a symbol or visual metaphor may serve to provide thematic information or commentary on the action of the play through its presence.

Henry Ossawa Tanner's painting *Spinning by Firelight: The Boyhood of George Washington Gray*, is an excellent example of the principles of emphasis and subordination in action. Here, size and placement are used to emphasize the figures of the woman, her spinning wheel, and the boy by the fire. They are set in the foreground, almost on the same plane, while the man is relegated to the background of the image. The woman and her spinning wheel are in the center of the picture plane and are posed so that

FIGURE 16-4 The Memorandum *by Vaclav Havel, costume design by Kaoime E. Malloy, set design by Jeffrey P. Entwistle, lighting design by R. Michael Ingraham, University of Wisconsin Green Bay, image credit R. Michael Ingraham*

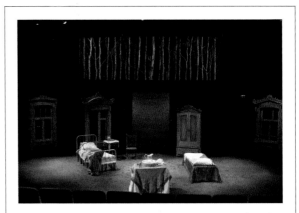

FIGURE 16-5 *Isolation—* Three Sisters *by Anton Chekov, scenic design by Frank Ludwig, lighting design by Chad Kolbe, Viterbo University*

FIGURE 16-6   *Single element in design— Dreamplay by August Strindberg, scenic design by Jeff Entwistle, lighting design by R. Michael Ingraham, costume design by Kaoime E. Malloy, University of Wisconsin Green Bay*

FIGURE 16-7   Spinning By Firelight: The Boyhood of George Washington, *Henry Ossawa Tanner, 1894 (image © Yale University Art Gallery)*

their visual weights combine to create one visual mass. The strong contrast of her dark clothing and the dark wood of the wheel against a pale background create more emphasis. The light coming from the fireplace surrounds both the boy and the woman, and is reflected off their faces, highlighting their expressions. The man looks towards the woman, creating a psychic line between them and focusing our attention on her. Even the diagonal lines on the floor lead to her. Together, the three figures create a triangular compositional mass that anchors the painting, grounding them within the format of the picture plane. Contrast supports the compositional emphasis: the wheel is dark; the faces of the woman and the boy are light and complete; the details of the wall, the male figure and background elements are blurred and soft. These parts of the painting have been subordinated so that our eyes will focus on the central figures and their actions.

The same principles can be seen Figure 16.8, a production shot of *Lysistrata*. In this scene, the women are taking the oath to refrain from sex with their husbands in order to end the war that is raging throughout Greece. Lysistrata stands on a raised dais in the center of the stage, holding aloft the jug filled with ceremonial wine. The other women move in a circle in front of her, hands joined as the ceremony is performed. Light illuminates their faces, but Lysistrata herself is the only one fully lit. She is the focal point, both by placement and contrast. The soft light that casts their bodies and the rest of the surrounding set details into blurred shadow subordinates the other women. As a group, however, they have more emphasis than the rest of the stage, which takes a backseat to the action at hand. Placement, isolation,

and contrast all contribute to the dominance of the group of women in the scene.

Emphasis and subordination are key principles for theatrical designers. Part of our role in creating the visual world of the play onstage is the careful manipulation of what is seen and what is not. By virtue of what we choose to put on the stage—and what we elect not to, either through the process of elimination or through editing our designs—we are creating a kind of emphasis and subordination through our process alone. Lighting designers make extensive use of these two principles through selective illumination, determining what to reveal through light and what not to reveal. Costume designers may choose to give main characters more detailed costumes to make them stand out and be identifiable, and give the costumes for chorus characters less detail in order to make them blend together as a group rather than stand out as individuals. A set designer might decide to decorate the office of an influential and successful businessman with brighter colors than that of his less successful rival in order to emphasize the differences between them. A sound designer may build a cue, purposefully manipulating the various components to make some louder, richer, or brighter in tone, while deliberately making others less distinct, relegating them to the background. A projection designer may choose to use images to frame one section of the stage space, thereby emphasizing both the area itself and any action that takes place there. Whichever design elements they are applied to, emphasis and subordination can be used in many ways to visually support the thematic content of the play.

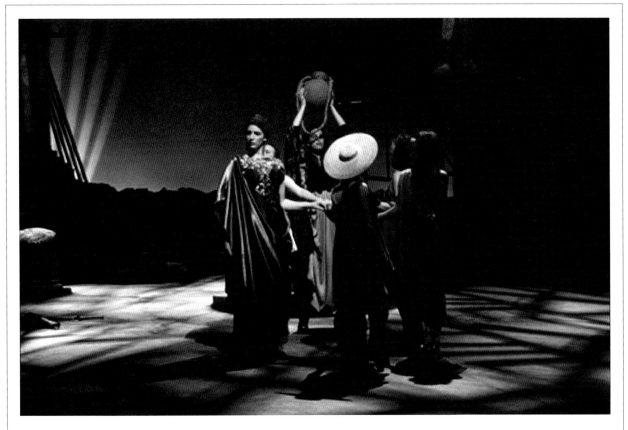

FIGURE 16-8 Lysistrata *by Plautus, adaptation by Wendy Knox, lighting design by Pip Gordon, costume design by Kaoime E. Malloy, set design by Robert Sunderman*

THE LANGUAGE OF EMPHASIS AND SUBORDINATION

Contrast: Visual differences within a design.

Convergence: The merging of visual elements, such as the meeting of perspective lines at a vanishing point.

Emphasis: Making one part of an image stand out from its surroundings, which attracts the attention of the viewer.

Focal point: A relatively small, clearly defined area of emphasis.

Isolation: Setting an object off by itself.

Placement: Where individual visual components are located within an image.

Radial design: A design with a central focus, where all other elements lead in or out from the center.

Single element: Using a distinct visual element as a focal point, usually set in isolation from the rest of a composition for a specific effect.

Subordination: Deliberately making parts of a composition less interesting visually in order to focus attention on the emphasized areas of the image.

PART FOUR

CORE PRINCIPLES FOR THE THEATRICAL DESIGNER

CHAPTER 17

COLLABORATION

WHAT IS COLLABORATION?

Theatre is, by its very nature, an inherently collaborative art form. In theatre, a group of artists with expertise in particular areas work together to create an engaging, entertaining, complete, and unified artistic realization of a playscript. Very rarely is an entire production created by one person alone. More often than not, an entire team of artists is required to bring a play to life. A collaborative design team is usually composed of: a producer or producers; an artistic director; a director; costume, scenic, lighting, and sound designers. Depending on the requirements of the show, there may also be a fight choreographer, musical director and choreographer. Each of these individuals will contribute to the final look, feel, and sound of the resulting production.

On the surface, a design team appears to be an assembly of related artists who are each experts in an individual area of theatrical art, gathered together to work on a project. They meet to talk about the play and the production as a whole, but go off by themselves to do their actual work. In reality, a design team does fit that simple description, but it is also much more. Not only do they work together *and* separately, they also inspire one another throughout the design and production process.

Essentially, theatre is an interpretive art form. Each member of the design team seeks to contribute to a collective interpretive vision of the playwright's ideas, one that allows its meaning to be communicated to an audience. Usually, these ideas take the form of a script, but not always. Operas and musical theatre plays rely on a musical score in addition to written dialogue, and shows can also be created through other collaborative means, such as improvisation, group writing, or

even without a written script at all. In the fine arts, the word "interpretation" sometimes carries negative connotations, where the personal expression of each individual artist carries a great deal of meaning and weight. There can be an implication inherent in the concept of interpretation that the resulting work that comes from it, work that starts from the source material of another artist, is not original or does not possess an individual voice. Nothing could be farther from the truth. In theatre, interpretation is the vehicle that facilitates meaning and understanding for the audience. The playwright is part of the collaborative process, whether they are physically present or not. The play itself is their contribution. Regardless of the fact that theatrical designers begin their artistic endeavor from a script, the end result is always unique, individual, and original. No two productions will ever be the same, even when a designer works on one play multiple times throughout their career.

As you grow as an artist and a designer, your experiences inform your work. This is true for all artists, regardless of the medium they work with. Your understanding of the play evolves and changes as you do. You learn new things and apply them to how you work. The members of the design team change, bringing new ideas and influences to the process. All of these factors affect the final interpretation of a script in each production, and the design choices will reflect those influences. A scene designer chooses each specific element of the set with care and deliberation to support a specific message. A costume designer makes choices that will support characters as individuals, down to the smallest detail, such as buttons. Lighting designers seek to make a statement with each cue and change in atmosphere. Sound designers pick effects and select music that underscores separate moments and facilitates communication. These are all individual and unique choices that reflect the individual voice of the designer and the collective interpretation of the collaborative team.

Collaboration is a word that can instill a great deal of excitement, or elicit an equal amount of apprehension. Excitement comes from the idea of sitting down with other likeminded, talented individuals who understand your art form, making discoveries about the play together, feeding off of each other's ideas. In a good collaboration, everyone on the design team works together to facilitate a creative, exciting, and engaging series of solutions for the challenges in the script. Meaning is discovered and presented to the audience in an engaging theatrical event. Apprehension arises because theatre as an art form has its own quirks and challenges that can be stressful enough on their own, and working with a group of people can exacerbate that stress. Unfortunately, teamwork doesn't always go smoothly. It can be multifaceted and unpredictable. Adding the dynamics of personality and behavior within a group of people can often make it more difficult. It takes practice and time to develop good collaboration skills and they are constantly evolving and changeable. Each experience is different, especially when members of the design team change from project to project.

Everyone has their own communication style. Designers are generally visual and sensory thinkers and are often best able to communicate their ideas through imagery in the form of research, sketches, finished drawings, rendering, and models or sound clips. This is not to say that designers are unable to articulate their ideas, only that they are trained to work with visual and sensory elements as integral components of their work, so they naturally respond and are drawn to images, sounds, and music. The language and vocabulary they use as they develop their conceptual approach and their final designs are based on aesthetic elements and principles. More often than not, designers are able to communicate with each other without too much difficulty. There are many directors who respond very well to this kind of input as they navigate their own process and who are able to connect to the visual world of the play through the materials that the designers bring to the meetings without difficulty. They are able to think in an abstract or speculative way, and can therefore visualize the ideas each designer is suggesting and discussing with them. They can make the leap between inspirational research and final product with ease and clarity. Other directors are very intellectual in their approach, offering detailed information regarding pertinent theories, philosophies, and analyses of the play through which they make their connections to the script. Since their methods

are different, they might not be as able to visualize the ideas of the designers from research alone. These directors might need detailed sketches, groundplans, renderings, projection samples, preliminary slideshows, and detailed sound files in order to understand the ideas the designers are bringing forth. Still others combine visual and intellectual processes into their way of working. No one way is necessarily better than the other, but designers should be able to adjust their process for the communication styles of the other members of the design team, or the collaboration will not succeed.

IMPORTANT CONCEPTS—WHAT MAKES FOR A SUCCESSFUL COLLABORATION?

Learn How to Listen

In order to take in all the director and your colleagues have to contribute in a design meeting you must do more than hear what they have to say; you must *listen*. It is a very important part of the collaborative process. Listening builds rapport with your colleagues, shows support and respect for their contribution to the process, and helps to facilitate the exchange of ideas and to find the meaning in the dialogue between collaborators. Listening is more than simply hearing what another person has to say. It is one part receiving information, one part comprehension, and another part evaluation.

Listening is not a passive activity. It requires you to be actively engaged in order to collect information. You must choose to pay attention and to direct your focus on the activity at hand. The trouble is that our attention is selective. Various stimuli compete for it all the time and what is most interesting to us usually gains our focus. Therefore, listening requires effort and desire to sustain it. You have to try and avoid distractions that might split your focus. Shuffling papers, doodling, and even the room temperature can interrupt your attention. Control what you can and try to keep your mind from wandering. It can help to maintain eye contact with whoever is speaking, although in a situation where you are also taking notes—like a design meeting—this can be more challenging. Concentrate on the main ideas in what is being said so you can write them down more easily and be sure to ask questions if you do not understand something.

In order to listen effectively, it helps to focus on the content of what is being said rather than how it is being said. This helps your comprehension of the material. Sometimes delivery and speaking style can affect how we absorb information and respond to it. Remember that the message is more important than the vocal nuances of the dialogue. Try to be objective and open-minded when you listen in a design meeting. If you are overly attached emotionally to what is being said, you may only hear what you want to hear rather than what is actually being said. You can miss important details that could potentially affect your design choices. You also cannot listen effectively if you are formulating your own response the entire time a colleague is talking, chomping at the bit to speak. No one likes to be interrupted and when you do, it often appears that you aren't listening. You can give your colleagues feedback to let them know you are really listening in other ways. Nodding, laughing, and smiling are all ways to let people know they have your full attention.

Think about what your colleagues offer to the collaboration. Digest it. Comprehension and understanding come from considering what was said, determining what it means and how it applies to your current project, challenge, or situation. Evaluation of the material gives you the opportunity to weigh what has been presented and figure out how the discussion will influence your next step in your design process and the choices you will eventually make.

Bring Your Own Ideas to the Table

There are going to be times when you walk into a design meeting for the first time, sit down, and listen as the director proceeds to give you a ton of information about the script, their understanding of it, the social and political events that surround and support it, what they want to emphasize in the production, and the direction they want to take the play visually. When this happens, it is wonderful. When a director has done this kind of research before the first design meeting, not only is a wealth of information shared among the members of the production team, it shows the director's investment in the play and the production, their enthusiasm for the project, and that in turn is transmitted to the designers working with them. Excitement is infectious; it spreads to everyone around it and revs up their creative juices, moving them forward and often providing direction. It helps to drive your own work and sets you on the path to discovery. Who wouldn't want that? But what happens when you walk into that design meeting, and rather than pouring out information, the director asks, "So, what do *you* think is important about this play? Why do you want to work on it?" What do you do then?

Collaboration is a process that requires all participants to contribute. Multiple minds working on the same problem in order to come up with evocative and insightful solutions is one of the exciting aspects of collaboration. Ideally, it is not a process where one person determines the final outcome for everyone else. Even though the director is the captain of the ship, as it were, it requires an entire team to sail it.

Collaboration is a fluid and dynamic activity that ebbs and flows with the contributions of the participants. In order to be effectively engaged in this process, you have to have your own ideas. You have to think your own thoughts about the play, and have your own opinions. And, above all, you have to bring them to the table, meaning that you have to share them.

There are always going to be situations where the director walks in and has a very strong vision of where they want to take the production, both in terms of the acting and the design components. In those instances, our job as designers is to work with that vision to produce the most effective and engaging production as possible. But, more often than not, the director and the other collaborators want to know what each of their colleagues thinks about the play they are working on in order to arrive at a solution together.

So come to the first design meeting and every one after it prepared not only to listen, but to talk. Read the play and write down your thoughts about it. Identify key themes and ideas in the script. Highlight important passages that support them. Discover the structure. Do research, uncover information. Note any questions you have about the play—chances are that your colleagues have questions too. The dialogue between all the members of the design team is important. It is the process by which the production comes to life. The creative dynamic that occurs when ideas are exchanged is what stimulates and encourages new approaches, solutions and ideas to develop. In the collaborative process, everyone's voice is valuable.

Do Your Homework

In order to actively participate in the collaborative process, you have to do your homework. You should come to each design meeting ready to be part of the dialogue between the members of the production team. Each successive meeting builds on what was discovered, presented, and discussed in the previous one. When you leave a design meeting, you do so with new ideas, observations, and information to explore, all generated by the discussion between you and your colleagues. These things will serve to guide you in your further exploration of the play, as well as the needs of your specific design area. It will lead you on a hunt for information to inspire you.

Between design meetings, a designer must reread the play, taking into account the information that has been passed on from the director. What the director has to say in the initial design meetings can often change your original interpretation and understanding of the play. It can reveal hidden themes, important plot points, provide insight into character and setting, and guide your research. The comments made by your collaborators will do the same. Do research to learn about the play, the playwright, the socio-political environment that surrounds the world of the play and the playwright's life as well as research that informs your particular design area. Seek to develop an understanding of the play as a whole and not just through your individual area. Gather information, do analysis, conduct investigations, and find images that speak to you. If you are expected to have drawings at the next meeting, then get them done. Then bring them to the next meeting to share with your colleagues.

Be Flexible and Adaptable

Everyone has a different collaborative style and this requires you as a designer to be both flexible in your process and adaptable to new situations and ways of doing things. Every director works through their process differently. So does each individual designer. Communication styles can differ greatly from person to person and there will always be challenges to successful communication. But beyond that, collaboration is a fluid and dynamic process that evolves over time. The place where the design team starts in their exploration of the script may not be the place they finally end up. As information is collected and shared, as ideas are generated and discoveries are made, designers may find that they need to adapt to the new thoughts and decisions that are brought up throughout the process.

In Zen Buddhism, there is a famous story of the Japanese Zen master Nan-in who was visited by a university professor who came to Nan-in to inquire about Zen. The master served tea to his guest, filling the man's cup, and kept on pouring. The professor looked on, watching the tea overflow, until he could no longer keep quiet. "The cup is full," he said. "No more will go in." Nan-in replied, "Like this cup, you are full of your own opinions and speculations. How can I show you Zen unless you first empty your cup?" This story is often used in the martial arts to illustrate the idea that the student must be open and

receptive in order to learn what the teacher has to teach. The same thing applies to collaboration. You have to open yourself up and be willing to listen to and consider the ideas and information that will come up in design meetings.

In part, this means being flexible enough to give new perspectives and ideas a chance to affect and influence you as you work on your designs. You may not eventually choose to use them, but in true collaboration, all things should be considered, even if they are quickly discarded for one reason or another. It also means not being so attached to your ideas that that you become unwilling to consider any other options. Sometimes, they are not quite right, or do not work with the approach to the play, or the director does not like them. In that case, a designer may have to do some judicious editing or even go all the way back to the drawing board and start over again in order to look for the best solution or the one that the director wants. Often collaborative design is about providing multiple options to the challenges the play presents. Being adaptable enough to work with this process can lead to exciting and dramatic results.

Successful and exciting collaboration relies on all of these factors as much as it does on the creative talent of the individuals involved. A good cooperative team challenges each member to do their best, and can do more together than they can as individuals.

THE LANGUAGE OF COLLABORATION

Collaborate: to work jointly with others or together especially in an intellectual or artistic endeavor.

Collaboration: The act of working with another or others on a joint project. Also, something created by working jointly with another or other.

CHAPTER 18

ANALYSIS

WHAT IS ANALYSIS?

When a designer sits down to start working on a play, what they are really beginning is an investigation. The script is a new and unknown territory and you are on a scavenger hunt, looking for clues that will help you to understand the play, hoping to make discoveries that will eventually influence and inform your design. These clues range from the obvious to the subtle and each offers another part of the puzzle that is the script. A designer has to read the play carefully, not only the actual lines of dialogue but also in between them, paying attention to the descriptions of the settings, the action, the characters, and any other information presented by the playwright in order to find all the information they need to do their work. These clues and the answers to the questions that you may have about the play can be found through the process of **script analysis**. It can be done in a very formal way, examining a play for its literary components and structure, or in a relaxed, almost conversational manner. For designers, analysis can essentially be described as a way of asking questions and looking for answers that expand your understanding of a script and the playwright's intent. It also serves as a way to develop a connection to the play, which is essential in order to create an effective and compelling design. The way to start is by reading the script.

READING THE PLAY

In the course of the design process, you will need to read the play several times in order to understand the story and the characters, the theme, the playwright's intention, to forge a connection with the script and, ultimately, to complete your

work. How many times? There is no definitive answer to that question. One designer may only need to read a play once or twice to glean all the information they need to do their work effectively. Another may need multiple readings to accomplish the same thing. There really is no prescribed number. What is important is to find a way of reading plays that works well *for you*. One person's process may be quite different from your own and your method may vary from one production to the next. Some scripts are easy to read and your ideas about the design may come quickly. Others are more challenging and the design problems they present might require more thought before you can determine the best solution.

The first reading of the play can be relaxed and easy if you like. Rather than actively seeking out information, during this initial encounter with the script you may choose to simply strive to learn the story and the plot, becoming familiar with both. A first reading can give you a picture of the play as a whole and how the characters and plot work together to tell a story. This allows you to become acquainted with the play without expectations and preconceptions or imposing your personal judgment, taste, or values on the script. During this reading, you will be able to identify characteristics of the script such as genre, the number of acts and scenes, and get a feel for the basic flow of the story. Ideally, you may find it helpful to read the play without taking notes, an activity that can get in the way of experiencing the script as a piece of dramatic literature. Some people find that reading a script in this manner gives them a better feel for the play. Others want to get down to the specifics of their work as designers right away. Taking notes about your initial impressions during and after the first reading is often very useful, and can help to focus your attention in any subsequent readings. Reading the play through in one sitting can also be a good idea. It gives you the chance to experience the uninterrupted flow and rhythm of the play. This is an important step in visualizing the play onstage.

A second reading can give you the opportunity to get to know the script in more detail and on a more intimate level. With this reading you should begin your investigation of the play in earnest, if you have not done so already. During this reading, pay attention to the stylistic aspects of the play, such as the use of language and dramatic structure. How is language used? In addition to their presentation, how are words and ideas *spoken*? Is there a rhythm present in the words or phrasing? Some plays are written in an easy and recognizable vernacular. This type of dialogue reads like natural, everyday speech. Others are written in a more formal stylistic manner, such as iambic pentameter or rhyming couplets and read more like poetry or song lyrics. Both forms of dialogue affect interpretation. Identify key phrases in each scene and record which character speaks them. In this reading, your understanding of thematic content may deepen, and you should note the repetition of key elements or catchphrases and observe how they progress throughout the play and what influence they bring to bear on the action and characters. Observe the nuances of interaction between the characters and how those relationships enrich your understanding of the play itself.

As you go through the script, take notes of important information, ask questions and underline or highlight key phrases in the dialogue that speak to you or that underscore important plot or thematic points. Note the transitions between scenes and the passage of time. Identify the various locations and the time period in which the action takes place. Pinpoint the protagonist and the antagonist. Identify what the primary conflict of the plot is. Mark entrances and exits. Once you have accomplished this, it is time to look for answers to more detailed questions. Later, you may also decide to read the play again after your first meeting with the director and the rest of the design team, so you can use the input of your director and colleagues to further guide your inquiry and analysis.

GENERAL QUESTIONS TO ASK OF THE PLAY

While each designer will have to discover the answers to very specific questions for their specific design areas, all of them will need to identify some key overall characteristics of the play and can benefit from discovering the answers to the following basic questions.

- *What is the play about?* What is the story? What element of the human condition does the play explore?

- *What is the genre?* Identifying the genre of the script can offer clues to interpretation. Genre can have a significant impact on the design. Visual aspects of the production should reflect and support the play's literary type. Different genres set the tone for and influence the visual look of the play and they can also set up certain expectations and characteristics regarding presentation that need to be addressed by the designers. Do you as a designer have any expectations regarding the genre of the play? Does it bring any particular image or aesthetic style to mind? Are there any colors, textures, or styles that are suggested by the genre?

- *What is the overall style of the play?* Like genre, the style in which the play was written will naturally influence the visual style. Is the action and the world of the play realistic, representing a real world with real characters and action that seems to take place in real time such as that of Ibsen's *A Doll's House*? Or is the script more stylized, with heightened action set in a world that is distorted or simplified, with characters that represent archetypes or stereotypes, as in Luigi Pirandello's *Six Characters in Search of an Author*? Perhaps the play is completely absurd in its presentation, with characters that live in a fantasy world and speak apparent nonsense, as can be found in *The Bald Soprano* by Eugène Ionesco. Structure and genre are both key characteristics to identify in the designer's search for an evocative and engaging visual interpretation of the play. They will affect the way you respond to the script and will have a big impact on how the audience reacts as well. A realistic play may require a realistic approach, while an avant-garde style could offer more options for interpretation, requiring more flexibility from the designers. Would it be possible to interpret the style differently or alter it in any way? If so, how would that change affect the play? Would it still support the intent of the playwright? Ask yourself if the style of the script suggests a particular visual approach—colors, shapes, visual textures—and let that inspire you as you begin your work.

- *What type of dramatic structure does the play possess?* Does the structure suggest or dictate any particular visual approach? Does the structure offer any clues to interpretation? How does it support the themes and ideas presented by the script? Does the nature of the structure itself offer any clues that might inform your visual choices? Is the story presented in a realistic manner, with linear scenes that progress from one to the next in a logical fashion? Or is the play episodic in style, jumping from one scene to the next with gaps in time or changes in location that are less linear and open to a looser interpretive style?

Or is the structure cyclical, with scenes that intersperse present time with flashbacks from the past that reveal more about the plot, but might also make the play's action more challenging for the audience to follow? Careful consideration of the structure can provide inspiration that informs your design.

- *In what time period does the play take place?* Is it possible to set the play in a different time period without adversely affecting the action and thematic content? If so, is it possible to identify elements within the play that would support the change in time or location? Or are the action, story, and message of the play dependent on the setting as written or on the context surrounding when it was written? Some plays may work just as effectively in a timeless or "no period" world where the suggestion of another time is communicated through costumes or settings borrowed from multiple historical aesthetics and eras. Others might flourish in an abstract world, an imaginary time and place, where each design element is carefully chosen for its potential to illustrate, support, or communicate specific ideas about the play. In these instances, careful collaboration with the director and other designers will be required to present a unified production.

- *How does the action of the play move through time?* Does everything take place in real time, over the span of the performance? Or does the action take place over the course of a day, a series of days, or even years? How does the passage of time affect the design requirements?

- *Where is the action of the play located?* Is the setting urban or rural? What kind of climate is dominant in this location? What is the culture of the location? Does the action move from one location to another? If so, do these locations need to be specific and well-defined? Or can they be suggested?

- *What is the season or seasons?* How does the season affect the action or the characters? How does it reflect the meaning and message of the play? Does it contribute to the overall mood? Do the seasons change throughout the play or remain constant? Is it necessary that the seasons be reflected in your design choices, colors, textures, or other visual components?

- *What is the overall mood of the play?* Is the mood constant throughout the play, or does it change as the action progresses, or due to the behaviors of the characters? Does the mood suggest any particular colors, textures, or visual style? Does it suggest a type of setting or an overall descriptive sense of the space, such as isolation, confinement, openness, fluidity, spatial tensions, representational, or nonrepresentational?

- *How are the characters utilized by the playwright?* Which character is the protagonist? The antagonist? What are the relationships between characters? This not only refers to familial relationships, but also how characters relate to each other. Some of these will provide support to each other character, while others will generate conflict. How do these relationships evolve over the course of the play and how do they influence the action?

- *What is the overall theme or message of the play?* What is the playwright trying to communicate to the audience? How does the theme support the story and vice versa? How are the themes and messages supported and revealed throughout the action? Will they need to be emphasized visually?

- *What is the essential conflict of the play?* Stories thrive on tension, on problems that arise and that need to be resolved. Conflict drives the story forward. Plays are no different. Where is conflict found in the script? Does it derive from the circumstances of the situation the characters find themselves in? Is there tension between characters that generates conflict throughout the play? What is the inciting incident? When did the conflict start? Did it happen before the play began, or does it manifest itself during the action of the play? How does character tension support or undermine the essential tension of the script?

- *Are there any patterns in the play?* These could be recurring images, patterns of behavior, or themes that surface throughout the play. If they are repeated, they are important and should be considered when developing a design approach.

- *What images come to mind as you read the play?* Is there one overall prevailing image that surfaces or several? Are they suggested by the action or are they tied to specific characters? Do they change from scene to scene? How do they relate to the thematic content of the play? Do they suggest or remind you of anything in particular or of a certain aesthetic style or artist?

- *Are you able to visualize any of the images suggested by the play?* Are you able to locate visual research that is evocative of these images or is similar in mood or other qualities? Do the images in the play need to be incorporated into your designs in some way?

- *How is humor used in the script?* Does the artist use humor to assist the communication of the plot? To aid character development? Is humor employed to relieve the seriousness and tension of the plot? Or is humor the main focus of the action?

- *What is the overall effect?* This question concerns how the audience feels, should feel, or how we want them to feel when they leave the performance. What will they be thinking about after experiencing the performance? What will their mood be? What state of mind will they be in once they have seen the play? Will their impression of the play be the same as it was at the beginning of the performance? *Should* it be? In essence, this question is to make you think about what the audience should take away with them after the show.

How many times will you need to read the play to answer these questions? That will of course vary with each individual, but you should be prepared to read the script as many times as necessary in order to find the information required to do your work effectively. Once you have discovered the answers to these questions you can begin to visualize each scene of the play or even generate a chart that illustrates the action of the play for your reference and for your individual design area as you move through the design process.

THE LANGUAGE OF ANALYSIS

Script analysis: a way of asking questions and looking for answers that expand your understanding of a script and the playwright's intent.

CHAPTER 19

CONCEPTUALIZATION

WHAT IS CONCEPTUALIZATION?

Conceptualization is a buzzword in theatrical design, the fine arts, graphic design, and applied design. It is a term that gets thrown about a great deal in design education as well. "Students need to learn to conceptualize" is an often-heard phrase in the classroom, but conceptualization is a word that is also hard to define. Look it up in a dictionary and you are likely to get caught on a never-ending circular path between "to form into a concept," or "the act of conceptualizing," "to interpret in a conceptual way," and various other forms of the word—conceptualize, conceptual, conceptualizing—without ever getting a real definition of the word. The key part of the word is *concept*. As designers, we seek to come up with a **design concept**, an idea or theme that will drive our approach to the play as well as the decisions about the visual aspects of our respective areas. The process of developing that idea is conceptualization. But, what does that really mean? What exactly is a design concept, and how do you come up with one?

THE DESIGN CONCEPT

Each time a designer begins working on a play there is a series of new problems to be solved, challenges to be met, and questions to be answered in order to craft the final design. In order to accomplish this, a designer has to have a plan, a way of going about finding solutions and making decisions about their work. Dictionaries define *concept* as: "1. A general idea derived or inferred from specific instances or occurrences; 2. Something formed in the mind; a thought or notion; 3. A scheme; a plan."

A design concept is an idea or series of ideas, themes, or aesthetic guidelines that serve as a framework to guide

you throughout your process. It will become the underlying reasoning and logic that motivates all of your design decisions.

A design concept may start out visually or verbally. In your initial investigation of the play, you might find yourself coming up with phrases that speak to your preliminary observations.

- "I really think that it's important to set this show in the time period in which it was written."

- "I want to underscore the tension between these characters and in the environment."

- "Movement is of key importance in this setting."

- "It seems like light should really define space in this play."

- "Fantastical moments need to look completely different from the more realistic moments and lighting can make that distinction."

- "The sounds should have an old-time radio show feel."

- "The setting needs to be realistic."

- "The evolution of the characters through the course of the play needs to be underscored in their costumes."

- "Music will be crucial in facilitating transitions between one scene and the next."

- "There should be a sense of sophistication in how this world looks."

- "The setting feels minimal."

- "In order to accommodate multiple locations, the setting will need to be flexible."

- "There's a very film noir feeling to this script."

Verbal ideas tend to be more abstract than visual ones, and tend to deal with the message that you are trying to communicate through the design, but they are very useful in leading a designer to discovering visual choices. All of the previous sentences can provide a designer with a place to start and a direction to guide them as they begin their research, which will lead to more specific verbal ideas as well as visual ones. Visual ideas are usually more tangible and specific and can also be the first step in coming up with a concept, but they also often come out of early verbal brainstorming. Visual concepts will actually convey your ideas to the audience in a readily accessible way.

- "I don't see much color in this world, but what color there is will be important and point out key ideas or moments."

- "Broken patterns and prints in the costumes will help underscore their individual, fractured personalities."

- "All the sound effects will need to be actor-generated."

- "I want to use cogs and other machine parts as decorative items in the set to underscore the mechanized feel of the world of the play."

- "Gobos of specific images will be used to suggest locations, like stained glass windows for the church scene."

- "In order to emphasize the organic nature of this play, I want to use curvilinear lines throughout the design, and eliminate straight lines and angles."

- "I plan to base the tile pattern on the floor on the artwork of Chagall, borrowing his love of abstract images and bright colors."

Verbal concepts tend to come before visual ones, especially early on in the design process when the focus is on discussing the play, in order to really understand it and what the design team is trying to accomplish. The visual is, after all, a realization of the verbal ideas generated through collaboration. But, that doesn't mean that one way or the other is better. Most designers will likely use both methods to come up with ideas.

PRELIMINARY WORK: WHAT TO DO BEFORE COMING UP WITH A DESIGN CONCEPT

Given that a design concept is an idea that allows you as a designer to solve the problems and challenges of a given production, the first thing you have to do before you can

develop one is to identify and define these problems. You cannot solve a problem if you do not know what it is. So, before you sit down and start to develop your design concept, you have to talk with the director and the rest of your design team. You have to get to know the play, inside and out. Determine what the basic requirements are for your design area. Ask yourself—and the play—some general questions.

- How many exits and entrances are needed?

- Are there multiple locations or just one?

- Does the set have to do any "tricks" or other special affects?

- What kind of theatrical space will the play be produced in?

- Will the lighting be motivated or general?

- What role will lighting take in this production?

- Does the play need to take place in a specific location?

- Is the play set in a specific time period?

- Does the action take place all on one day, or over multiple days/weeks/years?

- How many characters are there?

- How many costume changes are there?

- Are there any special makeup needs?

- How many sound effects are required?

- Can I find sound effects or will I need to create them?

- Is musical underscoring asked for throughout the play?

These kinds of broad questions will help you figure out what the basic needs of the play are, before you ever start making more specific inquiries about interpretation and realization.

No matter how good they are, the director will never be able to tell you everything that you want to know about a play or the production. You can ask questions and listen actively, because sometimes the answers you are looking for pop up in unexpected places, between the lines. You can find out what they hope to accomplish with the production. But ultimately you will have to do your own research in order to be able to make a connection with the play and to start imagining the visual world. Research will lead to inspiration, which in turn generates the ideas that will eventually become your design concept and approach.

INSPIRATION

For a designer, ideas are our bread and butter. Without them, we would be lost and each new project requires us to generate new ones. But, how do you do that? Where do these ideas come from? How do you find the inspiration to develop creative ideas in the first place? What is inspiration, anyway?

In the arts, **inspiration** is the source of creativity and innovation. Inspiration is what makes it possible to generate new and innovative ideas. For designers and imaginative people of all kinds, it is fuel for the mind and nourishment for the creative soul. In essence, inspiration has come to mean any influence, person, event, or action that provides the motivation to produce creative works or that moves the heart, body, and mind to a higher level of activity or feelings. But, there is also a spiritual component to inspiration. Originally, the word literally meant "to breathe in and be filled with the spirit of the gods." The myths of ancient Greece explained that all creativity had a divine origin, and that humans could only hope to make imperfect copies of what they were shown. Some artists and writers refer to their source of inspiration as their muse in recognition of this ancient connection.

The things that inspire us are as unique and individual as we are. What stirs creativity for one person may have little effect on another. What inspires us will also change with each production and as we grow as artists. So, where do you look for it?

Where Does Inspiration Come From?

- The *script* will be a primary source of inspiration. In it, a designer will find clues to guide them in their research. Plot, themes, underlying messages, and characters can all inspire you in the quest for ideas.

- *Art* is incredibly inspiring. Looking at the work of other designers and artists of all kinds is a great way to study composition and the elements that are used to create it. Looking at the work of other artists can provide inspiration about the use of color, line, balance, tension, texture, thematic content, context, style, artistic voice, and the aesthetic conventions of different time periods, all of which can be applicable to the design problems you are trying to solve and can influence your solutions.

- *Movies* provide inspiration through often amazing visuals combined with the magic of storytelling that engage and move us. Films can take us to places that we have only been able to imagine before, and even to some that we have never thought existed. Movies also provide access to the often stunning results of powerful image creation and editing technologies that can potentially be applied to theatrical design. Beautiful costumes, exciting locations, gorgeous animation, amazing lighting effects, and spectacular makeup with emotionally engaging music and sound effects created specifically for the film can all inspire and motivate us.

- Like movies, *television* can be a source of inspiration by telling stories, introducing the viewer to new worlds, creating emotional connections and providing fantastic images. Sets for some programs can be very similar to theatrical settings, playing to the audience in a particular location much like live theatre. Observing these sets can increase our understanding of space, movement, and traffic, which can later be applied to our own designs. Television also has commercials, some of which contain excellent examples of design.

- *Architecture*. Not only is looking at architecture an absolute must for scenic designers, it is a fantastic way to examine how space can be shaped and used to not only guide movement and traffic, but to create an impression and affect the surrounding area. Looking at architecture is also a great way to see how light is let into the structure both to illuminate the interior and to create mood. Historical trends in the construction and design of buildings is a necessary area of study for designers, in order to understand visual aesthetics from different time periods.

- *Interiors and décor* are just as important to the education of a designer as architecture, and equally inspiring. Not only is it important to learn which interiors go with which exteriors as well as costumes, both historically and stylistically, interior design also provides insight into the character and personalities of the people that inhabit that space.

- *Fashion*. Like architecture and interior design, fashion design can be a valuable source of inspiration. Costume designers need to study fashion and fashion history because it will be the main source of information for their area of design, but all designers can benefit from looking at fashion. Costume history provides information on what types of clothing are unified with specific styles of architecture and interiors as well as reflecting major stylistic shifts throughout history. It illustrates important historical details such as sumptuary laws and the patterns of social norms, illustrating what is acceptable and what is not for specific activities and times of day. It reflects occupation and social status. Clothing is also highly subjective and personal, and offers a great deal of insight into character, as the reasons why we wear clothing are fluid and dynamic.

- *Nature* is the ultimate source of inspiration. The natural world around us is full of color, pattern, rhythm, and beauty of all kinds. Being in nature stimulates the senses, rejuvenates the mind, feeds the soul, and relaxes the body.

- *Works of fiction* inspire us through the writer's ability to create pictures in the reader's mind and by immersing them into an entirely different world. Although theatre design is more visual by nature than fiction, they share the quality of interactivity, relying on an audience of one kind or another who will bring personal interpretation to their experience of the work. Children's books are doubly inspiring, because they often contain beautiful illustrations that draw the reader in and assist in telling the story.

- *Works of non-fiction* have the potential to teach us something new, whether that is about history, world events, the lives of influential or inspirational public figures, art techniques and history, and even help us to discover things about ourselves. Learning new skills and gaining new information increases our knowledge base and provides a well of material to draw from for inspiration.

- *Magazines* cover a wide variety of literary genres and subjects and can provide access to all kinds of information and inspirational images. It is also an artistic medium that has been using solid design theory and practice for a long time and it can be beneficial and inspiring for designers to see these principles in action in another format.

- *Theatre and dance productions.* One excellent way for designers to become inspired is to see as many performances as possible. Watching a show that contains clever and exciting production components and engaging performances can leave you feeling charged, renewed, and excited about your own work. A really good production can open you up to new possibilities, introduce you to new technology, and move you emotionally.

- *Museums and galleries.* A visit to a museum offers inspiration in the form of multiple exhibits that reflect diverse subjects, cultures, time periods, aesthetic styles, artistic conventions, and history. It is a chance to see and experience things that you might not be able to see anywhere else. Museums and galleries engage and educate their visitors, and stimulate interest in individual artifacts, time periods, cultures, and artistic expression. It is almost impossible to leave a museum without new information or insights.

- *Libraries.* With the omnipresence of the Internet, it becomes harder and harder to convince students about the importance of libraries and books, but they have many things to offer that the Internet does not. Libraries have collections of rare and out-of-print material that cannot be purchased elsewhere. People visit libraries from all over the world to see rare books and manuscripts and to do research. Although you may have to pay for a library card in some institutions, you can then check books out for free and even request materials from other libraries through interlibrary loan. You'll have access to an endless number of books, reliable reference materials, and book experts who can be invaluable in your quest for information.

- *Conversations* both online and in person are intellectually stimulating and inspiring and can lead to new ideas. Discussing current events, social conditions, the arts, philosophy, and other topics can introduce you to new information as well as different points of view. In addition, having someone to bounce ideas off of can help you to see your design challenges from a different perspective, and may open a designer up to new solutions.

- *Daily experiences and observations.* The people and things you come into contact with each day are another source of inspiration. Watching people is endlessly fascinating and can provide a great deal of insight into human behavior that can be incorporated into your design work, especially for costume designers. As you move through your day you might read an article that motivates you or see a picture that sparks an idea or engage in a conversation that provides insight into your current design project.

- *Music* can be exciting or soothing, and is a natural source of inspiration. With its own compositional elements that correspond to visual elements, it can teach a designer about rhythm, time, and progression as well as give insights into using and defining space. Lyrics add the element of poetry to our experience of music and can illustrate many of the same qualities. Wassily Kandinsky believed so strongly in the correlation between music and the visual arts that he developed a theory to explain these correspondences. His thoughts on the nature of art and color theory can be read in *Concerning the Spiritual in Art.*

- *Visiting historical sites and travel.* Looking at a famous cathedral or castle in a book is one thing; visiting it in person is another. Visiting historical sites, whether they are castles, mansions, museums, cathedrals, temples, or natural locations gives you a different perspective than viewing them on a printed page and leaves a lasting impression that contributes to your understanding and appreciation.

- *Spending time with other creative people.* Creative individuals tend to be drawn to one another. If you look through history you will see that many great artists, writers, musicians, philosophers, and great thinkers have known each other or worked together. Even people that worked in relative isolation were able to benefit from the work of others. Keeping company with other artists and designers offers a sense of camaraderie and support in difficult times, such as when inspiration is lacking. They can remind you that inspiration is all around you. You will also be able to see how others navigate their way through the creative process, from ideas to finished designs. You can learn and benefit from their experiences rather than having to reinvent the wheel with each project.

Creating a Personal Resource of Inspiration

In design classes, I continually stress the importance of creating a **personal visual library** as an inspirational resource with my students. This is a twofold process. One part involves creating a literal, physical library full of books, magazines, and other items that stimulate your creativity and support your research. The other part is an abstract library, creating and nourishing a reservoir of visual information inside your head that you can draw from when needed.

The kinds of material that are included in the physical library of a designer will probably differ from one area of specialization to another. For a costume designer, their library will likely include books on costume history, garment construction, fabrics, dyeing techniques and fashion design. For a scenic designer, books on architecture, furniture, interior design, and décor will be useful. A lighting designer may elect to include materials that focus on the use of light in a variety of applications. A sound designer might keep a library of sound effects in various formats. A projection designer might keep a reference library of art, nature, and inspirational images. All designers can benefit from books on drawing and rendering techniques, art history, individual artists, design methods, subscriptions to relevant professional journals and publications, and playscripts. What else you choose to include in your personal design library may be largely personal, based on your own particular interests or on research materials gathered together over the course of various design projects. Children's books, fashion magazines, art calendars, catalogs, software manuals and guidebooks, history books, biographies, pattern collections, books on various art forms or techniques, journals, websites, and sketchbooks are just some of the items that are likely to find their way into your collection.

One great way to start a visual library is to collect images that you find inspiring, either by clipping them out of magazines or by creating a digital file. With the Internet, smartphones,

and image blogs like Tumblr and Pinterest, it is easier than ever to gather pictures and articles no matter where you are and then organize them into categories. In the past, recording observations meant carrying around a sketchbook or a journal, and it still can. But a smartphone with a camera can also be used to take quick snapshots of people and things you have seen throughout the day. Most of these devices also have ways to take notes via typing or handwriting, applications that allow you to sketch and record. Whether it is a picture of a building, the texture of a stone wall, a scene from nature, or an idea that suddenly comes to you, anything you collect this way can be useful later.

Cultivating a personal knowledge base of inspiration inside your head is a little more involved and is a continually evolving process, but it is not any more difficult. The personal library that you carry within you is the sum of all your experiences, learning, and knowledge and it is incredibly important. It is unique to you and a powerful creative tool to bring to the table in the collaborative process. However, ideas do not suddenly appear out of nowhere or in a vacuum, you have to feed your creativity in order to be able to generate imaginative concepts and to enable your abilities, your problem-solving skills, and your artistic abilities to develop and improve.

Designers are natural observers of the world. Like all art forms, theatre reflects the world around us and the people within it, and presents the universal truths that permeate existence. Artists as a whole tend to be fascinated with the world around them and are constantly trying to understand it in more profound ways so that they can reveal these truths in their work. This inherent fascination with life and people can be used to build your library of experiences and knowledge. Try to look beyond your own art form and out into the wider world. The key is to make your inquiries, experiences, and observations as broad as possible. Shake up your everyday experience: take a different route to work or school; read journals and books outside of your field; take a workshop or a class in order to learn something new; go someplace that you have never been before; visit museums and art galleries; attend theatre performances to see what is going on in your field; go to music and dance concerts; take classes in various topics that interest you; *feed your soul as an artist.* If you do not maintain an inquisitive mind, one that constantly seeks out new information, images, and inspirational sources, then your designs will never grow. Given that theatre is an art form that reflects the morals, behavior, ideals, and values of the culture that creates it, paying attention to what happens around you is just as important as any other research you undertake. After years of nourishing your mind with a wide variety of diverse material, priming yourself for creativity by filling your inner visual library, your design ideas and solutions will be inspired, innovative, and extraordinary.

CULTIVATING THE CREATIVE PROCESS AND GENERATING IDEAS

There are many ways to go about the process of generating ideas. No one way is better than another. But there are steps you can take, and activities that can help you to get from point A to point B, from the script to a finalized design. Some or all of these techniques might be useful to you.

- *Gather information.* Listen to what your director has to say and what your colleagues have to say. Write it down and consider it fuel for the creative fire. Collect images that are relevant to the current project, ones that not only speak specifically to your design area, but also to the mood, history, culture, and world of the play. Take notes; gather up articles about the play and the author. All of this is source material that you can use to develop ideas.

- *Cultivate ideas through observation.* The best way to describe this activity is to keep a creativity journal. Write down your experiences, notice and log your emotional sensitivities. Write down quotes that inspire you. Finding connections between things that seem unrelated is all about cultivating your observational skills. You have to be constantly *looking* for these intersections in order to find them. The idea is to keep track of anything that might influence future design work. It doesn't have to be a paper journal; you can do the same thing in a digital blog, which you can tag and organize to make searching through it easy and simple.

- *Brainstorm.* Keep a small notebook or sketchbook with you and write down any idea that comes to mind. Keep one in your bag and another in your car. One word, two words, short phrases, anything that you think of, for the current design problem or not. Sometimes, just writing down anything you can think of related to the project at hand in a stream of consciousness can generate a wealth of ideas and potential solutions.

- *Do research.* Investigate and learn about your subject as well as the things that relate to it. Don't confine yourself to just the design area you are responsible for. Expand your search, refine your knowledge, and become invested in the world of the play.

- *Gather information and keep learning.* This is like doing research, but less specific to a particular project. Collect images, articles, artwork, and other information that speaks to you. Investigate things that fascinate you and follow your curiosity wherever it takes you. Then learn about things you are not as interested in. You might be surprised at the connections you discover between seemingly unrelated things. Creative people are constantly learning and anything can potentially provide inspiration for a future project. Learn as much as you can as often as you can.

- *Percolate and synthesize.* Once you gather information and do your research, you need to take some time to digest all that information. Like a good cup of tea, ideas take time to brew. Read the articles and books you have gathered. Jot down notes in the margins, underline pertinent passages. Look at the images you collected and arrange them into categories. Scribble ideas on the back of them and write down where you found them in case you need to go back to the source later. Lay it all out on the floor around you and take it all in. Think about it, let it percolate. Combine things, rearrange the order, see how they can be synthesized and applied to your current design project.

- *Look, see, and think visually.* Be on the lookout for subjects, images and various viewpoints and how these things can relate to or inform your work. Quotes, stories, poetry, news articles, images, and opinions can all potentially be translated into visual ideas. One great exercise to enhance this skill is to take a quote and create a visual image to illustrate or communicate its core idea. This gives you the opportunity to become fluent in the use of visual symbols and metaphors to represent abstract concepts. Metaphors are phrases that are used to compare things that have no apparent relationship. Symbols are visual images that are used to give concrete form to an abstract idea. Symbols can become a visual metaphor when they become invested with meaning and thereby come to represent something different from what they are. The translation of words into communicative images is the foundation of theatrical design. Consequently, a degree of fluency in the language and use of symbols and visual metaphor is very useful.

- *Alter your perspectives.* The defining characteristic of creative thinking is being able to look at something that everyone else is looking at and see it in a different way. In order to do this, sometimes you have to leave the safety of your comfort zone, discard your own opinion, and try to see things from multiple points of view. This will allow you to discover things about your project that you might not have seen otherwise.

- *Let go of your assumptions.* Like Neo in *The Matrix*, we can all benefit from freeing our mind from expectations and social constructs that imply creative activity functions in only one way rather than many. The idea that we have to set aside time to be creative and that we have to think outside the box is not true. The truth is that there is no box of preconceived notions and we can think creatively at any time.

- *Stay focused.* With all the distractions provided by technology it can be hard to maintain focus on your work. Sometimes, when a project is difficult or contains a lot of challenges, our frustrations cause us to force a solution, lose motivation, or to even to give up. It is harder to be patient, to work through the challenges, and to cultivate a solution but, in the long run, the end result is worth the effort.

- *Freeform writing.* This is like brainstorming, but is less a stream of consciousness generation of words and thoughts and targeted more towards phrases that address specific ideas, challenges, and potential solutions. Working through your ideas by writing them down, either on paper or in a digital document, can often assist you in narrowing your focus, combining or editing your thoughts, and making design decisions.

- *Sketching.* When words are not enough to explore your ideas, sketch them out. Sometimes concepts take shape visually rather than verbally in your mind. Drawing them out quickly records them for further exploration and

sharing with your collaborators. Keep a sketchbook with you at all times and sketch as inspiration strikes you.

- *Exercise your drawing and rendering muscles.* Drawing is a skill like any other. You have to practice to maintain your ability and to become better. Draw as much as you can. Copy work is a great way to exercise your drawing muscles and improve your skills. Work in a variety of media, wet and dry. Experiment with techniques and expand your repertoire. It does not matter if the work is theatre-related or not. The more you draw, the better your skills will be. Given that a designer communicates their ideas visually, drawing is a crucial and necessary ability.

- *Mind mapping* is a style of note taking that "maps out" your ideas around a central concept or image, putting them into a visual form that can help you to see the relationships between different things. All mind maps share a common organization structure. Main ideas are placed in the center and everything else radiates out from that idea in the form of lines, colors, words, images, and symbols. The main branches that connect to the central subject like roads that lead to the source are labeled with a key word or phrase that represents your primary ways of thinking or

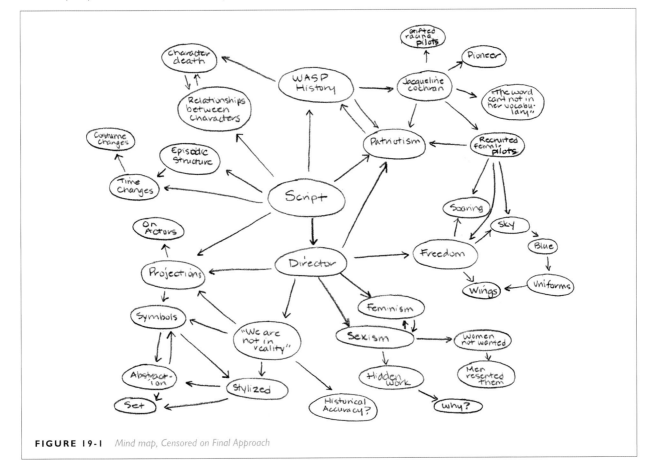

FIGURE 19-1 *Mind map, Censored on Final Approach*

main themes that apply to the central idea. Smaller "twigs" branching off from the main pathways represent ideas that are related tangentially. Mind maps let you visualize the structure of a problem and assist in the classification of ideas, brainstorming, decision-making, and problem-solving. It can be a very intuitive process and there are several types of software available to assist in their creation.

- *Plan ahead and budget your time.* Make sure that you have enough of the best materials you can afford in order to complete your work. Budget your time in order to meet your deadlines and complete your work on time. Rushing at the end is no substitute for careful planning and doing your work in a timely fashion. There are no shortcuts to a polished, high-quality design.

- *Ask your colleagues to respond to your ideas.* Collaboration is all about sharing ideas and interacting with your design colleagues. If you are having difficulties with your choices or need feedback on your idea, do not be afraid to enlist the help of your fellow designers. They have all been where you are and, more often than not, are happy to take a look at your work and offer their opinion.

- *Listen to what your colleagues have to say.* It can be difficult to remain open to criticism and see it as an opportunity to improve on what is working rather than a lecture on what was less successful. Every designer has different criteria for evaluation and they bring their individual observations, life experiences, values, and perceptions to each experience of another person's work and they are bound to be different from yours—sometimes very different. Rather than having a knee-jerk reaction, try to keep an open mind. You do not have to take the advice of a colleague, but you should do your best not to discount it without giving it some consideration. This is especially true in the collaborative process. Remember that you are all working on the same show and towards the same goal and your collaborators are your partners in achieving it successfully.

- *Be open to chance.* Sometimes accidental discoveries along the way can lead to exciting ideas that change your entire approach to your design. Be receptive to these opportunities and what they have to offer.

- *Confront your fear.* Fear and hesitation are natural parts of the creative process. We all want to do our best and we all have our comfort zones; but learning happens most when we test our boundaries and push our limits. Do not be afraid to explore your concepts and ideas and see where they take you.

- *Generate multiple options.* There is no rule that states that there is only one way to solve a design problem. If that

were the case, then every production of a play would look the same. There is no right way to design. Generating multiple solutions and variations not only allows you to fully explore your design ideas, it also gives your director options that they may not have considered. Using this method, you are also less likely to be 100 percent invested in one idea alone to the exclusion of all others, and therefore potentially unwilling to make edits or revisions or to see other possibilities.

- *Edit and make revisions.* Most ideas can benefit from a little editing in order to become stronger. Sometimes ideas need to be scratched altogether and new ones have to be explored as the collaboration progresses. Be open to making changes to your work in response to the natural ebb and flow of the creative process in order to strengthen the final design.

- *Finalize your ideas.* Even after careful editing ideas generally need some final polish to make them shine.

- *Learn from mistakes.* No one is perfect. If you make a mistake, see it as an opportunity to learn and move forward.

- *Evaluate your finished product.* No matter how happy you are with your final design, or how perfect the collaboration, there is always room for improvement. Taking a look at work objectively can be a useful tool in your growth as a theatrical artist. Take stock of what was successful and note what could have been more effective. Did the design concept work for the play? Were you able to communicate effectively to the audience through your design? Was the overall production enhanced by your contribution? Is there anything you would have done differently? Evaluating your work makes it possible to move on to the next production with confidence.

THE LANGUAGE OF CONCEPTUALIZATION

Conceptualization: Something formed in the mind; a thought or notion.

Design concept: An idea, series of ideas, themes, or aesthetic guidelines that serve as a framework to guide a designer throughout the design process.

Inspiration: The source of creativity and innovation.

Personal visual library: A combination of a physical library—full of books, magazines, and other items that stimulate your creativity—and an abstract library, creating and nourishing a reservoir of visual information inside your head that you can draw from when needed.

CHAPTER 20

THE DESIGN PROCESS

WHAT IS THE DESIGN PROCESS?

One of the most important aspects of education in theatrical design is learning the basic process of creating a design. This is different from learning how to work with the elements and principles of design. How does a designer progress from the unread script to the final, complete design? Where do you even begin? *Design process* refers to the steps a designer takes to get from the pages of the script to a finished design that is evocative, engaging, and that serves the intent of the play and of the current production. This chapter is intended to provide an outline of one way of developing a design, but it certainly is not the only way. As a designer develops their own way of working, their process will naturally evolve and change.

STEP ONE: THE SCRIPT

The beginning point in the design process for any designer is always the script. It is one of the main sources for information that will guide and inform you in your quest to create a visual realization of the world of the play. The script contains all of the details about the world the playwright envisioned when he or she wrote the play. Interpretation of that world is the job of the **production team**, also known as the design team.

Before going to the first design meeting, it is essential that a designer reads the play. The number of times a designer reads the play before meeting with the director and the production team is largely based on personal choice and individual working style. As stated in Chapter 18, your initial reading or readings of the play should lead you to start asking questions of and

about the script. These are questions you can ask yourself, but are also ones that you can bring to the first design meeting, to get feedback from the director and other members of the team. Questions about the script will undoubtedly come up throughout the entire design process, but there are a few key questions that always come up in the beginning. They lead you into a deeper exploration of the play. As a reminder, some of these questions might include:

- What is the main theme of the play?

- Are there any secondary themes?

- Whose story is being told in the action of the play? (Identifying the protagonist.)

- What is the main plot of the script?

- Are there any important subplots? (Secondary stories.)

- What is the main obstacle to the action of the play and the goals of the protagonist?

- What is more important – words or actions in the story? (Sometimes one might be dominant.)

- What is the central image of the play?

- What is the climax of the play?

- What moved you most when you read the script? Did you connect or empathize with any particular character or sequence of events?

- Were you unmoved by the script? If so, do you have any idea why?

- What does the director want to emphasize or visually support in the script? What do you think should be supported by your design choices?

Write down these questions as they come to you, so that you can bring them up in the first design meeting. Chances are you are not the only one that has them.

STEP TWO: THE FIRST DESIGN MEETING

The initial design meeting is full of potential. It presents many possibilities, both for you as a designer and for the production as a whole. At the first meeting between the director and the production team, everyone has a chance to talk about the play and share their impressions. Everything and anything is possible. What should you bring to this first meeting as a designer, and what can you expect?

The format and organization of this meeting, and likely all meetings to follow, will be different with each director. Each will likely have a slightly different process and an individual way of doing things. Some directors will do a considerable amount of preparatory work on the play before the first meeting: looking at previous productions; reading reviews of performances or scholarly articles about the text; learning about the author and their intentions in writing the play; researching the socio-political background of the author and the play in order to develop an understanding of the context of the script, both as it pertains to the world of the play itself and to the author and their background. They may gather information about the ideas and issues presented in the script, and do research to help understand these things in the context of the production. Usually, they have read the play many times before this first meeting, and they often have a great deal of information to share with their collaborators because they are so well prepared.

Other directors will want to set up a free-flowing dialogue between all members of the production team, and sometimes even the actors or other production personnel. This kind of collaborative process can be very exciting, because the environment and atmosphere is very open, and every member of the discussion feels that their ideas are being heard, and that they are actively contributing to the process. This type of open collaborative process can be especially rewarding for the actors, and has the advantage of offering up a lot of different ideas.

A designer should also be prepared for the first design meeting. You accomplish this by spending time with the script before the meeting, and doing your homework. The director and your fellow collaborators are as interested in your response to the play as you are in theirs, and they want to hear what you have discovered in the script. It is quite possible that you

have noticed something that they have not, or have a unique perspective that they have not considered. This is one of the most exciting things about collaboration. In some cases, the director might ask you to speak about your reaction, thoughts, and opinions before they give any feedback of their own. Designers must be able to hold their own in these conversations and be able to actively contribute to this part of the process.

What else should a designer do at this first meeting? In addition to participating in the conversation where appropriate, it is a good idea to take notes throughout the meeting, jotting down important points and ideas as they come up. Write down the information the director presents about the play so you have it for reference when you go back to the script. It is impossible to remember everything that is said at a meeting, so good notes can go a long way in helping you recall what your colleagues had to say and the points that were discussed. Ask the questions you have about the script, including any that may come up in response to what is said in the meeting. Take whatever you can away from the discussion, to use as you begin the next step in the design process.

STEP THREE: GOING BACK TO THE SCRIPT AND BEGINNING WORK

Armed with the information gleaned from the initial design meeting, you can start to dig more deeply into the script, and begin the work of developing your specific design approach. At this point, it is a good idea to read the script again, keeping the notes you took at the design meeting next to you as you read, so you can remember to look for points that were brought up in the discussion. This is especially true if the information you took away from the meeting is radically different from your initial impressions, or if the director is suggesting a conceptual approach that is challenging. Reading the script with these factors in mind will help you in the next part of the process, where you begin to make connections purposely tailored to the current production.

Depending on their approach to the play, the director might have given some very specific information during the first design meeting. They may have felt strongly about setting the production in a particular time period or location, wanted to point up a specific part of the plot or a thematic element, or had definite ideas about the conceptual approach they want to use to support the message of the play. It is the job of the designers to take all the input they are given and create an evocative and compelling design that suits the needs of the production, meets the challenges of the play, effectively supports the script, and brings the director's vision to life.

For this reading of the play, it is important to look at the script with a more discerning eye. This read-through is about noting details that will affect or influence the final design. Underline key information, such as time of day and year, locations, exits and entrances, passage of time, and what characters say about themselves and each other. Costume designers should also mark references made regarding costume needs and take note of how characters change psychologically over the course of the play. These changes may need to be reflected in their costumes. You may wish to start a **costume plot**, to chart the changes required for each character in each scene and over the course of the play. **Character analysis** sheets should be filled out, a convenient way to list overall qualities related to the character in a chart format, such as social status, general mood, notes from the script, and design thoughts such as line, colors, and texture. All designers might elect to create a **French scene chart**, a diagram that shows the entrances and exits of each character in each scene, making it possible to keep track of who is on stage at any given moment. Set designers should pay attention to scenic, furniture, and prop needs that are directly required by the script or suggested by the action. Lighting designers should note the overall mood of individual scenes and how it progresses from one scene to the next, noting any specific lighting requirements such as practical lamps and environmentally motivated light sources. Sound designers should consider specialized effects, ambient sound needs, and how to consider the pre- and post-show environment. Projection designers should note any mention of required images, static or moving, and make note of places where the director has indicated that they would like projections to be used.

What happens if you are having difficulty making a connection with the play? Or if, for one reason or another, you simply don't like the script? What if you strongly *dislike* it? Chances are, at some point in a design career or over the course of a design education, you will work on a play that you personally do not care for. Scripts do not always have universal appeal. The challenge in this situation is to not become ambivalent about the script. If you have a strong reaction—positive *or* negative—to a play, then you will be able to create an effective design. It is when you have no reaction *at all* that designing becomes difficult. In this situation, you need to find a way to become invested in the script. This might be through a particular character whose personality or qualities intrigue you, or that you identify with. You might become fascinated with the technical challenges of the play, or with the dynamics of the relationships between a set of characters. The stylistic challenge of the director's approach to the production might resonate strongly with you. Any route you can find that leads you into the play, and allows you to make a connection to the script will help you in your process, and lead you to a creative and suitable design.

STEP FOUR: PRELIMINARY RESEARCH

Once this specialized reading has been accomplished, the next step before attending another design meeting is to do research. This step can cover a lot of ground. It will not only include visual research for your specific design area, but will also most likely consist of contextual research about the world of the play and other factors that affect the people, locations, and actions that take place within it. If your director has chosen to impose a particular stylistic approach on the production, and/or if the script itself is from a highly stylized genre, you may also want to look at materials that can support these conceptual ideas.

Some of the things you may choose to research include:

- the time period of the play.

- the geographic location.

- socio-political factors of the time period, which can include historical events, religious influences, cultural factors, social structures, sumptuary laws, and artists and artistic trends.

TABLE 20.1 *French scene chart example.*

Character	Act I, Sc1, FS 1	FS 2	FS 3	FS 4	FS 5	FS 6	FS 7	FS 8	FS 9	FS 10	FS 11	Act I, Sc 2, FS 1	FS 2	FS 3	FS 4	FS 5
Jim	X	X		X	X		X			X	X					
Sally	X	X	X		X	X	X	X	X	X	X			X	X	X
Tom		X	X	X		X	X	X	X	X	X					
Mary	X	X	X	X	X	X	X					X	X	X	X	X
Anne	X	X		X	X	X	X	X			X		X	X		X

- the social classes of the characters.

- the architecture of the period.

- art and artists of the period (portraits are especially useful for costume designers).

- furniture and accessories of the period.

- clothing and accessories of the period.

- the playwright, including biographical materials as well as literary criticism of the work.

- previous productions of the play, including critical reviews.

- the literary style of the play—tragedy, comedy, farce, Restoration drama, absurdism, etc.

- information that informs and supports the literary genre of the script.

- information that supports the stylistic concept of the production.

- inspirational research materials, such as images that suggest mood, symbols, metaphors, or lighting looks.

A large portion of your research will undoubtedly be visual. Research images serve to guide and inspire your choices as a designer and also increase your internal visual library. They also help you communicate to the director and the production team in a clear, evocative manner. It can be tempting to concentrate on visual research to the exclusion of everything else. But do not overlook the nonvisual, contextual research. Many times, this is exactly what you need in order to understand the script itself, the world of the play, and the stylistic direction of the production.

For example, August Wilson's *Ma Rainey's Black Bottom* is a realistic script with a story that is outside the realm of experience of the average twenty-first-century person. The play is one of a ten-play cycle written by Wilson that chronicles the African American experience in the twentieth century. Set in Chicago in the 1920's, the play's action follows a day in the life of the famous jazz singer Ma Rainey, and explores issues of power, race, religion, art, and the exploitation of black recording artists by white producers in the height of the jazz era. In order to understand the action of the play and the issues that are raised and examined by the script, a designer needs to make themselves familiar with: the world of the 1920's; Ma Rainey's life, personality and experiences; jazz music; the realities of discrimination and the exploitation that faced African American recording artists; and African American history in the United States. This is in addition to research that addresses locale, clothing, lighting, the author, the genre, and the stylistic approach to the play. This research needs to be done in order to place

the play in its historical context. To not do so is to create an inauthentic design that is not true to the original source material and does not fully explore the intent of the author.

A useful tool for the designer is a **research or response collage**. This is a collection of images, words, and textures collaged together in a digital or two-dimensional format as a response to the play, its story, thematic content, or the ideas it presents. It can be a way to visualize your initial ideas about the script and to group images together in a way that helps you collect your thoughts about characters, scenes, or design goals. It is also a great visual tool for communicating these ideas to your director and the other designers.

But what if the play you are designing is removed from its historical context or the content is flexible enough to allow for a wide range of visual interpretations, such as the range of possibilities when producing a Shakespearean play? Is the research method the same? Yes and no. The method is the same, but the path from point A to point Z might take a few twists and turns along the way.

Using Shakespeare as an example, because his plays are so often adapted to other locations and time periods, we will examine the idea of taking a production of *Hamlet*, and imposing a drastically different design approach on the script. We will take it out of its time period and location, and thereby drastically alter the required visual approach. For the purpose of our examination of the design process, we will assume that the director has decided to set the play in feudal Japan, citing the parallels between Hamlet's quest to revenge the murder of his father, and the samurai's duty to exact retribution for his lord's death. It is now up to you as a designer to locate the necessary information to validate this approach for yourself as you work on your designs, and to find a way to make it work effectively for the play.

In your research, you would most likely examine the relationship between samurai and the lords they served in more detail in order to understand the obligations the samurai incurred and how this relates to and supports the task of revenge that the ghost of Hamlet's father sets for him. You might even suggest that Hamlet's current position makes him a *rōnin*, a masterless samurai who only lives to avenge the death of his liege lord. You may read the historical account of the 47 *rōnin*, once of the most celebrated stories in samurai history. You might watch a film adaptation of *Chūshingura*, the celebrated *Bunraku* play that is based on this beloved example of samurai loyalty. By examining Japanese mythology, you would discover the role of ghosts in Japanese culture, and learn how an angry ghost can seek out the living to avenge wrongs done to them in life. You might also investigate the shogunate in Japan to learn if the parallels between its structure and that of a feudal monarchy are strong enough for the play to be set in that society. You would look at the role of women in the samurai culture in order to explain Ophelia's behavior in the play, perhaps discovering that the filial duties required of samurai daughters provides a strong foundation for her actions, for doing as her father bids her without question.

As part of your investigation, you would learn that in feudal Japan, there was honor to be found in committing suicide, giving some background for Hamlet's famous monologue about life and death. By examining the religious traditions of Japan at this time, you would find Buddhist and Shinto traditions competing with the values of Christianity, newly brought to the country by European missionaries. You would find evidence of samurai embracing Christianity while still remaining Japanese; meaning that all three spiritual traditions lived side-by-side, but that the values and moral constraints of the new religion never overran the familial and cultural obligations of the individual in Japanese society. You might come to the conclusion that the conflicts between these religions provide another reason for Hamlet not to take his life, and to have doubts about doing as his father asks. In short, it is possible you would find all the information you needed to embrace the director's conceptual slant and to integrate it into your design approach, explaining how it supports the play.

FIGURE 20-1   Hamlet set in feudal Japan, costume designs by Kaoime E. Malloy

Primary versus Secondary Research

Given all the sources for information that are now available in an Internet-dominated world, it is worth discussing the value of different sources. When conducting research, images and content fall into two categories: primary research and secondary research. The differences between them are important, and can often be significant.

Primary research sources consist of visual images from the period being investigated: art work of all kinds; paintings; furniture; architecture; mosaics; stained glass; photographs (if applicable); clothing and other items; and photographs of these items. **Secondary research sources** are mainly comprised of drawings of primary research, and can include films and television shows depicting historical time periods. The distinction is important because primary research is far more accurate. Drawings by artists can easily miss important details and create inaccuracies. Secondary research can, however, provide additional information and still offer artistic inspiration.

The same kind of mistakes can happen in nonvisual research, especially on the Internet. While there is a great deal of good information to be had on the Web, there is also a lot of misinformation. Just because something has been published on the Web does not make it accurate. You should carefully consider whether or not the source you are using is reliable and this is especially important for information obtained from the Web. Many websites do not have independent, third-party verification of the information they contain and without it they can be questionable at best and completely unreliable at worst. If you have any doubts, cross-reference the information by checking against other sources that you know you can trust.

Popular literature—such as trade books, magazines, and the like—can be good sources of information. These authors often use the independent confirmation standard, and their sources are typically checked and rechecked by professional editors and other workers throughout the publishing process.

Academic books and journal articles are excellent sources of reliable information. Academic publishing has rigorous conventions governing the collection and evaluation of information. More often than not, academic publishers also require a peer review; that is, an evaluation and critique by other experts in the field. Now that so many academic sources are available on the Web, you do not even have to go to the library to take advantage of them. Many university libraries have subscriptions to online databases in a variety of fields, allowing you to examine information from all over the world at the click of a mouse button.

Historical accuracy might not be the eventual goal of every production. For stylistic reasons, or to support aspects of the

Primary

Secondary

FIGURE 20-2 *Primary and secondary research (Boris Stroujko, Pavila, Everett Collection, FCks / shutterstock.com)*

script, you might decide to take liberties with historical looks or to make subtle variations based on your research. But, starting from a good, accurate base assures that your choices are well reasoned and plausible.

Presentation of Research Materials

Organization is an important aspect of presenting your ideas and materials to your collaborators. It is also critical for keeping your research in an easily accessible format for your own use. Whether you choose to copy all your research and put it into a notebook, or scan it and create a digital reference file or slide show, it should be clearly organized and easily navigable. A research notebook might eventually include the following sections:

- A copy of the script.

- Script analysis.

- Director's notes.

- Design meeting notes.

- Concept statement.

- French scene chart.

- Character analysis (for costume designers).

- Costume plot (for costume designers).

- Prop list (for scenic and prop designers).

- Fashion research (for costume designers).

- Architectural research (for scenic designers).

- Interior and décor research (for scenic designers).

- Lighting research (for lighting designers).

- Sound research (for sound designers).

- Image research for projections (for projection designers).

- Research on the author.

- Production history.

- Relevant societal/cultural research, divided into sections.

- Inspirational images and research materials.

You might also choose to set up a website for your production team, in order to make the exchange of information easy and accessible. It can be a very useful tool if you are designing long-distance and are meeting by phone or using digital chat or conference software. Any site where you can add and share files, post links, and post comments to a message board—such as Yahoo groups or Google docs—makes sharing research convenient and instantaneous.

STEP FIVE: ADDITIONAL DESIGN MEETINGS

The next steps in the design process are usually a succession of design meetings for the production team; a series of back-and-forth exchanges between the director and the designers. During this time, ideas will be traded and discussed, research will be shared and evaluated, and concrete decisions regarding the conceptual approach to the show will be made. Designers might be asked to go back to the drawing board, and rethink their ideas or even start over. The exact number of meetings will vary from project to project. But once this crucial decision regarding the take on the production has been agreed upon, the designers can start making specific choices in their own areas.

At some point during or between these meetings, designers should set up private sessions with the director to discuss the concerns specific to their individual areas. At this time, you can show more detailed research and supporting materials as well as ask questions that are pertinent to your area alone. Costume designers can discuss individual characters, how they change over the course of the play, and present clothing images for each. Scene designers can discuss environmental needs, what the director requires from the set for actor movement and composition, furniture and props needs, and share the research they've done for each area. Sound designers can play audio clips of effects and music and discuss their suitability. Lighting designers can show images that suggest the looks for each scene and discuss color choices or show digital **light renderings**. Projection designers can go over their

designs for each image and discuss them in detail. One-on-one time with the director can be very productive and is an absolutely necessary part of the design process.

Undoubtedly, you will have several meetings as the production team works its way through the design of the production. The next steps in the design process will occur within the framework of continued meetings between the director and the various designers.

STEP SIX: PRELIMINARY SKETCHES

Once the initial investigative work has been completed, the play has been analyzed, the conceptual approach has been collectively determined and you've met with the director individually, it is time to put your ideas down on paper or another visible format. The easiest and fastest way to do this is by creating **preliminary sketches** or **thumbnails**.

Preliminary sketches serve several purposes, both for you as a designer and for your colleagues. Chief among them is the chance to work out your design ideas in a tangible fashion without the investment of a fully finished drawing. Beginning sketches are generally rougher (which is why they are often called **roughs**), usually contain fewer details, and are often smaller than the drawings you will make for your final, finished renderings. The first rough drawings convey the general idea of your design, and research images can be used to show the details that the sketches may be lacking. Consequently, they can take less time to do, and this gives you a certain amount of freedom to quickly explore options before making final design decisions. Sometimes you might have a very clear idea of how you want a character to be dressed, how a setting appears, how the lights work in a scene, or what image or images you want to project. Other times, you may have several ideas that you want to try out, to see which is more effective or which one you like better. Creating variations can help you to work through your ideas, find creative solutions to the design challenges and problems presented by the script and get a feel for the visual realization of the play. By making rough sketches, you can see if your choices are successful and engaging before taking them to your director.

Thumbnails for costume designs can be small, five or six inches high, showing the basic costume silhouette and the overall look without intricate details. You can use your research book to provide supporting details when needed, or even make a small side-sketch to show a key element of the design. In addition, you might choose to place daubs of color next to the sketches or on them, or even to attach swatches of fabrics to help convey your ideas more effectively.

Storyboards, a series of small sketches that show a progression of looks from one scene to another, are very useful for scenic, lighting, and projection designers to show their design

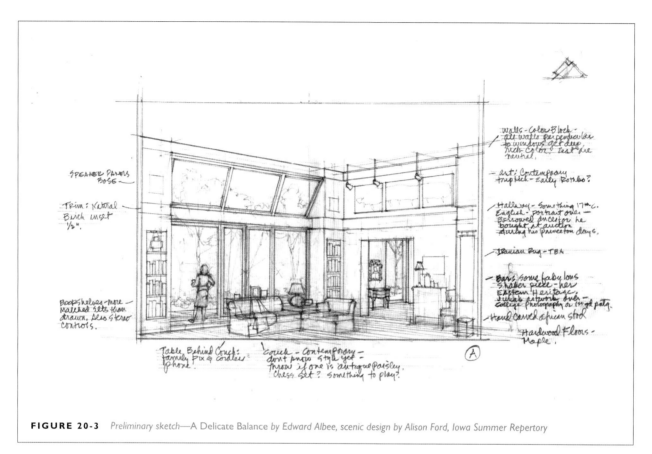

FIGURE 20-3 *Preliminary sketch—A Delicate Balance by Edward Albee, scenic design by Alison Ford, Iowa Summer Repertory*

FIGURE 20-4 *Costume thumbnails—Bedroom Farce (by Alan Ayckbourn, costume design by Kaoime E. Malloy, Iowa Summer Repertory)*

ideas for each scene. A **preliminary groundplan** is also required for the director to understand how the scenic space is being utilized and where key scenic elements such as furniture, exits, and entrances are placed. A groundplan is essentially a map that shows the placement of scenic elements and furniture. This gives the director an idea of how the space can be used for blocking, and whether or not the arrangement will work for what they have planned in terms of actor movement. You could also choose to create a **white model** to help convey your ideas in a three-dimensional manner. A white model is a very a basic model of the set made from white cardstock or foam core board, in scale (such as ¼-inch for every inch), that shows the set in miniature, with all the levels, entrances, exits, and furniture that will be present in the actual, realized set. Sometimes a designer might choose to draw additional details on the model to represent other elements that will be present, such as wallpaper, paintings, and light fixtures. Like a thumbnail sketch, it takes less time to construct than a formal, **detailed model**, but still conveys a great deal of useful information that might not be readily apparent in a two-dimensional drawing.

Once your preliminary sketches are completed, you will take them back to a design meeting and show them to the director and your production team colleagues. At this meeting,

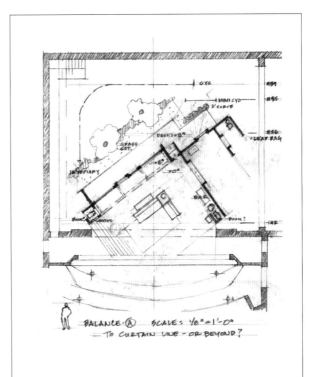

FIGURE 20-5 *Preliminary groundplan—A Delicate Balance by Edward Albee, Iowa Summer Repertory Theatre, set design by Alison Ford*

FIGURE 20-6 *White model—The Marriage of Figaro by Mozart, Krannert Center at the University of Illinois, set design by Alison Ford*

FIGURE 20-7   *Story boards—*Revenge of the Space Pandas *by David Mamet, set design by Kaoime E. Malloy*

you need to explain your choices, perhaps using your research to fill in the gaps and show your intent. Although you may be very happy with the choices you have made so far, it is still possible that you will need to make minor or even major changes to your designs in order for them to suit the production and the director's goals. Editing is a standard part of the design process and you should not be surprised or offended if you are asked to refine your ideas. More often than not, your revised designs will be better for the input you receive from your colleagues.

Sound designers may elect to put together a collection of sounds files to share with the director. These files should include the materials they are considering for all aural aspects of the production; sound effects, incidental music, pre- and post-show music and ambient sounds. Having several variations of each sound or musical piece gives the director multiple options and can help them find the choice that is most suitable for the production. At this point, the sound designer can also give examples of cues that they have built from their research for the director to listen to and evaluate. These sound clips and compositions serve the same purpose as rough sketches and thumbnails. They are preliminary tools that help the designer to work through their concepts and ideas and communicate them to the production team.

STEP SEVEN: FINAL DRAWINGS, RENDERINGS, PROJECTION FILES, AND SOUND CUES

Once your preliminary designs have been approved by the director, the next step is to create **final drawings**. By their very nature, these drawings will be more complete and contain a higher degree of detail than your preliminary sketches. When creating them, you will incorporate any changes the director asked you to make and consider the suggestions made by your design colleagues.

For the costume designer, the final drawings and the **renderings** they will become are very important. They will serve as construction blueprints for the costume shop, and should be able to answer questions about costume construction details when the designer is not present. Consequently, these drawings might include details such as seam placement in garments, accurate numbers of buttons, and additional detail drawings that show close-up construction details for the costume technicians. Final renderings need to be in color for the same reason. A colored rendering can answer more questions, and show exact details of the final costume design. It also communicates information regarding makeup, hair, and

FIGURE 20-8   *Final costume drawings and renderings— Ma Rainey's Black Bottom by August Wilson, Iowa Summer Repertory Theatre, costume design by Kaoime E. Malloy*

costume accessories such as hats, gloves, shoes, and purses. Final renderings should also have swatches of the fabrics you plan to use attached to them, in order to show what the actual, finished costume will look like as accurately as possible.

For the scene designer the finished drawings, renderings, and **paint elevations** will communicate the final look for each scene in the play in full detail. These drawings should show all the elements of the scenic design clearly—the overall space, colors, exits and entrances, windows and doors, furniture, wall treatments, and so on—in a realistic manner that conveys depth and implied space. Scenic designers might also choose to include final drawings of props, furniture, and other scenic items that will be included in the set. Or, in place of a rendering, they may decide to create a fully realized scenic model in full color and in scale. Directors often relish the opportunity to use such a model to develop blocking patterns, which can also allow them to visualize the space more easily. Scene designers should also include paint chips or fabric swatches to help the director envision their choices. Once a final design is approved, they will generate supporting paperwork and drawings that present the design in full detail for the scene and paint shops.

Building on the feedback they have received from the director throughout the design process, projection designers will

now finalize their images and get them into the proper format required for the projection equipment to be used for the production. Digital files can be edited to reflect the director's and designer's choices to build the final images and then saved in the correct file format and resolution. If needed, slides can be ordered for large format projectors as required.

Lighting designers might not elect to do final drawings, and instead opt to use digital programs such as Virtual Light Lab in order to create images that will convey their design ideas. Given that directors might have a hard time visualizing design looks without some kind of picture to look at, light renderings can be extremely useful when trying to communicate your ideas. In some instances, a lighting designer might choose to make a copy of the scene designer's final drawings, and then create light renderings from them, either by hand or digitally. Given that image editing software is readily available and relatively easy to use, it can be a very effective tool for the lighting designer to use in order to communicate their choices in an effective and appealing manner.

No matter your area, you may decide to hold off on coloring your final drawings until after your director has had a chance to see them, and give one final note of approval. Renderings take much longer to complete than rough or even

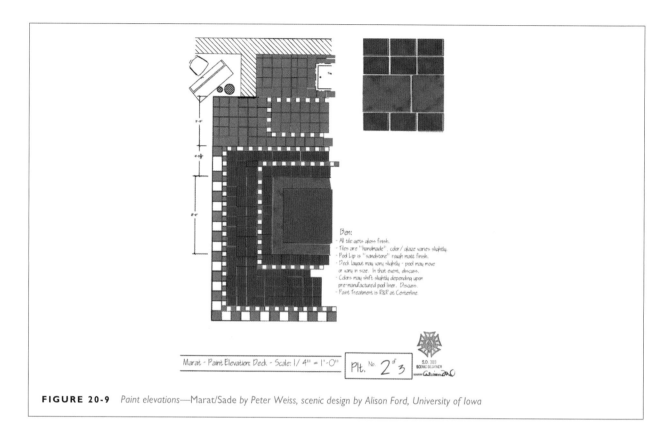

FIGURE 20-9 *Paint elevations—Marat/Sade by Peter Weiss, scenic design by Alison Ford, University of Iowa*

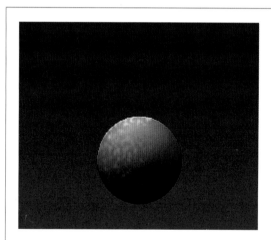

FIGURE 20-10 *Virtual Light Lab rendering*

final sketches, and you will be more invested in them and how people react to them because of this fact. Although changes can happen at any point in the design process up until opening night, if you can avoid unnecessary rework along the way, do so. Many designers choose to do their renderings digitally using Adobe Photoshop, Adobe Illustrator, or Corel Paint for this very reason. Even drastic changes are easily accomplished with digital editing software, making revisions quick and simple.

AN OUTLINE OF THE BASIC DESIGN PROCESS

Step One: The Script: Reading the play, learning the plot and the story, and asking questions.

Step Two: The First Design Meeting: Meeting with your production colleagues. Listening to the director, learning about their take on the play and the production. Sharing questions and ideas.

Step Three: Back to the Script and Beginning Work: Digging deeper into the script. Identifying design challenges for your area. Verifying information from the design meeting. Creating a deeper relationship with the script.

Step Four: Preliminary Research: Finding supporting visual and written material for the content and context of the world of the play. Looking at images to become inspired and informed.

Step Five: Additional Design Meetings: Sharing the information you've gathered with the production team. Showing images, asking more questions, developing an approach to the production, eventually sharing sketches and renderings.

> **Step Six: Preliminary Sketches:** Creating drawings of initial design ideas. Making variations. Using drawings as a visual shorthand to work out design choices. Presenting these ideas and drawings in design meetings.
>
> **Step Seven: Final Drawings and Renderings:** Creating finished, detailed drawings of design ideas. Coloring in the final, approved drawings. Sharing these drawings and renderings with the design team.

THE DESIGN PROCESS IN THE CLASSROOM

What if you don't have a director? What do you do then? If you are working on a script as a project, it is likely that you will not have the experience of an initial design meeting, although collaborative projects between design and directing classes do occur, often with very exciting results. What do you do instead?

Beginning design students should relish the chance to work without a director, for a number of reasons. Creating an effective, evocative, and engaging design is a challenging enough task for a young designer without adding in the additional considerations that a director brings to the mix. While having another person to discuss the play with and bounce ideas off of can be very useful, and is indeed the very nature of theatre as a collaborative art, you need to be able to come up with your own ideas first, without input. Developing your own process as an artist is just as important as learning to collaborate.

Working without a director provides the freedom to explore your own thoughts, try out different approaches, to take risks and to work without the potential limits and boundaries that can arise in future collaborations. A designer needs to be able to come up with ideas and be confident in presenting them. Working on unrealized projects in the supportive and safe environment of the classroom is a fundamental part of learning how to do this effectively. Enjoy the freedom of working independently now while you have it. Working without a director is not a handicap; it is a luxury that affords you the time you need to grow as a designer, and to become comfortable with your work and how you do it. Use the time working alone to develop your skills, and to create a way of working that promotes success. Find out what works for you and what does not. Learn how to budget your time efficiently. All of these things will make you a better collaborator.

Without a director, there are still ways to receive input on your work and your process. In a class situation, you might meet with your instructor to discuss the play and your ideas about it. This can be an opportunity for you to ask questions about the play, clarify things you do not understand, get feedback on your ideas and talk about the important elements you have discovered in the script. An instructor may give you suggestions about what to consider, things to research, or provide other constructive comments about your take on the play. Unlike a director, who is working with the designers towards creating a specific outcome, an instructor will support and guide you in the process, allowing you the freedom and the opportunity to make decisions and choices on your own, providing feedback to assist you along the way. You can also receive feedback from your peers, who can be excellent sources when it comes to the impact and effectiveness of your design choices. The process itself will essentially be the same. You will follow all the same steps as you work on your design, minus the regular design meetings. In the end, you still have a finished design for your portfolio with all the supporting research and preliminary sketches to show how you arrived at your design choices.

THE LANGUAGE OF THE DESIGN PROCESS

Character analysis: A list of the overall qualities related to the character in a chart format, such as social status, general mood, notes from the script, and design thoughts such as line, colors, and texture.

Costume plot: A chart that lists the changes required for each character in each scene and over the course of the play.

Detailed model: A scale model of the set that is fully painted, showing all the details and textures.

Final drawings: Drawings of a design showing all the fine details.

French scene chart: A diagram that shows the entrances and exits of each character in each scene, making it possible to keep track of who is on stage at any given moment.

Light renderings: Renderings that specifically show the desired effect of the lighting design on the set, costumes, and actors.

Paint elevations: Flat renderings of each scenic unit showing the details of the desired paint treatment.

Preliminary groundplan: An initial groundplan used to map out the locations of the various scenic components.

Preliminary sketches: Initial rough drawings that are used to sketch out your initial design ideas.

Primary research sources: Research taken directly from actual historical sources.

Production team: The creative team working on the design of the production, including the designers and the director. Sometimes referred to as the design team.

Rendering: A final drawing of a theatrical design including all major and minor details, in full color.

Research or response collage: A collection of images, words, and textures collaged together in a digital or two-dimensional format as a response to the play, its story, thematic content, or the ideas it presents.

Roughs: Another name for preliminary sketches.

Secondary research sources: Research taken from an intermediary source, rather than directly from a historical source.

Storyboards: A series of small sketches that show a progression of looks from one scene to another which are useful for scenic, lighting, and projection designers to show their design ideas for each scene or cue.

Thumbnails: Another name for preliminary sketches.

White model: A scale model of the set created in white card stock or foam core that shows the basic silhouette without the painted details of the design.

CHAPTER 21

THE ROLE OF THE CRITIQUE

WHAT IS A CRITIQUE?

Every person that has ever taken an art or design class of any kind has been through the process of having their work critiqued. Whether in a group, listening and responding to the observations of your peers, or one-on-one with your teacher, the critique can be one of the most challenging parts of arts education and one that can fill students with trepidation. Often a critique appears to be not only a criticism of your work but also an assessment of your personal worth as an artist. The impression is that a critique is very personal, and this is true. For those of us that work in creative fields, our artistic work is very close to our hearts and it can be difficult to separate criticism of the work from condemnation of our abilities as artists. Critique of our work can be so nerve-wracking that we do our best to avoid it at all costs. However, in theatre, receiving feedback on your contribution to the production is an integral part of the collaborative process, so it is essential that as a designer you learn not only how to take criticism well and use it to grow and improve your designs, but also how to give useful feedback to your colleagues so they can do the same and so that the production will benefit from the exchange.

A good critique process is more than criticism, and there is more to criticism itself than the relatively simple process of judgment—determining whether or not we like a design. Criticism is not a random discussion; it is instead an informed conversation about the work at hand with the intent of increasing our understanding and appreciation of the design and the choices that were made. A critique is a means towards an end. Through the process, observers can make a connection with a design. They come to understand the work and to recognize the components that contribute to that understanding as well

as those that detract from their comprehension. They also learn to appreciate the design and to identify the particular aspects that create that response. In a critique, a designer can receive feedback on the various characteristics of their work, which assists their creative process. Without feedback, there is no way to know if your design is truly effective. The entire production team receives feedback from the audience in every performance. In effect, the reaction of the audience is the ultimate barometer of whether or not the designers' choices were effective. But in the collaborative process, when the team is working together to come to a unified approach and make design decisions, who better to give this needed information than your fellow designers and colleagues?

THE CRITIQUE PROCESS

The critique process can be broken down into four steps: description, analysis, interpretation, and evaluation/judgment. These individual steps are taken from the techniques of formal analysis in the visual arts, but tailored and adjusted here for theatrical design.

Description

Description is discussing the visual aspects of the design without value judgments, analysis, or interpretation. It answers the question "what do you see?" The various elements that can make up a description include:

*   The *form* of the design, whether sets, lights, costume, props, sound, projections, puppetry, or other design area.

- The *intended medium* of the work—clay, stone, steel, paint, fabrics, leather, metals, sound effects, music (or the intended illusion of that material)—and the *actual medium*, along with the associated techniques or tools used. In theatre we know that it is unlikely that a stone wall will actually be made of stone, instead it will be made to *look* like stone, so we need to consider the desired effect or impression the designer hopes to convey as part of description.

- The *size* and *scale* of the design, including the relationship between the viewer and the individual elements as well as the actors and the individual components. Given that actors will inhabit the stage space, scale and size have a direct effect on the perception of the human body as well as the delineation of space. Scale also has an effect on the viewer and the context of the play. There can be an expectation regarding different genres and the scale of the design elements and this can have a direct effect on the perception of space and how the audience reacts to the design.

- *Individual elements* or general *shapes* used within the composition, such as an architectural structural system (like a Gothic arch) in a set, or an arrangement of shapes within the design, such as patterns in a costume or the melodic line in a sound cue.

- Description of the dominant *axis* whether vertical, diagonal, horizontal, etc.

- Description of *line*, including what types of line are used (contour, outline, implied, etc.) and the qualities of line present in the design (jagged, smooth, thick, thin, soft, hard, etc.).

- Description of how line is used to describe *shape*, *space*, and *volume*. This should include distinguishing between lines within individual objects and the lines that dominate the composition and carve out space.

- *Relationships between shapes.* Do they overlap; are they large, small, organic, geometrical, etc.?

- Description of the *color* and the overall *color scheme*. Is it predominately cool, warm, open, analogous, monochromatic, etc.?

- *Texture* of the various surfaces, whether real or implied.

- *Style* of the design. Is it realistic, stylized, romanticized, operatic, Brechtian, abstract, minimal, etc.?

- *Time period* of the design.

- *Context* of the design, such as the intended act, scene, or moment of the play. Is the design based on aspects of a culture outside of our own, and do we need to know about that culture in order to effectively understand and appreciate the work? The same question can be asked if the work is based on the style of a particular artist or historical aesthetic convention.

Analysis

Analysis is a step beyond description. It is the process of determining what the individual visual elements suggest and deciding *why* the designer used those features to convey specific ideas. It answers the questions "how did the designer do it?", "what elements did the designer choose?" and "how did they arrange them?" The various elements that constitute analysis include:

- The determination of the *intended location, character, act, scene,* or *moment.*

- Selection of the most *distinctive features* or characteristics of the design, whether that is line, shape, color, texture, value, etc.

- Analysis of the *elements and principles of design* in the composition and how they are used. Is the composition stable, rhythmic, symmetrical, harmonious, geometric, varied, chaotic, horizontally or vertically oriented, etc.?

- A discussion of how the elements or structural system contribute to the *appearance* or the *function* of the design. This can include speculation on style and how that enhances or detracts from the overall impression of the design.

- An examination of the use of *value* and the role of *color*. Is it high or low contrast, illogical or seamless, warm or cool, monochromatic or analogous, symbolic, suggestive, etc.?

- A discussion of the treatment of *space* and *volume* within the work, both real and illusory, including the use of the various types of perspective. Is the space compact, deep, shallow, naturalistic, random, fantastical, etc.?

- The depiction of *movement* and how it is achieved. This could also include the potential for movement within the design. Is there a sense of flow throughout, or is motion directed in a specific direction or deliberately cut off at chosen locations?

- The effect of the particular *medium* or media used. Does the medium mesh seamlessly with the design and the style of the object, or does it create tension? For example, consider the different effects of a ballgown made of stiff silk and one made of fur or burlap.

- Your perceptions of *balance*, *proportion*, and *scale*. How are they employed within the design and what effect does this have on the overall visual impression? Does the use of these visual components serve to create unity and harmony, or tension and divisiveness?

Interpretation

Interpretation establishes the broader context for the design you are critiquing. It answers the questions "why did the designer make these choices?" and "what does it mean or express?" Here, critique looks at what the design communicates to you, the observer. In theatrical design, this of course relates to how the design supports the needs of the play, but that can also include how the design works in terms of political, social, cultural, or intellectual history and whether or not those things are communicated to the audience. Interpretation may involve looking at multiple sets that are part of one production, multiple lighting or sound cues, or the transitions presented by costumes throughout the design in addition to looking at each item individually. It may also include a discussion of the political, social, intellectual, and cultural events that surrounded the designer and the author of the play itself and how they inform the design choices being made. The various elements that constitute interpretation include:

- The *main idea*, *concept*, or the *meaning* of the design. Here you are looking for the overall conceptual thread that ties the various individual parts of the design together.

- An *interpretative statement*. Can you express what you think the design is about in one sentence?

- *Evidence* that supports your take on the design. What supporting materials inside or outside of the design support your interpretation?

Evaluation and Judgment

Evaluation and judgment consist of deciding if the design is effective for the given play. Judgment answers the question, "is it a good design?" The elements of judgment include:

- *Criteria*—what criteria do you think are most appropriate for judging the design? Are they visual, contextual, or do they include other factors? Are they based on your own contextual bias—i.e., what you bring to the process of observation and evaluation—or are they external?

- *Evidence*—what evidence inside or outside the design supports your criterion? What have you found within the design that supports your conclusion?

- *Judgment*— based on the criteria and evidence, what is your judgment about the quality of the design? Is it good or bad? Are the designs effective? Can you see and comprehend what the designer wanted to communicate, or are those messages not coming across?

- *What does it mean to you?* Are you able to make a personal connection to the design? How does it affect you emotionally, intellectually and as an informed observer?

GUIDELINES FOR A SUCCESSFUL CRITIQUE

When preparing for a class critique or getting ready to show your work to the rest of the design team, it can be useful to figure out what *you* need from the critique. What do you hope to learn about your designs through the feedback process? Are you looking for a response to form alone, or do you want a response to content as well? Do you want assistance with a particular design challenge, an evaluation of individual elements, or a complete assessment of your designs for the show as a whole? Being clear about your expectations makes it possible to ask the questions you really need to have answered.

- *Listen.* In order to be able to grow as a designer, to refine and hone your craft and your ability to create effective designs you must be able to listen to what your colleagues and peers have to say in a critique. A critique is a unique form of dialogue. It is crucial that each participant be able to express their point of view without qualification in order to maximize the benefit of the process. Qualification includes such phrases as, "well, this is just my opinion," which can undercut what you have to say. This does not mean that debate is not usual or discouraged. Some of the most insightful comments about design are born out of heated discussions.

- *Critique does not mean the design is bad*. Rather, it is a meant to be a detailed analysis of the work that is presented and an honest discussion of what is and what is not working or successful. It should reinforce the positive qualities of the design as well as point out those aspects that detract from the overall effectiveness or which could use improvement. The point of a critique is to make better work, either in your revisions of the current design or in future work. Comments should reflect that goal. An evaluation of design work should not be a criticism of the designer.

- *Be specific.* Describe what you see. Do any adjectives come to mind? What visual elements affect your description? Is there one part of the design that stands out more than another? Does the technique of the design have an effect on what you see? Can you speak with certainty about any of the things you can see in the design? Is there a dominant style in the design? If there are multiple images in the design, can you compare one to the others? Do they look like they belong in the same show? Do they all work together, or do they struggle against each other? Analyze what you see. How are the individual visual elements being used? How do they affect the overall composition of the design? How does the pose in a costume rendering affect the costume itself? Is a sound cue long enough? Interpret what you see. Can you identify meaning in the design? How is this meaning expressed? Are you able to determine a difference between what was intended and what is actually communicated by the design?

- *Explain why you feel the way you do.* "It's nice," "I like it," or a simple thumbs up or down are not acceptable responses. Explain your observations. If, for example, you like the use of color in the design be clear about *why*. The phrase "I may not know art, but I know what I like" no longer applies to your methods of inquiry. Critique is a rigorous process where you and others look deeply at your work and dissect it piece by piece. Through this critical forum you will be able to take your work apart and put it back together again, and make it better than it was before. What personal context and perspectives do you bring to your interpretation? Biographical? Feminist? Comparative? Formalist? Archetypal? Psychoanalytic? Can you identify any cultural or socio-political influences that exist in the design?

- *Is this a successful design?* What is the internal context of the design? In other words, is it relevant to the play? How does the design support the technical needs of the script? Does it help to tell the story and reveal the characters?

Is the design original? Does it make you think? Has the design made you see the play in a new or different way, or revealed aspects of the play you had not considered before? Why do you feel the design is or is not successful? What criteria do you bring to your evaluation? Be very detailed and precise in your explanations.

- *Respect your colleagues.* This should go without saying. Your colleagues are your collaborators and peers and you should treat them the way you want to be treated. However, leave your ego at the door. The forum of a critique requires that each person speak openly about the issues at hand, and not only must you be willing to say what you think about the work of others, you have to be prepared to hear criticism that might be harsh about your own work. Remember that feedback offers an opportunity for growth, to make your designs better and this is true for your colleagues as well.

THE LANGUAGE OF CRITIQUE

Analysis: The process of determining what the individual visual elements suggest and deciding *why* the designer used those features to convey specific ideas. It answers the questions "how did the designer do it?", "what elements did the designer choose?" and "how did they arrange them?"

Description: Discussing the visual aspects of the design without value judgments, analysis, or interpretation. It answers the question "what do you see?"

Evaluation and judgment: Deciding if the design is effective for the given play. Judgment answers the question "is it a good design?"

Interpretation: Establishes the broader context for the design you are critiquing. It answers the questions "why did the designer make these choices?" and "what does it mean or express?"

CHAPTER 22

DRAWING AS OUR COMMON LANGUAGE

WHAT IS DRAWING?

Drawing is the creation of an image, usually on paper, using lines as the primary visual component. It is a familiar and intimate art form. Familiar because almost everyone over the age of two draws or has drawn at some point in their lives. Intimate because it is a personal way of recording the world around us, of capturing what we see on paper, and it can be done anywhere, at any time. Drawing is also one of the primary ways in which designers communicate their ideas and, as such, it is a skill they need to master to some degree.

Drawing is perhaps the most direct of all arts. The lines and marks laid down on the paper reflect the movement and skill of the artist, their hand and arm. We feel the presence of the artist when looking at a drawing. This aspect is different from the qualities of the lines themselves as a design element. In addition to all the qualities line is able to express, it can also be an evocative representation of an individual artist's unique style. Even if drawing is not the main medium an artist uses in their work, or the intended final product, most will use drawing for a number of different reasons. Designers are working in the same manner as any visual artist, using drawing as a powerful method to communicate their ideas to the director and their collaborators. Even a sound designer may use drawing to show the layout and arrangement of sound sources and distribution patterns.

HOW DRAWING CAN BE USED BY A DESIGNER

Personal Notation

A designer may study forms and make sketches in preparation for rendering them in another medium, or as part of planning a design for visual research. Many designers keep a sketchbook as a visual diary, making sketches of interesting objects they see during their day for later use. This process can be part of creating a personal visual library to be used for inspiration as well as simple practice to maintain drawing skills.

Preliminary Sketches or Rough Drawings

Designers often make several **preliminary drawings** or **rough sketches** in order to work out the composition of a set, costume, or lighting composition before they actually begin to do a final drawing and render it in another medium. They may use drawing to explore various design elements: composition, pose, gesture, volume, mass, or variations in the design. In this way, they can think visually on paper and create multiple options for the director. Working in this manner also helps to refine and edit your ideas.

Detail Drawings

A designer may need to make **detail drawings** of their designs as part of the production process. Detail drawings are comprehensive drawings, usually in scale, that provide additional information about the appearance of the design. A set designer may do a series of **front elevations** for individual elements of the scenery, properties, or the entire set to scale, which show all of the scenic elements in detail along with measurements. They may do a detailed black-and-white scale drawing of the set. Further **technical drawings**, which serve as blueprints for the construction of the scenery and properties, are executed by the technical director. A costume designer may add drawings that provide construction details to their renderings, or provide

FIGURE 22-1   *Sketchbook/research drawings by Kaoime E. Malloy*

FIGURE 22-2   *Rough drawings—Much Ado about Nothing, by William Shakespeare, costume design by Kaoime E. Malloy, Grinnell College*

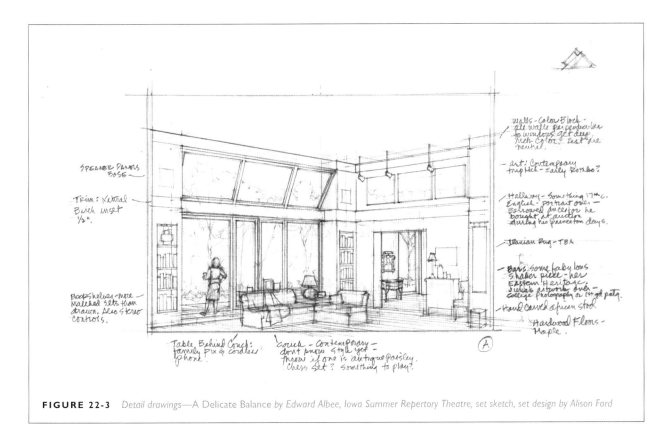

FIGURE 22-3   *Detail drawings—A Delicate Balance by Edward Albee, Iowa Summer Repertory Theatre, set sketch, set design by Alison Ford*

such drawings separately. A lighting designer may do their own **light plot**, a technical drawing that conveys all of the information that a lighting crew will need to hang, focus, and circuit the instruments. Sometimes these types of drawings are collected and considered works of art in their own right.

Final Drawings

For the designer, **final drawings** are an artistic presentation of their designs in a completed form without color. All of the final details are included in the image, ready to be colored with the designer's media of choice.

THE MECHANICS OF DRAWING

The beginning stages of drawing education always begin with techniques that foster the recreation of realism. At first glance, this may seem counterintuitive. After all, some of the greatest artists of the past two centuries have worked outside the confines of realism. Many great stage designers have also pushed the boundary of realism beyond its limits, producing renderings that are vibrant and dynamic yet highly stylized. If it is good enough for them, why not for us as well? What we have to realize is that an artist chooses to express themselves in a preferred style in order to present their ideas in the most

communicative and effective way possible. Picasso and van Gogh also possessed excellent realistic drawing skills, which they perfected long before embarking on the work for which they are recognized. Even they understood the value of developing technical skills in drawing; they simply preferred to express themselves in a different style. The techniques that are learned and the abilities that are developed when learning how to draw realistically form the basis of drawing in general, and will serve you no matter what you seek to put on paper, regardless of the style.

As theatrical designers, our drawings also have a goal that an artist working in a different medium may not always share. Our drawings need to be **representational**. Rough sketches, thumbnails, conceptual, and final drawings all need to present an accurate illustration of what the final set, costume, prop, makeup, projection, or lighting composition will look like onstage. In order to do this effectively, a degree of realism is required. This does not mean that drawings cannot have style or an individual voice. All artists will develop their unique visual style. It means that a designer needs to keep in mind that their drawings are not just representations of an idea, but also serve as blueprints for the respective shops that will bring those ideas to life. They need to be clear enough to provide answers when the designer is not present. Providing realistic detail ensures clear visual communication along with the designer's artistic interpretation. Shape, light, shadow, and perspective are the foundations of representational drawing.

Although it takes time, effort, and practice to master the techniques associated with the various forms of drawing media, one of the biggest hurdles in learning to draw effectively is learning how to see. Drawing requires careful observation of your subject and then drawing what is *actually* there—rather than drawing what you *think* is there or what your mind tells you *should* be there. Learning to see is about trusting the information conveyed to you by your eyes. Part of this is noting the way light moves over a subject and how it is reflected back to the viewer, recognizing the pattern it makes and how it defines the object's shape and mass. Another part is the understanding of how to translate a three-dimensional object into a two-dimensional shape in order to transfer it to paper. Still another part is technical; knowing how to create the illusion of three-dimensional shape on a two-dimensional surface. The final component, is realizing that even the most complex object and composition can be broken down into a framework that is made up of only four basic shapes; and if you can draw those four shapes, then you can draw anything, from observation, memory, or imagination.

LEARNING TO SEE

Learning to see involves two basic steps: letting go of what your mind tells you about an object you are drawing so that you can pay attention to what you are actually seeing, and cultivating your observational skills. If an object is familiar, it can be even more difficult to override the information that our brain tries to tell us. Relying on what you know about your subject rather than what your eyes notice about it can lead to mistakes in proportion, perspective, scale, and other details. In order to accurately draw an object, you have to learn to forget what it *is* so that you can concentrate on what you *see*. Once you forget what your subject is, you can instead focus on the shapes that make up the composition, dividing it into smaller, more manageable sections that will be easier to draw. Doing this also allows you to observe the relationships between the individual parts of a composition and within separate objects, understanding how they share edges and interact with positive and negative space.

TRANSLATING A THREE-DIMENSIONAL OBJECT TO A FLAT SURFACE

When we begin to draw, we initially begin by sketching an outline of the forms we see or wish to record on the paper. **Sketching** is a quick method of drawing and while it can be

quite evocative, using very expressive lines that create beautiful images, a sketch generally is not very realistic. We live in a three-dimensional world, and what we admire in realistic works of art is the illusion of depth and three-dimensional form on a two-dimensional surface. Shading—modeling form with **light** and **shadow** to create volume—is what produces this illusion and in order for that to happen, the outlines around an object have to be eliminated. Creating this illusion may not always be the primary goal of a theatrical drawing as a designer may choose instead to employ a range of stylization to convey their ideas. However, they still need to understand how to convey volume and the suggestion of three-dimensional forms to create a representational image.

THE ANATOMY OF LIGHT

Creating the illusion of three-dimensional forms convincingly on paper is based on both the construction of an accurate outline sketch using the principles of perspective and an understanding of how light moves over an object and is reflected back to the viewer. Using highlight and shadow to model the subject and moving past shape to create volume defines the form in three-dimensional space. The way light strikes an object and is reflected back to the viewer can be divided into several distinct patterns, all of which contribute to the illusion of mass and volume.

- The **light source** is where the illumination hitting the subject is coming from. This may be a lamp or a lighting instrument, ambient or diffuse light from a window, or direct light from the sun. The light source has direction, angle, and distance from a subject and how it strikes an object has a direct effect on our perception of its form.

- The **highlight** is the brightest amount of reflected light striking an object and is created on the part of the form directly in the path of the light source. The brighter the light, the closer it is to the object or the more reflective the object's surface, the brighter and more distinct the highlight becomes. On a very reflective surface, it may even be possible to see the shape of the light source on the object. The highlight is always the lightest value in a drawing.

- **Midtones** are the transitional values between the highlight and the core shadow. They are created by light reflecting off the object, but demonstrate that this part of the object is beginning to move away from the light source.

- The **core shadow** occurs on the form where the reflected light ends and the shadow begins. It is the darkest

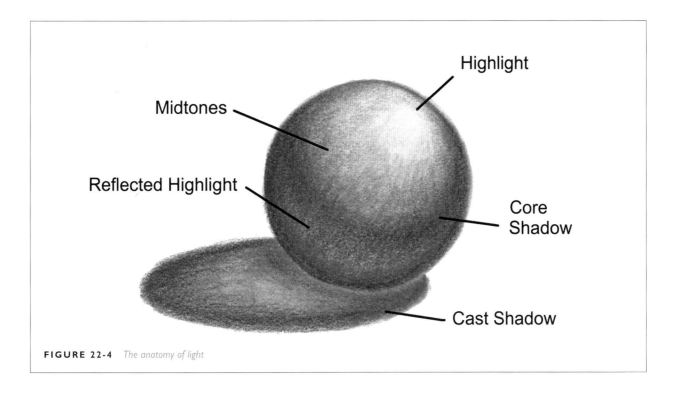

Highlight

Midtones

Reflected Highlight

Core
Shadow

Cast Shadow

FIGURE 22-4   *The anatomy of light*

area of value and the part of the object that can be the most challenging to get right. It can appear counterintuitive to put a dark shadow in the middle of your subject. Many beginning artists will place the darkest shadow at the edge of their subject, but this will only flatten the form rather than create volume.

- **Reflected light** is the light that is reflected off the surface underneath an object, which then strikes the form underneath the core shadow. It is a complementary highlight to the core shadow, rounding off the form of your subject, but should never be as bright as your highlight. It should be subtle and soft. Think of it as moonlight rather than the sunlight of the light source.

- A **cast shadow** is the shadow created by the object in the path of the light coming from the light source. Adding a cast shadow to a drawing increases the sense of realism by adding additional depth. A cast shadow is like an orbit moving around an object, back and forth through space. If it only extends out behind the form, it will flatten the image and ruin the effect. Strong light casts equally strong shadows. Diffuse light creates a softer, more diffuse shadow. It is important to remember that a cast shadow possesses midtones as well as darker values to create depth and that there should be a difference in value between the front and the back of the shadow, based on the location of the light source.

- **Backlight** is a light source striking the object in a drawing from behind. While not absolutely necessary in a drawing, backlight can provide a sense of the object continuing beyond what the viewer can see, completing its shape and mass and increasing the illusion of three-dimensional form.

THE FOUR BASIC SHAPES

Part of learning to see is cultivating the ability to break down even the most complex composition and objects into recognizable shapes. Doing this divides a large drawing into a smaller, more manageable framework. It also speeds up your drawing method by creating a kind of visual shorthand that serves to simplify the process of committing information to the paper. There are four basic geometric shapes that form the fundamental building blocks of any composition—spheres, cubes, cylinders, and cones. These are simple shapes that anyone can draw with practice and using them as a basis for your compositions will allow you to create sketches quickly and create realistic compositions.

Compare the photograph of the armchair with the drawing of the chair in in Figure 22.6. At first glance, the chair might appear to be a complex and daunting shape. But the simple outline drawing shows that the chair is in fact a combination of simple shapes. While on first glance the chair seems to be a complex form, the drawing shows that it can

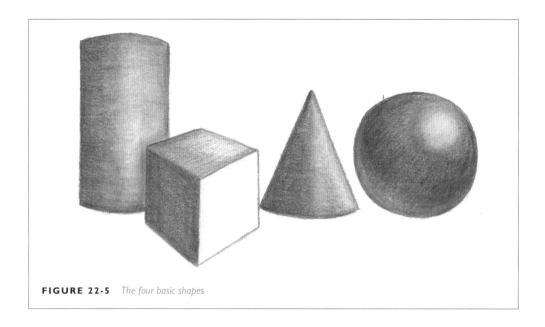

FIGURE 22-5 *The four basic shapes*

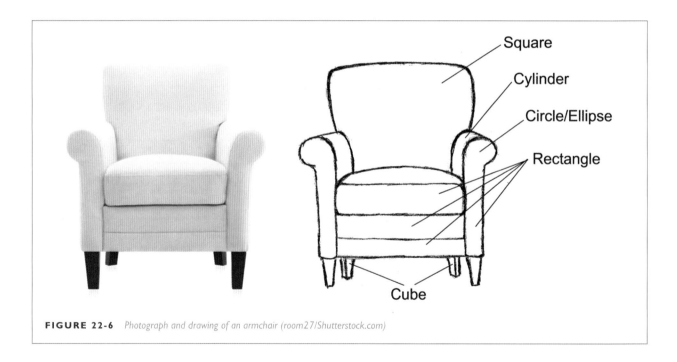

FIGURE 22-6 *Photograph and drawing of an armchair (room27/Shutterstock.com)*

be broken down into a series of smaller, readily identifiable shapes. By focusing on the geometric shapes that form the underlying structure of your subject, drawing becomes simpler and easier.

Spheres

The sphere is one of the simplest of geometric forms, yet it presents several challenges in terms of rendering it effectively in three dimensions on paper. Learning to draw a sphere convincingly, creating the illusion of three-dimensional form, is an excellent way to practice the techniques for creating light and value patterns. This will also make it possible for you to draw other shapes that are based on the sphere. Once you can render a simple sphere realistically, you will then be able to recognize them in more complex shapes and compositions.

Observing a Sphere

The basic outline of a sphere is a circle. Value and shading must be added in order to give a sphere dimension. Linear perspective is of little use in rendering a sphere, as it is the only shape that is not affected by your eye level or the horizon line. Instead, your perception of it is based on the direction of the light source. Whether you view it from above, below or the side, a sphere always looks the same. Spheres and ovoids form the basis for many other forms, including parts of furniture and architecture, heads and faces, and the joints of the human figure. When using a sphere as the basis for drawing an object, you start by sketching in the outline and then modeling the sphere as required for the light source in the drawing. Once the basic form is created, details can be added as needed.

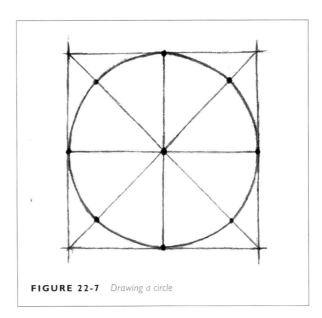

FIGURE 22-7 *Drawing a circle*

Exercise: Modeling a Sphere

In order to draw a sphere, it is essential to develop the ability to draw a reasonably accurate circle freehand. It is certainly possibly to draw a circle with a template, and there are some types of theatrical drawings that require that kind of accuracy, but not all of the drawing you will do as a designer will demand that degree of rigor. One way to draw a sphere freehand is to begin with a square. Begin by finding the midpoint along each line of the square and connecting them with light strokes. Lightly draw lines diagonally across the square from the upper to lower corners. Using the intersection of the lines as a midpoint, make a set of marks along the diagonal lines to either side to mark the length of the sides of the square. Then draw a circle inside the square that touches all of the points that you have marked and then adjust the shape as needed. Another way is to start by holding the pencil in a relaxed grip, and then trace a circle on the paper with light, multiple strokes, going over the lines several times. By doing this, you can take the fear of drawing a circle the "right" way and pick out the final shape from the light lines you have created.

To add volume to the sphere, modeling the form with highlights and shadows, first pick a direction for the light source and indicate it on the paper with an arrow, so you can remember while you are drawing. Next, add in a general overall light tone to the sphere with your pencil or charcoal, blending with a **tortillion** or paper stump. Carefully erase out a round shape for the area of the brightest highlight and smoothly blend the edges. Then draw in a darker value for the middle value tones halfway down the sphere. Remember that you are working on a round form so your marks need to follow and reinforce that three-dimensional shape. They cannot simply go straight across and support the form; they must

follow the curve of the sphere. The darkest values can then be placed along the bottom of the sphere, again following the curve. The next step is to carefully blend the values, creating a smooth transition between the tones from light to dark. Remember that light continues to travel around an object, so even at the lightest value near the light source, there will be a line of shadow that serves to carry the eye around the form. Some light will also be reflected off the surface the sphere rests on, creating a reflected highlight in the darkest shadow. Using an eraser, carefully remove some of the shadow, following the lower curve of the ball and then blend the edges in with the tortillion.

To create the cast shadow underneath the sphere, begin by drawing a loose ellipse underneath the sphere, extending away from the light source. The shadow of the form is distorted because it is closer to your eye level. Although there will be less contrast between tones in the cast shadow, there will still be a range of value. Start by filling in the ellipse with a middle tone and blending it throughout the shape and up to the sphere. Be sure that the value of the cast shadow is lighter than the value of the sphere. Add darker values to the edge of the ellipse and blend, leaving a lighter area of reflected highlight near the sphere.

Cubes

A cube is a box consisting of six equal sides that meet at right angles. For the purpose of their use in creating compositions, boxes with unequal sides—rectangular objects—are also considered cubes. Because the appearance of a cube is altered as the angle at which you view it changes or when your eye level moves, the principles of linear perspective are important

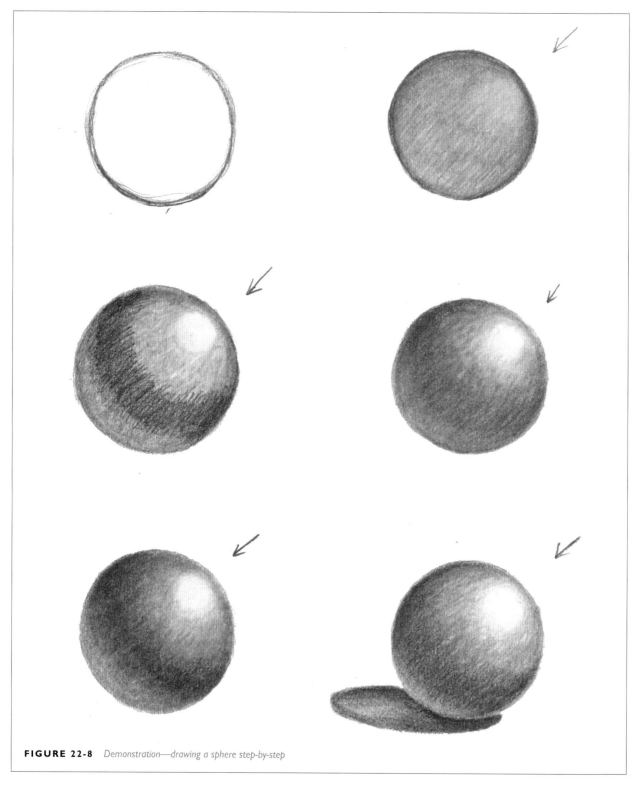

FIGURE 22-8   *Demonstration—drawing a sphere step-by-step*

tools that must be used to render it realistically. Whether you use one- or two-point perspective is determined by the angle at which you are viewing the cube. When using a cube as a basis for drawing another object, you start by creating a basic cube and then modifying it as needed for the proper angle and view. After that, volume and detail can be added as required.

Observing a Cube

Although a cube is made up of six sides of equal dimensions, those sides will never look the same. The sides of a cube will appear to be different based on the angle from which you view it. By placing a direct light source on the cube, its volume will be revealed and defined through the values of light and shadow. As with all forms, the edges of the cube are defined by the boundaries of the light and dark values of the planes rather than by outlines. Outlines are simply a visual tool to enable understanding of form—they do not exist in reality. The greater the contrast between the values on the planes of the cube, the more those intersecting edges will appear to come towards the viewer, while lower contrasting edges appear to recede into the background, providing depth.

Exercise: Modeling a Cube in One- and Two-Point Perspective

To begin drawing a cube freehand you can use a ruler to establish your lines and ensure that they are straight, but it is not required. This is more critical when drawing a large cube than a small one, where the chance of the lines becoming crooked over a longer distance is greater. Begin by drawing the lines that will set the angle of viewing for the cube in either one- or two-point perspective. This will determine whether your cube will have one or two vanishing points.

When drawing a cube in one point perspective, you will initially draw a square parallel to the horizon line. Take time to make sure the sides are even in length and that they come together at 90-degree angles. Make a mark in the center of the horizon line. This is your vanishing point. Using a ruler, draw a light line from each corner of the square to the vanishing point. These lines will dictate the shape of the sides of the cube that you can see in this view. Draw a line that connects the vanishing lines above the top of the square to form the top of the cube at your desired width and connect the vanishing line on the side with the one leading from the bottom of the square. Then connect the smaller lines that mark the edges between the planes of the top and side of the cube.

To create a cube in two-point perspective you will initially establish the angle of the bottom of the cube in order to set the two vanishing points on the horizon line. Draw in the horizon line above the space. Using a ruler, draw a light line from each of the angles of the cube out to the horizon and make a mark where they intersect. These are the vanishing points. Next, extend a vertical line up from the intersection of the cube's bottom angle to the desired height. This establishes where the two planes of the cube that can be seen in the angle of view intersect. Use your ruler to connect the top of the vertical line to each of the two vanishing points to establish the top edge of each of the two planes of the cube. You will now need to draw two more vertical lines to create the edges of the cube between the vanishing lines. If the cube is

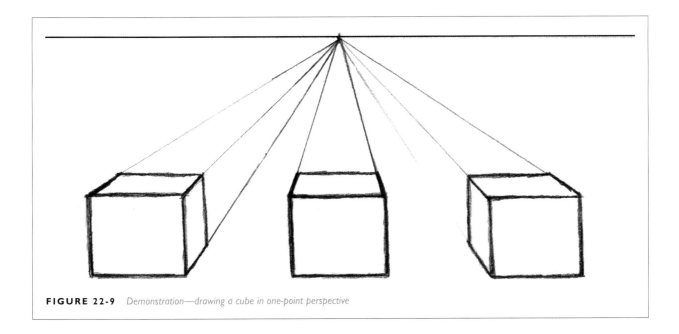

FIGURE 22-9 *Demonstration—drawing a cube in one-point perspective*

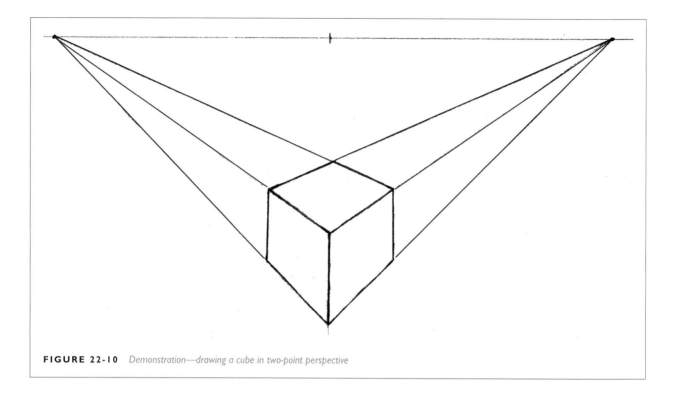

FIGURE 22-10   *Demonstration—drawing a cube in two-point perspective*

in the center of the drawing, both of these sides will be equal. However, if it shifted to the left or right, keep in mind that you will see more of the side closest to the center. Once you have set these edges, you will then draw a vanishing line from the tops of these vertical lines to the two vanishing points in order to define the top plane of the cube. In two-point perspective, these vanishing lines cross over each other, as they do in Figure 22.10. Once all these lines are in place, you can now go over the lines as needed to fill in the three-dimensional form of the cube.

As with adding volume to a sphere, you will want to indicate the direction of your light source with an arrow. Lightly sketch one in to help you remember where the light is coming from. In Figure 22.11, the light source is coming from the upper right hand corner. The top plane of the cube will receive the brightest light and so retains the lightest value. You can either leave it uncolored if using white or light paper, or fill it in with a light value, using a tortillion to blend the tone evenly across the plane. With the light source in this position, the right side of the cube will receive a middle range of light. Use your pencil to color in a middle value tone, making sure you maintain a crisp edge between the planes on the top of the cube and the front of the cube. Blend to create an even surface. The plane facing the viewer receives the least amount of light and will therefore be the darkest in value. Use your pencil to color in a tone that is

darker than the one used for the side, carefully maintaining crisp edges between the planes of the cube and then blending for an even surface. Once you have these three values in place, you can go back in with your pencil and add darker tones to the edges of the cube where the planes are furthest from the light to add more depth. To create the cast shadow coming from the cube, begin by drawing a line that extends from the furthest point on the bottom plane at roughly a forty five degree angle. As the front plane of the cube becomes more parallel with the horizon line, the shallower this angle becomes. Next, draw a line that is slightly less than parallel with the back plane of the cube, extending out towards the line you just drew. The cast shadow should echo the shape of the object, but the direction of the shadow, its length, and the hardness all depend on the angle and strength of the light hitting the cube. For the purpose of this exercise, you will be creating a soft shadow. Fill in the space between the lines with a dark value, letting the edges be soft rather than hard. Use the tortillion to blend and create an even tone, feathering out the edges of the shadow away from the cube. Once you have created the main bulk of the shadow, use your pencil to draw a dark line around the base of the cube to show that that shadow is wrapping around the object, which will enhance the illusion of depth and realism by anchoring the cube to the surface on which it sits.

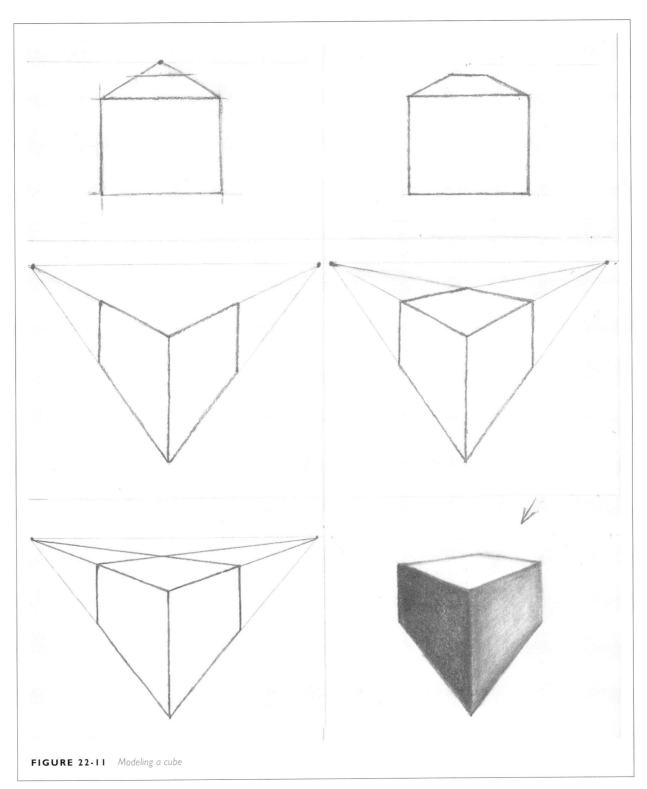

FIGURE 22-11   *Modeling a cube*

Rectangular Objects and Proportion

Like a cube, a rectangular object has six sides, but unlike a cube, these sides are not all the same size. The sides of a rectangular object may be tall or short, narrow or wide. There is an infinite number of variations. Observing a rectangular box requires that you pay attention to the height of the rectangle and how that affects the appearance of the top side of the box. Remember that in linear perspective all parallel lines meet at the same vanishing point, so both the top and bottom planes of the box will have the same vanishing points. When the top of a rectangular object is above the horizon line the vanishing point will be below the top of the box and the edge of the top plane will angle down towards the horizon line. This defies what your mind knows about the box, so you have to trust what you see in order to draw it realistically.

Exercise: Modeling a Rectangular Object

As with drawing the cube, drawing a rectangular object begins with determining the angle of view and then lightly drawing in the horizon line. Sketch in the angle of the base of the box and then extend those lines to the horizon line using a ruler. Place a mark where they meet the horizon line to establish the vanishing points for either one- or two-point perspective. Next, draw a vertical line up from the intersection of the box's bottom angle to the desired height. For this exercise, do not extend this line above the horizon line. Use your ruler to connect the top of the vertical line to each of the two vanishing points to establish the top edge of each of the two planes of the box. Now, draw two more vertical lines to create the edges of the box between the vanishing lines at the desired width. For the purpose of this exercise, the box has been placed to one side of the center line of the image, so that the two sides will not be equal. Remember that the plane closer to the center line will be wider. Once you have set these edges, you will then draw a vanishing line from the tops of these vertical lines to the two vanishing points in order to

define the top plane of the box. Remember that in two-point perspective, these vanishing lines will cross over each other. Once the boundaries of the form have been created, you can then go over them with your pencil in preparation for adding volume with value.

Modeling a rectangle follows the same steps as modeling a cube. Determine a direction for the light source and sketch in an arrow to remind you while you are drawing. The plane that receives the most light will have the lightest value. The side of the box below the direct light source receives less light and therefore has a darker value. The side of the box furthest away from the light has the darkest value. Fill in each plane with the appropriate level of value and then blend with a tortillion to create a smooth tone. Be sure to maintain crisp edges between the three planes in order to create the illusion of a hard edge. Then, you can add in darker values at the receding edges to assist in creating the illusion of depth. The cast shadow created by a rectangular object will be similar to one made by a cube. The main difference is that the shadow will be longer and extend farther behind the box in order to mirror the shape of the object. Begin as you would for a cube, drawing a line out from the corner furthest from the light source. Draw another that leads from the hidden corner of the bottom plane directly opposite, parallel to the first and then fill in the area with a dark value. Blend to even out the tone, using a tortillion to soften and feather the edge of the shadow.

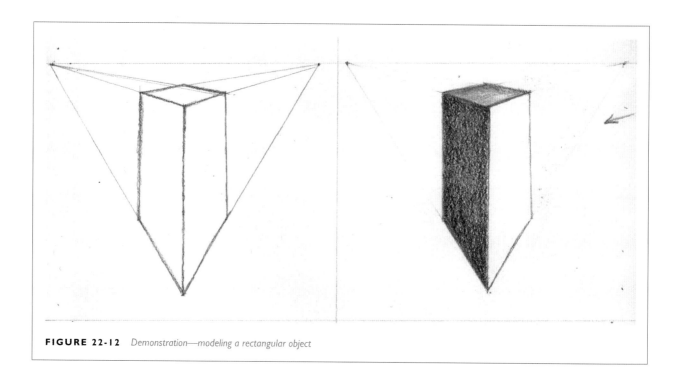

FIGURE 22-12   *Demonstration—modeling a rectangular object*

Cylinders

A cylinder is a three-dimensional form consisting of two circular or elliptical shapes connected by a plane that follows the curves of both shapes. Cylinders have parallel sides and can be short or tall, narrow or wide. Many forms are purely cylindrical in shape, such as a roll of paper towels or architectural columns, and others are based on cylinders, such as coffee cups, bannisters, the arms of chairs, and the neck, legs, arms, fingers, and toes of the human figure. Cylinders combine aspects of both spheres and cubes. Like a cube, realistic rendering of a cylinder requires the use of perspective techniques, because the shape of the form will change depending on the angle of viewing and eye level. In addition to the way the parallel lines are affected by linear perspective, you must also understand how the two circular planes on the ends of the cylinder are affected by foreshortening and elliptical perspective.

If you look at a circle from directly above or directly below, the size and the outline of the shape does not change. But, as the edge of the circle comes closer to our eye level, either by raising or lowering it, or by tipping it away from us, the circle will become an ellipse, flattening until finally it becomes nothing more than a line. You can observe this effect directly by placing a soda can on end in front of your eyes and slowly turning it away from you. Note how the circular top of the can slowly appears to change shape until it finally it is just a flat line. This is essentially the same visual effect that takes place on the top of a cube or rectangular object in one-point perspective when the angle of perception is changed. The difference is that there are no parallel lines to follow to a vanishing point, but a square or rectangle can be used to help determine the boundaries of a circle when a cylinder is viewed from the side. When using a cylinder as the basis for drawing other objects, start with a basic cylinder in the view you require and then modify it as needed, giving it volume and then adding detail.

Observing a Cylinder

The biggest obstacle to accurately drawing a cylindrical object is the knowledge we already possess about cylinders as a three-dimensional form. This understanding will often try to influence your drawing in favor of what you think you know over what you are actually seeing. A cylinder always contains two ellipses that need to be rendered; one on the top and one on the bottom. You will only see the front half of the bottom ellipse unless the cylinder is transparent. Because of where your eye level sits in relation to the cylinder, how much what you see of each ellipse will be different and the curve of the two ellipses will not look the same. This will be more apparent in a tall cylinder than a short one, where the distance between the top

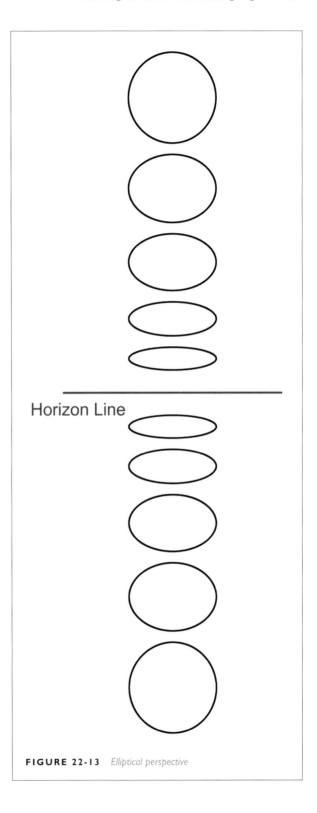

FIGURE 22-13 *Elliptical perspective*

and the bottom is greater. Just as in the example of the effect of foreshortening on a circle, the top ellipse is flatter because it is closer to your eye level.

When a cylindrical object is on its side with one end closer to the viewer, drawing it is more complicated. Both the

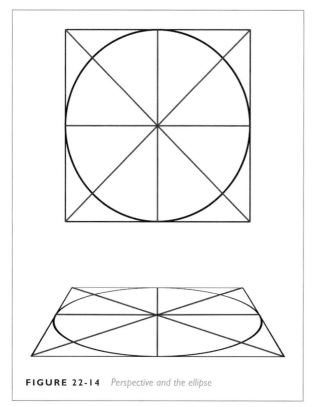

FIGURE 22-14 *Perspective and the ellipse*

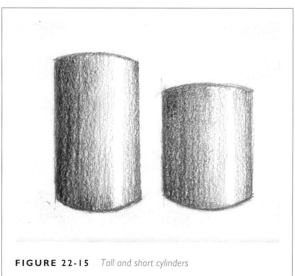

FIGURE 22-15 *Tall and short cylinders*

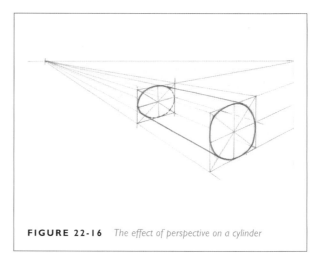

FIGURE 22-16 *The effect of perspective on a cylinder*

Exercise: Modeling a Cylinder

In order to draw cylinders you need to develop the ability to draw a reasonably accurate ellipse by hand. As with drawing a sphere, holding the pencil lightly and using it to trace a loose ellipse shape by creating lines with light pressure, going over them several times, makes it possible for you to pick out the final shape. One of the easiest ways to draw a cylinder and ensure that the two ellipses on the ends are properly curved is to draw it inside a cube or rectangular box, using it to maintain correct perspective.

To draw an upright cylinder, begin with a cube. Once you have the shape of the cube defined, you will draw in lines to establish the guidelines for the correct linear and elliptical perspective. As we know, when we view a circle at an angle, what we see instead is an ellipse. The angle of the tilt is called the degree. An ellipse has two axes, the major axis and the minor axis. The major axis divides the ellipse across its widest part into two equal halves and the minor axis divides the ellipse across its narrowest part into two equal halves. The two axes always cross each other at a 90-degree angle. However, when you put an ellipse into linear perspective, the major axis will shift from the perspective center, which can be confusing.

Lightly draw lines across the top and bottom planes from one corner to the other, forming a cross across the surface. This establishes the perspective center of the cube and the ellipse. Next, draw a light vertical line from the center of the intersection on the top plane to the center of the intersection on the bottom plane. This line forms an imaginary central axis of both the cube and cylinder. It will also form the minor axis of the ellipse. Then lightly draw a horizontal line across the top and bottom planes of the cube perpendicular to the vertical axis and intersecting the inside corners. These lines form the major axes of the two

eye level and angle of viewing have changed and therefore elliptical and linear perspective are required in order to draw it realistically. This will affect both the size and the shape of the two ellipses on either end of the cylinder. In this position, the two parallel lines that make up the sides of the cylinder will now have a vanishing point, moving closer together as they move away from the viewer. The ellipse that is closer to eye level, further away from the viewer, will appear smaller and flatter; while the ellipse closer to the viewer will appear to be rounder and larger.

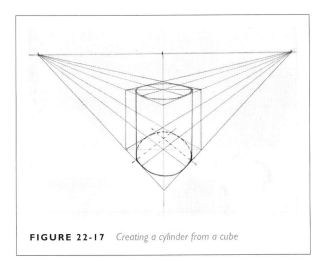

FIGURE 22-17   *Creating a cylinder from a cube*

ellipses. Note that they do not lie on the cube's perspective midpoint, but sit in front of it instead. Using the axes and the squares as guidelines, draw in the ellipses on the top and bottom of the cube. Because the top ellipse is closer to the viewer's eye level, it appears flatter. Connect the two ellipses at their outside edges with two vertical lines to create the cylinder.

To draw an ellipse on its side with one end close to the viewer, begin by establishing the horizon line on your paper. Then draw a line for the central axis at the angle you desire extending all the way to the horizon line to set the vanishing point for the sides of the cylinder. Then, draw a line perpendicular to the central axis on either end of the cylinder at the desired length. You can draw a square at either end to use as a template to create the ellipse, or create both freehand. Once you have established the ellipse closest to the viewer, lightly trace lines from the top and bottom of the ellipse to the vanishing point on the horizon line to find the sides of the cylinder. You can go over the lines you have sketched in to pick out the shape of the cylinder, refining the outline and cleaning up the edges in preparation for adding volume.

Modeling a cylinder with highlight and shadow is similar to creating volume for a sphere, as the surface of a cylinder is also round. The strongest highlight exists where the cylinder is struck by the light source and the value decreases as light travels around the object. The greatest contrast between tones exists where the cylinder is closest to the viewer, helping to draw it toward the eye, creating depth. The elliptical plane of the cylinder that is visible will be shaded much the same way as the flat planes of a cube, either highlighted or shadowed depending on where the light source is striking the object. A cast shadow on an upright cylinder is nearly identical to the cast shadow

of a sphere, extending back from the object in an elliptical shape. The shadow will move outward at an angle from the form, with an even value that has soft edges. The cylinder's height will determine the shadow's length. By drawing a thin dark line around the base of the form, you will carry the shadow around the entire cylinder, anchoring it to the surface underneath it and increasing the sense of depth. The cast shadow of a cylinder on its side is almost rectilinear in shape. Imagining a rectangle around the edges of the four sides of the cylinder casting a shadow below it will assist you in drawing the right shape. The lines of the shadow will run parallel to the two elliptical planes on the top and bottom of the cylinder as well as the lines of the sides of the form, extending out slightly in front of the curve facing the viewer and a bit more behind the cylinder. With each shadow, fill in the area with an even value and then blend, leaving the edges soft.

Cones

The cone is the last of the four basic shapes and, like the cylinder, combines aspects of both the cube and the sphere. A perfect cone consists of a circle at one end and a point at the other. Its basic volume is round, like a sphere. Like a cube, the same shading techniques are required where the plane of the ellipse meets the cone in order to bring the edge forward.

Observing a Cone

Like a cylinder, a cone looks very different standing upright than it does when it is lying on its side. When it is lying on its side, a cone is subject to linear perspective, much like a cylinder, which serves to distort some of its features. Again, trusting what you see rather than what you know about the form is important in order to capture the object realistically. Casting light onto a conical form will reveal its volume. The strongest highlight will appear in a direct line from the center of the light source. The greatest contrast in value occurs where the light meets shadow as it travels around the object. In an upright cone, the base of the object is closest to the viewer so the shadow underneath that part of the object will be the darkest, bringing it towards the viewer and grounding it on the surface on which it rests. Cast shadows from an upright cone will follow the shape of the base, stretching out to mirror the height of the point. A cone resting on its side will have a more complicated highlight and shadow pattern, depending on the direction of the light source and the position of the form.

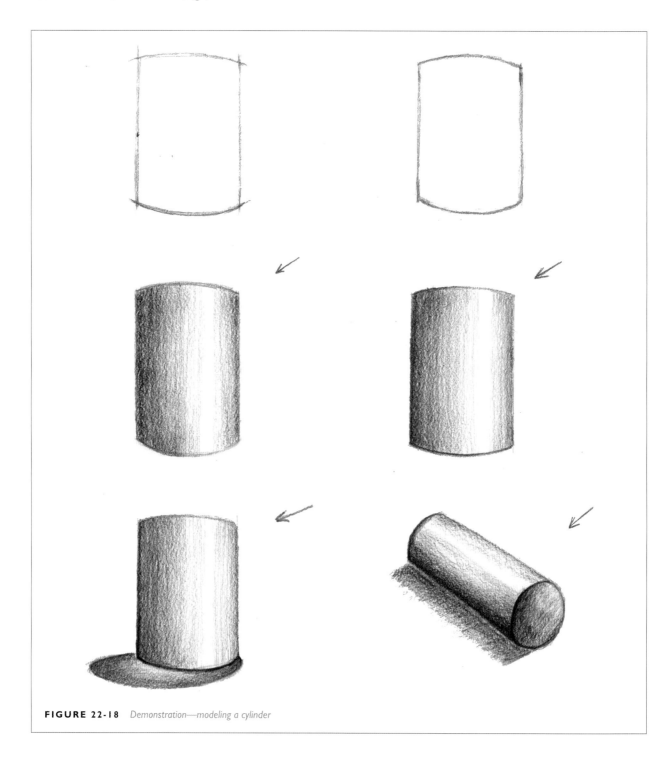

FIGURE 22-18 *Demonstration—modeling a cylinder*

Exercise: Drawing and Modeling a Cone

Drawing a cone accurately requires a combination of observation and an understanding of elliptical and linear perspective.

The biggest challenge in drawing an upright cone is making sure that both sides are the same. To prevent it from becoming lopsided, begin by lightly drawing a vertical line to serve as a guideline. This line will make sure that you center the tip of the cone above the center of the base. Determine the height of the cone from tip to base and set marks at either end of this plumb line to indicate the top and bottom of the form. Lightly draw a line perpendicular to the guideline roughly a half-inch up from the base to use for the width of the cone. Make a mark on either side of the center line at equal distances to establish the width. Draw a straight line between these marks and the point on the center line to create the sides of the cone. The closer your eye is to the base of the cone, the shallower the curve will be. Adjust this horizontal guideline as needed. Next, draw a curve that connects the two sides, touching the mark on the centerline that is the bottom of the cone, creating the base. If it is easier, you can lightly sketch in a full ellipse, touching all of these points. Once you have the

basic shape sketched in, you can model the form as you did for the cylinder.

To draw a cone lying on its side, you will need to establish a horizon line on your paper in order to apply perspective to the form. Once you have it established, sketch in a central guideline in the direction you want the cone to face order to correctly line up the base with the tip. Next, make two marks

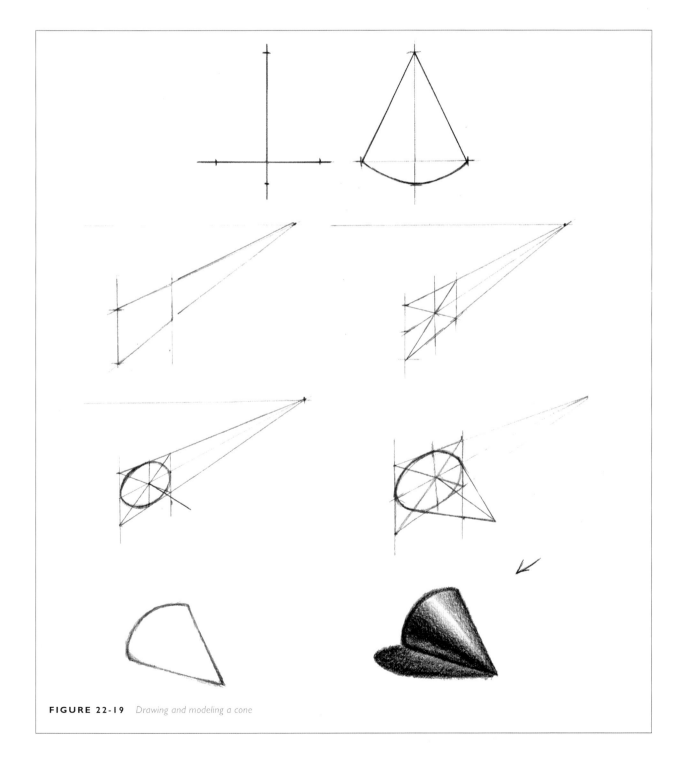

FIGURE 22-19   *Drawing and modeling a cone*

on the central line to indicate the length of the cone. The next step is to draw a line perpendicular to the guideline at the end closest to the horizon line to create the central axis for the ellipse that forms the base of the cone. This axis will extend all the way to the horizon line, establishing a vanishing point for the base. Now you need to determine the proportion of the width of the ellipse in relation to the length of the cone. Mark the width on the axis line. Then determine the depth of the cone and mark it on the central guideline. Once you have these marks, determine the height of the base. You can sketch in the ellipse, tracing lightly over the lines until the shape is correct and then connect the edge of the ellipse to the point of the cone. From here, the volume of the form is ready to be modeled with highlight and shadow.

DRAWING MEDIA

An important part of drawing concerns a purely technical aspect of the visual arts, the **medium**. A medium is the material that the artist uses to create a piece or work—pencil, clay, wood, stone, ink, fabric, film, music, theatre, etc. **Media** is the plural form of medium, and some works will contain multiple media. These are often referred to as **mixed media** pieces. Each medium has unique characteristics that can be seen and appreciated in the works that utilize them. Each has advantages that can be exploited, and limitations that must be worked with or around. There are some artists who are so skillful with their chosen medium that their effort is invisible. They transcend the limitations of the medium in order to shape it and make it perform as they want as they create their artworks. This can be true whether the medium is a traditional one such as paint or charcoal, or a modern, digital one like Photoshop or ZBrush.

There are many different types of drawing media, and they generally fall into one of three categories:

1. Dry media

2. Liquid media

3. Mixed media

There are so many different types of drawing media that it can be overwhelming. Visiting an art store can be like a trip to the candy shop, full of an infinite variety of tempting choices. There is no one type of drawing media that is right for everyone. Most artists will use different media to achieve a variety of effects and one medium might be more suited to a particular project that another. It is important to experiment with different types of media in order to find out what you like, what you do not and what materials work best to achieve your goals.

Dry Media

Some traditional dry media that may be useful to a theatrical designer include:

- Graphite and graphite pencils

- Mechanical and drafting pencils

- Charcoal

- Chalk

- Pastels

- Crayons

- Colored pencils.

Graphite pencils are similar to the pencils used for writing and most designers will use them at some point in their process. Artists' pencils are made of thin rods of graphite, a soft form of carbon that is mixed with clay and baked in a kiln before being encased in wood or some other form of holder. The amount of clay determines the hardness of the pencil. The amount of graphite determines the value and thickness of the resulting marks. The more clay, the harder the pencil and the lighter the line it will produce. The graphite or lead pencil was not commonly used in art until the end of the eighteenth century, when the technique of adding clay to vary the hardness was invented. The value created by the pencil depends on the hardness of the pencil, the pressure applied by the artist, the way in which the pencil is held and the speed of the marks being made. Graphite can also be purchased as a loose powder, in order to cover large areas of a composition using a cloth or paintbrush.

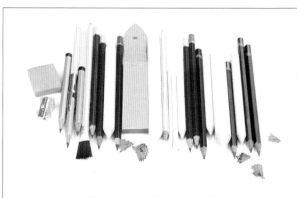

FIGURE 22-20   *Drawing pencils (Africa Studio / Shutterstock.com)*

Colored pencils come in a variety of forms, including:

- Artist grade pencils
- Pastel pencils
- Pigmented sketching pencils
- Watercolor pencils.

Colored pencils contain an inner core made of pigment mixed with wax and other fillers surrounded by wood or plastic. They are available in a wide range of colors and different hardness, and can be blended together on the work surface to create new colors, delicate shading and effects. In the hands of a skilled artist, colored pencils can be used to create extremely lifelike drawings. Colored pencils can also be true to their origin as pencils, and be used to create marks that are very linear and readily identifiable, using successive layers to create a depth and intensity of color, dimension and value.

Charcoal is made of charred wood or vine in sticks of varying widths and hardness. It is a medium that moves very freely across the paper, creating broad, soft lines in a range of values. Marks made with charcoal are easily smudged and blended. Consequently a charcoal drawing requires a **fixative** to set it to the paper. A fixative is a type of glue that binds pigment particles to a surface. Charcoal is thought of as a very forgiving medium, as it is easily erased and reworked over and over again, making it possible to refine a drawing continuously. It is also a very free medium, meaning that it can be worked in a variety of ways—in stick forms like a pencil, rubbed and blended with a cloth or the fingers, or with sponges and other tools. It can also be crushed and used as a powder for broad washes of value. Charcoal can be very useful to the theatre designer for quick light sketches and storyboards to give a rough idea of the visual composition for a specific look or scene.

FIGURE 22-21 *Colored pencils (anaken2012 / Shutterstock.com)*

Artists' chalk is made from naturally occurring deposits of calcium carbonate and various mineral pigments. The chalk is ground to fine powder, mixed with a binder and then compressed into sticks. Chalk has a long history of use as a soft drawing medium. Renaissance, Baroque, and Rococo artists used white, black, and red chalk to work up and down the value scale on a tinted surface that served as a middle value. Today, chalk can be purchased in a range of tones from black through white and is a convenient way to draw quick value studies and light renderings.

One of the most versatile forms related to artist's chalk is **pastels**. Pastels come in soft, hard, and oil varieties. Soft pastels are often confused with chalk, which is harder. Soft and hard pastels are made by combining pigment with filler that is bound together with a small amount of gum or resin. Hard pastels can also made into pencils. When rubbed into paper with enough "tooth," or abrasive texture to hold the particles of pigment dust, pastels deposit masses of color on the paper. Pastel drawings have often been thought of as paintings, because the artist can lay down areas of color like they can with paint, blending it to a smooth and even consistency. Pastels can also be used in a linear fashion by making lines as with a pencil. Pastel drawings and paintings are very fragile until treated with a fixative. If they are shaken or moved before fixing, some of the powder will fall off. If too much fixative is used, it can deaden the color or spot the drawing. Pastel paintings and drawings are often worked in layers, with fixative in between each successive layer to hold the pigment in place. To gain permanence, pastel drawings are placed under glass. Pastels are often associated with pale tones, (hence the name, pastel), and pale pastels are well suited to creating light effects, and romantic images. Pastels are very soft, so most artists smudge and blend them. For the theatrical designer, pastels can be used to lay down quick areas of color that can be blended to create soft effects that are evocative of fabric and filled with movement. They can be very useful for costume renderings for dance. Combining them with markers can help fix them to the paper.

Several different media carry the name "crayon." **Conte crayons** bear the name of the man who invented them in the eighteenth century. They are a finely textured, grease-free sticks made of powdered graphite and clay to which red ochre, soot or blackstone is added to give it a red, black, or brown color. They are somewhat powdery in texture, but nowhere near as soft as charcoal. However, Conte crayons can be used in much the same way to create gently shaped areas and tones of value, making them very suitable for light renderings and storyboarding, although crayons in general tend to skip across the paper and allow more of the paper's texture to show through. Conte crayons can also be used in a linear fashion, to create bold, distinct marks similar to pencil.

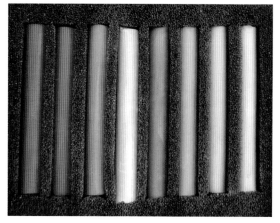

FIGURE 22-22 *Soft and hard pastels (Studio Barcelona, Kulish Viktoriia / Shutterstock.com)*

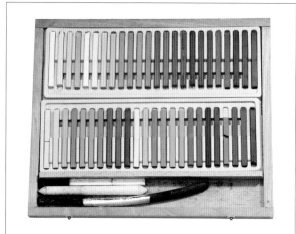

FIGURE 22-23 *Conte crayons (Shutterstock.com)*

Liquid Media

The primary liquid media used for drawing is ink, applied with either a brush or a pen. Today's inks are made of pigment particles, shellac, and water. In ancient China, Japan, and in Europe, ink was made by combining lampblack with weak glue. In Japan this type of ink is still made and is called *Sumi.* Ink is usually applied with pens made of steel, quills, reeds, or bamboo. Ink applied with pens is essentially a line medium. Depending on the shape of the tip, or nib, the pen can produce lines of uniform width or lines that vary in width according to the direction and pressure of the pen. Pen and ink can be a difficult medium to control, because the point of the pen may catch on the surface of the paper, causing the ink to splatter unpredictably. Modern technical pens can help prevent this, creating a similar control to ballpoint pens. But they can still be unpredictable.

There is a wide variety of professional artists' pens and markers available on the market for artists to use in their work. Markers contain a reservoir of soluble ink that is wicked onto a drawing surface through a felt or nylon tip. With the exception of archival markers, most markers are not lightfast, even if they are classified as permanent. Some markers are also water soluble, allowing the artist to work with them like watercolor paints. Technical pens for graphic illustrations have precise tips in a variety of sizes and are archival quality. Felt tip markers—such as Prismacolor and Copic—come in a huge range of colors, and have a wedge-shaped tip on one end and a fine point tip on the other, which offer several surfaces to make different kinds of marks. Some markers even have a brush tip that can be used like a paintbrush.

Ordinary writing pens, such as ballpoint and gel pens are also used by designers and artists alone or in mixed media applications. However, many are not lightfast and fade very quickly compared to professional artists' pens. Markers and pens make it possible to work very quickly and linearly, adding color, value, emphasis, and dimension by building up successive layers of marks. Markers can also be used to create highly detailed, painterly renderings for theatrical design.

FIGURE 22-24 *Markers (drpnncpptak / Shutterstock.com)*

Mixed Media

A designer may also choose to combine media in order to create the effect they want in a drawing. Pencils, pens, markers, and ink may be used interchangeably throughout a drawing in order to create a range of value or other visual effects that enhance the overall look of the image, create mood and atmosphere or communicate emotion or other artistic intent.

THE LANGUAGE OF DRAWING

Artists' chalk: Calcium carbonate mixed with mineral pigments.

Backlight: A light source striking the object in a drawing from behind.

Cast shadow: The shadow created by the object in the path of the light coming from the light source.

Charcoal: Charred wood or vine in sticks of varying widths and hardness.

Colored pencils: Pencils that contain an inner core made of pigment mixed with wax and other fillers, surrounded by wood or plastic.

Conte crayons: A finely textured, grease-free stick made of powdered graphite and clay to which red ochre, soot, or blackstone is added to give it a red, black, or brown color.

Core shadow: The location on an object where the reflected light ends and the shadow begins.

Detail drawings: Comprehensive drawings, usually in scale, that provide additional information about the appearance of the design.

Drawing: The creation of an image, usually on paper, using lines as the primary visual component.

Final drawings: Drawings that are an artistic presentation of the designs in a completed form without color, including all the final details.

Fixative: An agent that seals the surface of a piece, "fixing" the media in place.

Front elevations: Scenic drawings that show the full details of the entire set, properties, or scenic elements from the front, along with measurements.

Graphite pencils: Thin rods of graphite mixed with clay and baked in a kiln before being encased in wood or some other form of holder.

Highlight: The brightest amount of reflected light striking an object.

Light plot: A technical drawing that conveys all of the information that a lighting crew will need to hang, focus, and circuit the instruments.

Light source: Where the illumination hitting the subject is coming from, such as a lamp or a lighting instrument, ambient or diffuse light from a window, or direct light from the sun.

Media: The plural form of medium.

Medium: The material the artist uses to create a piece or work.

Midtones: The transitional values between the highlight and the core shadow.

Mixed media: Images created using multiple media.

Pastels: Pigment mixed with filler that is bound together with a small amount of gum or resin.

Preliminary drawings: Drawings made in order to work out the composition of a set, costume, or lighting composition before they actually begin to do a final drawing and render it in another medium. Also called rough sketches or thumbnails.

Reflected light: The light that is reflected off the surface underneath an object which then strikes the form underneath the core shadow.

Representational: A design that is composed of recognizable images, however distorted or stylized.

Rough sketches: Sketches made in order to work out the composition of a set, costume, or lighting composition before they actually begin to do a final drawing and render it in another medium. Also called preliminary drawings or thumbnails.

Shadow: The absence of light.

Sketching: Quick, loose drawing meant to record ideas.

Technical drawings: Highly detailed drawings, usually in scale, that serve as blueprints for the construction of the scenery, properties, the hanging and focus of lighting instruments, which may provide costume construction details, rigging specifications, or other information.

Tortillion: A paper stump used to blend drawing media on a surface.

CHAPTER 23

RENDERING

WHAT IS A RENDERING?

A **rendering** is a final drawing of a theatrical design including all major and minor details, in full color. Renderings are typically created by scenic and costume designers as part of their design process. A set designer may do additional renderings for properties that also need to be built, such as furniture, stained glass windows, specialty items, and paint elevations. Costume designers may do separate renderings for armor, hats, costume props, or other accessories. Lighting designers may also do renderings, but the prevalence of digital lighting programs has largely replaced rendering by hand, making it possible to render multiple looks quickly and easily. In the film industry, renderings are executed by a wide range of artists from production, costume, lighting, set, and makeup designers to production and conceptual artists, special effects artists, miniature and

FIGURE 23-1 *The Foreigner by Larry Shue, Merrimack Repertory Theatre, set sketch, set design by Alison Ford*

properties artists, modelers, animators, weapons designers, storyboard artists, and more.

Renderings are an important step in the design process. They provide a complete visual representation of the designer's final choices, illustrating what the finished designs will look like on the stage. They communicate the designers' intent and vision to the director, the actors, and the shops that will bring the designs to life. They are the midway point, the culmination of the initial phase of the collaboration between the director and the designers. It is important that they present an accurate picture of the set, costumes, lights, projections, or other design elements, both in terms of visual representation and overall tone. Renderings are most effective when they include a touch of atmosphere and mood, a sense of character that evokes emotion and communicates something about the play or the characters. Ideally they should engage the viewer in much the same way as the realized designs are intended to onstage.

SURFACES

The **surface**, or **support**, refers to the material on which paint or other media is applied. There are a number of different supports available to a designer to use for painting, including

illustration board, papers, cotton and polyester canvas, linen, Masonite, prepared boards, aluminum wood panels, and plywood. Which surface you choose depends largely on what type of media you are using. Heavier media require more substantial supports than light media. Theatrical designers also need to consider portability when creating their renderings; consequently artists' papers and illustration boards will most likely be the surfaces you use. Always consider the longevity of your artwork when selecting the surface for your renderings. Papers and boards should be acid-free and archival quality in order to preserve your work.

When choosing papers make sure they are substantial enough to support the medium you are using. Papers are made specifically for different types of media, but that does not mean you have to strictly adhere to their intended use. There are dozens of different types of paper, each with unique characteristics. Some have textured surfaces while others are smooth. Experiment with different types and different media to see which ones you like. Boards are also made for specific media, both smooth and textured. Both papers and boards also come in a wide range of colors.

COLOR MEDIA

There are many different types of color media that can be used to create renderings. Each one has its advantages and disadvantages. The range of media is extensive and every beginning designer should experiment with different media in order to find which ones work best for them. Being proficient in more than one type of color media can bring greater flexibility and variety to your renderings. It also makes it possible to tailor the media you use to the genre and style of each production in much the same way you might choose to vary the style of your drawings to suit the tone of each play or the overall conceptual approach of your design. Being familiar with several media also allows you to combine multiple techniques in your renderings, which can create dynamic visual effects and enrich their overall appearance.

It is beyond the scope of this book to examine all the possible color media available to a theatrical designer. There are advantages in having skills in one portable medium and one liquid medium, so one of each are covered here. The techniques available to a designer by being fluent in at least two media provide greater artistic flexibility with regards to rendering. In addition, being able to use one digital image-editing software program with a degree of proficiency can speed up the rendering process and make any necessary editing quick and easy.

COLORED PENCILS

Colored pencils are an excellent medium to use when you are first learning to apply color to final drawings. They are a

FIGURE 23-2 *Art papers (Kaoime Malloy, Colour59 / Dreamstime.com)*

clean, flexible, and easy to use medium that is highly portable, so they can be used anywhere. Because they are pencils they lend themselves to any technique applicable to drawing and can be used in much the same way to lay down color and model light and form. Even though they are primarily a linear medium, and value is built up through layers of multiple marks and strokes, because colored pencils are wax-based it is also possible to use solvents to create washes of color to speed up the process of working with them. Colored pencils are available in dozens of different hues and are relatively inexpensive when compared to other media. They also come in a variety of forms. The same pigment found in pencils can also be purchased in sticks and in hard and soft options. Although the main form of this media is wax-based pigment, colored pencils are also available in oil and watercolor forms, making it possible to blend colors and create washes quickly. Intensity and saturation of hues are easily changed by varying the amount of pressure with the pencil and color mixing can easily be created by **layering** colors on top of each other. In addition, to a certain extent, they can be erased, which allows for the correction of mistakes.

The main disadvantage of colored pencils is that it takes time to build up an even, saturated area of color through the application of multiple layers of pencil. Adding multiple areas

of color along with the necessary modeling needed to add volume and lighting effects to create mood and atmosphere can be very time-consuming. The temptation to rapidly build up color by using firm pressure as a shortcut can etch grooves into the surface underneath the pencil that will remain in the finished rendering. However, because colored pencils are a semitransparent medium, layering can also produce luminous color with incredible depth. Each layer of color shines through the next, whether the pencils are used to create linear strokes or broad areas of color.

Whether or not colored pencil becomes a medium of choice for your renderings, learning the techniques that will allow you to use them effectively is very useful for the theatrical designer. In mixed media applications, pencils are excellent tools to add targeted highlights and shadows and fine details to a rendering.

Tools and Supplies

There is a wide variety of artists' paper and board available for use with colored pencils. Different surfaces accept the pigment of pencils in different ways and all will affect the final look of a rendering. It is important to know what kind of look you want to create in the final image in order to pick the surface that will work best. Paper and boards also come in a variety of colors and since large parts of the paper may show through in a rendering, color has an effect on the overall look of the finished product. Although white and lighter colors are the best for creating the smooth, painterly look that is possible with colored pencil, a designer may wish to choose a paper color that reflects the mood or theme of the production. Selecting a neutral colored paper also makes it possible to use it as a middle value in your rendering, which can speed up your process. Black paper can also be used to create vivid light renderings with colored pencil.

Paper for colored pencils should always be heavy enough to withstand multiple applications of the pigment as well as erasing and other texture techniques. It needs to have a medium "tooth" or texture so that it can hold on to successive layers of pencil pigment. Heavily textured paper is not suitable for colored pencils as the texture can show through your marks. It should also be 100 percent acid-free and archival quality in order to make sure it lasts as long as possible. Renderings not only serve as important tools for the current production; they also go into your portfolio, where they serve as a showcase of your work and abilities, helping you to get more work.

Pencils for the fine artist basically fall into one of three categories: wax based, water based and oil based.

FIGURE 23-3 The Mountain Giants *by Luigi Pirandello, costume design by Kaoime E. Malloy*

- **Wax-based pencils** are made by combining pigments with wax binders. They are a semitransparent medium that can be used to create smooth lines, bold areas of color through multiple layers, and they can be burnished to a lustrous surface. Some brands offer both hard and soft versions of the pencils in their lines. The only drawback to wax pencils is that they can develop a hazy **wax bloom** on their surface, but it easily removable through the light application of solvent, burnishing, and **fixative** to set the color.

- **Water-based pencils** are made by combining pigment with water and a water soluble gum as a binder. They are very flexible because they can be used dry like a traditional pencil, or blended with water to create watercolor-like effects.

- **Oil-based pencils** are made by combining pigments with oil as a binder. The colors are vibrant and a bit more opaque than wax pencils. They can be used to create linear marks or blended with oil paint mediums and solvents to create washes and other effects. They combine well with wax pencils and oil pastels.

Every type of pencil is different, although all are semitransparent, making it possible to layer one color over another yet still see the underlying layers, providing optical color mixing along with depth of shade and tone. Every brand of pencil has its own color palette and range, and some brands have a much wider offering of colors than others. One brand may feel buttery smooth when you make marks on the paper and another might feel hard and crisp. The only way to know which brand you prefer is to experiment with several and see which one responds best in your hand.

Additional tools that you will find useful when working with colored pencils include:

- *Colorless blenders*: A **colorless blender** is a colored pencil with no pigment. With a colorless blender, you can blend or burnish layers of pigment together without changing the hue. Blenders come in oil and wax based formulas and both can be used with all wax based pencils.

- *Pencil sharpener*: It is worth investing in a good pencil sharpener of your choice. Whether that is electric, hand, or crank is up to you. Some pencil manufacturers make sharpeners that are specifically made to work with their pencils and they can save money in the long run by sharpening your pencils efficiently and not grinding them down to nothing.

- *Erasers*: Erasing is a necessary part of working with colored pencils, either to remove pigment as part of the drawing process or to keep your work surface and drawing clean. Having several different types of erasers gives you maximum flexibility-although it is important to remember that colored pencil can stain papers and boards so it is not always possible to remove it completely. Kneaded erasers can be shaped to work in small areas and will not create much residue even when kneaded and reused multiple times. Erasers made of vinyl and white plastic come in several shapes and sizes and can easily be cut with a mat knife into various shapes and sharp points as needed. Always remember that erasers create residue that must be brushed away, and that renderings can be smudged in the process.

- *Power eraser*: A **power eraser** can be useful for removing pigment from large areas and often gives better control than a handheld eraser, which may just push the pencil around rather than remove it. A small, battery-operated eraser is a great tool for picking out highlights. Combining it with a plastic straight-edge or ruler gives you a lot of control for tight spots. It can even be used as a drawing tool to add detail and lines in the areas of color.

- *Straight-edges*: Rulers, triangles, or T-squares are useful for drawing straight, vertical, horizontal, parallel, and perpendicular lines. They are also useful guides for erasing.

FIGURE 23-4   *Colored pencils (Lissandra Melo / Shutterstock.com)*

- *Craft knife*: A sharp craft knife is great to sharpen pencils in shapes that a pencil sharpener cannot, and to shape erasers. It can also be used to scratch marks into the surface of a pencil rendering to add highlights or textures.

- *Solvent*: **Solvent** can be applied with a cotton swab, brush, or pad to quickly cover a large area or to blend colors together. Solvent works by dissolving the wax and allowing the pigment in the pencil to flow into the paper's grain. Weber Turpenoid Natural® is nontoxic alternative to traditional painting solvents, but should still be used with adequate ventilation.

- *Fixative*: Fixative is an important final step to seal your renderings once they are complete. This will preserve your rendering and make it last longer. You can also use fixative to eliminate wax bloom.

- *Desk brush*: Working with any kind of pencil creates pencil dust, especially when you use heavy pressure to lay dark areas of color or to burnish layers. Having a soft drafting brush to wipe down your table will keep your work surface clean and prevent stray pigments from staining your work.

- *Color lifters*: Masking tape, a kneaded eraser, or even mounting putty can be used to lift color from the surface of your rendering. Simply knead the eraser or putty, press it down into the surface and then gently lift up to remove the color. Repeat until you achieve the desired results. Tape works well for large areas, where you can lay down overlapping strips, etch into the tape with a tool such as a ballpoint pen, and then gently peel back the tape to remove the pigment.

Techniques

With any medium, *how* you apply it to the chosen surface is as important as the medium itself. There are as many different ways to apply colored pencils to paper as there are artists. You can work with pencils in a soft manner, using loose, light strokes that maintain their linear properties, or they can be applied in a dense style with a smooth surface like a traditional painting. When experimenting with the medium, you need to learn what kind of stroke to make, how much pressure to use, and how sharp the pencil needs to be to achieve your desired effect.

Choose the Right Pencil Point for your Desired Task

A sharp point is mainly used to apply layers of color to the paper. Start with a sharp pencil and sharpen your pencil often as you work. A sharp pencil dips into the valleys of the paper's texture, giving a better, more even coverage whereas a dull pencil deposits the pigment on the top, which can leave parts of the paper showing through. A dull, rounded pencil point creates softer, uneven textures where you want the paper to show through. It can be very useful when creating fabric, wood, or other layered textures that require multiple colors. A blunt, angled point is used for **burnishing**, where you will use heavy pressure to both blend layers of color together and polish the wax surface, making it shine.

Select the Right Stroke to Create the Effect You Want

- A **circular stroke** creates a smooth, even area of color. Keep your pencil point sharp and overlap your strokes in small circles to build up an area of color. Do your best not to move in an obvious pattern or create a definite line. The idea is to create an even area of color with no visible lines when you are finished.

- **Linear fill strokes** are applied all in the same direction with a sharp pencil, overlapping as you layer them on top of each other to fill in an area with color. As with circular strokes, the intent is to fill in the area of color without leaving a definite mark. Be careful to keep the layers even so that you do not wind up with one part of the area darker than the rest. All marks should be even and smooth when you are finished.

- **Multidirectional fill strokes** are small overlapping linear marks that move in multiple directions. Using a sharp pencil, first fill in the area with overlapping vertical strokes, then with overlapping horizontal marks, and then overlapping diagonal strokes, and finally overlapping diagonal strokes from the opposite direction. Turn your paper as needed to help you get even coverage. Repeat each step as needed to create a smooth, even finish. You may not have to go in every direction to completely fill in the area.

- **Pure linear strokes** retain their shape, creating visual texture. This type of mark has a pointillism-like effect, creating optical mixing through close proximity of individual strokes in addition to the color blending that naturally occurs with colored pencil due to its transparent qualities. It is important that this type of linear mark follows the form of your subject, whether that is a door, a chair, a face, a beam of light, or the folds of a skirt in order to maintain and reinforce the shape and volume of that object. Otherwise, the pencil lines can contradict the perspective of the drawing underneath.

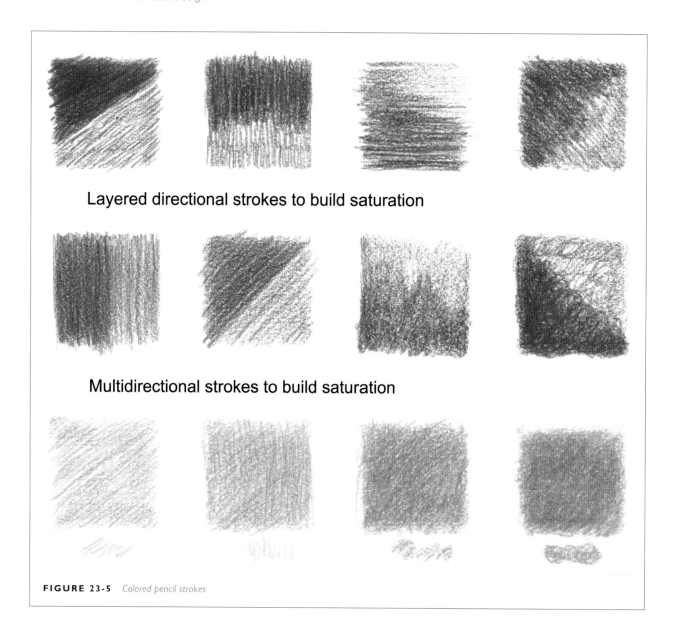

Layered directional strokes to build saturation

Multidirectional strokes to build saturation

FIGURE 23-5 *Colored pencil strokes*

Pressure is Important

It takes some practice to master applying color with pencils. Using the right amount of pressure is critical when laying down color with pencils. Light pressure with a sharp pencil demands a looser stroke that allows you to push the pigment in between the grain and texture of the paper as you build up successive layers of color. Heavy pressure with a rounded pencil blends the color as you add pigment but flattens the texture of the paper as you work. Pressure is important for two related reasons. Because colored pencil is a semitransparent medium, you can see through each layer to view the color below. Careful layering produces vibrant effects and dimension.

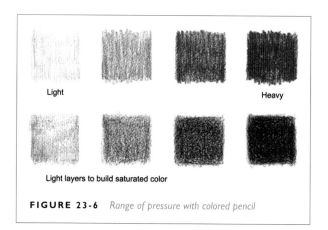

FIGURE 23-6 *Range of pressure with colored pencil*

But because pencils are oil- or wax-based, there comes a point where the surface becomes saturated with the material, making it impossible to add any more. Therefore, adding color with light pressure, depositing less wax makes it possible to add a maximum amount of color, far more than is possible with heavy pressure.

Layering Color for Luminous Effect

Take advantage of the semitransparent nature of colored pencils to build up layers of color. Layering pencils gives their colors more depth and brilliance because light is able to penetrate the multiple layers and reflect a greater range of color back to the eye. Layering hues generates more visual interest than a single color and creates beautiful new colors in the process. Burnishing the final surface further enhances the effect.

- *Layer complementary colors for rich, vibrant neutrals*: When working with any color media, combining complementary colors creates a chromatic gray by neutralizing the two hues. Rather than the cool, true neutral tone made by mixing black and white in varying degrees, a chromatic gray possesses hue by virtue of how it is created. Because of this they are more vibrant, lustrous, and dynamic. When created in pencil, by layering, both colors shine through the final gray tone with a bright, luminous quality. Figure 23-7a shows the richness of color in chromatic grays.

- *Layer complementary colors for lustrous blacks*: In paint, it is possible to purchase a variety of different blacks, each possessing a different underlying color tone. Some have a green cast, others seem red, still others glossy, embodying a "true" black. Pencils generally do not offer more than one option for black, but you can still create your own rich, beautiful chromatic blacks by layering certain complementary colors. In paint, one way to do this is by combining quinacridone red with phthalo green. In pencils, similar colors are brick red and teal green. Combining tertiary complements is the best way to create these rich, velvety dark tones. Figure 23-7b shows this technique.

- *Layer analogous colors to add richness and depth*: Layering colors that are analogous, ones that sit next to each other on the color wheel and share a primary, can serve to add depth and vibrancy to the desired hue. Whether the top color is darker or lighter depends on the effect you want to create, but even a light color can shine through a dark one due to the semitransparency of the medium. Figure 23-7c demonstrates this technique.

- *Burnish for luminous color*: Burnishing not only blends the layers of the colors together, it also pushes the pigment into the paper and polishes the surface, creating a vibrant shine. In Figure 23-7d, the top of each swatch is burnished with a colorless blender, while the bottom is left unburnished. As you can see, burnishing creates a sense of light and vibrancy in the colors.

Highlight and Shadow with Analogous Colors for Greater Depth

Simply shadowing an object with a darker version of the base color creates minimal depth and volume and can actually make the subject appear flatter. Highlights and shadows possess color, particularly within the lighting world of theatre, and judiciously using analogous colors that share a primary with your main color will make the subject appear more three-dimensional. Shadows can be layered under the main color for a more subtle effect, or layered on top for a more dramatic look. Highlights underneath the main body of color can shine through the form due to the transparent nature of colored pencils or can be applied on the top for burnishing and precise highlighting, to pick out details.

Use Sticks to Fill In Larger Areas

The pigment in colored pencils is also available in stick and woodless form, both of which can be used in much the same manner as pastels. While the tips of these **art sticks** can be sharpened like any colored pencil, their greatest advantage comes in breaking them into convenient lengths and then using them to fill in larger areas of color with light, circular strokes. This makes it possible to quickly establish a base color and then go in with standard pencils to work the details into the composition. Given that pencils are a relatively slow medium to work with, anything that speeds up the process is useful.

Create Washes with Solvent

Because pencils are essentially a linear medium, they do not at first glance appear to lend themselves to laying down large areas of color. While it is possible to quickly sketch in large areas of color with stick forms of the medium, using solvent to dissolve the wax or oil base of the pencils can fill in big parts of the composition as well as create beautiful effects. Weber Turpenoid® in the blue can or Weber Turpenoid Natural® natural both work well for

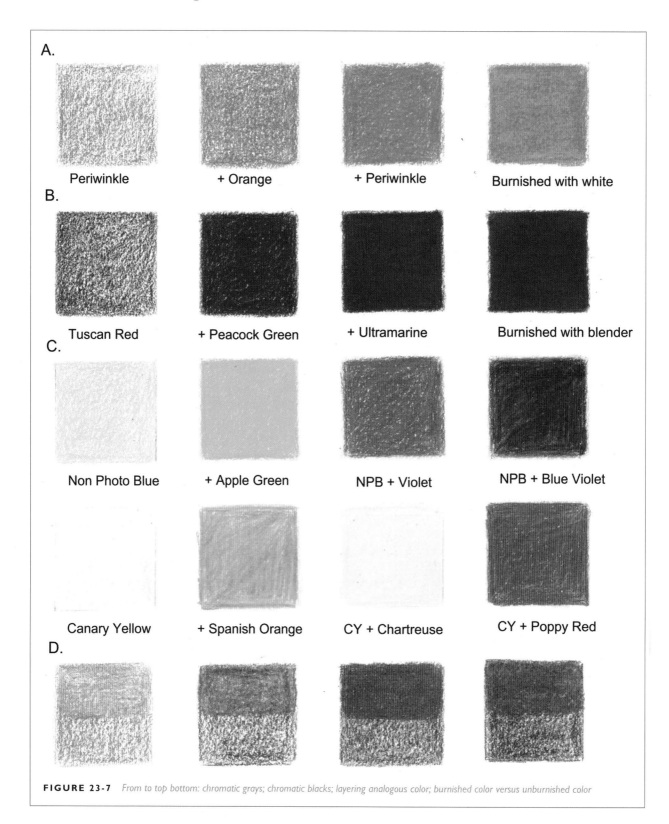

A.
Periwinkle   + Orange   + Periwinkle   Burnished with white

B.
Tuscan Red   + Peacock Green   + Ultramarine   Burnished with blender

C.
Non Photo Blue   + Apple Green   NPB + Violet   NPB + Blue Violet

Canary Yellow   + Spanish Orange   CY + Chartreuse   CY + Poppy Red

D.

FIGURE 23-7   *From to top bottom: chromatic grays; chromatic blacks; layering analogous color; burnished color versus unburnished color*

this process. The solvent can be applied with a cotton swab or a paint brush, although very little is needed to dissolve the wax. Make sure that you have enough pigment on the paper before you begin. Dip the brush into the solvent and pat off the excess on a rag or paper towel and then go over the entire area to be blended with circular strokes. Color can be feathered out into

FIGURE 23-8 *Analogous colors for highlights and shadows—blue, purple, navy blue, turquoise, white, applied in three different ways*

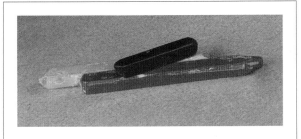

FIGURE 23-9 *Art sticks*

FIGURE 23-10 *Creating washes with colored pencil and solvent*

the paper at the edges for a subtle lighting effect, which is very useful for light renderings and backdrops on scenic renderings. If you wish to reapply color and work in layers, be sure to let the paper dry completely in between layers of solvent. Once you have achieved your desired wash effect, the resulting color can be burnished, worked with more pencil on top, or even lightly erased to create fog-like tones. You can also erase shapes and details into the wash with an electric eraser.

To Burnish or not to Burnish?

Burnishing is the process of going over all the layers of a pencil rendering with a blunt colorless blender or another color using hard pressure to blend the colors and burnish the surface, making the pigment shine. In the process, all of the pencil will be pushed into the paper, flattening its texture. One of the goals of burnishing in a colored pencil painting is to create the smooth, even look of a traditional oil painting. This may not be a goal for the theatrical designer when using pencil. A designer may choose to use pencil because they like the roughness of the marks made by the medium, and want to exploit that quality to represent and illustrate an idea in their design. Burnishing the final rendering might remove that texture and make the final image less evocative. Another designer may want to burnish precisely because they want the smooth, shiny surface that the technique creates in their rendering. Another might use it selectively in their rendering; in some parts of the composition, but not others. Either way, the technique is available, and can be employed in three ways. In each method of burnishing, color can be reapplied and burnished over and over, until the desired look is achieved. The amount of color and the degree of pressure will vary slightly with each layer. Too much pressure and you can put grooves in the surface of the paper or board. Your strokes can be linear or circular, as long as they overlap. A little experimentation is required to become proficient at the technique.

- *Burnishing with a colorless pencil*: Several brands of colored pencils offer a colorless blender as part of their line. Burnishing with this product blends the pigment and creates a smooth, brilliant surface without adding any additional color or changing the saturation of the hue.

- *Burnishing with another color*: Burnishing with another color blends the top color with whatever color or colors are underneath in addition to creating the shine that comes from the pressure of the technique. This method often creates dramatic new colors that are vibrant and visually interesting.

- *Burnishing with white*: Burnishing with white will lighten the underlying color as it buffs the pigment. However, you can add more color and repeat the process to get back to the color you want until you reach the paper's saturation point.

A Word About Wax Bloom

Once you start working with pencils in depth, you will inevitably come up against the phenomenon of wax bloom. Because pencils are wax-based, once they have been burnished several

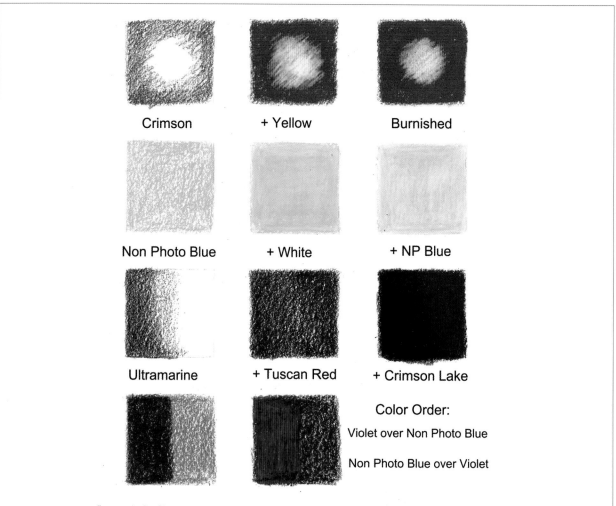

Crimson + Yellow Burnished

Non Photo Blue + White + NP Blue

Ultramarine + Tuscan Red + Crimson Lake

Color Order:

Violet over Non Photo Blue

Non Photo Blue over Violet

FIGURE 23-11 *Four methods of burnishing: with colorless blender; with white; with another color; using multiple colors and linear strokes*

times the wax has a tendency to rise to the surface of the drawing, where it forms a gray, hazy film that dulls the color. This can easily be corrected by lightly buffing the surface of the rendering with a soft cloth and then spraying it with fixative, which will prevent the bloom from returning permanently and seal the rendering from smudging and other damage. Fixative is a final step, so it should only be done when the rendering is complete. Oil-based pencils do not develop wax bloom.

ACRYLICS

Acrylic paints were brought about by an enormous development in chemistry in the early twentieth century. Sooner or later it had to affect artists' studios. By the early 1930's, chemists had learned to make strong, weatherproof industrial paints using a vehicle of synthetic plastic resin. By the 1950's, chemists had made many advances in the new technology, and had adapted it to an artist's requirements for permanence. For the first time since its development, oil paint had a serious challenger as the principal medium in Western painting. These new synthetic artists' colors are widely known as acrylics. Acrylic polymer is more accurate. The vehicle consists of an acrylic resin that has been polymerized, meaning that its simple molecules have been linked into long chains through emulsion in water. They are water-soluble until dry. As they dry, the resin particles coalesce to form a tough, flexible, waterproof film.

Acrylics are a very versatile paint medium, and are well-suited to the creation of theatrical renderings. Depending on how they are used, they can mimic the effects of several other different kinds of paint, including watercolor, oils, gouache, and even tempera. The can be used on almost any surface: wood, plaster, canvas, paper, art boards, Masonite, and even on fabric.

They can be layered in heavy impasto like oils, and they can be thinned into transparent washes like watercolor. Like tempera, they dry quickly and permanently. There is a wide range of mediums that can be added to them to create special paint effects and textures. Acrylics are now available in exciting new colors and metallics that allow for beautiful visual effects. Daniel Smith has a line of duochrome and interference acrylics that change color under different light angles and on light and dark colored papers. Their range of metallic colors is also impressive. Lumiere has a line of metallic acrylic colors made for fabric that contain metal, making them rich and highly reflective. Acrylics are also far less expensive than oils and watercolor, making it possible to have a wider range of colors in your artists' kit. The biggest disadvantage of acrylic paints is that you have to work quickly when using them. Once they are dry, they are permanent and cannot be reworked. While it is possible to add mediums to acrylics that slow their drying time, this fact cannot be changed. You also have to clean your brushes right away or rest them in water while working to prevent the paint from hardening on the bristles and ruining the brush. However, the flexibility of the medium and the range of effects that can be created with it more than make up for its quick drying time.

FIGURE 23-12 *Slavs! by Tony Kushner, costume design in acrylic by Kaoime E. Malloy, Iowa Summer Repertory*

Types of Acrylics

There are several different types of acrylic paints on the market and the main difference between them is their **viscosity**. Viscosity is simply how thick or thin the paint emulsion is. Thick paints have a high viscosity; thin paints have a low viscosity. Which type you choose to work with will largely be based on preference.

- **Heavy body acrylics**: Heavy body acrylics have a very high viscosity. They are thick enough to hold a brushstroke and to be applied with a palette knife and retain the shape of the stroke. They are available in both matte and glossy finish. Most acrylic paints fall into this category and it is likely these will be the main paints in your kit.

- **Open acrylics**: Open acrylics are so named because they contain an additive that prevents them from drying as quickly as traditional acrylics, allowing for a longer working time. They are intended to be worked in thin, multiple layers using traditional blending techniques and have a creamy texture.

- **Fluid acrylics**: Fluid acrylics are thin enough to be poured but contain the same pigment load as heavy body acrylics.

- **Airbrush colors**: Airbrush colors have the thinnest viscosity, similar to ink. They have a slower drying time than most acrylics owing to the need to pass through an airbrush and have a higher degree of translucency. They can almost be used like a dye to stain surfaces, especially fabrics and canvases.

Important Things to Remember about Acrylics

- *Acrylic paints are water soluble.* Acrylic is a water-based paint and can be cleaned up with soap and water. The paint can also be thinned with water to change the saturation level of the pigment. Doing so also dilutes the acrylic binder, making the paint more transparent and dulling the sheen. In this state, it can be used much like watercolors to create translucent washes and to build up thin layers of color. Even when thinned, acrylic is still permanent when dry.

- *Acrylic paints have a range of opacity.* Some acrylic colors are transparent, some are semitransparent, and others are opaque. The opacity of colors is determined by the type of pigment used to create it. Modern or organic pigments are usually translucent and have a high chroma

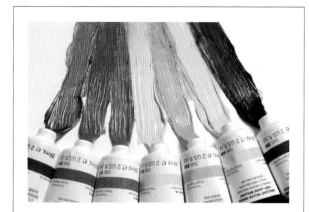

FIGURE 23-13 *Acrylic paints (R. Gino Santa Maria / Shutterstock.com)*

value. They produce vibrant tints and glazes because of their high pigment content. Mineral or inorganic pigments are generally opaque, have a low chroma value and their tinting strength is low because of the lower amount of pigment. They are easily recognizable because their names reflect their mineral origins. Burnt sienna, raw umber, and violet iron oxide are all examples of mineral pigments.

- *Acrylic paints are inherently glossy.* Acrylics have a natural sheen. Matting mediums and varnishes can be used to dull the paint's finish. They contain a fine white powder that creates this effect, but it can cause colors to lighten and become cloudy underneath the medium. The thicker the use of the medium, the more pronounced this effect can be. Acrylic paints labeled "satin" or "semi-gloss" already contain a matting agent, just in a lesser degree than matte medium and varnish.

- *Acrylic paints dry quickly.* This is both an advantage and a disadvantage. When emulating oil painting techniques, the quick drying nature of acrylics makes it possible to apply several layers in one painting session. This also makes it possible to work quickly when using acrylic like watercolor, layering thin, transparent washes, without lifting up the previous layer with each new one. But you have to work quickly while the paint is wet to lay and blend color.

- *Acrylic paints shrink when they dry.* The polymer emulsion of acrylic paint will shrink in volume as it dries. Thick layers can shrink by almost a third and pull on the surface of a rendering or a model. When working in thin layers this is not noticeable.

- *Acrylic paints darken as they dry.* Most acrylics are noticeably lighter when they are wet. This is because the binder in the paint is white when wet, but clear when dry. Windsor and Newton Artists acrylics have a clear resin base, so

there is virtually no color shift between the wet and dry paint. It is also important to remember that the more mediums and gels you add to acrylic paint, the greater the color difference will be between the wet and dry paint.

- *Acrylic paints have a two-step drying process.* Acrylic paints dry in two phases. In the first step, the paint surface becomes dry to the touch, forming a skin due to the evaporation of water from the emulsion. The second part of the drying process takes place over the next few days or even weeks while the acrylic emulsion cures. The curing process is dependent on environmental factors such as humidity and temperature as well as the thickness of the paint film. When working with thick layers of paint, keep in mind that a piece should not be wrapped tightly in plastic or stored in a closed environment, and it should be kept from extreme temperatures until the paint has fully cured.

- *Acrylic is vulnerable when "tacky."* Acrylics go onto the surface in a smooth, buttery fashion with both brushes and palette knives and are workable until they begin to dry significantly. At this point in the drying process acrylics develop a skin on their surface that is thick and sticky to the touch. If you continue to work the paint at this point you can damage the surface and create unwanted effects. However, a hairdryer can be used to speed the drying process if needed.

- *Do not let acrylic paint freeze.* Oil painters will sometimes freeze paint on their palettes to conserve paint but this is not a viable option for acrylics. Although they contain propylene glycol to keep them from freezing, the paint becomes unstable after several freeze and thaw cycles. A better option to conserve your paint from one painting session to the next is to buy a palette with an airtight lid. That will keep your paint fresh for several days at a time.

- *You must soak your brushes in water as you paint.* Paint brushes much be cleaned thoroughly with soap and water after each acrylic painting session to remove excess pigment. Soaking them in water in between each use during a rendering session prevents any deep-set paint from drying before you can clean them.

- *Mix paint with a palette knife, not a brush.* Brushes are made for painting, not for mixing large amounts of paint. Using a brush for this purpose drives paint up into the metal ferrules where you cannot clean it and shortens the lifespan of your brush.

- *Acrylic products are intermixable.* You can combine any acrylic paint, medium or gel with any other acrylic product. Matte medium can go over glossy medium, gels can go over sand medium, and paint can be used over all of them.

You can repeat any number of layers with acrylic products as often as you want. Just keep in mind that each product affects the look of the previous layer you cover.

- *Acrylics can be combined with other media.* Acrylics can be combined with other media to create new and interesting visual effects. However, other media should be worked on top of acrylic rather than the other way around. For example, oils can be worked on top of dry acrylic, but acrylic will not adhere to an oil-based surface. It also is not advisable to combine acrylic and other paints when they are wet, as the pigments are suspended in different binders and have different drying speeds.

- *Acrylics work as glue.* Both acrylic paint and mediums can be used as glue to adhere objects to the surface of your rendering or model to create collage images or embed texture. Once dry, they can then be over painted with more color.

Tools and Supplies

- *Paints*: Acrylics are available in a wide range of colors. How many you keep in your paint kit is up to you. At a bare minimum, you should have each of the three primary colors, a black of your choice, titanium white, yellow ochre and burnt sienna for mixing flesh tones, and burnt umber. Dioxazine purple and hooker's green are useful adjuncts to supplement your color range as are any duochrome, metallic or interference colors you might want to use for special effects.

- *Palette*: If you plan to save your paints from one work session to the next, a paint palette with an airtight lid is a great investment to keep your paints fresh over several days. Otherwise, there are several types of artists' palettes available, from flat trays to options with cups for different colors. An old plate from the thrift store works just as well. There are also disposable palette pads of waxed paper that make cleanup quick and easy.

- *Brushes*: The brushes you keep in your kit will be based on the type of rendering you do and personal preference. Brushes for acrylics are often made of synthetic bristles and these will hold up longer when sitting in water. The same is true of brush handles made of plastic rather than wood, which will swell when wet and shrink when dry, eventually loosening the ferrule. Select a range of brushes in multiple sizes to suit your needs. Flats for laying in color; filberts for soft edges, adding contours and rounded forms; brights for details when you need control; fan brushes for textures like grass, fur, hair, and lace; and rounds for lines and details.

FIGURE 23-14   *Paint brushes (Marie C Fields / Shutterstock.com)*

- *Palette knife*: Keep at least one flat palette knife in your kit for mixing paint. Palette knives come in a wide range of shapes and sizes for use as painting tools and you may choose to keep some in your kit for impasto techniques.

- *Supports*: As with colored pencils, there many different types of paper that will support the application of acrylic paint. Paper is primarily suitable when you plan to apply the paint in a light, watercolor style or by building up multiple thin layers of paint. Bristol paper and pastel paper are both suitable choices. For heavy paint treatments, untextured illustration board is a better choice. Both should be acid-free and archival quality in order to preserve your renderings over time. Acrylics are suitable for any surface that is not oily or greasy. They will adhere to wood, metal, plastic, canvas, Masonite, prepared painting boards, and fabric.

- *Rags*: Keep a couple of clean rags nearby your work area to use to clean brushes in between colors, to keep your hands clean as you work, and to pick up color from the painting surface as needed. Cotton cloths work best for their absorbency. An old flannel sheet torn into squares is excellent.

- *Mediums*: At the bare minimum, keep a bottle of **matte medium** and one of **gloss medium** in your kit. Both can be used as glue to add collage elements to your rendering, to affect the finish of the paint, and to seal the rendering when you are finished painting. If you think that you will be working texturally with the paint, heavy gloss and heavy matte gels are good additions to your set of acrylic mediums.

- *Cups for water*: You will need a couple of large containers for water while you are painting. At a minimum, keep one for rinsing and cleaning your brushes and one for diluting the paint as you work. Change both out often. The idea is to keep your mixing water as clean as you can so that you do not inadvertently add color from the water into your paint as you work.

- *Ruler*: Having a ruler makes it possible to draw straight lines with your brushes. Place several poster mounting tabs on the underside of the ruler to raise it up off the painting surface to prevent paint from running under it from the paintbrush. Ideally, the ruler should be high enough that the ferrules touch the straight edge rather than the brush.

Mixing Colors

Color mixing with acrylic is relatively easy, provided that you start with true primaries in a professional brand of paint that offers real artists' pigments. Student-grade paint, while less expensive, provides either nontoxic substitutes for artists' pigments or a lesser concentration of them in the emulsion. If every color in the brand is the same price, that is a clear sign of the paint being student-grade. Artists' pigments range in cost, so good quality paint should have a price that reflects the cost of each pigment. Learning to mix color is an important part of learning to paint a rendering and working with the best paint you can afford, with real pigments, will help you succeed—and prevent you from becoming frustrated when you cannot mix the color you want because of poor pigment quality. Your initial experimentation with color mixing should be with primaries rather than secondary or tertiary colors so that you can clearly see the effect of adding one hue at a time, along with white and black. Remember that each time you mix in a new color you are removing the amount of light that can be reflected back to the eye. Mixing with secondary and tertiary colors removes a greater amount of light than a primary because they contain more colors. The resulting mix can become dull quite quickly.

Most brands of paint will indicate which of their colors they consider to be their primaries, based on their pigment concentration and their ability to reflect light. In pigment, the three primary colors are red, blue, and yellow, and these colors are often sold in acrylic sets. I encourage my students to avoid them, as I generally do not agree with the color choices in these kits. I prefer to work with fuchsia, turquoise, and lemon yellow as the primary colors. These three colors are difficult to mix from red, blue, and yellow, but it is easy to mix red, blue, and yellow *from* them. These colors roughly correspond to cobalt or cerulean blue, deep magenta, and cadmium yellow light or cadmium lemon in several brands. True cobalt and true cadmium are both potentially toxic pigments and should be handled with care. If you prefer not to work with them, cadmium and cobalt colors are both available

in nontoxic hues that mimic the color of the real pigment, but their colors are not quite as vivid and they will not be as concentrated in tints.

In theory, mixing a secondary color from two primaries is as simple as blending each primary in a 50/50 ratio. In reality, the ratio of one color to the other is variable depending on the pigments in each primary. Color mixing and matching takes practice and you have to develop your eye in order to figure out what color or colors to add to your mix to make the final color you desire. If you have a large area to paint one color in your rendering, or a series of renderings that require the same color, it can be useful to mix up a large amount of the color and keep it in a closed container in order to ensure the color matches throughout the image or images.

Brushstrokes

As with pencils, the marks you make on a surface with a paintbrush are dependent on several factors. The amount of pressure you use when pressing the brush against the surface determines how much of the bristles comes into contact with the paper. Heavy pressure bends or compresses the bristles, allowing for a broader stroke, while light pressure only brings the tips of the bristles in contact with the paper, resulting in a lighter mark. The amount of paint on your brush has a direct effect on the marks made with each stroke. A saturated brush makes it possible to create a long, solid stroke with even color throughout, whereas a brush that is only lightly loaded with paint may create a shorter, less consistent mark. The dilution of the paint will change the value and viscosity of the marks made by the brush. Paint heavily diluted with

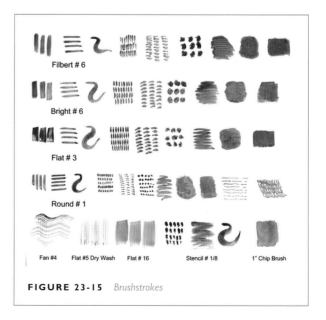

FIGURE 23-15 *Brushstrokes*

water will be less saturated, more transparent, and thinner in viscosity. Undiluted paint will be thicker, more opaque, and darker in value. Different brush types make marks of different shapes and each type of brush comes in a range of sizes. A large brush will make larger strokes and can fill in large areas on a rendering, while a small brush will be more suitable for fine details. The appearance of a brushstroke can be altered by holding the brush at different angles from the painting surface, making it possible to use each side of the brush to make marks of varying width and texture. A brush will make a different kind of mark based on whether you make your stroke with the edge of the bristles or the full width. It is also possible to turn the brush in the middle of a stroke, altering the position of the bristles to make a dynamic, shifting mark.

Paint in Sections

When working with acrylic, it is useful to divide your rendering into sections to make it easier to paint them. This not only includes breaking a large rendering down into individual parts—a set into the floor, walls, furniture, steps, backdrop, set decorations, and so on—but dividing each *part* of the rendering into smaller, more manageable sections. For example, a costume rendering may be broken down into the face and skin tones, individual garments and shoes. But garments can be further divided into individual folds of a skirt or legs of a pair of pants, the arms and sides of a coat or blouse, skin tones into faces, necks, décolletage, arms, legs, and hair. This makes the paint easier to control in each area. And, given that larger objects are made up of smaller shapes, it lets you deal with the way light is striking each section of the rendering and the objects within those parts in detail to create volume, depth, and a sense of realism.

Working in Layers

Laying down acrylic in layers makes sense for painting renderings whether you are working with thick or thin paint. Applying paint in layers gives you more control over the application, which is especially important when working with thick acrylic. When working with thin paint, layering lets you build up translucent color that blends together to create depth, vibrancy and luminosity. When working with thick, it allows you to create even areas of color with or without surface texture.

Working Thick

When working with thick acrylic straight from the tube it is best to use illustration board for the surface in order to support

FIGURE 23-16 *Painting in sections with acrylics—The Lucky Spot by Beth Henley, costume design by Kaoime E. Malloy, Iowa Summer Repertory*

the layers of paint. Paper is not thick enough to maintain its shape when the paint shrinks during the drying process, or to support the layers of paint without buckling. When working with paint straight from the tube, you will be dealing with the paint in its highest opacity. It is likely you will be covering the illustration board completely. Therefore, you cannot rely on the translucency of layering to create depth and volume. Instead, you will have to paint in all the highlights and shadows yourself, either in individual layers, or through wet blending.

When working on a dark colored board, it is beneficial to begin by laying down several thin layers of white, cream, or neutral gray in order to provide a lighter surface for the paint. Otherwise, you will be fighting the deep color of the board throughout the painting process and it will limit the amount of light that can be reflected back from the surface of the rendering. Lighter colored boards do not require this preliminary step before they are painted. This is especially important for areas where you intend to paint with light colors, such as light flesh tones in a costume rendering. Without this layer of underpainting, you will have to lay down additional layers of paint before you reach the intensity and value of color that you desire, increasing your working time.

FIGURE 23-17 *Heavy acrylic—The Magic Flute by Mozart, costume design by Kaoime E. Malloy*

Even when the end goal is to build up thick layers of paint, start thin. Your first two or three layers in each section of the rendering should be relatively thin. Thin layers coat the surface of the board, effectively priming it for the heavier layers that will come after. As you work each section, use these layers to fill in each area as you desire with your base color, taking care to create a smooth, even coat of paint. Subsequent layers of thick paint will glide more smoothly over this primed surface and make it easier to create even layers and blended colors. There are many different painting techniques that can be used with undiluted acrylics.

- **Wet blending** is the process of blending two or more colors of paint while they are wet. The goal may be to create a smooth transition between colors or to develop a more textural appearance. Wet blending can be accomplished by laying down the colors with separate brushes and then using a clean brush to blend the colors together, or one brush can be loaded with two or more colors and used to fill an area on the rendering and then blended. This creates a less controlled, more abstract effect.

- **Impasto** is a textural technique where paint is built up in a thick manner on the painting surface. Brushstrokes and palette knife marks are often clearly visible in the surface of the paint. Impasto is useful for creating texture on both renderings and models. There are no hard and fast rules for using the technique. The best way to become comfortable with using it is simply to experiment and find what works for you.

FIGURE 23-18 *Underpainting on dark board*

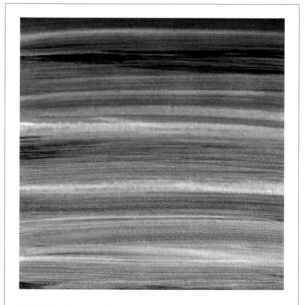

FIGURE 23-19 *Wet blending with acrylic (solarbird / Shutterstock.com).*

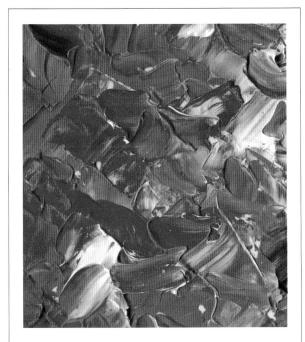

FIGURE 23-20   *Impasto (alexcoolok / shutterstock.com)*

FIGURE 23-21   *Sgraffito (Laurin Rinder / shutterstock.com)*

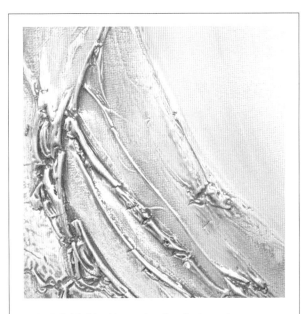

FIGURE 23-22   *Heavy gel medium (Louisanne / Shutterstock.com)*

- **Sgraffito** is the process of etching into a wet of coat of paint over a dry layer to reveal the color below. It can be used to add texture or as a design element in and of itself. To use this technique you must first create an underlayer of paint. Once that layer is completely dry, cover it with another layer of paint. While the top layer is still wet, use a brush, eraser, comb, or other object to pull the paint from the surface of the rendering, making the desired marks and revealing the color underneath. Then allow the top layer to dry completely.

- **Gel medium** is a thick gel that increases the viscosity of acrylic paint. This makes the paint extremely thick and it can be used in a very three-dimensional way. The surface of a rendering can be built up with heavy impasto strokes that retain the impression of the brush or palette knife and they can be sculpted into the shape you want. Gel medium is available in regular and heavy viscosity and glossy and matte finishes. Gloss finish gel dries clear so it does not affect the color of the paint, but matte gel dulls the sheen of acrylic just like matte medium. Unless you plan to use small quantities, gel mediums should be used on board or another rigid surface due to the shrinkage of the paint.

- Gel and fluid **retarder** is used to extend the drying and working time of acrylics. Gel retarder has a high viscosity and will produce more textural effects. Slow-Dri blending fluid from Liquitex lets you add up to 50 percent retarder to the paint without affecting the strength of the pigment and it increases the working time as much as 40 percent. Retarders are transparent and dry clear. If you want your paints to remain open and workable for longer periods, adding retarder to them before applying them to your surface will give you more time to work.

- Paint companies make a number of different **texture mediums** that can be added to acrylics to create various texture effects. Sand medium, black lava gel, glass bead gel, iridescent tinting medium, tar gel, crackle medium, and other mediums can all be used to affect the texture of the paint.

- **Modeling pastes** allow you to build up thick, hard surfaces on renderings and models. They can be used to create texture and sculpt surfaces that can be sanded, carved, and worked with other tools. They can be mixed with acrylics or painted after application.

Working Thin

Thinning acrylic paint allows you to treat the medium like watercolor, applying color in light, transparent layers. By painting in this manner you can create depth, volume, lustrous color, and beautiful textures. Fluid acrylics are ideally suited to this technique, as they have a lower viscosity than heavy body acrylics but contain the same amount of pigment per ounce. It requires far less water to create a thin paint consistency and therefore the resulting color retains its brilliance. However, any type of acrylic can be thinned and used in this manner. Remember that thinning with water dilutes the binder in the paint, dulling the color. To retain the sheen of acrylic, thin with gloss medium instead or add gloss medium when thinning with water. If a duller finish is desired, you can thin the paint with matte medium to further reduce the paint's gloss.

Like watercolors, thinned acrylic paints will stain and granulate. **Staining** occurs when the pigment seeps into the painting surface and dyes the material. **Granulation** is a visual texture produced when paint settles into the grooves of the surface (microscopic or visible), creating a pattern mimicking the appearance of grains of sand or rice. Inorganic mineral pigments are denser and heavier than organic pigments and, consequently, when the paint is diluted, they will float out across the water in the dilution to settle in the crevices of absorbent surfaces. In contrast, modern organic pigments will stain any and all parts of the surface when diluted, creating even strokes of color. There are many different ways to work with acrylic in a thinned form, including the most basic watercolor techniques.

- **Washes**: A wash is a thin, even coat of color. To create a wash, thin the paint to the desired consistency and then wet the area of the rendering to be painted with a clean brush and a thin layer of water. Apply the paint in long strokes from one edge to the other, overlapping with each stroke until the area is filled. Once you are finished applying the color let the area level and even itself out. Once the wash is complete, leave it to dry. Resist the temptation to go over a drying wash and rework it. The result is usually less than satisfactory. Once a wash is dry, more layers can be added as needed to achieve the desired effect. Acrylic flow release is a medium that breaks the surface tension of water, which can be added to acrylics prior to painting on the rendering. This increases the paint's ability to soak into a porous surface, resulting in a more even wash.

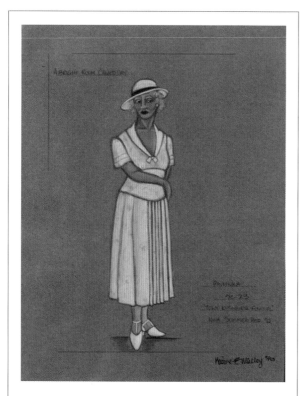

FIGURE 23-23 *Layered acrylic—A Bright Room Called Day by Tony Kushner, Iowa Summer Repertory, costume design by Kaoime E. Malloy*

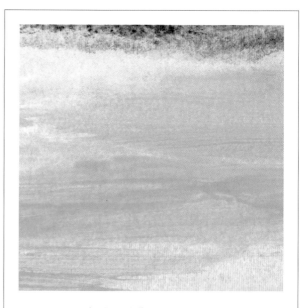

FIGURE 23-24 *Acrylic wash (Rudchenko Liliia / Shutterstock.com)*

- **Glazing**: Glazing is a similar technique to a wash that uses a thin, transparent pigment to layer color over an existing dry color. The purpose of a glaze is to adjust the color and tone of an underlying area, though they can also be used to deepen the value of shadows. Glazing is done with a darker color over a lighter color. Glazes can be made by mixing the paint with water, or with acrylic glazing medium.

- **Scumbling**: Like glazing, scumbling is accomplished by applying a thin, transparent layer of paint on top of a dry area of color. Scumbling is usually done with a lighter color rather than a dark one and because of this it can flatten out the underlying layers of color. It is very useful for adding beams of light or concentrated highlights to reflective surfaces.

- **Wet in wet**: Working wet in wet is simply applying thinned paint to a wet surface. This produces softer, blurred marks and unrefined shapes based on the wetness of the paper. These types of soft marks are very useful for creating a sense of atmospheric perspective in the background of a rendering. Simply wet the area of the rendering you wish to work in and paint in the wetness. Be sure that any color underneath is completely dry first or you can pull up the paint in the process.

- **Dry brushing**: Dry brushing is almost the exact opposite of painting wet in wet. In dry brushing, a brush loaded with paint is lightly dragged over a completely dry surface. Marks made in this fashion usually have hard edges and appear crisp. Dry brushing is an excellent method for creating texture on the surface of your rendering, including wood grain, siding, stripes in fabric, and other linear marks.

- **Dropping in color**: This is a simple process where thinned paint is dripped onto a wet surface and allowed to spread without interruption. The results are unpredictable, but the shifting edges of the paint can produce beautiful feathering textures and shifts of color that cannot be created by other methods.

- **Spattering**: Spattering is created by loading a brush with highly diluted paint and quickly running a finger or palette knife across the bristles to disperse a fine spray of color across your painting surface, producing speckles of color. Spattering creates visual texture that breaks up larger areas of color.

FIGURE 23-25 *Glazing (MoinMoin / Shutterstock.com)*

FIGURE 23-26 *Wet in wet (solarbird / Shutterstock.com)*

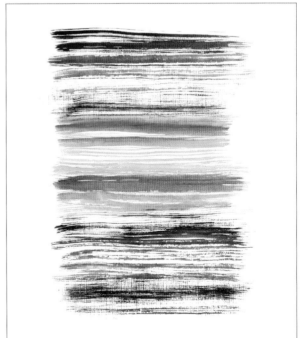

FIGURE 23-27 *Dry brushing for texture (solarbird / Shutterstock.com)*

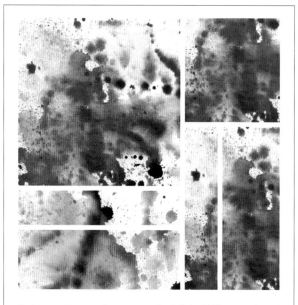

FIGURE 23-28 *Dropping in color (solarbird / Shutterstock.com)*

FIGURE 23-30 *Modeling with analogous colors—red, burgundy, yellow orange, and yellow ochre*

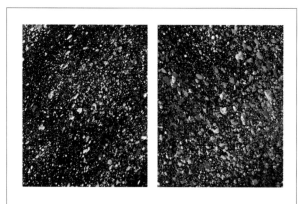

FIGURE 23-29 *Spattering (Africa Studio / Shutterstock.com)*

Highlight and Shadow with Analogous Colors

Just as when working with colored pencil, using analogous colors for highlights and shadows in acrylic rather than a darker shade of the base color creates more depth and volume. Using tints and shades alone actually makes the subject appear flatter. Remember that highlights and shadows possess color as well and that stage lighting seeks to recreate that effect. When working with thinned acrylic, shadows can be layered under the main color for a more subtle effect, or layered on top for a more dramatic look. In acrylic, highlights will be more effective on top of the paint layers, even when worked in thin layers, so that they can be seen clearly. Thicker paint demands that both highlights and shadows be placed on top of the base color or wet blended into the main paint layer. Both highlights and shadows can be used to pick out details and add dimension with precise, thin lines as part of the painting process.

MIXED MEDIA

Mixed media is the practice of applying multiple types of media to a rendering. The advantage of using different types of media is that you can apply a variety of techniques to your image, taking advantage of all the positive aspects of each. The end result is a rendering that looks exactly the way you want it to. Colored pencils may be layered over acrylics. Graphite pencils can be used to model form and pick out detail over colored pencil, acrylic, or marker. Markers can be used to add depth and dimension to paint and pencil. Pastels can add highlights on top of paint. There really are no rules with mixed media beyond the limitations of the media themselves and your imagination.

DIGITAL

If you are looking for maximum flexibility, nothing beats digital rendering. Using an image-editing program such as Adobe® Photoshop®, Adobe Illustrator®, CorelDRAW®, or Autodesk Sketchbook® Pro allows you to create and edit your renderings with the click of your mouse. These are powerful programs that offer a multitude of brushes, patterns, textures, tools, and other options to apply color and lighting effects to your rendering. In particular, Sketchbook® Pro offers a library of digital Copic markers and specialized drawing tools that mimic the intuitive feel of hand-drawing. You can even draw your sketches within the programs using a digital pen tablet, a digital stylus on a tablet computer, or a digitizing pen like the Bamboo® Stylus. A digital stylus mimics the feel of working with a traditional pen or brush,

FIGURE 23-31 *Mixed media*—Cloud 9 *by Caryl Churchill, University of Iowa, costume design by Kaoime E. Malloy*

FIGURE 23-32 *Digital rendering*—bobrauschenbergamerica *by Charles Mee, costume design by Kaoime E. Malloy, University of Wisconsin Green Bay*

responding to the pressure of your hand against the tablet or screen to alter the marks made in the program. Sketches can be made with the Wacom® Inkling®, a traditional ballpoint pen that allows you to sketch on paper, simultaneously digitizing your drawing for transfer to a computer. You can even create multiple layers as part of the drawing process with a simple touch of a button. It is also possible to scan

in a hand drawing and use the programs to add color and dimension. However you begin your drawing, with a little practice you can use digital tools and editing programs as easily as you would pencils or paint.

Demonstration: Digital Painting with Adobe® Photoshop®

This demonstration is executed using Adobe® Photoshop® on a Windows PC. Some of the shortcuts may be different on a Mac and some of the tools may be in different locations on the tool menu. Hand-drawings for digital renderings will be easier to work with if they are drawn on white paper with heavier line weights. This makes them scanner-friendly and eliminates the need for extensive cleanup before you can paint. Textured and speckled papers are challenging to scan and touch up and might prevent the color from filling the spaces evenly in the final image. If your drawing style is loose and "sketchy," you might want to go over your final drawing with felt-tip pen and then erase your pencil lines to ensure a clean image with unbroken lines.

Step One: Preparing the Image for Coloring

1. Begin by creating a black-and-white image folder on your computer. You will use this to save your images during the grayscale steps in this process.

2. Scan your original black and white drawing at 400–600 dpi and save it as a .tiff file in your black-and-white folder. It is important that your original drawing is clean with clear, even, and unbroken lines before you scan it in order to save on cleanup time before painting.

3. Open your .tiff image in Photoshop®.

4. Open the history dialogue box by clicking on "window" in the toolbar and selecting "history" from the dropdown menu.

5. Most line drawings will need to be prepped and cleaned before they can be painted with the program. If there are any speckles or marks on the background, select the eraser tool, adjust the tool size on the menu above the work window and then swipe your cursor over the area with the left mouse button held down to remove them. Release the button after each pass of the cursor.

6. If the lines of your drawing are too pale, darken them by adjusting the levels. Go to: Image > Adjustments > Levels and then move the slider to the right to darken the lines and clean up the background until you reach your desired level of contrast.

7. Check to be sure your image mode is set to RBG color. Go to: Mode > RGB Color.

8. Check your drawing for any line breaks. Noncontinuous lines will allow the color to spill out into the background or other areas of the image. It is important that any area you intend to pour color into be sealed up as an individual cell. If you have openings, select the paintbrush or pencil tool, choose an appropriate size and hardness from the tool's menu, select black as the color, and then close the line by drawing with your cursor, holding the left mouse button down.

9. Duplicate the layer. Go to: Layer > Duplicate Layer. You can also right-click on the layer in the layer palette.

10. Delete the background. Select the magic wand tool from the tool menu. Left-click on the background of the image.

Delete the background (Ctrl + X). The image now stands alone on a transparent background.

11. Save the new image in the black and white folder as "silhouette" or "outline."

12. Use the magic wand tool on the background again. Go to: Select > Inverse. Now the silhouette/outline of your image is selected rather than the background.

13. Create a new Photoshop document. Make the new document 11 × 14 and 400 dpi.

14. Using the move tool, drag the image to the new page and center it on the canvas.

15. Select flatten image from the layer dropdown menu and merge the layers.

16. Name and save this new file.

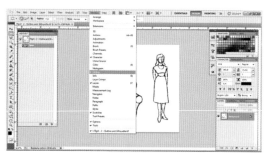
Step 4 - Open the History dialogue box

Step 5 - Clean the image

Step 6 - Adjust the levels

Step 8 - Close any line breaks

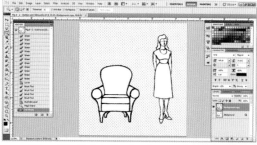
Step 10 - Delete the background

Step 14 - Drag the outline to the new image

FIGURE 23-33   *Preparing a digital image (Adobe® product screen shots reprinted with permission from Adobe Systems Incorporated.)*

Step Two: Painting the Image

When painting the image, it is definitely possible to work on just one layer and add all your color, texture, and lighting effects to that layer to create the rendering. However, you will have greater control over the individual parts of the image, including the ability to step backwards and forwards using the history layer interface by assigning a new layer to each part of the image. Working in layers also makes it possible to hide parts of the composition, making them invisible so that you can see one layer individually and work on it by itself. Having multiple layers also allows you to edit the rendering as many times as you like, so if your director requests changes there is no need to draw an entirely new sketch. You can simply recolor your design, save it with a new file name, and you will have both the old and the new version readily available. You can keep all the individual layers separate until you are ready to merge them together to create one single image or never merge them. The choice is yours, although multiple layers do generate larger files.

1. Open your newly cleaned and prepped file. Notice in the layer dialogue panel that this new merged image is now called "background."

2. Duplicate the background layer. Rename this layer "silhouette."

3. Magic wand the background on the silhouette layer. Delete the pixels (Ctrl + X). If there are any small areas of background mixed in with the object in the image, such as between an arm and the body in a costume drawing, be sure to delete those pixels too.

4. Duplicate the silhouette layer. Rename it "silhouette 2."

5. Using the magic wand tool, click on each individual cell in the image and delete the pixels inside it. You can also use the magic eraser tool to erase the pixels. The magic eraser tool is located in the eraser palette on the toolbar. You may need to zoom in on the image in order to select small areas with the magic wand. Use CRTL + to zoom in and CTRL – to zoom out. The reason we want the image totally transparent is that when working in layers, it is easy for a layer with greater opacity to completely obscure a layer with lesser opacity. By making them all transparent to begin with, you are free to choose the opacity on each layer as needed. In order to see which cells you have cut, click on the eye icon next to the background and silhouette layers in the layer menu to make them invisible.

6. Duplicate the silhouette layer as many times as you need for each part of the image. Rename each layer with an easy identifier so you know which part of the rendering it applies to, such as "skirt," "face and hair," "floor," "walls," or "chair." This process is called *flatting*.

7. Fill the areas with color, working on each layer individually. The easiest way to do this is with the paint bucket tool. Choose the color you want by clicking the color swatches at the bottom of the tools menu to open the color picker. Scroll through the color slider on the right hand side of the dialogue box to choose a color range and then click on the color you want in the dialogue box. You can also select colors in the color palette, though the selection is limited there. For flesh tones, you can find an image that has the colors you want, and use the color picker tool to select colors as desired. On the toolbar, select your opacity between 100 percent and 1 percent. Select the paint bucket tool from the tools menu and then click inside the area of the rendering you wish to color. The tool will fill the area, up to the boundaries created by the lines. Repeat until all areas are filled for the layer. Be sure that the layer you want to work on is highlighted in the layer palette.

8. Add dimension to each layer. This can be accomplished in several different ways.

   a. Use the bevel and emboss tool: This tool will quickly add dimension to the entire layer. To access the tool go to: Layer > Layer Style > Bevel and Emboss. This opens the dialogue box for the tool which has a number of qualities that can be adjusted. These values will all be set at their default settings when you open Photoshop. Here you can adjust the opacity of the tool, the shape of the marks it makes, the style, the direction, the highlight and shadow modes, the texture, and the softness. Once you make your adjustments, you can also save the style as a new style to be used again later. A preview swatch is displayed on the right-hand side of the dialogue box for you to see how your changes will affect the tool's appearance. Select OK when you are ready to apply it to your layer. The tool will automatically apply a somewhat stylized version of highlights and shadows to your image. You can also do this to the entire image after you have combined the layers.

   b. Use the dodge and burn tools: Dodge and burn are transparent highlighting and shadowing tools, respectively. They apply lighter and darker versions of the color in any area with each stroke. Unlike the bevel and emboss tool, they needed to be applied manually to the individual parts of the image you want to model. Layering strokes will intensify their effect. Like the paintbrush tool you can alter the size, hardness, texture, and opacity of the mark they make. These tools are grouped together on the tools menu along with the sponge tool, which produces a gray version of the underlying color when used. This tool can be used to blend dodging and burning marks into the colors beneath them.

c. Color dodge and burn: Color dodge and color burn are modes available on the paintbrush tool menu under mode. Selecting them from the dropdown menu on the toolbar allows you to apply colors to the dodge and burn effects through the paintbrush tool so you can model form with color rather than tints and shades alone. Like the dodge and burn tool, this mode applies the color transparently, so you can apply color with full saturation without losing your drawing details underneath it.

d. Add highlights and shadows with the paintbrush tool: Using the paintbrush tool gives you full access to the paintbrush mode menu of effects. With the paintbrush tool you can achieve full opacity of color if desired and still dial it down for transparent washes.

Remember that the effects of dodge, burn, color dodge and burn, and painting with color are cumulative, meaning that each successive layer will build color on the layer underneath it, just as you would with real paint, increasing saturation and value.

9. Color the background. Once you have the main parts of your rendering colored, you can apply color to the background using the paint bucket tool. Pattern and texture can be applied to the background if desired by using one of the texture brush presets on the paintbrush tool menu and another color.

10. Add lighting effects to the background layer. Photoshop® has several powerful rendering tools in the filter menu:

a. Lens flare: Lens flare allows you to add a flare of light to the image. To access the tool, go to: Filter > Render >

Steps 3 & 5 - Delete the pixels

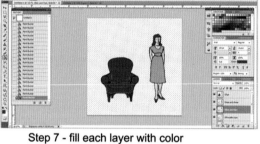

Step 7 - fill each layer with color

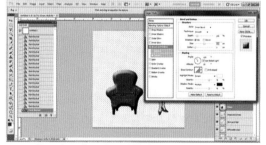

Step 8a - Bevel and Emboss

Step 8b - Dodge and Burn

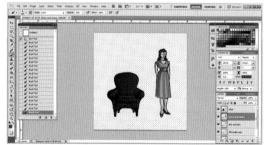

Step 8c - Color Dodge and Burn

FIGURE 23-34 *Painting a digital image (part one) (Adobe® product screen shots reprinted with permission from Adobe Systems Incorporated.)*

Lens Flare. In the dialogue box that opens you can select the type of lens effect, adjust the brightness and the position of the flare in the image.

b. Lighting effects: Photoshop® offers 16 different adjustable lighting styles in the lighting effects filter. To access the tool, go to: Filter > Render > Lighting Effects.

In the dialogue box you can select the style of filter you want to use as well as the light type, its intensity, focus, properties, and texture. In addition, in the preview pane you can adjust the light positions, shape, and spread of each "instrument" in the effect. It is even possible to mix the light color.

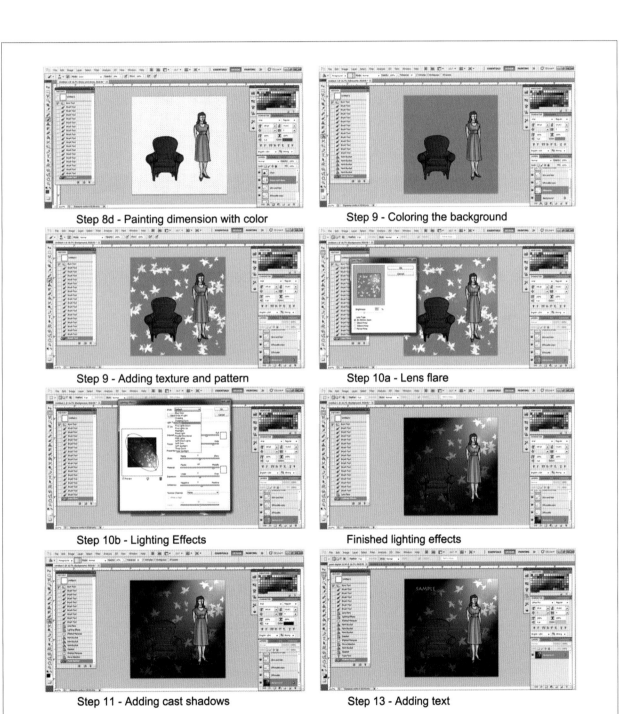

Step 8d - Painting dimension with color

Step 9 - Coloring the background

Step 9 - Adding texture and pattern

Step 10a - Lens flare

Step 10b - Lighting Effects

Finished lighting effects

Step 11 - Adding cast shadows

Step 13 - Adding text

FIGURE 23-35 *Painting a digital image (part two) (Adobe® product screen shots reprinted with permission from Adobe Systems Incorporated.)*

11. Add cast shadows to the background layer. Once your lighting effects are in place, you can add shadows underneath objects in the rendering to enhance the sense of dimension and depth with the elliptical marquee tool. By putting shadows on the background rather than any other layer, you can be sure that they will be underneath any other objects in the rendering where they belong. Select the elliptical marquee tool from the tools menu and then use it to select the location and shape of shadow you want under an object. You can adjust the location while the shape is selected by clicking inside the shape and dragging it to position it where you want. Set the color to black and the opacity to 50 percent. Using the paint bucket tool, fill the ellipse with color. Deselect the ellipse and repeat the step for each object you want to shadow.

12. Merge the layers together. Once you have all of the layers painted the way you want, you can either save the file and leave them separate for later editing, or you can merge them into one layer, producing a smaller file. To do this, you can either flatten the image, or merge the layers down. Go to: Layer > Flatten image. The program will automatically compress the layers together. Notice in the layer palette there is now only one layer.

13. Add text if desired. Using the text tool, you can add the title of the play, act and scene numbers, and any other information you wish. The text tool allows you select font, color, and adjust size and placement as well as add effects through the layer tool menu just as you could for any other layer.

Some Tips for Working with Layers

In using Photoshop for coloring renderings there are a few things you will want to remember and get in the habit of doing as you work to make your painting process easier and more fluid.

- *Save your file often.* This will prevent any loss of progress.

- *Remember that you can undo and redo steps.* With the history window visible, you will be able to see your last steps so that you can quickly jump back and "erase" your work. You can also jump forward to redo steps. Be aware that once you manually make a change in your image after an undo, you will delete all the "erased" steps from the history window and they cannot be recalled.

- *Use the "eye" icon next to each layer in the layer palette to make a layer invisible.* Sometimes it is useful to make some layers invisible while you work on another. Clicking on the visibility icon is a quick way to hide and reveal layers. Remember that a layer must be visible to make any adjustments.

- *Right-click on a layer in the layer palette to duplicate it.* This is a little faster than using the layer dropdown menu.

THE LANGUAGE OF RENDERING

Airbrush colors: Acrylics with the thinnest viscosity, similar to ink.

Art sticks: Wax colored pencils in stick form.

Burnishing: Using a wax pencil with heavy pressure to both blend layers of color together and polish the wax surface, making it shine.

Circular stroke: Overlapping pencil or brush marks applied in a circular motion.

Colored pencils: Pencils that contain an inner core made of pigment mixed with wax and other fillers, surrounded by wood or plastic.

Colorless blender: A colored pencil or marker with no pigment, used to blend colors together on the surface of a rendering.

Dropping in color: A simple process where thinned paint is dripped onto a wet surface and allowed to spread without interruption.

Dry brushing: Dragging a brush loaded with paint over a completely dry surface to create surface textures.

Fixative: An agent that seals the surface of a piece, "fixing" the media in place.

Fluid acrylics: Acrylics that are thin enough to be poured but contain the same pigment load as heavy body acrylics.

Gel medium: A thick gel that increases the viscosity of acrylic paint.

Glazing: A similar technique to a wash that uses a thin, transparent pigment to layer color over an existing dry color.

Gloss medium: An acrylic additive that increases the sheen of the paint.

Granulation: A visual texture produced when paint settles into the grooves of the surface, creating a pattern mimicking the appearance of grains of sand or rice.

Heavy body acrylics: Thick acrylic paint with a high viscosity.

Impasto: A very thick, highly textured application of paint to a surface where the marks of the brushes, individual strokes, or painting knives remain visible.

Layering: Placing colors or media on top of one another for effect.

Linear fill strokes: Pencil or brushstrokes applied all in the same direction, overlapping, and layered on top of each other to fill in an area with color.

Matte medium: An acrylic additive that dulls the natural shine of the paint.

Modeling paste: A heavy medium that can be added to acrylic paint for thick impasto techniques or to create sculptural forms which can be carved and sanded.

Multidirectional fill strokes: Small overlapping linear marks that move in multiple directions.

Oil-based pencils: Pencils made by combining pigments with oil as a binder

Open acrylics: Acrylics containing an additive that prevents them from drying as quickly as traditional acrylics, so that they remain "open" longer.

Power eraser: An electrical eraser.

Pure linear strokes: Linear pencil or brush marks that retain their shape, creating visual texture.

Rendering: A final drawing of a theatrical design including all major and minor details, in full color.

Retarders: Additives used to extend the drying and working time of acrylics.

Scumbling: Applying a very thin coat of opaque paint over a painted surface to produce a soft or dull effect.

Sgraffito: The process of etching into a wet coat of paint over a dry layer to reveal the color below.

Solvent: A chemical that can dissolve the binders of various media so they may be thinned or manipulated to effect.

Spattering: Loading a brush with highly diluted paint and quickly running a finger or palette knife across the bristles to disperse a fine spray of color across the surface of your painting surface, producing speckles of color.

Staining: When paint pigment seeps into the painting surface and dyes the material.

Support: The material on which paint or other media is applied. Also called a surface.

Surface: The material on which paint or other media is applied. Also called a support.

Texture mediums: Acrylic additives that change the texture of the paint.

Viscosity: The thickness of the paint emulsion.

Wash: A thin, even coat of color.

Water-based pencils: Pencils made of pigment combined with water and a water soluble gum as a binder.

Wax-based pencils: Pencils made by combining pigments with wax binders.

Wax bloom: A phenomenon where wax rises to the surface of a colored pencil drawing, where it forms a gray, hazy film that dulls the color.

Wet blending: The process of blending two or more colors of paint while they are wet.

Wet in wet: Applying thinned paint to a wet surface.

PART FIVE

INDIVIDUAL DESIGN AREAS

CHAPTER 24

COSTUME DESIGN

WHAT IS COSTUME DESIGN? A BRIEF HISTORY

Clothing is one of the most easily recognizable and accessible parts of any production and through it the audience can connect with the characters on an intimate and familiar level. As human beings, we all know what it is like to wear clothes and we can easily relate to what they communicate about a character, because we make our own clothing choices for many of the same reasons a character might. As human beings, we all understand the desire to want to look good in what we are wearing, or to be comfortable. We have all experienced dressing for work or to engage in a sport or other activity. We have chosen an outfit in order to impress or attract others. We have selected clothing to protect us from the elements, and we know what it is like to dress up for a special occasion. All of these experiences contribute to our appreciation and understanding of how costume reveals and supports character. And, because costumes are inherently tactile in nature and very often beautiful, they have the ability to both impress and delight the audience, providing another way to draw them into the performance.

The moment an actor walks onstage, an impression is made. The audience immediately gains crucial information, both about the production as a whole and the character themselves A costume is a transformative garment, one that assists an actor to become, for a time, someone else. By working in harmony with the emotions, movements, imagination, and skill of the actors, a costume helps to create and express the characters of the play to the audience, revealing subtleties of personality, behavior, class, social standing, profession, and other nuances of identity. It enhances the actors' performance and helps to tell the character's story. It is not uncommon for an actor to say that the moment they put on the costume they truly felt their character come to life.

Costumes have a long history, both inside and outside of theatre. Before theatre had developed into a recognizable art form, people the world over were wearing articles of clothing to assist in the telling of stories, to establish and delineate rank among groups, and to perform ceremonies and rituals.

FIGURE 24-1 The Memorandum by Vaclav Havel, costume design by Kaoime E. Malloy

Shamans donned animal skins and headdresses made of feathers, antlers and bone to magically transform themselves into mythic and otherworldly beings and to enhance their connection to the spirit world. So dressed, they could summon the spirits and ask for their assistance in the hunt, to influence the weather or the luck of their people, or to encourage fertility of crops and humans alike. People have created makeup, jewelry, and garments of special significance and skill to honor leaders and people of import, distinguishing them from the rest of the community. Religious leaders developed garments that became ritualized over time, turning into uniforms that are as important to the relevant spiritual activities and ceremonies as the activity itself. Armies have designed uniforms to help identify their members, to elicit fear, or to command respect. Throughout time, standards of dress have been used to delineate professions and social classes and have even been regulated and codified based on activity and time of day. In short, clothing not only identifies who we are, but how we fit into our society and how we wear it communicates how we feel about ourselves.

THE FUNCTIONS OF COSTUME

The primary function of costume is to assist the actor in the creation of character. If we define a costume as any clothing item that is worn on stage, then our real concern as a designer becomes how to create an *effective* costume, one that does several things at once. An effective costume is one that enhances and underscores the physical and emotional choices made by the actor, by assisting and complementing their performance and the character that they have developed. The well-designed costume defines and enriches the character visually and helps to establish and anchor them in the world of the play. A compelling costume should engage the audience, communicating information about the character in an understandable way that simultaneously draws them into the production. A careful and thoughtful costume design speaks to the audience, delving into their own personal context to draw on their individual understanding of clothing in order to help them identify and comprehend who the character is, often before they ever speak—and even if they never have *any* dialogue over the course of the play. An effective costume is also one that contributes to the overall mood, theme, and visual approach to the production, helping to establish unity with the other design elements, enhancing the entire experience of the performance and the play.

FIGURE 24-2   Halcyon Days *by Steven Deitz, Plymouth State Theatre, costume design by Alison Ford*

CREATING AND DEFINING THE CHARACTER

When we say that a costume must define a character visually what we mean is that when an actor walks onstage, the audience should be able to identify who they are, what position they hold within the world of the play, and what kind of individual they are. Even if their identity is a secret from the rest of the characters, or if they are meant to be in disguise, the audience should generally be able to figure out who they are and what purpose they serve. Some plays will require this more than others, as there are entire genres of theatre that rely on easily recognizable stock characters to tell their story. In these plays, character identification is crucial. Each character also needs to be unique, with enough difference between them and the rest of the characters to allow the audience to gain and understand crucial information about them as individuals. However, costumes are also an ideal way to illustrate and support the relationships between characters, tying them together visually in subtle or obvious ways to assist in communicating these connections. With all of these goals, costume designers have a tall order to fill long before costume designers begin to consider how their work will tie in with that of their design colleagues.

In order to define the character, a costume has to deliver a variety of information by providing visual answers to several different questions. These questions address specific qualities that all have the potential to influence the look of the character onstage and it is no accident that these questions are similar to the ones that an actor tries to answer when developing their approach to the character. Character analysis for the costume designer and the actor are comparable. The characters in the play are people like you, living in an imaginary world that might be very similar or quite different than the one we live in, but they will often make their choices regarding what they want to wear

FIGURE 24-3 The Importance of Being Earnest *by Oscar Wilde, University of Iowa Theatres, costume design by Kaoime E. Malloy*

for the same reasons we do. In fact, thinking about costumes as clothing for people that live in these other, imaginary worlds might be a more useful way of approaching the task of costume design than referring to these items as a "costume."

INFORMATION COMMUNICATED BY COSTUME

Gender

Throughout history and in all cultures all around the world, there have been distinctions in fashion between genders. For the costume designer, these differences can be used to reveal, conceal, or even confuse the gender of a character, as required by the script. In the West, we have largely come to associate dresses, skirts, high heels, and other "feminine" garments with women, and pants, suits, jackets, ties, and similar "masculine" clothing with men, but this is not the case for all cultures worldwide, nor is it strict rule in Western culture. What is masculine or feminine varies greatly from one country and society to the next and there are also some cultures that have clothing traditions for individuals outside the gender binary. Careful research is always necessary when addressing gender in a production, especially in modern plays, where gender identity can be fluid, highly personal, and affected by multiple social and political influences.

Age

Costume designers are often required to consider age as one of their requirements when making design choices. Age is, after all,

a crucial aspect of character and can sometimes be drastically different than the age of the actor. In addition, there may be characters that need to age over the course of the play, starting out as children or young adults and sometimes becoming significantly older as the play progresses. Costumes can help to reveal those changes by reflecting the time period as the character progresses through the play. Costumes can illustrate the differences in fashion, hair and makeup styles, variations in the character's taste and personality over time and how these are reflected in their choice of clothing. They can show changes in their standard of living and profession and also general fluctuations in health and appearance over time.

Health

Some characters are vibrant, strong, and healthy, living their lives at the peak of physical health, while others are seriously ill. Some may suffer the effects of a terrible accident, such as a limp or confinement to a wheelchair, while the physical appearance of others may reflect a life lived completely inside or underground, never having seen the light of day. A character may start out healthy and become ill during the action of the play or vice versa. They may gradually lose their sanity or suffer an injury in the play. A character may need to appear as if they've lost or gained weight, or become pregnant. These are all things that can be supported and revealed through costumes and makeup and therefore must be taken into consideration by the costume designer.

Personality and Mood

Who we are and how we feel about ourselves is often reflected in the clothing choices we make and the same is true for characters in a play. There is an almost unlimited number of factors that might influence a character's mood. How we dress when we are happy, well-rested, and having a good day is usually very different from the way we dress when we are tired, sick, feeling down, or having a difficult day. We might choose brighter colors when we are feeling better, or clothes that accentuate our features. If we are tired or feeling ill we might base our choices on comfort rather than style, opting for older clothing items that are well-worn, faded, or even darker or more neutral in color that may draw less attention. When we want to impress someone then that desire is often reflected in our clothing choices as well. We might select better-made or more costly items from our wardrobe, pieces of clothing that make us look more sophisticated and appealing. What we wear when we do our laundry is probably very different. Our clothing choices can also demonstrate our level of taste and degree of professionalism.

When it comes to communicating a character's mood, how we wear clothing and the condition of those garments is as important as what items we choose to wear. An expensive, well-tailored fine wool suit that is clean and crisply pressed conveys one impression about the person wearing it, while an old, cheaply made polyester suit that is stained, wrinkled, missing buttons, and looks like it has been slept in says something else entirely. Finely made clothing can be "dressed down," or worn in such a way that is in direct contradiction with the quality of the clothing, thereby communicating a different idea about the character wearing it or making a deliberate statement about their state of mind or situation. Conversely, it is also possible to dress a character in well-worn clothing that has been carefully mended and cared for without making them look completely threadbare, and everything in between. Often, how a costume piece is worn may be highly influenced by input from the individual actor and this kind of attention to detail is very useful in showing character progression over the course of a play.

Culture

The society in which a character is born and the one in which they reside can have a significant influence on their manner of dress. The word "culture" embodies a variety of influential attributes, including the prevailing philosophy, morals, codes of behavior, aesthetic conventions, spiritual beliefs, forms and styles of art, music and literature, and standards of behavior of a group of people, all of which can have an effect on the design of clothing. Characters reflect the environment in which they are raised and live, which can help to create a sense of belonging and build relationships with other characters in the same location. Using these same ideas, it is also possible to point out differences between characters and heighten their separation. When a stranger arrives in a community, they may stand out like a sore thumb, as much for their clothing as for their mannerisms, values, or way of speaking.

Time Period

Costumes can instantly communicate the time period of the play. Fashion silhouettes throughout history are distinctive and recognizable and help to bring the audience into that world. Changes in historical fashions over the course of the play are also a useful way to show the passage of time in a production. It goes without saying that a costume designer needs to possess an intimate knowledge and understanding of fashion history in order to be able to do their work.

Time of Year

Clothing needs differ from one season to the next and fashion follows those requirements. Garments for the winter are warmer, heavier, and usually darker in color than those for summer. They cover more of the body. Conversely, summer garments are made of lighter fabrics, employ lighter colors, and may show more skin on both men and women, depending on the time period. These differences can easily indicate the time of year and changes in the types of garments worn can also be used to indicate the passage of time throughout the production.

Location

The clothing we choose to wear depends largely on our environment. Someone that lives in the desert southwest of the United States is going to dress quite differently than someone that lives in the Arctic Circle. Location will also have an impact on culture as it pertains to clothing, as characters may be strongly affected by local fashion traditions or even just the opposite. A character might be an outsider or a stranger to the community, and need to clearly appear that way. Location also has an effect on the clothing worn in individual seasons, as summer in a northern country is very different from one near the equator.

Social Status

Social status is commonly reflected in not only the way clothing looks and whether or not it is the latest style or how much it costs, but in the cut and fit of each article, the age of the items, and the materials and workmanship of the garments. A character with a great deal of money or one born into a high-ranking family is likely to have an extensive wardrobe, one that reflects their wealth or taste and perhaps an interest in the things that money can buy, while one without the means to acquire such things will probably have a smaller, less populated wardrobe, perhaps filled with older items that are out of style or have seen better days, carefully mended in order to remain wearable. Certain time periods or cultures may also have distinct and highly codified standards of dress between social classes, social customs that dictate the manner of dress throughout the day or for specific occasions, or sumptuary laws that are used to distinguish one strata of society from another. Taking advantage of these factors and variations in dress will provide opportunities to highlight distinctions between characters and accentuate where the character fits into the hierarchy of the play.

Occupation

What a character does for a living can have a tremendous impact on how they dress. Over the course of history, occupation has dictated dress to such an extent—either through social conventions, propriety, regulations, traditions, or the concern for safety—that certain professions now have easily recognizable uniforms that allow us to identify individuals as members of that group. In some cases, these uniforms have become highly codified and now must adhere to specific standards. Nurses, doctors, firemen, judges, chefs, the military, members of the clergy, and airline personnel are all examples of professions where clothing readily identifies not only their occupation, but often their professional affiliation as well. These are obvious examples, but there are other, less palpable or classified standards of dress that can suggest what a character does for a living. For both men and women, the suit has become synonymous with white-collar, corporate or office jobs where a standard of dress is required as part of fitting into the business environment and culture. In the corporate business world of Japan, the suit has evolved to the point of being a uniform with so little variation in color and style that the individual becomes as visually subordinate as the company worker is jobwise to their boss. In other occupations, clothing is chosen for the suitability to the tasks performed by the worker rather than the culture of the workplace. Originally manufactured to meet the needs of gold prospectors for a durable, long-lasting garment in the middle of the nineteenth century, blue jeans have become acceptable work attire for individuals whose jobs require a comfortable, strong garment that will last through multiple washings. As jeans have become more accepted as a standard garment they have increasingly worked their way into the workplace in numerous permutations. Now, jeans are worn by construction workers, factory personnel, landscapers, painters, hairdressers, retail workers, and everything in between. Determining whether or not your character's profession will affect their clothing choices, or if their profession needs to be revealed through clothing, can add a tremendous amount of depth to your costume choices.

Character Changes and Development

There are very few characters that remain the same throughout the entire play. Many will change dramatically over the course of the action. These changes can be supported by modifications in costume, whether they are physical, mental or emotional.

FIGURE 24-4 Love's Labours Lost *by William Shakespeare, costume design by Kaoime E. Malloy, photo by R. Michael Ingraham*

QUESTIONS TO ASK/WHERE TO START

Given all of the things that costumes can communicate to the audience and contribute to the production, how do you go about finding out that information? The first place to look is the play itself. By reading the script with the goal of looking for this material in mind, the costume designer can ask specific questions and find the answers that are needed. Some of these answers will apply to the play as a whole—such as location, time period, and time of year—and will be part of your overall script analysis. But a costume designer will also need to do a more in-depth, specific character analysis for each individual character in order to design costumes that are effective and appropriate. After the play, the next source of information is the director, who will be able to add additional perspectives and information on the world of the play along with the direction they wish to take the production. So, what kinds of questions do you want to ask? The first questions that you want answers to are the same ones that guide you in script analysis:

- What is the genre of the play?

- What is the overall style of the play?

- What type of dramatic structure does the play possess?

- In what time period does the play take place? Are there multiple time periods that might influence costumes?

- How does the action of the play move through time? Does the action take place over a few hours? Days? Weeks? Months? Or years?

- Where is the action of the play located? Are there multiple locations that will affect costume choices?

- What is the season or seasons?

- What is the overall mood of the play?

- How are the characters utilized by the playwright?

- What is the overall theme or message of the play?

- What images come to mind as you read the play?

- Are you able to visualize any of the images suggested by the play?

- Which character is the protagonist? Whose story is being told?

- What are the major conflicts in the play? What or who is preventing the protagonist from getting what she or he wants?

- Which characters play the major roles in the story?

- Which characters are secondary or supporting?

In order to answer these questions, you need to read the script several times, but the information you gather will provide a solid foundation from which to begin your investigation of each character. This information also becomes the basis for the discussions you will have with your director and collaborators as you work to develop your visual approach to the play. But, in order to make decisions about the costumes for the individual characters, you will have to dig deeper, and do a character analysis for each one.

CHARACTER ANALYSIS

The **character analysis** completed by a costume designer is very similar to the one done by an actor. Building on the basic questions asked of the play, a character analysis seeks to answer more specific questions, and in more depth, to discover the things that motivate the characters. Of course, an actor is going to continue to make discoveries about their character throughout the rehearsal process. But given that clothing and how it is worn is so tied to the individual and personality, it makes sense that both actors and costume designers are looking for similar information within a script.

Many of the questions we seek to answer as costume designers have to do with the functions of costume and how they relate to each character precisely. But there are also things we want to find out that suggest specific visual aspects of the character, ones that might serve to guide us as we make choices about the costumes.

- *What is the character's gender?* Is this different from their apparent gender?

- *What is the character's age?* Does this change over the course of the play?

- *What is the character's social status?*

- *What is their occupation?*

- *What is the state of their health?* Does that change over the course of the play?

- *Does the author make any reference to their appearance?* What is the character's height, build, hair, and eye color? Are any of these things mentioned by any of the other characters?

- *What is the character's overall mood?* Does that change throughout the play?

- *What is the character's dominant personality?*

- *Does a predominant color come to mind when you think of the character?*

- *What is overall line of the character?* What type of line best represents them? Straight? Curvy? Diagonal? Vertical? Horizontal? Zigzagged? Broken? Jagged? Thick? Thin? Think of this question as a metaphor for describing who they are, which might translate into a guiding principle for the costume.

- *What is the principal shape of the character?* In fashion, the general shape of a garment is often referred to as **silhouette**. Although you may not be able to fully identify the character's silhouette until a time period for the production has been established, the character's overall shape speaks to the basic physical build suggested by the playwright. Words that describe silhouette include: round, rectilinear, blocky, wide, narrow, bell shaped, hourglass, constrained, restrained, tight, open, and so on.

- *What is the value or visual weight of the character?* Some characters, by virtue of their personality or their function in the play seem to be light and airy, and their costumes should reflect that. Others are darker and heavier, and their costumes should support that aspect of their character.

- *What is the overall texture of the character?* This can be used to describe both their personality and their appearance. Some characters seem "rough around the edges," or have an "abrasive personality." These are qualities that can be supported visually.

- *If you could cast any actor in the part, who would you cast?* While certainly not required, identifying an ideal actor who epitomizes the character can be a useful way of discussing them with your colleagues and the director. Because of the kinds of roles that famous actors routinely play, we as audience members have perceptions formed about them in our heads, so when you say "I could really see Anne Hathaway playing this part," that gives a very different feeling and connotation than if you were to say "When I see this character in my head, I imagine Jennifer Lawrence." Both women are very different in appearance, and both have played very dissimilar roles. Chances are, the minute you read the names of those two actresses, you immediately saw them in your mind, and they conjured up very different qualities along with them. This can be a very useful tool, especially for a beginning designer.

- *If the character were an animal, what would they be?* Based on actor exercises, this is another question that is not required, but can be quite valuable. Associating a particular animal with a character can provide clues to movement, personality, color, behavior, and other physical and psychological factors that could inform your visual choices later.

- *Are there any costume or makeup requirements for the character in the script?* Does the character have a scar? Are they missing a limb? Are they confined to a wheelchair? Are they blind?

Do they have an extensive costume transformation that has to take place? Does a garment need to perform a trick or contain a special effect? These are important character and costume considerations that should be noted.

- *Notes from the text.* As you read through the script, it can be useful to write down anything that is said by the character that directly relates to their personality, behavior, or appearance as well as anything that is said by any of the other characters about them. This allows you to note not only how the character feels about themselves, but also how other characters perceive them.

For ease of reference and future discussions with your colleagues, it can be beneficial to log the answers to these questions on a chart, divided into individual categories, leaving plenty of room to write in information. Having two columns on the page allows for you to write in your observations on one side and those of your director on the other, making it easy to cross reference them as you work.

TABLE 24-1 *Character analysis chart.*

Play _____ Time period _____

Character		
Gender		
Age		
Height/weight		
Hair color		
Eye color		
Health		
Culture		
Personality and mood		
Social status		
Occupation		
Color		
Line		
Shape		
Value or visual weight		
Texture		
Animal		
Ideal actor		
Text requirements		
Text notes		

FIGURE 24-5   The Mountain Giants *by Luigi Pirandello, costume design by Kaoime E. Malloy*

BASIC COSTUME ELEMENTS

When a costume designer makes decisions about what a character will wear and how they will look onstage, they are really dealing with multiple layers of garments and accessories in order to design a complete outfit. These items can be divided into categories in order to understand their function, but also to consider them in terms of what department will be responsible for them in a professional shop.

Undergarments are costume items generally worn underneath everything else, close to the actor's skin. This includes items such as underwear, slips, brassieres, dance belts, petticoats, undershirts, girdles, and other foundation garments. In a period show, where undergarments help to provide the silhouette of the time period or dramatically affect the actor's movement, the director and designer may choose to use historically accurate pieces to achieve a more authentic look and feel. Even when undergarments comprise the entirety of a character's costume, additional items are usually provided to the actor for modesty and comfort.

Main garments often make up the bulk of the character's costume. Shirts, sweaters, suits, blazers, frock coats, skirts, pants, T-shirts, dresses, leotards, uniforms, caftans, pajamas, bathrobes, smoking jackets, nightgowns, tuxedos, knickers, and blouses are

all examples of principle garments. Their style, cut, and fit will all be reflective of the time period in which the play is set.

Outerwear consists of those items worn over the main costume layers and as the name suggests, is often meant to add warmth or protection to the wearer from the elements when outdoors. Coats, capes, cloaks, and jackets are all examples of outerwear and vary greatly in cut in style from one time period to the next. Whether or not outerwear is needed to lend authenticity to a production is something that a costume designer has to work out with the director and in careful observation of the script requirements.

Costume **accessories** is a broad term applied to a wide variety of clothing items. Accessories can be thought of as items that enhance the overall look of the outfit, but do not take the place of the costume itself. Hats, shoes, belts, jewelry, glasses, ties, spats, armor, masks, purses, scarves, bags, gloves, socks, stockings, pantyhose, corsets, bustles, and military accessories such as gun belts and holsters fall into this category. Often, undergarments are placed here as well.

There is also a blurred line in theatre between properties and **costume properties**, leading to extensive conversations regarding which designer is responsible for a certain item. Often, the distinction lies in whether or not an item is worn as part of the costume, a sword belt for example, which is usually considered a costume prop, or whether it is carried, such as the sword and scabbard itself, which is relegated to properties. Purses are generally a costume prop, but the items inside of it—keys, a wallet, money, lipstick, a shopping list, cell phone, and so on—may be more properly considered a true prop. There are some items that are clearly in the costume designer's purview because of their relationship to clothing: pocket watches, parasols, handkerchiefs, gun holsters, and compacts, for example. As a general rule of thumb or guiding principle, when in doubt, if an item is carried by an actor and needs to coordinate with their costume, then at the very least, the costume designer should have some input on the design or selection of the item in question.

There are many scripts that have nonhuman characters or require some form of **special effects** over the course of the action. Lizard tails, angel wings, animal heads and bodies, lightning-fast changes from one costume to the next, pregnancy padding, fat suits, oversized body parts, characters on stilts, transformational makeup effects—any or all of these could be necessary to assist the dramatic action. Designing these pieces requires innovative thinking on the part of the designer, sometimes looking so far outside the box that it is as if the box never existed. But finding creative solutions to the problems posed by a script is where the real magic of design takes place.

FIGURE 24-6 Aloha Say the Pretty Girls *by Naomi Izuka, costume design by Kaoime E. Malloy, set design by Jeff Entwistle, lighting design by R. Michael Ingraham, University of Wisconsin Green Bay*

FIGURE 24-7 *Bottom's head,* A Midsummer Night's Dream *by William Shakespeare, designed by Kaoime E. Malloy, constructed by Kelly Keiler, University of Wisconsin Green Bay*

Just as a scenic designer has to make decisions about decorative elements and props that will be used onstage, a costume designer is required to make similar choices regarding **decorative notions** on each individual costume. These notions can be thought of as icing on the cake, final decorative elements that may be functional as well, and that enhance the overall look and feel of each individual costume piece. These items include buttons, decorative snaps, beads, feathers, patches and appliques, lace, ribbon, and other types of trims, rhinestones, and sequins. The clothing of some historical periods is highly ornamental and dependent on significant decoration, but even a modern dress shirt will require the designer to select buttons appropriate for the garment and the production. These small choices affect each garment and the overall look of the entire range of costumes as a whole.

THE ART OF THE COSTUME DESIGNER

By necessity, a costume designer must possess a variety of skills in order to accomplish their work. They must be part fashion designer, able to understand the influence of fashion and garments have on the wearer, their ability to affect mood, reflect personality, show status, reveal or conceal gender, and shape the body. Like a fashion designer they have to understand the language of fabric—the fiber content, how it moves, how it responds to manipulation, how to modify, alter, and dye it. They need to have a thorough knowledge of fashion history in order to be able to understand the changes not only of garments throughout time, but also the socio-political factors that have precipitated those changes, sumptuary laws, cultural codes of behavior, and their influences on fashion and the effects of technology on garment production. A knowledge of fashion history also helps a designer understand how garments were worn, allowing this to be communicated to the actor. They should also have a working knowledge of garment construction, **draping** and **pattern drafting** in order to comprehend how a piece of clothing is manufactured, in order to be able to communicate construction details and preferences to a costume shop and the artists within during the production process.

Costume designers are often required to have highly specialized knowledge and skills in the area of costume crafts, which can include **millinery** design and construction, creature fabrication, armor manufacturing, jewelry making, fabric painting and dyeing methods, ageing and distressing techniques, and the construction of various costume accessories from corsets to parasols. In order to include them in their designs, a designer may benefit from having basic skills in knitting, crochet, weaving, beading, applique, quilting, ribbon art, and other decorative fabric embellishment techniques. Often, a costume designer is also required to serve as the makeup designer for a production and consequently needs to have an understanding of makeup and hairstyles throughout history and a degree of skill in application procedures and special effects techniques.

A costume designer is also an artist, able to communicate their ideas through thumbnails, rough sketches, detailed drawings, and fully painted renderings. In some cases they may be talented sculptors, creating detailed, three-dimensional maquettes of their designs. Increasingly costume designers are also being asked to be computer literate, able to use computer painting programs like Photoshop® or ZBrush, or three-dimensional pattern creation programs such as PatternMaker or Fashion Cad. As with all designers and artists, costume designers are constantly seeking to keep up with new technology and materials and to learn new techniques, in order to create more evocative work in a more efficient or safer manner.

FIGURE 24-9 *Fabric modification - painted abstract camouflage. The Balkan Women by Jules Tasca, costume design by Kaoime E. Malloy*

FIGURE 24-10 *Makeup design created in ZBrush. Kaoime E. Malloy.*

FIGURE 24-8 *Thumbnails—The Importance of Being Earnest by Oscar Wilde, costume design by Kaoime E. Malloy, University of Iowa*

TABLE 24-2 *Character analysis chart—example.*

Play: *Dracula* by James Balderson   **Time Period:** 1900

Character	Dracula
Gender	Male
Age	Centuries old, appears to be 50.
Height/weight	Tall, with an athletic build that speaks to the warrior he was in history, capable of wielding a sword and engaging in combat.
Hair color	Dark, perhaps even black.
Eye color	Light, piercing, mesmerizing.
Health	Undead, but can pass among the living at night. Paler complexion. Sculpted cheekbones. Immortal, heals.
Culture	Originally from Transylvania. Still possesses a sense of the "old world" and all that entails. Is able to fit into the current time period but has a slight anachronistic feel. Continental flavor.
Personality and mood	Mysterious, seductive, reclusive, dangerous, sensual, intriguing, brooding, coiled, tense, resilient, waiting, patient, impatient, dangerous, suave, cold, complex.
Social status	A count. Landed aristocracy, wealthy.
Occupation	Has no need to work. Socialite.
Color	Dark colors. Navy blue, charcoal, black, burgundy, crimson, red.
Line	Flowing, vertical, flexible, moving, clean, slim, contained, tight.
Shape	Rectilinear.
Value or visual weight	Dark, heavy. Occupies space and demands focus and attention.
Texture	Sensual, slick, smooth, refined, silky.
Animal	Raven, spider, bat.
Ideal actor	Mark Strong
Text requirements	Enters in evening dress and cloak. Bares teeth—makeup requirement? Lifts up Renfield. Is staked
Text notes	A tall, mysterious man. Polished and distinguished, Continental in appearance and manner. Aged 50. Seward: Very kind of Dracula with his damned, untimely friendliness. His English perfect but his accent foreign. A struggle between science and superstition.

THE LANGUAGE OF COSTUME DESIGN

Accessories: Items that enhance the overall look of a costume, but do not take the place of the costume itself.

Character analysis: An examination that seeks to answer specific questions about a character, to help the costume designer understand them as individuals and to discover the things that motivate them.

Costume properties: Costume items carried by the actor, such as watches and glasses.

Decorative notions: Trims, buttons, ribbons, sequins, feathers, and other decorative items that are used to enhance the costume's overall look.

Draping: A method of creating a pattern for a garment by wrapping fabric on a dress form and arranging it to the appropriate shape, cut and fit.

Main garments: The bulk of the character's costume.

Millinery: The design and making of hats.

Outerwear: Garments worn over the main costume layers often meant to add warmth or protection to the wearer from the elements when outdoors.

Pattern drafting: A method of creating a pattern on a flat piece of paper by using measurements to determine the shape, cut, and fit of the garment.

Silhouette: The overall shape of a costume.

Special effects: Any special need required of a costume.

Undergarments: Costume items generally worn underneath everything else, close to the actor's skin.

COSTUME EXERCISES

Project #1: Research Project

Project Goals

This project is intended to give you an opportunity to examine nonvisual research that informs, expands upon, and supports the themes, ideas, and concepts in a playscript, as well as to discover information that expands your understanding of the world of the play in additional to costume and fashion focused research. This may include but is not limited to material focusing on:

- Time period
- Locale
- Historical details
- Societal conventions
- Social class and associated conditions
- Religious views and influences
- Manners and morals
- Political structure
- Critical essays about the playwright or the play itself
- Thematic elements
- Plot elements
- Ideas presented in the script.

Assignment

Your task is to research the role of women in feudal Japanese society. The Feudal Era in Japan spans the twelfth to nineteenth centuries, and includes the Kamakura, Muromachi, Azuchi-Momoyama, and Edo periods.

Requirements: Source Material

For each category of information, visual and nonvisual, you must have:

- A minimum of *five* total sources of information. You may have more.
- A minimum of *three academic sources*. Academic sources are ones that have withstood third-party verification and include textbooks, scholarly articles, most magazines and museum articles, and websites.
- A minimum of *two book sources*.

Organize copies of your source material by sections in a binder or folder or in a digital format with pertinent material highlighted in the texts for ease of finding them later. Organize visual reference material by gender and topic—for example, men, women, children, kimono, obi, fabric, ornament, hairstyles, etc.

Project #2: Art as Inspiration

Inspiration can come from many different places and in several forms and one source can be used to inform design choices on multiple projects. The objective of this assignment is to play with an inspirational image, using it to stimulate your creativity to design two completely different costumes.

Materials

- One abstract art image, no smaller than 3 × 5 and in color
- Color media of choice—paint, colored pencils or markers
- Bristol paper 9 × 12
- Pencils, eraser.

Method

1. Search online for a work of abstract art that inspires or you are drawn to.

2. Identify the key elements and principles of design in your image and observe how they are used. For your designs you can choose to use them in the same manner or manipulate them to create a look that is reminiscent of the original. The idea is not to copy the original image wholesale, but rather to use it as a starting point for your creative process and explore variations of the visual elements and forms. Start with your image and expand your ideas from there.

3. Design #1—design a red carpet dress inspired by your piece of art.

4. Design #2—design an alien creature inspired by your piece of art.

CHAPTER 25

SCENE DESIGN

WHAT IS SCENE DESIGN? A BRIEF HISTORY

Like clothing, the way in which we choose to arrange the environment around us is familiar, understandable, and accessible. We have all purchased furniture for our homes, set it up in each room over and over, trying out different configurations in an attempt to create a pleasing setting that utilizes the provided space with efficiency and yet creates a sense of harmony and flow. We have picked out carpet and selected drapes; searched for the perfect piece of art to complement a room; put up posters of our favorite rock band in a dorm room in college. As with clothing, the choices made about how we outfit our home and work spaces can be very personal, reflecting our tastes, personality, and cultural and social influences. Onstage, these choices are another way for an audience to connect with the characters in a play and connect to them. We as human beings are also able to relate to a variety of different interior and exterior locations whether they are urban or rural. We know what it is like to move freely through empty space, to have our movements affected by the arrangement of furniture in a room, the layout of a shopping mall or the floorplan of a large government building. We know what it is like to have the route of our morning commute dictated by the arrangement or roads and freeways as they move around houses and urban landscaping. We have been to parks, gardens, museums, police stations, in subways, airports, and our grandparents' house. Scenery can transport us to these and any number of other locations, both real and imagined. Sets can be fully realized and completely realistic, down to the last piece of china and running water in the kitchen sink, or they can be stylized, symbolic, and fragmented, merely suggestive of the places they represent. Even a bare stage can be engaging and evocative when used correctly.

The moment the curtain rises, revealing the set, or—as is often the case in modern theatrical performances—the moment the audience walk into the theatre and sees the set on the stage, an impression about the play's location begins to develop. The audience immediately gains important information about the production as a whole, about the world of the play, the environment, the location, the time period, and the characters that inhabit this world. The scenery is magical—it transports us, for a time, to another place. A place that may be very much like the world we live in or that might be incredibly different, where miraculous and astounding things can happen. It can carry us back in time, to a place in history that we would never otherwise be able to visit. It can whisk us halfway around the world to a country that we've never been to and immerse us in the lives of the people that live there. Or, it can take us to a place that only exists in the imagination of the playwright, a place that can only come to life on the stage at that precise moment to be experienced by an audience in a unique, interactive way.

Settings, scenery, and the various trappings that can go with them—such as furniture and other properties like curtains, pillows, dishes, silverware, and further items—have a distinguished history both inside and outside of theatre. For countless centuries around the world, people have used a range of settings, pageantry, and various props, from the ordinary to the opulent, to celebrate important events, tell stories, honor dignitaries, perform spiritual ceremonies and rituals, decorate their homes, identify social status, and to impress others. As storytelling progressed into theatre, the rear wall of the stage itself became the scenery and the location of each scene was often explicitly spelled out in a character's lines. Individual furniture pieces or other small set elements might also be used to assist the action. In the West, scenery as we know it today is largely a product of the Italian Renaissance, due in large part to the application of linear perspective and other three-dimensional painting techniques from the world of architecture to the creation of theatrical sets. The development of theatre building was also influenced by the discovery of *De architectura* in 1414, a treatise on architecture written by the Roman architect Vitruvius whose ten volumes included substantial information on Roman theatres, along with detailed information on the scenery used for classical plays. It is from this treatise that the terms "upstage" and "downstage" originate. Using this information, several recreations of Roman theatres were built finally culminating in the construction of the Teatro Olimpico in Vicenza.

In the Renaissance court theatre, located in an existing room in a palace, linear perspective was applied to the scenery, designed to provide the royal seat, located on an elevated dais at a precise location in the center of the room, with the perfect view of the set, which was conceived of in architectural terms and not meant to be moved or shifted during the performance. The floor, level at the front of the stage, gradually rose on a gentle rake as it moved towards the back to suggest receding distance and increase the illusion of depth. The scenery was placed on the sloping portion of the stage, and consisted of four sets of **wings**. The first three sets consisted of two planes, one that would face the audience and the other that angled upstage. The final set was entirely flat, and placed parallel to the audience, all of which would be placed in front of a flat backdrop. The wings and drop would be painted using one point perspective in order to provide a convincing illusion of realism and depth to the primary seat in the audience. As the Renaissance progressed, wing and drop sets were built with

multipoint perspective, in order to create the same effect from more points in the audience.

When we step into a room, we are often immediately aware of its purpose, based on the décor and the items included within the space. A kitchen contains a stove, a sink, cabinets, and counters, often with other appliances suitable for the preparation of food. A bedroom usually contains a bed for sleeping, perhaps with a nightstand beside it, and dressers to hold clothing. While a conference room and dining room both hold a table and chairs where people can gather around and sit, a conference room is a business space, designed to be less personal and more utilitarian. The average dining room is a place for a family to eat together in a home, and will likely reflect the tastes of the people that live there.

THE FUNCTIONS OF SCENERY

The primary function of scenery is to create a space for the action of the play to take place. But within this simple goal are several other functions that have to be taken into consideration when designing a set, as the designer is concerned not only with the function of the design, but also its appearance. Many of these functions also communicate crucial information about the play and the production to the audience and require careful coordination with the other design areas in order to present a unified picture.

- *Defining the performance space*: Scenery defines the performance space by establishing the distinction between **onstage** and **offstage** areas. Onstage areas are those that will be used for the dramatic action of the play. These regions can be defined in a number of ways, through the use of floor treatments, flats, drapes, platforms, line, shape, color, light, or other methods. A designer may choose to employ **masking** to hide the offstage spaces from the view of the audience, so that actors, technicians, and objects in those spaces cannot be seen; or they may choose to leave the view into the offstage areas open, acknowledging the theatrical space as a stage with additional areas beyond the performance space. In an arena or thrust configuration, the audience itself may serve as the demarcation line between the performance space and the offstage area. It is also possible for the theatrical space to be variable, allowing for the audience to be intermingled with the acting spaces, providing a different kind of experience for actors and audience alike. Often determining the limits of the acting space will also define the audience space, as the two go hand-in-hand, especially in a black box or arena theatre.

- *Creating a floorplan*: A scene designer seeks to create a **floorplan**, a layout of the stage space that provides a

FIGURE 25-1 *The theatre of Aspendos, near to Antalya, southern Turkey (mountainpix / Shutterstock.com)*

variety of acting areas for the director to use to stage the action. Given that the acting area can be organized in a variety of ways, developing a floorplan requires careful communication and collaboration between the director and the scene designer to develop one that will be suitable for the production. The acting area or areas should offer multiple opportunities for movement in the form of interaction between the characters, stage business, dance (if required), and visual composition. A floorplan will show the locations of all flats and set walls, doors, exits and entrances, windows, furniture, levels and platforms, the location or absence of steps—both onstage and off; in short, all of the elements of the visual arrangement of the set.

- *Creating an environment for the performers and the audience*: Because the set is usually the first thing that the audience sees, often long before the start of the show when no curtain separates them from them from the stage, scenery plays a crucial role in establishing the overall look and feel of the production. In the design for Vaclav Havel's *The Memorandum* in Figure 25.2, the audience is introduced to a monochromatic, grayscale world where line and shape have been pared down to a simple, basic level. Accents of color are few and far between, and restricted primarily to red.

Although the room itself might be recognizable as an office, the overall effect is utilitarian and off-kilter. The audience may suspect that they are entering a dystopian world, one where individuality is far less important than fitting in.

- *Setting the tone and character of the acting space*: Scene design is responsible for setting the overall tone of the acting space and, through it, the production, giving the set character and flavor along with creating a floorplan. The manner in which this is accomplished is dictated by the overall design concept. A realistic approach to the design may require that the various locations in the play be represented in a convincing manner. If this is desired, it is likely that the designer will select furniture, architectural details, and décor from a specific time period or location. They may even go so far as to have working appliances and practical lights. *Crimes of the Heart*, for example, is a play that requires running water in the kitchen sink as part of the dramatic action. Another design concept may only require the suggestion of a realistic space in order to establish the location. A few realistic pieces may be juxtaposed with fragmentary sections that serve to create the environment. Other plays may rely on employing images, symbols, or stage

FIGURE 25-2 The Memorandum *by Vaclav Havel, set design by Jeff Entwistle, costume design by Kaoime E. Malloy, lighting design by R. Michael Ingraham, photo by Kaoime E. Malloy*

conventions from the time period in which they were written. The design concept can also be based on the idea of dramatically altering the locale and time period of the original play, as is often done with classical plays, setting them in a period and location that resonates with the thematic content of the play, perhaps making it more accessible and relevant to a modern audience. When a play has multiple settings and locations, such as with Shakespeare's works, it can be very challenging to provide realistic environments for all the scenes and settings the play asks for. One possible solution is to make the set **nonspecific**, providing multiple levels, stairs, doors, ramps, or other scenic elements that permit the playing space to be **flexible**, allowing for the various scenes to be played out without interrupting the continuity, rhythm, and pace of the dramatic action, which might be adversely affected by the demand for realistic scene changes.

- *Distinguish realistic from nonrealistic theatre*: The set design also has the ability to help the audience understand the level of reality in the world of the play. Given that the genre of the script will inform and influence the

design choices, visual elements can assist the audience in understanding the dramatic action and story. In the design in Figure 25.3 for *bobrauschenbergamerica* by Charles Mee, the set takes the form of a shadow box, with items that represent ideas and themes from the artist's life arranged in a visually pleasing way. This presentation of a familiar piece of artistic Americana resonates with the audience, but is undeniably nonrealistic, letting the audience know that the play they are about to engage with is nonrealistic as well. In contrast, the set design in Figure 25.4 for *Twelve Angry Men* is much more realistic, with architectural details that are evocative of the time period of the play, suggesting a real jury deliberation room in an urban courthouse. The implication is that the action of the play taking place in this space will be as realistic as the environment.

- *Setting the mood and atmosphere of the production*: The elements of the set design should also visually support the mood and the tone of the play. This communicates information about the genre, action, and overall nature of the script to the audience, helping them to understand what kind of play they are about to experience. A tragedy

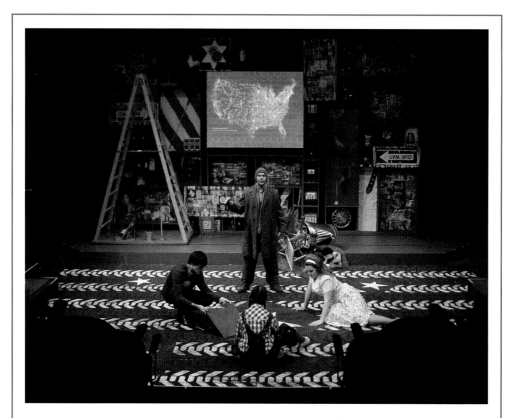

FIGURE 25-3   *bobrauschenbergamerica by Charles Mee, set design by Jeff Entwistle, costume design by Kaoime E. Malloy, lighting design by R. Michael Ingraham, photo by R. Michael Ingraham*

FIGURE 25-4 *Reginald Rose,* Twelve Angry Men, *set design by Jeff Entwistle, costume design by Kaoime E. Malloy, lighting design by R. Michael Ingraham, photo by R. Michael Ingraham*

might benefit from a dark and foreboding atmosphere, one that creates visual tension to support the dramatic action; a farce from a light, bright, and airy mood that complements the fast pace and heightened style of the genre.

- *Setting the style of the production*: Realism and nonrealism are not the only stylistic choices when it comes to visual aesthetics or genre. In all areas, design choices are able to reflect, enhance, and support the overall conceptual approach to the production by reinforcing it visually. Even a realistic play may employ stylized scenic elements, such as fragmentary scenic units in order to suggest the flavor and character of a time period coupled with realistic furnishings to anchor the dramatic action in a pseudorealistic framework. Some genres may also lend themselves to a more heightened, stylized approach than absolute realism, or be so far removed from realism in their literary style that a realistic visual presentation would be confusing. In the design for *A Funny Thing Happened on the Way to the Forum* in Figure 25. 5, the set designer has used the broad style of cartoons as inspiration for his choices, using curved shapes, bold colors and outlines to present a humorous take on the world of the play, one that lends itself to the farcical nature of the musical.

FIGURE 25-5 A Funny Thing Happened on the Way to the Forum *by Sondheim, Shevelove, and Gelbart, set design by Jeff Entwistle, costume design by Kaoime E. Malloy, lighting design by R. Michael Ingraham, photo by R. Michael Ingraham*

Whatever the stylistic choice, it should always support the thematic content of the play and serve to help engage the audience rather than create a barrier for them to overcome.

- *Establishing locale*: The set design should establish where the play takes place, whether that location is a kitchen, a dining room, a house, a temple, a forest, or a factory. Even when the design is nonspecific, there should still be a suggestion of location to ground the action of the play, making it plausible that what occurs throughout the play belongs there.

• *Defining time period*: A good set design should also define the time period of the play, letting the audience know whether the play takes place in the past, the present, or even the future. Furniture, wall treatments, décor, fixtures, and other set elements should reflect the historical time period chosen, supporting the overall production concept. Even when the design concept calls for "no time period," there should still be some attempt to unify the elements of the set so that they work together cohesively and support the content of the play.

• *Support the overall production concept*: Each of the design areas should work together to support the overall conceptual approach to the production, unifying the visual elements and presenting a cohesive picture to the audience. All of the design elements need to be coordinated in order to show that the world of the play is complete and whole. If one element of the design appears to not belong, it can undermine the entire experience of the performance or make it confusing for the audience.

• *Presenting a central image or overall interpretive statement*: Design has the ability to communicate to the audience subliminally, through images and metaphors. Each design area can incorporate the ideas to reinforce the overall production concept, but set design can often present a strong central image or overall statement that serves to interpret important thematic points of the play and present them in visual terms. In the design for *The Balkan Women* by Jules Tasca in Figure 25.6, the set reinforces the idea of the brutality of the women's situation through the use of strong vertical lines, crumbling foundations, and a segregated playing space. The women are kept in one area, away from the men, symbolically representing the ethnic lines that separate the prisoners from their captors, and metal grating in the open arches turns the space into a cage, from which there is no escape.

• *Solve practical design problems*: Scripts have scenic requirements in order to facilitate the action of the play. Doors, windows, staircases, furniture, places to sit, and sometimes special effects may all be required. The set of *Blithe Spirit*, for example, needs to be able to do specialized tricks near the end of the show in order to show the displeasure of the ghosts. Paintings spin on the

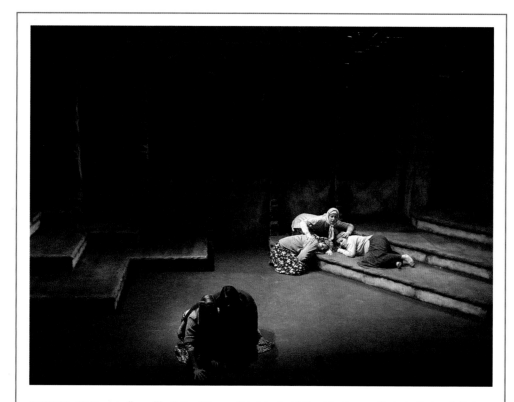

FIGURE 25-6 *Jules Tasca.* The Balkan Women. *Set design by Jeff Entwistle. Costume Design by Kaoime E. Malloy. Lighting design by April Smet. Photo by R. Michael Ingraham*

walls, the mantelpiece falls apart. Farces often require multiple practical doors in order to enable the quick, fast-paced action of the play. The scene designer needs to be sure to incorporate all of the required elements into their design in order to meet the needs of the script.

- *Communicate information about character(s)*: An evocative set design can provide information and clues about the characters that inhabit the space. This is particularly true when the environment created onstage is home to one or more characters, or particular set items belong to certain individuals in the play. Just as our own homes reflect our personal tastes and choices, those of the characters in a play will also be influenced by their likes and dislikes, their social class, morality and values. Willie Loman's home in *Death of a Salesman* should embody all the hardship he has faced. The cart that Mother Courage drags along with her from town to town carries her entire life with her; what it looks like is a direct reflection of her life and the choices she has made.

BASIC SCENERY ELEMENTS

In order to produce an effective and engaging set design, most designers rely on using several basic kinds of set units. It is important to be familiar with these basic building blocks of scenery in order to combine them together in a creative manner to produce a final design that is practical as well as evocative. Being familiar with the construction, potential and limitations of each type can assist you in making your design choices.

- **Framed units**: A framed scenic unit is one that possesses a frame on all four sides for support, which can be made of wood or metal. Framed units can be covered with wood or cloth and are generally rectilinear in shape, though the tops of each unit may be shaped to provide a different profile, depending on the design concept. These units are often referred to as **flats** and can be placed together in multiples in order to create walls that are then painted, treated with texture or trimmed with architectural pieces. Flats can be open, with windows or doors build into their frame, built without any opening, or shaped to resemble a particular silhouette. Flats generally require some kind of support in order to stay in place, either secured to the floor or braced. A specialized type of flat called a **groundrow** is a framed piece, often made entirely of lumber or Masonite, placed upstage in front of a cyclorama or a backdrop to hide the bottom and to provide a horizon line, further enhancing the illusion of depth with the sky beyond. They can be as simple as

a plank painted the same color as the stage floor, or as elaborate as a miniature landscape or city skyline. Another type of framed unit is a **screen**, which provides a surface for the projection of still or moving images on the set. A screen can be covered with cloth, wood, or special projection material, be built into a flat or be a separate unit entirely that hangs or is mounted in the space, or even flies in at the appropriate time.

Three-Dimensional Scenery

Although flats and architectural trims are also three-dimensional, the term *three-dimensional scenic units* usually refers to set pieces made to support the weight of the actors, becoming part of the playing space. These pieces can take several forms, including platforms, ramps, stairs, rakes, and other representational pieces.

Directors often appreciate having multiple levels in a set because it allows them to create interesting movement and visual compositions with their blocking. Platforms make it possible to have a variety of levels. A **platform** consists of a rigid frame constructed of wood or metal, mounted on top of a series of supports called **legs** that add height, and covered with a rigid surface on the top. In order to support weight, platforms are constructed with a series of ladder-like rungs spanning the length of the frame at two-foot (61-centimeter) intervals called **joists**. Platforms can be built in any number of shapes as needed and legged to any height, though many theatre companies will keep a stock of standard sized platforms that are four feet (1.2 meters) wide by eight feet (2.4 meters) long, which can be used over and over. Another type of platform, called a **wagon** is fitted with casters on the bottom rather than legs so that it might be moved on the stage, either as a freely moving unit, or as part of a **slipstage**, a wagon that moves back and forth in a track and has a limited range of motion.

Stairs and **ramps** allow actors to move easily from one level to another, either by traversing a series of steps at regular heights or by walking up and down a slope or inclined plane that links two levels together. Designers need to consider the rise of individual stairs and the steepness of any ramps in their design in order to make it possible for the actors to navigate the stage safely. A designer may also choose to angle the stage floor so that it rises in height as it moves away from the audience. This configuration is called a **rake** and is often applied to the seating in theatres to provide a better view. A rake can be simple, with the entire playing space rising at the same rate, angle and to the same height, or it can be **compound**, where the floor is divided into several platforms, each with their own rate and angle of incline. A rake can also be built with a steep incline and a curved surface, similar to a skateboard park. This type of stage unit is referred to as a **curved deck**.

In addition to these pieces, three-dimensional scenic units can be built to replicate other objects, such as rocks, bridges, fountains, statues, fences, tunnels, trees, or any other scenic item that might be required.

Soft Units

Soft units are made from fabric, suspended above the stage, and are typically unframed. Some of these pieces are used for masking, to conceal the offstage areas from the audience's view, while others are part of the onstage scenery. Draperies are the most common form of soft masking unit, made of black, light absorbent velour or duvetyn fabric. Masking drapes typically come in three varieties: **legs**—tall narrow drapes that are hung on either side of the stage, parallel to the proscenium, to mask wings; **tabs**—long, narrow drapes hung side-by-side and perpendicular to the proscenium to mask the wings; and **borders**—shorter, narrow drapes that run the entire length of the stage and are used to conceal stage lights and battens from view. A theatre may also have a single black curtain that spans the width of the stage to use as a masking unit, hung upstage so that it can sit behind a set. Collectively, masking curtains are often referred to as **blacks**. **Teasers** and **tormentors** are cloth-covered hard horizontal and vertical masking units placed directly behind the proscenium in order to create a small, false portal, thereby reducing the size of the opening.

A **backdrop** is a painted cloth, often encompassing the entire width of the stage, which is used as part of the scenery. A drop can give the feeling of enclosing the set by providing an ending point or back wall. Backdrops can be used to show large, dramatic vistas, adding depth through painted perspective and soaring height. A backdrop may be framed at the top and the bottom in order to keep the fabric straight and taut. It may also have cutouts incorporated as part of the design.

A **scrim** is a drop made from an open-weave fabric that appears opaque when lit from the front, but becomes transparent when lit from behind, or if an actor or object behind it is lit. When lit correctly, a scrim can appear to be as solid as a backdrop only to magically become transparent with a change of light. A scrim is usually black or white, although the fabric can be dyed if desired. Painting the fabric fills in the open-weave and reduces or eliminates its transparency. The fabric can be hung in folds like a curtain or stretched on a frame for a variety of effects and uses.

A **cyclorama**, or cyc, is a large, continuous curtain made of white or neutral fabric that is tightly stretched and hung at the back of the stage. Often, a cyc is curved so that it wraps around the stage space and is primarily used as a canvas for the lighting designer. It creates a broad vista that can be used to achieve dramatic effects, especially the illusion of a sky.

Stretch shapes are three-dimensional pieces made by stretching fabric over a frame. They are available in a wide variety of two-dimensional units called **splats**, as well as framed circles and rectangles, which can be linked together to form walls, ceilings, used as projection surfaces or for simple decoration, either directly or with other scenic elements such as pipe and frames. They are also available in many three-dimensional shapes, including columns, snowflakes, icicles, crystals, stars, irregular pieces, and wall components. Stretch shapes are lightweight, collapsible, and can be customized with a variety of fabrics and digital printing.

SET DECORATION AND PROPERTIES

In addition to the scenery itself—walls, platforms, stairs, doors, windows, and other pieces that make up the playing space—the scene designer is also responsible for selecting the furniture, set decoration, and properties that make the design complete. Although a properties master may be the person in charge of making, purchasing, or locating the props, the designer is ultimately in charge of ensuring that they are suitable and fit in with the overall production concept. Properties usually fall into one of two categories: **set props** (or **set decoration**) and **hand props**.

Set properties are those items that are attached to or are an integral part of the set. They include carpets, drapes, furniture, and wall-mounted décor, such as lighting fixtures and paintings. Hand props are items that are used by the actors in stage business. They might include items like dishes, flowers, books, weapons, letters, money, keys, and other pieces that can be picked up and carried.

QUESTIONS TO ASK/WHERE TO START

Given all of the things that scenery can communicate to the audience and contribute to the production, how do you go about finding out that information? The first place to look is the play itself. By reading the script with the goal of looking for this material in mind, the scene designer can ask specific questions and find the answers that are needed. Some of these answers will apply to the play as a whole—such as location, time period, and time of year—and will be part of your overall script analysis. But a scene designer will also need to look for specific information relating to the dramatic action of the play in order to design an environment that is effective and appropriate. After the play, the next source of information is the director, who will be able to add additional perspectives and information on the world of the play along with the direction they wish to take the production. So, what kinds of questions do you want to ask? The first questions that you want answers to are the same ones that guide you in your script analysis:

- What is the genre of the play?

- What is the overall style of the play?

- What type of dramatic structure does the play possess?

- In what time period does the play take place? Are there multiple time periods that might influence the set design?

- How does the action of the play move through time? Does the action take place over a few hours? Days? Weeks? Months? Or years?

- Where is the action of the play located? Are there multiple locations that will affect the set design?

- Is the location an interior or an exterior? Or are both required? What rooms are required for the action of the play?

- Are complete scene changes required to facilitate the action of the play?

- If this is an interior location, what type of structure does the action take place in? A private home? A public building? A garden? A palace?

- Which character owns the location? (If applicable.)

- What is the social status of the character that owns the location(s)?

- What practical problems are presented by the script? How many entrances and exits are needed? Is furniture specified? Are there any special effects that the set needs to perform in the course of the performance?

- Will the set be permanently installed on the stage, or does it need to come apart for touring?

- Would the play be better served with a nonspecific, flexible setting? If so, what playing areas are required? How many levels are needed? What scene changes will be required to change locations?

- What is the season or seasons?

- What is the overall mood of the play?

- What is the overall theme or message of the play?

- What images come to mind as you read the play?

- Are you able to visualize any of the images suggested by the play?

- Which character is the protagonist? Whose story is being told?

- What are the major conflicts in the play? What or who is preventing the protagonist from getting what she or he wants?

- How are the characters utilized by the playwright?

- Which characters play the major roles in the story?

- Which characters are secondary or supporting?

THE SCENE DESIGNER'S ART

A scene designer needs to possess a wide variety of skills in order to accomplish their work and communicate their ideas. Like an architect, they need to be able to conceive of structures to be used by people, and understand how to sculpt space through the use of levels, steps, stairs, and other set components. In order to accomplish this, an understanding of building techniques is highly useful. As scenic designers, we are concerned with not only the appearance and the arrangement of the space onstage, but also its purpose and how it functions. Because the organization of the space and the various elements that are included will affect the director's work and the blocking and the movement of actors through the set, we have to think of the traffic patterns that are established by the design we develop. A designer has to be aware of the needs of the actor as they use the set, not only to ensure their safety, but also to understand what kinds of characters live in the space and how they influence its look and feel.

A scene designer is also a historian who needs to be familiar with the history of architecture, furniture, and décor. They must have an understanding of various historic and artistic styles in order to be able to draw on their visual aesthetics and incorporate them into their designs. They are partially an interior decorator, someone who is familiar with the conventions of décor, furnishings, decorative motifs, and interior design; understanding the stylistic conventions from one period to the next; able to visualize the setting as a whole, reflecting the tastes and personality of the characters that inhabit it. They must also have an understanding of theatre history and how the conventions of other cultures, locations, and time periods affect the presentation of plays onstage. They must be sensitive to the possibilities and limitations of various stage configurations and how that affects their design choices, whether proscenium, arena, thrust, or experimental in nature.

A scene designer is also an artist, able to communicate ideas through rough sketches, detailed drawings, painted renderings, white models, and painter's elevations. They should

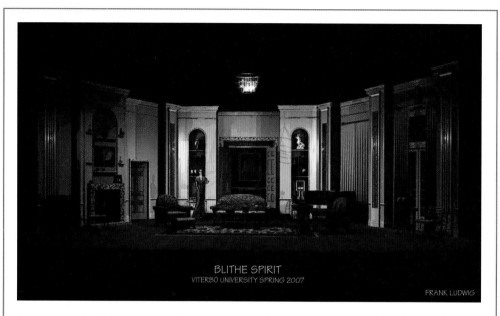

FIGURE 25-7   Blithe Spirit *by Noel Coward, set design by Frank Ludwig, created with Adobe Photoshop® and Vectorworks with Renderworks, Viterbo University*

FIGURE 25-8   Revenge of the Space Pandas *by David Mamet, throne room, scenic design by Kaoime E. Malloy*

have a working knowledge of how to paint scenery. They are part draftsman, able to draft floorplans and other working construction drawings in order for the set to be built, and, increasingly, they are required to be computer literate, able to use computer-aided drafting and painting programs as part of their design process. Like all designers, we are constantly learning about new materials and technologies in order to create better, more evocative work.

THE LANGUAGE OF SCENE DESIGN

Backdrop: A painted cloth, often encompassing the entire width of the stage, which is used as part of the scenery.

Blacks: The stage drapes used to mask the offstage areas.

Borders: Short, narrow drapes that run the entire length of the stage and are used to conceal stage lights and battens from view.

Compound rake: A rake that is angled in more than one direction.

Curved deck: A rake built with a steep incline and a curved surface, similar to a skateboard park.

Cyclorama: A large, continuous curtain made of white or neutral fabric that is tightly stretched and hung at the back of the stage.

Flats: A framed scenic unit used to form walls.

Flexible set: A set that is nonspecific, allowing for multiple scenes to be played out without slowing down the action with multiple realistic set changes.

Floorplan: A layout of the stage space that provides a variety of acting areas for the director to use to stage the action. Also called a groundplan.

Framed units: A scenic unit that possesses a frame on all four sides for support, which can be made of wood or metal.

Groundrow: A framed scenic unit placed upstage in front of a cyclorama or a backdrop to hide the bottom and to provide a horizon line, further enhancing the illusion of depth with the sky beyond.

Hand props: Items that are used by the actors in stage business.

Joists: A series of ladder-like rungs spanning the length of the frame of a platform at regular intervals.

Legs: Tall narrow drapes that are hung on either side of the stage, parallel to the proscenium, to mask the offstage areas. Also the name commonly used to refer to the supports for platforms.

Masking: Pieces of hard or soft scenery that are used to hide areas of the theatrical space from the audience's view.

Nonspecific set: A set that provides multiple levels, stairs, doors, ramps, or other scenic elements that permit the playing space to be flexible, allowing for the various scenes to be played out without interrupting the continuity, rhythm, and pace of the dramatic action, which might be adversely affected by the demand for realistic scene changes.

Offstage: Those areas of the theatrical space, usually hidden from the audience, which are not used as acting areas.

Onstage: Those areas of the theatrical space, visible to the audience, which will be used for the dramatic action of the play.

Platform: A rigid frame constructed of wood or metal, mounted on top of a series of supports that add height, and covered with a rigid surface on the top.

Rake: Angling the stage floor so that it rises in height as it moves away from the audience.

Ramp: A gradual incline leading from one level to another.

Research collage: A collage of research images created in response to the content of the play.

Screen: A framed scenic unit that provides a surface for the projection of still or moving images on the set.

Scrim: A drop made from an open-weave fabric that appears opaque when lit from the front, but becomes transparent when lit from behind, or if an actor or object behind it is lit.

Set decoration: Soft goods such as curtains, pillows, throws, wallpaper, and other items of décor.

Set props: Items that are attached to or are an integral part of the set, such as furniture and light fixtures.

Slipstage: A wagon that moves back and forth in a track and has a limited range of motion.

Soft units: Scenic pieces made from fabric, suspended above the stage and typically unframed.

Splats: Two-dimensional stretch shapes.

Stairs: A set of steps leading from one level to another.

Storyboards: A series of small sketches that show a progression of looks from one scene to another which are useful for scenic, lighting, and projection designers to show their design ideas for each scene or cue.

Stretch shapes: Three-dimensional pieces made by stretching fabric over a frame.

Tabs: Long, narrow drapes hung side by side and perpendicular to the proscenium to mask the wings.

Teaser: A cloth-covered hard horizontal masking unit placed directly behind the proscenium with a pair of tormentors in order to create a small, false portal, thereby reducing the size of the opening.

Tormentor: A cloth-covered hard vertical masking unit placed directly behind the proscenium with a teaser in order to create a small, false portal, thereby reducing the size of the opening.

Wagon: A platform fitted with casters on the bottom rather than supports so that it might be moved on the stage.

Wings: The backstage area on either side of a proscenium stage, unseen by audience. Also refers to flat scenery that projects into the stage space from the side.

SCENE DESIGN EXERCISES

Developing a Central Image

One of the most difficult parts of developing an evocative design is creating a central image for the play, an interpretive visual statement that can be used throughout the design to subtly support the script's thematic content. For this series of exercises, you will be working with an active idea rather than a play in order to develop conceptualization skills without worrying about the playing space in fine detail. The idea that you will be working with is "conflict," something that we can all relate to and understand on several levels. Your job as the scene designer is to develop a design concept/approach to the idea, research that idea, work through several variations of your approach to the topic and finally, to create a scenic collage rendering representing an environmental set on a proscenium stage. This project will take place in several steps.

Step One: Research and Research Collage

Considering the topic of conflict, the first step in the process is to do a variety of pictorial and contextual research that provides information in both visual and conceptual terms. Consider the following questions as you look for applicable information and visuals:

- What is *your* definition of conflict?
- What definition of conflict will you be using for your project?

- How is conflict looked upon in your time period?
- How has conflict been viewed in other time periods?
- How is conflict perceived in our culture? What about other cultures?
- Is conflict necessary? If so, for what reason? If not, why?
- Is there any beauty to be found in conflict?
- How does conflict affect society?
- Are there any positive side effects of conflict?
- What are the negative effects of conflict?
- How do you perceive the idea of conflict?
- Do you know anyone that has participated in combat?
- Could you participate in combat if required?
- How has conflict affected you personally?
- What are your personal feelings about conflict?
- What kind of work have artists created in reaction to conflict?

Find at least 20 visual images that speak to you, ones that are evocative and illustrative of the topic. In addition, do nonvisual research to help you become familiar with the topic.

Taking your research images, create a response collage to conflict, no smaller than 9 × 12 inches (22.86 × 30.48 centimeters). Anything smaller limits you in terms of image size, making them less useful. This is a beginning step towards your final design, not the end product itself. It will by nature be raw, perhaps unfocused, contradictory, and lacking unity. That is perfectly fine for this initial collage. The first step after collecting information is responding to the images that you have gathered. There is no right or wrong way to do this step. **Research collages** are meant to be a way to think out loud in a visual format, and can include drawing, painting and other artwork as desired. A collage is an assemblage of images, cut and pasted securely to another surface. Simply making copies of images found in books, magazines, and online can be a simple way to make a collage and allows you to shape and organize them any way you like. They can also be done digitally, in Photoshop® or other CAD programs, and then printed out or shared with your production team through email or other means. Remember that at this point, the more images you look at the better. You are feeding your internal visual library, fueling your creative furnace and looking for inspiration.

Step Two: Using Storyboards to Edit and Refine Your Idea

A storyboard is a small sketch of how to organize a story and a list of its contents. A storyboard helps you:

- Define the parameters of a story within available resources and time.

- Organize and focus a story.

- Figure out what medium to use for each part of the story.

They are a very useful tool for working out ideas or for set designs and multiple scene sets. In this part of the exercise, you will use storyboarding as a method of exploring the images you found in your research to develop your central image, and adapt it to a scenic environment. A rough storyboard doesn't have to be high art—it is just a sketch. And it is not written in stone; it is just a guide. You may very well change things along the way towards your finished design.

Some questions to ask yourself when working to discover your central image include:

- What is the essential story I want to tell?

- Is my story linear, nonlinear, episodic, or circular?

- What do I want to communicate?

- What mood do I want to create?

- How will I draw the audience in?

- Do I want to create distance from the audience?

- Will the audience be part of the final space or outside of it?

- What part of the story is best told through images?

- What part of the story is best told through graphics?

- What part of the story is best told through text?

- What colors best illustrate my ideas?

Using your visual research collage as a starting point, identify three parts of the collage that exemplify the approach you wish to take to the idea of conflict. Use storyboarding as a way to explore these central ideas by zeroing in on each image and playing with the elements and principals of design to alter them with the goal of creating a final scenic space. Ideally you should create two small sketches for each selected image, no smaller than 6 × 6 inches, but you may find you need more in order to work through your ideas. These sketches can be in

pencil, marker, black-and-white, or color as needed. They can even be created as collage images or assembled digitally by selecting parts of your conceptual collage and manipulating the images to create the individual sketches.

Step Three: Final Scenic Collage

You will need:

- Illustration board no smaller than 18 × 24 inches

- Gluestick

- Paints and other color media

- Xeroxed images in black and white or color

- Scissors

- Pencils as needed

The final scenic collage will be created on a sheet of illustration board, no smaller than 18 × 24 inches. Boards are usually sold in this size, so you can spare yourself the trouble of cutting the board and buy the size you need if you want to save time. Color does not necessarily matter, as you will likely be covering most of the surface with your collage rendering; but if you plan to leave any part of the board showing through, select a color that will work with your overall design concept.

The advantage of a collage rendering is that you can manipulate images in Photoshop® or other image-editing programs, or even with a copier, in order to adjust them in terms of size, perspective, and angle before you incorporate them into your rendering. This can save a great deal of time, allowing for intricate details to be added with ease and is especially useful for the beginning designer.

Begin by setting up a proscenium framework and stage area on your board using simple one-point perspective. You'll want to give yourself enough space to have a clear indication of a proscenium arch without overly limiting the playing area. Using Figure 25.9 as a guide and with a ruler, lightly draw a line parallel to the longest side of the board at three inches from the bottom to mark the front of the proscenium and the curtain line. Be careful not to score the surface of the board. Next, draw a line one inch from the edge of your board, beginning at the first line you drew, on either side of the short edge. Then draw another line 1.5 inches from the top to define the shape of the proscenium arch. Next, divide the board in half and draw a light line from the top to the bottom, marking the centerline of the composition and the stage.

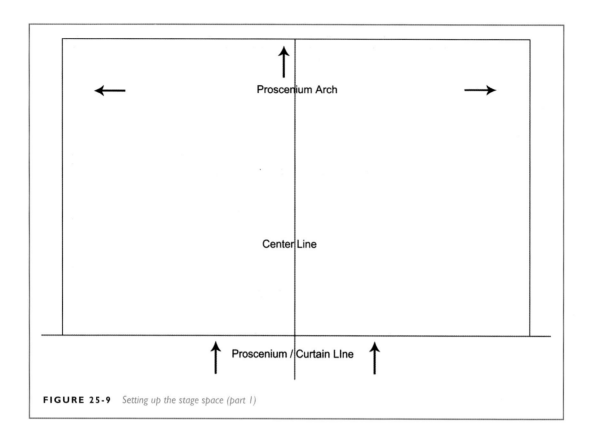

FIGURE 25-9 *Setting up the stage space (part 1)*

Next, still using Figure 25.9 as a guide, set up a horizon line and central vanishing point in order to use one-point perspective to define the mass of the proscenium and define the stage space. Begin by drawing a horizontal line between the proscenium opening three inches above the curtain line. Where this line intersects with the center line is the central vanishing point. Now you can draw in faint lines from the corners of the proscenium arch to the vanishing point as guidelines to draw in the rest of the proscenium, framing the stage space. Draw lines one half inch away from the proscenium on either side of the board, connecting the two vanishing lines. Then, using Figure 25.10 as a guide, draw a line 0.5 inches below the top of the proscenium, from the two vanishing lines, beginning and ending where the vertical lines you just drew intersect them. Reinforce the mitered lines between the edges of the proscenium walls and the bottom of the wall where it meets the stage floor and you are ready to begin the rendering. Add a rounded or shaped apron to the area in front of your proscenium arch if desired, as shown in Figure 25.10.

Once your proscenium and apron are created, begin to assemble your collage within the space, based on the ideas you explored in your storyboards. Your final design can take the form of a stage backdrop, three-dimensional set pieces, or any combination thereof. Keep in mind all the questions you have asked yourself about the topic throughout the exercises. Remember that this is a stage space and that actors have to be able to walk through it. Do you require levels? A flat stage floor? Walls?

Consider the elements and principles of design throughout your design process. How will they be used to tell the visual story you wish to communicate? How can they be manipulated for effect? How will the audience connect with your design?

Once your collage is assembled, begin to apply color as needed to flesh out the design. It will help if you select a light source for the final image in order to help you convey the illusion of three dimensional forms with light and shadow. Once you have added all the elements and colors you want, applying a final coat of matte or gloss medium will help seal all your materials to the board.

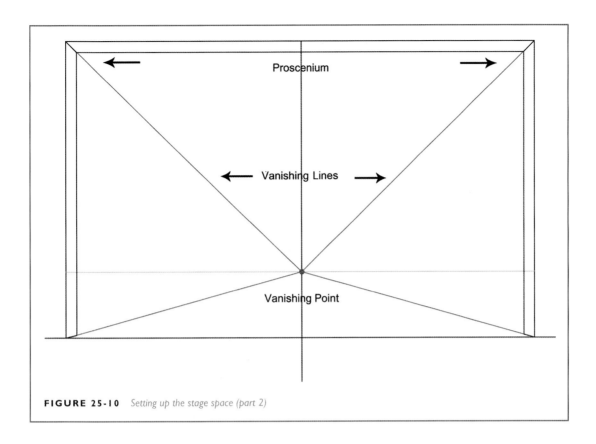

FIGURE 25-10   *Setting up the stage space (part 2)*

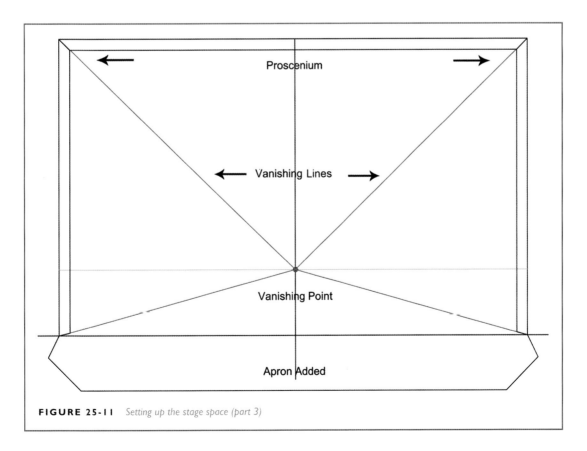

FIGURE 25-11   *Setting up the stage space (part 3)*

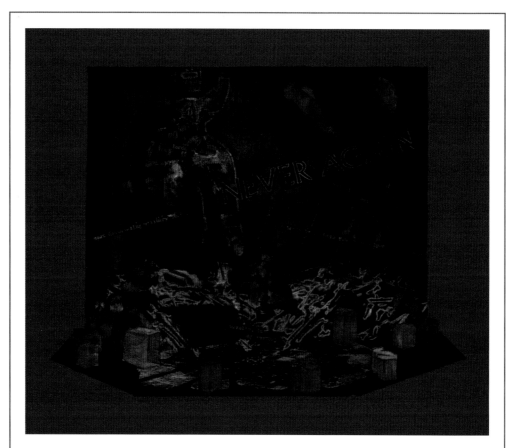

FIGURE 25-12 *Setting collage rendering—conflict set design example, Kaoime E. Malloy*

CHAPTER 26

LIGHTING DESIGN

Painting with light is an art form that requires the ultimate understanding of what is seen versus what should not be seen—in characters, in text, in our complex world of imagery, in our minds, and most importantly in our shared human experience of the heart. It also requires that you work in the eye of the hurricane where you know your craft well enough to paint with audacity and vulnerability despite the myriad of the moving parts of set, sound, costume, projections, playwrights, and directors. Being a lighting designer requires you to jump off the proverbial cliff hundreds of times in a tech rehearsal knowing that you will either land on your feet or learn how to fly. Theatrical design—any and all of it—requires a breed with courage to take such daily leaps of faith, especially in the first ten out of 12 tech rehearsals with a stage manager looking sideways with that look—that look of… "give me the damn cue." "Working…"

Pip Gordon, lighting designer

WHAT IS LIGHTING DESIGN? A BRIEF HISTORY

Lighting design as we know it today is the use of light to shape and sculpt space, illuminate the actors on stage, produce special effects, and to create mood and atmosphere. The use of light in theatre may be as old as the art of formalized theatre itself. The Greeks aligned their large, outdoor theatres—such as those at Dionysus and Epidaurus—with the sun in order to take advantage of natural lighting. This preparation for the effects created by natural lighting could be characterized as design. Over the following centuries, lighting design developed extensively, first using natural and then artificial sources. Sunlight, moonlight, candlelight, oil lamps, gas lamps, torches, limelight, and electric arc light have all played a part in early lighting for theatre. Many of the principals of modern lighting design were established during the Italian Renaissance. Lighting design as we know it today began to flourish with the invention of the incandescent light bulb in the late nineteenth century. With this invention came the development of small, portable lighting fixtures that could be placed anywhere in the stage space. It was also possible to control these instruments remotely with an electrical **dimmer** system to adjust the levels of light at any given moment. Not only did this offer the lighting designer more control and flexibility, these instruments were also much safer than the previous gas or oil lamps. The technology of lighting design continues to develop, offering new light sources, **instrument** types, controllers, and a rainbow of color media for the designer to explore.

In the theatre, the lighting designer is responsible for the design of all of the lighting components for a production. This includes the overall design approach to the play, individual looks from scene to scene, any **practical** lighting effects—light **fixtures** that are included in the set that must turn on and off as part of the action—and, occasionally, any projections that are included as part of the design, although increasingly projections are being considered a separate design area. A designer also typically produces several documents that are used to hang and focus the instruments, program the **light board**, and create the composition of each individual look. Although lighting design relies heavily on technology—more so than costumes and scenery—it is important to remember that, like those other areas, it too is an art. It can be easy to get caught up in the technology, to the point that it becomes your focus rather than on creating a design that meets all the needs of the play and is also evocative, engaging, and moving. A similar analogy would be a costume designer that focuses exclusively on fabric rather than character, or a scenic designer that gets caught up in building materials over the needs of the play, conceptualization, and imagery. The lighting designer is as much of an artist as an actor, director, musician, or any other designer. Of course a lighting designer needs to understand and master the science of their design area; but they also need to be a good interpreter and collaborator. They must understand the psychological aspects of light, aesthetics, style,

and the elements of visual composition. As with all areas of the production, a lighting designer can take great satisfaction in knowing that they have fulfilled the needs of the play, provided adequate illumination, and supported the overall conceptual approach of the production. But, as an artist, it is far more gratifying to know that, by painting the stage with light, through careful control and planning, you have met all of your objectives and moved an audience in the process.

Lighting design is somewhat different from the other areas of design in that it can be challenging to show what the final design will look like in another medium, such as a rendering or a model. While it is possible to do exquisitely beautiful light sketches and renderings, and various software programs such as Virtual Light Lab make it possible to demonstrate how you plan to apply lighting to the stage and the actors, none of these techniques and tools can completely replicate seeing the design onstage with the actual instruments.

FIGURE 26-1 The Balkan Women *by Jules Tasca, lighting design by April Smet costume design by Kaoime E. Malloy, scenic design by Jeff Entwistle, photo by R. Michael Ingraham*

The reason for this is that light is our actual medium as lighting designers and it can be difficult to represent effectively through indirect means. In addition, light interacts and reacts with the objects it touches, sometimes in unpredictable ways and that cannot be learned until the lighting is seen onstage. However, unlike sets or costumes, it is relatively easy to make adjustments in a lighting design. Even something as far-reaching as changing the entire color scheme is a simple matter of switching gels on the instruments, and the controllable qualities of light are infinitely adjustable throughout the rehearsal process.

THE CONTROLLABLE QUALITIES OF LIGHT

We have talked about the elements and principles of design and how they can be applied to visual composition. All of them can be applied to lighting design, but there are also some descriptive attributes that are particular to light that we need to add in order to communicate effectively about our design choices. These attributes make it easier for use to discuss light in terms that are understandable, setting up comparisons between various types of light and lighting effects and how they might be applied to a particular production. There are several core attributes of light that are controllable. Manipulating them effectively, it is possible for the lighting designer to paint the stage with light.

Intensity and Brightness

When we discuss the intensity of light, we are actually talking about three closely related qualities. **Intensity** is the term used to describe the strength of the light. Luminous intensity is measured in **candela**, which describes and measures the power emitted by a light source in any particular direction. **Illumination** or illuminance describes the amount of light falling on any particular object or surface. Illuminance is measured in **footcandles** or **lux** (metric). Finally, **brightness** describes the visual effect created when a light source interacts with an object, and how that effect is perceived by the eye. Together, these phenomena make up intensity. Although intensity can be measured, this aspect of light is often discussed in comparative terms, such as "the moon lit up the night as bright as day" or "the light was as bright as the sun." Onstage, we as designers are concerned with the **relative intensity** of light, in order to ensure that the stage and actors and can be seen and that they in turn can see well enough to navigate the stage space. Whether we describe it in measureable units or comparative terms, intensity is an important quality that directors can

easily understand and relate to, making it a useful tool for communication of ideas about your design.

Color

The **color** of light is determined by the wavelengths that are present in its composition. Color is often considered to be the most dynamic quality of light and it certainly is a feature with a far-reaching effect, both visually and emotionally. Light affects the perception of color of any object it touches, a combined effect of the wavelengths of the light hitting it and the intrinsic color of the object itself, which determines its ability to reflect that color back. An object that shares wavelengths with the color striking it possesses the ability to reflect that light making its color appear richer, brighter, and more saturated. But if no wavelengths are shared, then the color of the object will be distorted, becoming duller, flatter, grayer, or even black as it absorbs the light rays striking it rather than reflecting them. The color of light from lighting instruments is easily modified by the use of colored media made of glass or plastic. Other materials such as fabrics and fluids have also been used to alter the color of light. Generally, the media is placed in a frame that holds it in front of the instrument so that light may pass through it on its way to the stage, thereby filtering the light. For this reason, color media for lighting is often referred to as a **filter**.

Gel is the most common form of colored media used in lighting. Originally made from animal gelatin, gel is now made of transparent plastic, comes in a wide range of colors and can be cut to size for each individual lighting instrument. Unlike gelatin, plastic colored media is made to withstand the temperatures of modem lighting instruments, is of a higher quality with consistent color throughout the media, is relatively inexpensive, and easy to replace. However, the name *gel* persists regardless of the actual material. There are also several different types of glass filters available, typically used for long-term projects, as gels do eventually burn out over time, or to achieve specific effects. Many of these glass filters specifically alter the physical quality of the light, creating differences in textures and diffusion patterns in addition to or in place of color.

Distribution

Although Stanley McCandless described **distribution** as form, most lighting designers consider distribution in terms of two distinct properties: angle (or direction) and quality. *Angle* describes where the light is coming from—front, back, side, top, bottom, and so on. Where is the main source light? Where are the highlights coming from and where do the shadows fall as a result? A lighting designer must always keep in mind how an object will be affected by the direction of the light source.

FIGURE 26-2 Picasso at the Lapin Agile *by Steve Martin, lighting and scenic design by Pip Gordon*

As human beings we relate to light naturally occurring from an overhead source. The sun is high in the sky and most lighting fixtures are above our heads. Because of this experience, we tend to see light that comes from other directions as more dramatic or unnatural. Consequently placing lighting instruments in other positions can be used to provide dynamic and vivid effects.

Quality describes the texture and the overall characteristics of the light. Light can be sharp and crisp or soft and diffuse. It can be hot, harsh, stark, even and clear, without texture, like bright sunlight on a cloudless summer day in the desert, washing the stage in a broad stroke of color. Or it can be cool, muted, dappled, uneven, broken, and heavily patterned, resembling the light falling through a dense forest on a rainy, cloudy day in winter, painting the stage floor with texture. Changes in texture are accomplished with the use of **gobos**, metal frames cut with patterns that are inserted into the lighting instrument that filter the beam as it is cast, changing its shape. Light can be shaped, drawing the beam into a tight configuration that adds dimension, showing tight parallel beams; or it can be loose and unfocused, filling the space with light that is ambient and non-motivated.

Movement

Movement describes the changes in light from scene to scene or moment to moment. Movement is dynamic and fluid and has the potential to bring lighting to life when used effectively. Changes in movement can happen in a variety of different ways. One type of movement is the actual movement of the light source itself. On a very basic level, this can be illustrated by the idea of watching a candle or a flashlight being moved from one place to another by an actor. Movement can also refer to observing the light move without seeing the source itself move. A prime example of this effect would be a **followspot** following a soloist onstage. Another type of movement is simply the changes that occur within the lighting over time. Examples of this include changes in color, intensity, and distribution. Movement may be rapid, quick, and intense, or it can be slow, languid, and subtle. Movement of all kinds is usually tied to the transitions between **moments**, **looks**, or individual **cues** in the play, translating to changes in the overall visual appearance of the design from one static composition to the next. Movement can also be achieved by the use of moving lighting instruments, which can be programmed to create rapid changes in focus positions, colors, and filters during a performance. They are dynamic tools for composition, but it is important to understand the underlying quality you are seeking to manipulate and the effect you are trying to achieve before getting caught up in all the toys, bells, and whistles that the technology has to offer.

THE FUNCTIONS OF LIGHT

There are several functions associated with the use of light onstage, although its main purpose is to reveal the actors and the environment. The communication of emotion is largely dependent on our ability to see a person's face, to see their expression and hear the tone of their voice. If the actors cannot be seen, then the story of the play cannot be told and experienced effectively. In order to address the various functions of light and create an evocative and effective design that meets the need of the script, the controllable qualities of light are modified, combined and manipulated.

Visibility

Visibility is defined as the principle of revealing an object using light. Many lighting designers would argue that this is the most

important function of lighting design. Initially, when lighting was first introduced to theatrical performances, the designer's job was simply to ensure that there was enough light for the audience and the actors to be able to see. The general philosophy towards design was "more is better," and that the more light sources you had in a space the better your visibility was. Modern lighting design is based on the idea of **selective visibility**, using light to reveal only what needs to be revealed to the audience. Showing less may be more dramatic and hence more interesting. It may do a better job of supporting the play, setting the mood, and telling the story. It is far more frightening when we cannot see the monster, when it creeps slowly out of the shadows or is half hidden in them than if it appears in bright light. Using selective visibility, low values, high contrast, silhouettes, and shadows become important compositional tools for the lighting designer. Actors need to be seen, they should stand out from the background, and they need to be modeled in order to reveal their form. Visibility is affected by a number of other factors, such as the angle of the light, its color, and its intensity.

Setting the Scene

In theatre, lighting helps to communicate important information about the play and the environment that is being created onstage

FIGURE 26-3   Dreaming of Forests by Doug Bedwell, lighting design by R. Michael Ingraham, costume design by Kaoime E. Malloy, set design by Jeff Entwistle

FIGURE 26-4   *Honk by Anthony Drew and George Stiles, lighting and scenic design by Pip Gordon, Orpheum Theatre Center*

to the audience. This includes critical material such as time of day, season, and geographical location. Together with all the other elements, lighting helps to present a cohesive, unified picture to the audience. This can be collectively referred to as *setting the scene*. If a scene occurs at night, and the overall conceptual approach to the play is realistic, then the scene should be lit in a manner that suggests night. There are, of course, other questions to answer. What time of night? Is it an interior or exterior scene? If exterior, is the sky cloudy, or are the stars visible? What about the moon? If the scene takes place inside, are there lights on inside the structure? If there are, what kind of lights are they? Light from a fire looks different than light from lamps, for instance. Gaslight has a different quality than electrical light or candlelight. Finding the answers to these kinds of specific questions help you to create looks for each scene that are suitable, engaging and evocative.

Creating Focus

Focus is the practice of creating emphasis by directing the audience's attention to a particular area, element, person,

or group. One of the lighting designer's tasks is to guide the audience's perception, showing where it should be concentrated at any given moment. Without this guidance, a member of the audience might look wherever they wished and miss important parts of the action. While a lighting designer may create multiple areas of focus in any composition onstage, **primary focus** is given to the most important part of the stage picture, making it more prominent. This in turn creates **secondary focus** on the remaining elements onstage.

There are a number of ways to create focus. Raising the intensity of the light on an actor, an area or an object, making it lighter and brighter, is a simple way to create focus. An example of this is the use of a followspot on an actor. An actor can also be highlighted by a single **special**, a light focused on a precise mark onstage to create focus for a specific moment, such as a monologue. Lights can be brightened on groupings of furniture in order to create focus, thereby subtly directing attention towards the action taking place there or, as another example, on a door in order to create focus on the actors when they

FIGURE 26-5   *Something's Afoot, lighting design and set design by Pip Gordon, Orpheum Theatre Center*

enter or exit. It is also a valid choice to create focus by reducing intensity, altering the relative brightness of the light onstage. Choosing to darken all the areas around an area or actor and leaving lights focused on him alone also directs attention and, depending on the scene, might be more desirable.

Establishing Mood and Atmosphere

Next to visibility, creating mood is the function of light that has the greatest effect on the audience. Light is an incredibly influential design element when it comes to establishing mood and creating an emotional response. Over the course of any performance, the mood of the lighting may change several times, adjusting to each individual scene in order to support the dramatic action and following the rhythmic pace set by the script. Lighting can be energetic, uplifting, light, carefree, romantic, comfortable, and inviting. Or it can be dark, oppressive, foreboding, heavy, static, depressing, or passive. The potential is limitless. These changes may be so subtle that the audience is entirely unaware of them or quick and easily recognizable.

Modeling Form

Sometimes referred to as *sculpting*, **modeling** is using light to enhance the three-dimensional qualities of the objects that are onstage, whether they are sets or actors. We are able to understand form best when we observe how light moves around an object, paying attention to the highlights and shadows. Raised areas on an object catch light from the source and reflect it back to the viewer, while recessed areas are passed over, receiving no light and thereby creating shadows. Makeup artists can model incredibly detailed patterns of light with highlights and shadows in order to accentuate or change the shape and details of the face. Lighting designers can use light to do the same thing, producing clarity and recognition of objects, surfaces and actors.

As a general rule, light that comes from the side of an object is the best for revealing the three-dimensional qualities of a form. Angled light that comes from the front or behind tends to create a profile effect, flattening the object and making it more two-dimensional. The angle of vertical light can also have a tremendous effect on our perception of form. As an experiment, shine a flashlight upwards directly under your chin,

FIGURE 26-6   Vinegar Tom *by Caryl Churchill, set and lighting design by Pip Gordon, costume design by Kaoime E. Malloy, Grinnell College*

or on a piece of decorative architectural molding from different angles, noting how the change in direction alters the shape and dimensions of both. Light coming from the front, straight on, can often flatten out all sense of dimension in a three-dimensional object.

Creating Visual Compositions

Composition, as we have discussed, is the arrangement of visual elements into a harmonious picture. In terms of lighting design, the visual elements in question are the contributions of all of the designers as well as the actors as they have been blocked on the stage by the director. The lighting design combines all of the visual elements of the production into a complete package, but they do so in a unique way. Not only does the lighting designer choose *what* elements are revealed to the audience, they also choose *how* those elements are revealed. Does the lighting design need to be **motivational**, appearing as if the light is coming from realistic or practical sources, such as the sun streaming in through a window or lamp fixtures in a room? Or will the design be **non-motivational**, focusing on the use of angles, instruments, and color, seeking to create a sense of emotion, a mood, or a

particular response to themes presented in the script? Will the set be revealed all at once, or one section at a time? Will the lights go down all at once, in a quick **blackout**, or will they fade out slowly? The stage can be revealed in an infinite number of ways. We know that our perception of objects and of color is entirely based on light and that objects can appear very different under different lighting. It only takes a few small adjustments to change how a set or costume looks under light in order to alter their appearance and mood. Because it has such a far-reaching effect on the visual look of a production, lighting has the potential to be the single most influential unifying design aspect of the production, tying all the visual elements together.

Staging the Story

This refers to the nuts and bolts of creating the kinds of visual compositions and effects you want to achieve with your design. Just as a costume designer selects costume pieces and fabrics and a set designer chooses how many and what kinds of levels they will use, what furniture will be on the stage, and so on, a lighting designer must decide what form the lighting will take for the production. This includes determining how transitions

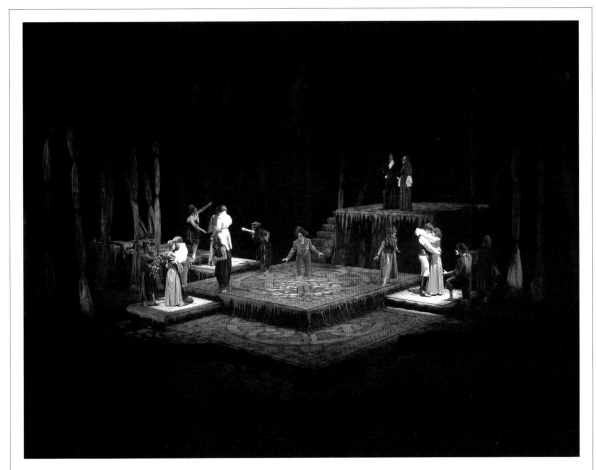

FIGURE 26-7   A Midsummer Night's Dream *by William Shakespeare, scenic design by Jeff Entwistle, lighting design by Zak Viviano, costume design by Kaoime E. Malloy*

will be handled, whether or not full blackouts will be used, what kinds of theatrical techniques will be employed, how the space needs to be defined with light, and what instrument types are needed to accomplish that effectively and efficiently.

Creating Rhythm

In lighting design, **rhythm** relates to the staging of movements and transitions from one look to the next. Depending on the play and the style of the production, transitions may be very subtle or they can be dramatic. Sometimes, the rhythm of the lighting changes may relate simply to the staging of the story or the logistical needs of the play and that may be the best choice for supporting the production. For another play, it may be more appropriate for the lighting transitions to follow the dramatic tensions and changes in the script itself. It is important to determine which approach will support the flow of the action rather than being disruptive.

Another type of rhythm relates to the various changes that naturally occur based on the movement of the actors onstage and the changes in focus, mood, or other factors that might have an impact on or require a change in lighting. Like all the design areas, lighting should serve to underscore the dramatic action and conflict as it progresses through the play and support the thematic ideas within the script. An effective lighting design will serve the needs of the play, be dynamic, engaging, and evocative.

Supporting the Visual Style of the Production

As with the other design areas, style in lighting design refers to a guiding principle or aesthetic convention of representation that serves to inform the overall visual look of the design. It can be a specific historical, literary, or artistic style, or an overall pervasive quality that is used to influence the visual elements of a production. The style of the production should be developed collaboratively between the director and the members of the design team in order for them to share an understanding of the common idea and so that they will be able to realize a final product that is unified and consistent, with all elements working together in harmony.

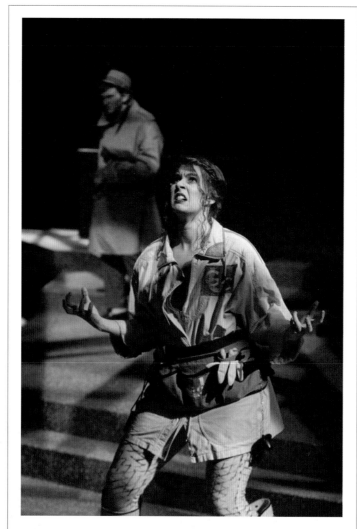

FIGURE 26-8   Urinetown *by Mark Hollmann and Greg Kotis, lighting design by Pip Gordon*

THE ART OF THE LIGHTING DESIGNER

A lighting designer must possess a wide variety of skills in order to be able to design effectively. They need to understand the rules of visual composition and how they relate to light in order to apply them to their designs and to create compelling and engaging visual pictures. As lighting designers, we are not simply concerned with providing enough light to see the stage and the performers; we are also concerned with the quality of that light, how it is perceived, how the audience relates to it, and how they react. We must think about not only what needs to be seen but how it should be revealed and that requires an understanding of the psychology of light, including our perceptions of it and how it affects us as human beings.

A lighting designer must be a good listener, able to hear and understand what the director is asking for in terms of light in order to translate that into a workable design and to make adjustments throughout the rehearsal process. He or she needs to be able to do effective text analysis and research, to understand the lighting requirements of the play in both practical and artistic terms and to be able to locate inspirational images that can be shared with their collaborators and inform their design choices. The designer needs to be familiar with the history of lighting, including the changes in fixtures, lamps, and the various light qualities produced by each so that those characteristics may be recreated onstage with modern instruments. They must understand the principles of stage blocking and how to notate it in a concise and effective manner so that they understand where light is needed for the actors throughout the production.

Lighting is a technology-driven field—much more so than costumes or scenery—and consequently, a lighting designer must continually strive to stay on top of new developments in the technology. They must understand the science and physics of light as well as the art in order to paint with light and mix color, predicting how it will be perceived by the human eye. They must be part electrician, with a basic understanding of electricity, electrical theory and safety, power distribution, and the ability to make basic electrical calculations for each theatrical venue.

A lighting designer is also a visual artist, communicating ideas through selective research images, storyboards, light renderings and cue sheets. They are part draftsman, able to create detailed **light plots** and **cross-section drawings** in order for the lights to be hung and focused. Increasingly, they are required to be computer literate, able to use computer-aided drafting and virtual lighting programs as part of their design process. Like all designers, a lighting designer must constantly learn about new materials and technologies in order to create better, more evocative work and stay current in a rapidly changing field.

LIGHTING THE ACTOR VERSUS LIGHTING THE STAGE

Because the actor is the main focus, most lighting designers will approach lighting the actors and the set separately. Even in highly stylized, dramatic, nonrealistic, or tragic scenes, the actors must stand out from the background. All aspects of their form should be visible, especially their face, in order to communicate emotion. In order to ensure that the actor is lit effectively, most designers will divide the playing space up into a series of acting areas, composing the light for each individually. Instruments are distributed as needed throughout these areas in order to achieve the desired level of visibility, to make sure that the individual actors are separate and distinct from the scenic environment and that their forms are revealed and adequately modeled. Each area can be lit with a combination of several different types of light. In practice, most areas are lit with a number of different instruments, making it difficult to identify the specific location of the lighting source.

FIGURE 26-9   *The Marriage of Figaro by Mozart, lighting design by Pip Gordon, scenic design by Frank Ludwig, Viterbo University*

TYPES OF LIGHT

- *Front, key, and fill light:* The main light for an area is called the **key light**. It may or may not be provided by a single fixture and seeks to provide the main light for the actor's face. The main light for any area usually comes from the front of the acting space, and for this reason may also be called **frontlight**. Key light produces a good deal of contrast in a theatrical space, largely due to the nonreflective surfaces that are typically found there. If there is only one key light then the contrast between the highlights and shadows as the light hits an object can be extreme and dramatic. Both the set and the actors may also be struck by **fill light**. Fill is essentially ambient light that exists in the space. Usually, its direction cannot be determined and it is rather diffuse in quality. Sometimes fill light is provided by additional fixtures that are used to "fill in" the starkness created by key lights, reducing the amount of shadow on an actor or object, often to accentuate the actor's facial features. Fill is different from **spill**, stray light that spills over from lighting instruments into the stage space. A delicate balance between key and fill light results in good actor visibility without flattening their features.

- *Downlight:* Lighting instruments mounted directly overhead create **downlight**. Downlight is important because it brings a sense of drama into a lighting composition. It is one of the most dynamic lighting angles, largely due to the strong shadows cast by the lights in this position. Downlight creates strong highlights on top of an actor or

an object, but the shadows that are cast can distort facial features and may look unrealistic. It can also have the effect of making the subject appear shorter or compressed.

- *Backlight:* **Backlight** is cast by instruments that are mounted behind an actor. Its purpose is to help the actor stand out from the scenic background. It also helps to model the actor's form, making them appear more three-dimensional, which also prevents them from blending into the scenery. Backlight may come from directly behind an object or at an angle, called **diagonal backlight**.

- *Sidelight:* Coming from instruments positioned on either side of an object, **sidelight** is used to model the subject, provide depth and to reveal shape and form. It accentuates the entire side of an actor's body from head to toe, highlighting their movements. For this reason it is especially useful in dance. Sidelighting fixtures may be placed on various structures and at different heights, focusing on different areas of the body. When placed on the floor, sidelights are often called **shinbusters**.

There are many different theories and systems for lighting the scenic environment. An essential task of any successful lighting design is to provide **general illumination** for the set as well as the actors. This translates into creating a system that provides consistent, even coverage of light throughout the entire stage, based of course on the needs of the play and the overall production concept and style.

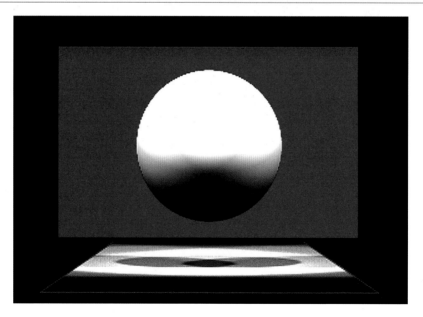

FIGURE 26-10   *Frontlight*

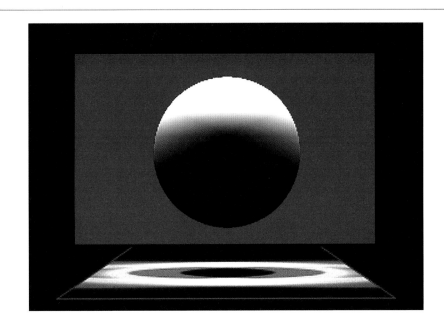

FIGURE 26-11   *Downlight*

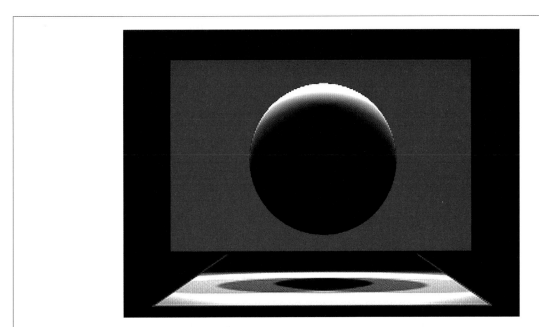

FIGURE 26-12   *Backlight*

In order to provide this, a designer may choose to employ techniques of general lighting, using **washes** to fill the stage with light, or **area lighting**, which provides light to more specific locations in addition to general illumination, or a combination of the two. The locations and angles of the instruments used to create general illumination are largely dependent on the stage space, but all of the same types of lighting positions used for actors may be used to light the set. A designer will be required to divide the stage into smaller, more manageable areas, taking into account the number of **luminaires** in their inventory, where they can be positioned and hung, how much control is desired for the design concept, the blocking created by the director, and what levels of illumination are required for the production.

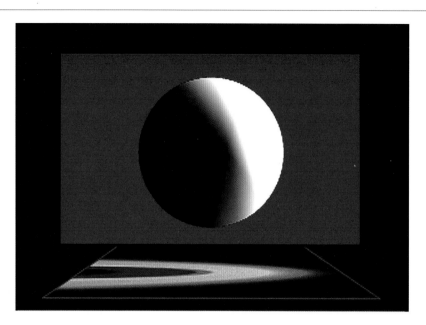

FIGURE 26-13 *Sidelight*

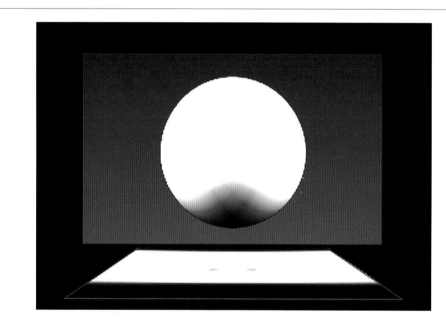

FIGURE 26-14 *General illumination and area lighting*

SCRIPT ANALYSIS—GENERAL QUESTIONS TO ASK OF THE PLAY

- What is the genre of the play?

- What is the overall style of the play? Will it be served best by motivational or non-motivational lighting?

- What type of dramatic structure does the play possess?

- In what time period does the play take place? Are there multiple time periods that might influence the lighting design?

- How does the action of the play move through time? Does the action take place over a few hours? Days? Weeks? Months? Or years?

- Where is the action of the play located? Are there multiple locations that will affect the design?

- Is the location an interior or an exterior?

- What are the sources of light? Are they natural or artificial?

- Are there any practical lighting instruments installed on the set? Will they need to be supplemented?

- What is the season or seasons?

- What is the overall mood of the play?

- What is the overall theme or message of the play?

- What images come to mind as you read the play?

- Are you able to visualize any of the images suggested by the play in terms of light?

- What part does light play in the dramatic action? Is light ever asked to take the place of scenery?

- Will the play begin or end with a blackout?

- What kinds of transitions are required between scenes?

- Which character is the protagonist? Whose story is being told?

- What are the major conflicts in the play? What or who is preventing the protagonist from getting what she or he wants?

- How are the characters utilized by the playwright?

- Which characters play the major roles in the story?

- Which characters are secondary or supporting?

ADDITIONAL CONCERNS FOR THE LIGHTING DESIGNER

In addition to the questions that will form the basis of the analysis of the play, the lighting designer also needs to take a few other relevant bits of information into consideration in order to create an effective design.

- *Become familiar with the set and costume designs:* Lighting design does not occur without something to light. Although the lighting designer is an equally valued member of the collaborative team who should be part of the conversation from the beginning, often they come into the design process late, after key conceptual decisions have already been made. Regardless of when he or she joins the process, a lighting designer must become acquainted with the work of their colleagues in order to light it effectively. Look at the set drawings, renderings, and paint elevations. If there is a model, taking a digital photograph of each scene can assist you during the design process. Look at the costume sketches, renderings, and fabric swatches. Visiting the costume shop to see the actual costumes can also be very useful. Pay attention to the color schemes used by both scenic and costume designers, how the elements and principles of design have been employed, and how style has been applied to their designs. These are all things that can inform your work as you proceed. This is not to say that lighting design is merely reactive to the design work that has already been completed; it is not. But it does serve as a distinct unifying element in the entire production that will have a profound effect on the work of the other designers and as such, their choices need to be taken into consideration to produce a cohesive picture.

- *Become acquainted with the venue:* What kind of stage space is the production taking place in? Proscenium, thrust, arena, black box, or outdoor theatre? The lighting designer needs to know the theatre and the lighting and rigging positions in order to make design decisions. They will need access to the structural plans in order to create a light plot. They need to know what instruments are in the inventory, what fixtures are permanent, and detailed information about the dimming and control equipment, as these will all have an influence on what can or cannot be accomplished in the space.

- *Attend rehearsals:* In order to light the stage and the actors effectively, the lighting designer needs to know the blocking created by the director and there is no better way to do that than by attending rehearsals. While the lighting designer must learn to take blocking notations on paper for their own use, they are not an adequate substitution for watching the actors go through the action of the play onstage. No matter how good the communication and collaboration is between the designer and the director, changes happen during the rehearsal process and the only real way to understand the visual picture being created is to see it firsthand. A lighting designer needs to attend several run-through rehearsals to not only get a sense of the blocking, but also to get a feel for the pacing of the show. By doing this, they will be able to determine their lighting areas as well as the timing of transitions between scenes.

Lighting is a very evocative design element that is crucial to the production as a whole. Its potential to create mood and atmosphere is limitless. The ability of light to model space and form is unrivaled. It touches all of the other visual elements in a production, including the actors. A skilled lighting designer who understands what light is capable of accomplishing, who is sensitive to the needs of the play and able to paint the stage with light in a thoughtful and evocative manner, will unify all the visual elements of the performance, bringing them together to form a cohesive whole.

THE LANGUAGE OF LIGHTING DESIGN

Area lighting: A lighting system that divides the stage into smaller, individual areas and lights them separately.

Backlight: Light that comes from fixtures mounted behind a subject.

Blackout: A transition to complete darkness onstage.

Brightness: The visual effect created when a light source interacts with an object, and how that effect is perceived by the eye.

Candela: The unit of measurement that describes the power emitted by a light source in any particular direction.

Color: The hue of light, determined by its wavelengths. Also may be used to refer to a color medium.

Cross-section drawing: A technical drawing that shows the theatre and lighting positions from a side view.

Cue: A static lighting composition or look created by a combination of lights, their angles, and mixing.

Diagonal backlight: Light that comes from a fixture both behind and at an angle from a subject.

Dimmer: A device that controls the intensity of light.

Distribution: A controllable quality of light, most often considered in terms of angle and quality.

Downlight: Light that comes from a fixture from directly above a subject.

Fill light: Ambient light in a theatrical space, or additional light used on a subject to soften high contrast and shadows.

Filter: Color or diffusion medium for a lighting instrument, which alters the appearance of the beam of light.

Fixture: A lighting instrument.

Focus: The practice of creating emphasis by directing the audience's attention to a particular area, element, person or group.

Followspot: A spotlight that is used to follow actors as they move onstage.

Footcandles: A measure of illuminance based on the amount of light found one foot from a candle.

Frontlight: Light that comes from fixtures mounted in front of a subject.

Gels: Transparent plastic colored lighting filters.

General illumination: A lighting system that provides basic illumination across the stage as a whole.

Gobo: A metal frame cut with a pattern that is inserted into the lighting instrument that filters the beam as it is cast, changing its shape.

Illumination: The amount of light falling on any particular object or surface. Also called illuminance.

Instrument: A lighting instrument. Also fixture.

Intensity: Strength of a light.

Key light: The main light for an area.

Light board: An electronic device used to program cues and control multiple lighting instruments at once.

Light plot: A technical drawing that conveys all of the information that a lighting crew will need to hang, focus, and circuit the instruments.

Looks: Changes in the overall visual appearance of the design from one static composition to the next.

Luminaire: A lighting instrument or fixture.

Lux: The metric measure of illuminance equal to one lumen per square meter.

Modeling: Using light to enhance the three-dimensional qualities of the objects that are onstage. Also called sculpting.

Moments: Changes in the overall visual appearance of the design from one static composition to the next.

Motivational light: Light that appears to be coming from realistic or practical sources.

Movement: The changes in light from scene to scene or moment to moment.

Non-motivational light: Light that focuses on the use of angles, instruments, and color, seeking to create a sense of emotion, a mood, or a particular response to themes presented in the script.

Practicals: Light fixtures that are included in the set that must turn on and off as part of the action.

Primary focus: Creating emphasis on the most important part of the stage picture, making it more prominent.

Relative intensity: The comparative relationship between the intensity of two light sources.

Rhythm: The staging of light movement and transitions from one look to the next.

Secondary focus: Deliberately subordinating parts of the stage to make other areas stand out.

Selective visibility: Using light to show only what needs to be revealed to the audience.

Shinbuster: Low sidelights, placed on the floor and typically used in dance lighting.

Sidelight: Light cast from a fixture mounted to the side of an object.

Special: A light focused on a precise mark onstage to create focus for a specific moment.

Spill: Light that "spills" over from an instrument.

Visibility: The principle of revealing an object using light.

Wash: Light that fills a large area of the stage.

LIGHTING DESIGN EXERCISE

Observing Light in Compositions or Spaces

The purpose of this exercise is to develop your observational skills: to identify light sources, note their effect on the objects in the environment and how light models form.

Materials

- Advertising images with clear light sources
- Tracing paper
- Pencils.

Method

Advertising images for print digital publication are carefully composed compositions designed to showcase products and communicate information about them to the viewer. Lighting is often used to dramatic effect in advertising design, not only to illuminate the product, but also to make it look appealing and desirable. They are, after all, trying to sell a product. But there are often other goals that are desired, which can lead to interesting and engaging lighting. A company may seek to educate the viewer, making them aware of important or uncomfortable facts, presenting them in a manner that makes them personal and real to the viewer; or they may seek to generate sympathy. They may wish to create the impression that their product is sophisticated and forward-thinking. Select two or three images to use for this exercise and identify the following aspects of the lighting in each and write them down:

- How many light sources are there in the image?

- Where are the light sources located? Can you identify their direction as they hit the objects in the image? What visual clues help you to answer these questions? Cast shadows? Concealed forms? Practical light sources in the image itself, or something else?

- Which light source is the key light?

- Which light source or sources serves to sculpt the subject(s), providing dimension and depth?

- Is there fill light? If so, which direction is it coming from?

- Is the lighting motivated or non-motivated?

- Is the lighting realistic or stylized?

- What colors of light are being used?

- How do the colors of the light affect the objects in the image? Do they enhance their color or diminish it?

- Is the overall composition of the lighting high contrast or low contrast?

- What is revealed by the light in the image, creating emphasis?

- What is concealed in the image and therefore subordinated?

- What mood is created by the lighting? What about the lighting helps to create that feeling? Color? Intensity? Direction?

- Does the lighting help to establish a location? If so, what is that location?

- Does the lighting suggest a season? What qualities contribute to that impression?

- Does the lighting suggest a time of day? What aspects of the light suggest this time? Color? Angle? Direction? Intensity?

- How do you respond to the lighting in the image? How does it make you feel? Does it make you think of anything in particular?

- Are there any other aspects of the light that you notice?

FIGURE 26-15   *Marat/Sade by Peter Weiss, University of Iowa Theatres. Set design by Alison Ford, lighting design by Bryon Winn, Costume design by Kaoime E. Malloy.*

CHAPTER 27

SOUND DESIGN

WHAT IS SOUND DESIGN? A BRIEF HISTORY

Sound design is the selection, manipulation, arrangement, and composition of all the aural components of a production. Despite the sound designer's place as a relatively recent, and sometimes still not fully understood part of the design team, sound as an integral part of the theatrical experience is not new. Sound has been used to accentuate and underscore religious, ceremonial, and theatrical events around the world for thousands of years. Drumming, chanting, and music have been and still are used as a core component of funerals, weddings, and other celebrations in a variety of cultures. Music resonates with us in multiple ways, particularly on emotional, primal levels and we live in a world colored by sounds of all kinds. We are affected by sound on an unconscious level every moment of every day. In our modern world, we are bombarded with sound. Silence is at a premium.

Music and sound effects were an important part of theatre in the ancient world, even when scenery and properties were minimally used. In ancient Greek theatre, sound was designed to act as a character in the performance, used to point out specific moments in the action and arouse the emotions of the audience. Choral elements were an integral part of Greek plays, so much so that three books were written on the subject of music design by one of Aristotle's followers. *The Principles of Harmonics* by Aristoxenus, dealt with the subjects of pitch, scales, notes, intervals, and the movement of voice. His second volume, *The Elements of Rhythm*, gives detail on meter and pace. Music and sound are no less important in the ancient theatrical forms of China, India, and Japan, where both are fully incorporated into the performance as a vital artistic component, essential to the experience and telling of the story.

In the Western world, medieval European theatre developed many of the conventions and devices of sound that would become commonplace in the theatre of the English and Italian Renaissance. *Commedia dell'arte*, employing easily identifiable stock characters and slapstick comedy techniques, used plentiful music and sound effects as reinforcement for its farcical style, as well as music before and after the performance. Offstage sound effects were a necessary component for Shakespeare's plays. It was not possible to show the audience all of the actions that the characters experienced, but any sound heard by the characters could also be heard by the audience. There were indications in scripts from this period of offstage sound effects: gunshots, clocks, bells and alarms, barking dogs, the sounds of combat, or rain and storms. In this way, it was possible in Elizabethan theatre to create atmosphere, mood, and special effects, and to assist the transitions between scenes of a play. Characters often arrived onstage with a fanfare that helped the audience to understand their importance and created a dramatic effect beyond this simple understanding of social status. Stage directions in prompt books from this period sometimes contained directions for the musicians hired for the productions, instructing them to make the instruments sound solemn, sweet, or doleful in order to set the tone or mood.

In the seventeenth and eighteenth centuries, as sets, costumes, and lighting became more elaborate, sound was no longer relied upon to establish various production details, and the use of music and sound effects went in and out of fashion. With the invention of gas lighting in the early nineteenth century, scenery became something more—a detailed, realistic set for plays that contained equally realistic, conversational dialogue. Plays presented a slice of life onstage, which demanded the use of realistic sound and lighting. Playwrights included descriptions of sound and lighting as part of their narrative in order to develop the world of the play. Sound effects were created by a combination of offstage and onstage effects, sometimes produced by the actors themselves, contributing to the effect of realism.

The use of recorded sound and music in the theatre was limited until the mid-1930s when the technology became widely available and the quality of prerecorded sound was greatly improved by the invention of the long playing record (LP) in 1948. Using the LP, the amount of material that could be stored on one disk was vastly increased, even though it seems incredibly limited by today's standards. In the 1950s the tape recorder began to replace the LP, although it took some time for the new technology to take hold in the theatre as there was already a large library of sound effects available on vinyl, and it was more affordable. Still, it was hard to convince Broadway directors to incorporate large-scale sound design into theatrical productions on the same scale as it was used in film, as the technology could be unreliable and the general quality was often poor. Sound was often the last consideration in the design process and if it was found to be a distraction rather than an enhancement, it was cut without an attempt to refine or adjust it. Thankfully, the advancement in sound production technology has removed many of the complications that early **sound engineers** and designers had to deal with.

Sound designers now have a remarkable set of tools at their disposal. Synthesizers, samplers, high quality loudspeakers, wireless microphones, computer-assisted playback systems, digital assisted workstations (DAW) that can create and adjust cues with ease, CDs, and high capacity flashdrives are all now readily available. Using them, a sound designer can produce a design with a very high level of quality and sophistication. There are also some forms of sound that have been developed specifically for use in the theatre. One of these is the **MIDI** (musical instrument digital interface). A MIDI provides both

hardware and software control of prerecorded musical scores, synthesizers, drums, and samplers and makes it possible to synch sound cues with light boards, coordinating them seamlessly. Composers can use them to create music and cues. There are even wireless MIDI devices that can be used by an actor to trigger a sound cue with a gesture, blurring the line between performer and operator. The possibilities for sound now are almost limitless.

THE CONTROLLABLE QUALITIES OF SOUND

We have discussed the elements and principles of design at length and how they are applied to visual composition and the areas of costume, set, and lighting design. They can also be employed in sound design, but there are also some descriptive attributes of sound that we need to add in order to understand how sound may be manipulated by the designer. These terms also help us to communicate more effectively about our design choices. Controlling these characteristics with precision and skill, it is possible for the sound designer to create aural compositions that are every bit as detailed and influential on the audience's experience of the play as the visual ones. There are five main controllable properties of sound.

- **Distribution** deals with where the sound comes from onstage and how much coverage there is in the space. Distribution is determined by speaker location, their position and direction, the location of **practical** sound sources onstage, and the position of any equipment used for sound reinforcement, such as microphones. A sound designer must consider speaker position carefully as part of their design, as their location has considerable influence on acoustics and the audience's perception of sound throughout the performance.

- **Volume** refers to the loudness of a sound, voices or music. Volume is easily controlled through both manual and mechanical means. Actors and musicians are able to control the volume of their instruments directly, and a sound designer can regulate their volume and the balance of sound when their output is being reinforced mechanically. The volume of individual cues can be set manually and the volumes of the various components that make up each cue can be set through **mixing**.

- **Movement** describes how sound travels through a space. Movement is an important quality because it relates to the location and position of sound sources and directly influences the perception of realism and believability. If an exterior noise is heard by a character in an interior location onstage, then in order to appear realistically

FIGURE 27-1   *Screen shot of QLab 3 courtesy of Figure 53*

motivated, the sound should originate from a believable location outside the interior space. In addition, that sound may travel through the space as the source moves. For example, an airplane flying overhead will not remain in one place. The sound will travel as the plane moves through the sky and the sound cue should contain that movement and shifting source in order to be believable. Conversely, a lack of movement or movement that contradicts a realistic motivation can create a sense of abstraction or stylization, which may be desired.

- **Duration** is how long an individual sound or a **sound cue** lasts. The length of a sound cue is generally set by careful collaboration between the sound designer and the director. In a cue built with multiple sounds, the length of each needs to be determined individually and set as part of the design process and part of the cue's development.

- **Quality** refers to the characteristics and features of sound and describes how it is perceived by the listener. There are multiple factors that affect sound quality and ways in which sound can be perceived.

  - **Timbre** is the overall tone or quality of a sound, instrument or voice. In terms of the visual compositional elements it most closely resembles color. Timbre makes it possible to distinguish one sound from another. Timbre can be changed by altering the pitch of a sound or the instrumentation.
  - **Pitch** is the highness or lowness of a sound, relating to the notes on a musical scale. Pitch can be altered by changing the tempo and **frequency** of a sound, making the sound vibrate at a different rate.
  - **Rhythm** is the element of time in sound and music. It is marked and measured by beats or counts that are used to determine the tempo, timing and pace.
  - **Tempo** is the rate or speed of sound cue or music, how fast it occurs, and is one way of describing rhythm. Tempos can be slow, fast, and everything in between. Choosing the appropriate tempo for a cue or sequences of cues is an important consideration, given that sound reflects and reinforces the concept and themes of the production as a whole and can be used to drive the action forward.
  - **Timing** is the pace of sounds and cues, the rate of which they happen in a sequence. Timing is very important in sound design, as cues are often linked with the actor's movement, lighting changes or other onstage action and must be carefully planned and rehearsed.

  - **Reverberation** is an effect that occurs when sound bounces off of hard surfaces, such as floors and walls and then blends together. It can also be created by processing sound through mechanical equipment. It is different than an **echo**, which is simply the repetition of sound with no blending.
  - **Layering** is using multiple sounds to build a new sound or effect. Through careful balancing and mixing, the result can be quite spectacular. The musical artist Enya layers her voice as many as 300 times in her recordings to achieve her signature sound. The resulting music is ethereal and otherworldly.
  - **Composition** refers to how sound is arranged. This can apply to individual cues, a sequence of cues and to the entire sound design as a whole. Composition takes into account all of the controllable qualities of sound as well as its function and the designer's intent, taste and artistic choices.

THE FUNCTIONS OF SOUND

Consider the fact that in a script, every word has been carefully chosen by the playwright for its effect. It has been selected for its meaning, the way it links together with the other words in a sentence, paragraph, or monologue, for how it travels back and forth between characters in a scene, creating meaning as they weave together. It has also been chosen for how it sounds, and actors and directors will allocate reason and value to every action and everything they say. Costumes are designed to underscore and reveal the inner lives of each character. The lights are carefully composed to reveal the set and the actors and to underscore the mood of the play. The set has been crafted to provide an appropriate physical environment in which the action can take place, meeting the requirements of the script and sometimes communicating additional information about the character in the process. It is the same with sound design. Any audio elements, whether **preshow** music, **sound effect**, musical underscoring, or even silences are deliberately chosen, aesthetic decisions. As with any other designer on the collaborative team, every choice made by the sound designer has meaning and purpose and is made with a specific goal in mind.

Sound reinforcement provides mechanical enhancement of the actor's voices and/or the musical ensemble in order to enhance the audience's experience. This includes subtly boosting the volume and enriching the quality of the sound as well as carefully mixing the voices and music to create a balanced effect.

Underscoring is the use of music in a scene, playing quietly underneath the dialogue or the visual elements, to establish mood, tone, or theme. It is sometime referred to as incidental music, although this implies that no thought has been given to its selection, which is far from the truth. All sound choices are made with careful thought and deliberation. Underscoring can be used to enhance the action at any given moment, or it can be used to establish a theme for an individual character. Underscoring cannot be heard by the characters in a play, so it does not necessarily have to fit in stylistically with the other sound choices, although this will depend on the overall design concept. An example of underscoring would be the ominous music used to build tension in a thriller or horror film as the hero walks into a dark room that may contain something dangerous.

Transitional sounds—the transitions between scenes in a play are movements in the dramatic action between locations or through time that link one scene to the next. They exist outside the main action. Transitional music or sounds can be used to help facilitate these transitions by providing a shift in mood, tone, or theme to point up the change, emphasizing the change for the audience. It can cap one scene, giving it a sense of closure or tie it to the next by continuing into it. It can signal the end of an act or the play itself. Transitional sound and music can precede a scene, announcing its beginning, or even the arrival of a character. By choosing similar themes in music, transitional cues can help to drive the action forward, helping the audience to understand the progression of the action. It can also be used to help fill the time needed for a scenic change. A sound designer can also help to move time and action forward within a scene by using a **segue**, a sound cue that helps to take the audience from one place in a scene to the next. A segue might be used if there is a change in time or location without a complete scene change, reinforcing the transition in a tangible way.

Specific cues are those **required** by the script and generally provide information that assists the dramatic action. They may be mentioned in the stage directions as written by the playwright, or the characters may refer to them directly in the dialogue. If a character says that they hear a doorbell ring, or hounds baying, or a gunshot, then those sound cues need to be there to reinforce the action. Leaving them out would be obvious and distracting, leading the audience to ask questions about their omission. Specific cues should also follow the stylistic conventions of the production. When they deviate from the production style, they become abstract. Specific cues fall into one of five categories: spot effects, ambient sound, required music, voiceovers, and progression.

- **Spot effects** are sound cues that have to happen at specific moments in the play and enhance or facilitate the dramatic action. They may be humorous or serious,

realistic or stylized. Gunshots, storms, lightning, thunder, breaking glass, doorbells, telephones, barking dogs, and explosions are all examples of spot effects. These are cues that are timed to happen at specific points in the action and include motivated sounds that come from objects on the set, such as televisions and telephones. If a series of spot effects are joined together in a sequence that serves as a background effect, they can become ambient sound.

- **Ambient sound** is noise that exists naturally in the environment. This can apply to the sounds that occur in the theatre space itself, but it also applies to the sounds that would naturally occur in the world created within the scenic environment onstage. For example, to reinforce the sense of being outside in the country at night, a designer may choose to include the sound of crickets and the wind in the trees. For a scene taking place in a factory, the sound of running machinery or a ticking clock may be appropriate. They can be considered in terms of background, foreground, or middle ground, referring to their level of intensity and the amount of **focus** they are meant to receive. But in reality all ambient sound serves as background in some capacity, as it is meant to provide color and mood over a longer period rather than serve as a spot cue. However, spot cues and ambient sound can be effectively combined to create an evocative and engaging atmosphere and sense of place.

- **Required music** is simply music that is required by the script, usually at a particular moment in the action. A playwright might be very specific in the choice of music, listing the exact song they want to be used in a specific moment. Or they might speak about the music in terms of genre and flavor, indicating what kind of mood and atmosphere they want the music to create at a given point in the play.

- **Voiceovers**—a voiceover is a prerecorded or live disembodied speech which can be used for a number of reasons. Most of us are familiar with a recorded preshow announcement, used to give general information about the venue to the audience before a play begins. But voiceovers can also appear during the course of the performance. Whether they are heard by the characters or not depends on the script requirements. A voiceover can present information or communicate thoughts and be reinforced with additional sounds for a dramatic effect. Artificial reverberation can draw more focus or alter the scale of the voiceover, giving the impression of importance or the suggestion of an otherworldly source. Conversely, presenting a voiceover in a realistic manner can ground the effect and make it appear more natural.

- **Progression** is the advancement from one cue to the next. As cues move through the show, a cohesive sound design develops a through line, coming together to tell a story of its own that serves to support the dramatic action of the play, thematic content, and the overall design concept.

Some of the many functions of sound and music include:

- *Creating mood*: Music speaks to our souls. We respond to it on an emotional level and whether it is used for the preshow, underscoring, or a spot effect, it has the potential to heighten and emphasize the dramatic action, drawing the audience's focus. Different sounds can also elicit a variety of emotional reactions and can be used in the same manner.

- *Establishing time*: Musical styles are very distinctive and, because of this, the careful selection of preshow, post-show, and additional music for a production can assist in establishing the time period of the play. Sound effect creation can likewise be indicative of specific time periods, as they can be highly influenced by the relevant technology of any given period. Recording technology is also connected to specific time periods, so the quality of a recording can also be used to showcase a given era as well.

- *Establishing location*: Sound can be used to establish location by providing both ambient and spot effects that serve to identify where the action is taking place. The soft sound of waves rolling against the shore can help to establish a beach location. Tolling bells might indicate a church. The sound of traffic passing by outside an apartment can anchor its location in a busy city.

- *Psychological intent*: When creating a specific cue, the sound designer always needs to take the psychological intent behind it into consideration. It is possible to imbue a sound effect with human qualities, allowing for it to have an emotional effect on the characters in the play and on the audience. Just as some people can appear intimidating and threatening, there are storms that are terrifying and menacing, with strong winds, loud and ominous thunder, and strident lightning that sounds like it could tear down everything around it. The tempo, timbre, and rhythm of rain can also be gentle and comforting. Consider the simple sound of a car horn. A car horn sounds different depending on the model and make of the car, but how it sounds is also dependent on the person using it, and

how they are using it. If you are driving, and another car suddenly swerves into your lane, you make strike the horn reflexively and hard, holding it down in order to warn the other driver of your presence, resulting in a continuous sound. If you are sitting in traffic, and the light in front of you changes from red to green but the car in front of you does not move, you may strike the horn a couple of times out of frustration, to get the driver's attention, resulting in a handful of short, quick bursts of sound. But if you are sitting outside a house to pick up a friend, and they have kept you waiting for a half hour, and now you are going to be late for an appointment, you may hit the horn over and over, using a combination of long and short strikes, taking out your frustration and irritation at being made to wait for so long, imbuing the resulting sound with the same characteristics. These are the kind of psychological qualities that can be built into a sound cue.

In our everyday lives, sound may go largely unnoticed; in a theatre production it is a dynamic design element that enriches the environment and the experience of the performance. Its effects are sensual and evocative, startling and compelling. Sound can help create the world of the play from the moment an audience walks into the theatre space by quickly establishing time, place and mood. It speaks to us as individuals on emotional and intellectual levels. A thoughtful and creative sound designer has the ability to use their medium to great effect, engaging the audience through a sense beyond sight to support and enhance the production in a unique and distinctive way.

SCRIPT ANALYSIS—GENERAL QUESTIONS TO ASK OF THE PLAY

- What is the genre of the play?

- What is the overall style of the play?

- What type of dramatic structure does the play possess?

- In what time period does the play take place? Are there multiple time periods that might influence the sound design?

- How does the action of the play move through time? Does the action take place over a few hours? Days? Weeks? Months? Or years?

- Where is the action of the play located? Are there multiple locations that will affect the design?

- Is the location an interior or an exterior?

- Are there any required sound effects in the script? Required music?

- What are the sources of the required sounds? Are they natural or artificial?

- Are there any practical sources of sound on the set?

- Do any of the characters refer to any sounds or music?

- Do the stage directions refer indirectly to any possible sounds or music?

- Are there any hidden clues in the script that suggest the need for sound?

- What is the season or seasons?

- What is the overall mood of the play?

- What is the overall theme or message of the play?

- What images come to mind as you read the play?

- Are you able to visualize any of the images suggested by the play in terms of sound?

- What part does sound play in the dramatic action? Is sound ever asked to underscore or enhance the environment?

- What kinds of transitions are required between scenes? Will sound be required for these transitions?

- Are there any segues with scenes?

- Which character is the protagonist? Whose story is being told?

- What are the major conflicts in the play? What or who is preventing the protagonist from getting what she or he wants?

- How are the characters utilized by the playwright?

- Which characters play the major roles in the story?

- Which characters are secondary or supporting?

- Do the characters require any sound reinforcement, themes or other sound effects to enhance them?

- What is the overall stylistic approach to the production? Will sound need to adhere to this approach at all times?

OTHER THINGS TO CONSIDER

In addition to all the questions a sound designer has to ask of the script in order to discover the key themes of the play, to develop a conceptual approach, and to identify all the required, implied, and hidden sound and music cues, there are several things they need to keep in mind when developing each cue.

Function

What is the function of the cue? Is it meant to provide information? Support a specific moment of the play's action? Provide atmosphere? Create mood? Establish location or time? Serve as ambiance? Underscoring? Preshow music? Knowing the desired function of the cue will help you to make creative and effective choices with the design.

Intent

Is there a psychological intent behind the cue, and if so, what is it? Since psychological intent deals with how character affects a particular sound effect, determining intent comes from two places: the script and the director. Is the cue meant to have an effect on the audience alone, or is it intended to have an effect on a character or multiple characters in the play itself? If we go back to the example of a car horn, we know that the sound can be used to express a character's emotion in a given moment. If a previously seen character has said they are going to go wait in a car for another character, and later we hear the sound of the car horn, one interpretation of that effect is the expression of impatience or frustration at being kept waiting. But the intent behind the sound of the horn could be to summon the other character and get them to come to the car. Or, the intent in blowing the horn could be to make the other character angry, triggering a reaction. Whatever the intent, it has an effect on how you choose to design and execute a cue. There may even be a point where an offstage sound effect almost serves as an additional character. For example, our irritated horn-blowing character might irritate a neighbor that is never seen in the course of the action of the play, but who comes out to argue with him over his behavior and can be heard onstage and by the audience.

Onstage Action

A sound designer needs to consider the level of interaction between the actors and their cues. Sound may be so integrated with the dramatic action that it becomes an additional character in the play. Actors need to be able to work with the cues prior to technical rehearsals in order to coordinate the interaction of their work with the sound design. Consequently, a sound designer needs to consider if a cue needs to be coordinated with any onstage action in terms of its execution. Will actors be relying on this cue as an integral part of the dramatic action or to move the scene forward? Will this cue be used to start a scene change? Careful discussions with the director are necessary to coordinate and integrate sound with action.

Emotion and Contrast

For every cue, careful consideration needs to be given to what kind of emotion you want to convey. Once you identify the emotional quality that is appropriate for each cue or scene, you can then start thinking of sound in terms of human qualities, applying those textures to the effect in order to illustrate the emotion with sound. You can alter all of the controllable qualities of sound to create the effect you desire, until you have a cue or sequence of cues that supports the action and creates the effect you want. It can also be a powerful choice to use a sound, a piece of music or effect that provides a contrast or counterpoint to the main emotional content of a scene.

Style

Like all the other design elements, sound needs to follow and conform to the overall stylistic approach to the production, but there is another level of style that must be considered with regards to the basic approach to your design as it will affect all of your choices. That is the decision to approach the design in a realistic or stylized manner. Both choices leave room for interpretation with in their framework. A realistic design style can be cinematic in its feel and highly detailed, or it can be representational and selective.

In pure realism the goal is to be true to life, paying attention to factual detail. Music and sound choices support that approach. Characters are aware of sound that emanates from practical sources, which are motivated, realistic, and appropriate. Ambient sound and underscoring supports the action but usually does not influence it and consistency and unity are important unless a comic effect is desired. A cinematic approach takes it clues from the sound conventions and styles of film, where ambiance is used liberally and underscoring is sumptuous and lavishly detailed. Music follows the action closely and consistency is vital. Once themes have been established and linked to action it is essential they are maintained throughout the production. In a cinematic style, the sound designer uses music and audio to paint a vibrant picture that fills the environment with sound. In a representational style, sounds are realistic and motivated but the design is sparse, specific, and selective. Cues only occur when absolutely necessary, but still follow the conventions of realism. The challenge with this design approach is in the careful selection of cues, choosing only what you need without fleshing out every single nuance of sound.

Stylization is a shift from absolute realism that emphasizes design rather than the exact representation of reality. It uses qualities such as exaggeration, distortion, abstraction, and conceptualization to distort and alter reality. A sound designer might choose a stylized effect or approach to heighten or emphasize the dramatic action.

Appropriateness

Appropriateness speaks to how well the cue, music, or effect fits into the world of the play and with the production concept. In a realistic production set in the 1920's, for example, it would make no sense to have the offstage sounds of *Star Wars*-style laser pistols when the script called for gunshots, or the revving engine of a Ford Mustang rather than a Model T.

Consider the following short line as an example for the basis of an offstage sound cue:

The caretaker walked down the long hallway of the mansion, pulling his master set of keys from his pocket and then opened the library door.

For a designer, this short sentence generates a multitude of questions in terms of how to ensure the cue is appropriate. What is the age of the caretaker? What is the caretaker's gender? What is their health? Do they move slowly or quickly? What kind of shoes are they wearing? How old is the mansion? When was it built? Is it currently being lived in? What is the floor made of, stone or wood? What kind of keys are they carrying? Modern keys or skeleton keys? Are they made of steel or iron? Are they on a keychain or a ring? How large is the door to the library? Single door or double door? What is the door made of, wood or metal? What kind of lock, tumbler or deadbolt? How long has it been since the lock was unlocked? How long has it been since the door was opened? Are the hinges rusty? Should the door squeak? If so, should the squeak be ominous? Is there anyone or anything behind the door? Should this sound cue be scary? The list could go on and on, and a designer must ask as many questions as they need to in order to ensure the cue fits the production.

THE ART OF THE SOUND DESIGNER

Like lighting, sound design is technology-dependent. We are largely working with the capture, manipulation, recreation, enhancement, and recording of sound via mechanical means, so a sound designer must be familiar with and reasonably fluent in the relevant technology and skills. They need to be able to use the available software for sound design such as QLab and be familiar with the various types of digital files that can now be used for sound formatting. They must understand the physical qualities of sound and **acoustics** and be skilled in manipulating them for effect. In some cases, a sound designer may also be a musician and **composer**, writing original music for a production that is customized and tailored to the individual needs of that play. But a sound designer also needs to be an artist, planning out an aural composition in the same way a visual artist visualizes a painting.

The visual artists in the theatre work with the elements and principles of design in their individual areas to create compelling and engaging visual compositions, ones tailored to the individual needs of the production. Costume designers work with fabrics that exemplify these qualities in order to create silhouettes and garments that exemplify, illustrate, and support the identifying qualities of each character. Set designers use building materials, painting techniques, fabrics, and textures in order to create the most suitable environment for the dramatic action to take place. Lighting designers use light, manipulating color, intensity, texture, angle, and direction to reveal and conceal, create mood and atmosphere, and frame the action. Sound designers have the same options at their disposal. All of the elements and principles of design can apply to sound creation, composition, and cue development.

The sound designer must learn to both interpret and visualize with their ears. We are taking clues from the script, some of which may be visual, others not, and trying to come up with audio interpretations. In some cases, we need for them to represent and recreate actions occurring out of sight of the audience or the characters onstage. Those interpretations need to paint pictures in the minds of the listeners as clearly as the other design elements present concrete images onstage. Sound is invisible, but it is not intangible. It can have a powerful effect on our other senses. The effect of stimulating one sense and eliciting a reaction from another is called synesthesia. Sound can have a powerful synesthetic effect. How many times have you heard a sound that scared you, only to have it activate your sense of touch, raising the hair on your arms or the back of your neck? Have you listened to a piece of music and seen a color behind your eyes or been taken back to a point in time, reliving a personal memory? Or, listened to a sound when you could not see the source, one that was complex, made up of several sounds, and tried to visualize what was happening to create that sequence of noises? Maybe you even saw a picture in your head as you imagined what was going on. Then you have experienced the incredible capacity sound has to affect us on an emotional, sensory level.

As humans, we tend to auto-associate sounds with emotions. Running water, whether in a brook or as a gentle, light rain, can be soothing and relaxing to us. Our response may be to slow down, become calm, breathe deeper as we let the sound infuse us with the same quality. The siren of a fire engine or an ambulance, however, generally has an opposite effect. It can make our heart beat faster as adrenaline rushes into our system. It can generate fear or anxiety. The sound of the flames of a

fire crackling can be comforting or frightening depending on the context. A crying baby may make us worried, tense, concerned, or bring out a sense of empathy. As designers, we not only have to create sound cues that allow for this kind of visualization, we often have to layer them together as if painting with sound to create complex compositions that provide engaging aural interpretations of ideas in the script that may be abstract or elusive. We have to be careful and sensitive editors, treating each layer of sound and music with a gentle touch to shape and craft it into an end result that matches our conceptual idea. This takes sensitivity and awareness and above all, the willingness to take the leap beyond the technology to the art of sound, because that is where the connection to the audience is made.

The sound designer is in a unique position. It is not possible to draw out what your design for the show will look like. You cannot make rough sketches of your ideas. But that does not mean there are not ways to work through your ideas. There are ways to gather reference material and share it with the director and the other designers. The ready availability of digital audio files in MP3, WMA, AAC, and other formats make it possible to transfer your preliminary design work from one computer to another or to transferrable storage media such as CDs or flashdrives. Even though the volumes, duration, and levels will not be the same as during the actual performance, sound files can easily be played in a production meeting with a laptop computer. Making a sample disk of sound effects, collections of music and cues as you build them is great way to let the director listen to the materials that you have collected as part of your research and live with them for a few days to see if they resonate with their approach to the play. Just as a costume designer might make multiple thumbnail sketches of a garment, showing different variations for the director to choose from, a sound designer can compose multiple versions of a cue, giving the director several options to choose from. Once a version of a cue or effect has been selected, you can then work on refining the cue to ensure it meets the needs of the script and fits in with the style of the production. A sample disk of cues and music is also an excellent tool for the director to take into rehearsal so that the actors can work with the sound design for the show before the technical rehearsals in order to work out timing with the blocking or other action.

THE LANGUAGE OF SOUND

Acoustics: The generation, transmission, and reception of sound.

Ambient sound: Sound that serves as background, creating mood and atmosphere, and enhancing the overall environment.

Composer: An individual that writes music.

Composition: How sound is arranged.

Distribution: Where the sound comes from onstage and how much coverage there is in the space.

Duration: How long a sound lasts.

Echo: The repetition of a sound over and over.

Focus: Creating emphasis with a cue.

Frequency: How many times a pattern of sound repeats in a given time period, usually one second.

Layering: Using multiple sounds to build a new sound or effect.

MIDI: Musical instrument digital interface.

Mixing: Manipulating the various qualities of sound and blending them together to form a balanced finished product.

Movement: How sound travels through a space.

Pitch: The highness or lowness of a tone or sound.

Practicals: Motivated sound cues that emanate from an object on the set.

Preshow: Music and sound that occurs before the action of the play begins.

Progression: The natural movement of cues throughout the design.

Quality: The characteristics or features of sound.

Required effects: Those sound effects that are required by the script.

Required music: Music that is required by the script.

Reverberation: An effect created when sound is reflected off of a hard surface, such as floors or walls, and then blends together. It can also be produced through mechanical means.

Rhythm: The element of time in sound.

Segue: A sound cue that helps to take the audience from one place in a scene to the next.

Sound cue: The introduction of any aural element into a production.

Sound effect: A sound used to convey information or to support the action.

Sound engineer: A sound technician.

Sound reinforcement: Providing mechanical support for the controllable qualities of the actors' voices or the musicians in a production.

Specific cues: Required effects that present information.

Spot effects: Sound cues that have to happen at specific moments in the play and enhance or facilitate the dramatic action.

Tempo: The speed of a sound cue or music.

Timbre: The overall tone of a sound, comparable to color, that distinguishes one sound from another.

Timing: The pacing of cues.

Transitional sounds: Sound effects and music that are used to assist the transitions between scenes.

Underscoring: The use of music in a scene, playing quietly underneath the dialogue or the visual elements, to establish mood, tone, or theme.

Voiceovers: Disembodied speech, either live or prerecorded, that is used to convey information or fulfill dramatic action.

Volume: The loudness or softness of sound or music.

SOUND DESIGN EXERCISES

Exercise #1: Noticing Sounds in an Environment

As a sound designer, you need to be aware of the full range of sounds at your disposal. Once you are able to perceive the various layers of sound that exist around you, you will be able to utilize a full spectrum of sound when creating a design. The purpose of this exercise is to develop your sensitivity to the sounds that are around you. In any room, space, or location there will be sounds that exist on various levels, adding aural texture to your perception of your surroundings. Even in a quiet space, there will be sound, whether from the ventilation system, computer, or other appliances, the wind outside the windows, pets, or even your own breathing. Some sounds will be more prominent, existing in the foreground of your awareness. These sounds help to identify your location. Others will exist in the middle ground, drawing less focus but still contributing a layer of interest. There will also be sounds in the background, perceived on a more subliminal level but still adding another layer of color.

As a simple exercise, close your eyes and concentrate on the three levels of sound in your current location. Spend several minutes focusing first on the foreground sounds, those that capture your attention first, either because they are louder, more distinct or occur more frequently. Think about what they offer to your perception of the space. Take a moment to write them down. Then, close your eyes again and shift your focus, paying attention to the sounds in the middle ground, those sounds that are less distinct, softer, quieter, and occur less often. What do they contribute to the overall sense of the space around you? Once you have identified them, write them down as well. Then, shift your focus again and with your eyes closed once more, try to concentrate on the noises in the background, those sounds that are peripheral, ambient, and subliminal. What sort of texture or color does this layer of sound add to your experience of the environment? Would your understanding of it be significantly altered if any of the sounds you noticed were missing?

Exercise #2: Visualizing Individual Sounds

The purpose of this exercise is to imagine and identify the individual sounds that make up an environment in order to consider how to build a sound cue or series of cues that can emulate a complete setting, providing atmosphere, location, mood and style.

Below are several different locations. Using them as a starting point, think about what environmental qualities come to mind when you picture them. When you imagine being in each of these places, what comes to mind? Spend a moment visualizing each location until you can see it clearly in your mind. What do you hear? Make a list of those sounds for reference. It doesn't matter whether your idea of each of these locations comes from actual experiences or from other sources, such as movies, radio, or television. By writing down everything that comes to mind when thinking of each of these locations, you will create a list that you can apply your taste and artistic judgment to, editing it to remove all the extraneous information as you determine what is necessary and appropriate to illustrate each with sound.

- Jungle
- Beach
- Forest
- Busy metropolitan city.

Using the jungle as an example, once you are able to see the acres and acres of tall trees and exotic plants and feel the heat and humidity surrounding you, what sounds fill out the space? The call of exotic birds? Monkeys? The rushing water of a river or waterfall as it flows over a cliff? The patter of rain on the leaves? The buzz of insects in the air? Try to be as specific and detailed as you can.

Once you have a list of sounds, make a table that divides them into ambient sounds and spot effects, with a column for adjectives that describe the qualities that you attribute to each of them. Distinguishing between spot effects and ambiance helps you to identify how the individual sounds will be used to build the cue. Applying descriptive terms makes it possible to think about how you may need to manipulate sound to create a desired effect.

TABLE 27.1   *Sound design exercise example*

Location	Ambient Sound	Qualities	Spot Effects	Qualities
Jungle	Rain	Soft, patter, constant, soothing	Monkeys	Variations in pitch, duration, and volume; loud and sharp.
	Waterfall	Medium volume, variations in pitch, constant	Birds	Used as punctuation. Varies in duration, pitch and volume. Startling. Sudden.
	Insects	Buzzing, low volume, constant, rising and falling in pitch		

CHAPTER 28

PROJECTION DESIGN

WHAT IS PROJECTION DESIGN? A BRIEF HISTORY

Projections are a rapidly developing design area in theatre that includes film, video, slide shows, static and moving computer images, multimedia, and live video that is created or tailored specifically for each production. Projection elements are presented and integrated into the living environment of the performance and, like any other design element, are used to support the world of the play, the action onstage, and to assist in good storytelling. They can be used to heighten emotional moments in the action, underscore thematic content, reinforce key points in the action, impart information, create special effects, and can also create the impression of a three-dimensional space, serving as scenery. Live images of actors can be projected from other locations to interact with the actors onstage. It is an exciting new aspect of stage design.

Despite the increasing prevalence of projections as a scenic and lighting element in theatrical productions, projections themselves are not a new technology. A **projection** is the display of an image by a device, such as a **projector**, and there are many different types of projectors. Slide, film, video, digital, and overhead projectors are all examples of projection devices. Although we now have highly sophisticated devices for the projection of images, the basics of image creation have been known for hundreds of thousands of years; image projection has probably been known for at least 2,000 years. Certainly, the origin of shadow puppetry and shows is linked to the discovery of fire, and no doubt hands were used to create cast shadows of animals and monsters to tell stories, entertain, and educate just as they are now. In Indonesia, Malaysia, Thailand, and Cambodia, shadow puppetry is a refined form of theatre that employs flat,

articulated figures made of paper or leather whose shadows are cast onto a translucent scrim or screen suspended between the audience and the puppets by the application of a light source. The puppets are highly detailed and capable of a wide range of movement. A skilled puppeteer can make the puppet appear to walk, dance, laugh, nod, engage in combat, and move in a variety of ways. There are more than 20 countries around the world that have shadow puppet traditions. In ancient China and Japan, "magic mirrors" were used to project images onto a wall or screen. Made of highly polished bronze, the magic mirror was used to reflect light from a bright source, producing an image, although no image appeared in the surface of the mirror itself.

One of the earliest known projection devices is the **camera obscura**. The word *camera* is Latin for "room" and the word *obscura* is Latin for "dark," and these two words explain how the device works. By going into a completely dark room and then making a tiny pinhole in the covering of a window it is possible to project an image of the world outside the window in full color and movement on a wall opposite the window, upside down. Although the term *camera obscura* was first used by Johannes Kepler in the seventeenth century, who used the device to make astronomical observations, the first mention of this type of device was in the fifth century BCE by the Chinese philosopher Mo-Ti, who observed and then recorded this image projection effect in a darkened room which he referred to as a "collecting place" or "treasure room." The principle of the camera obscura was also known to Aristotle in the fourth century BCE, who observed the image of a partially eclipsed sun through the holes of a sieve projected onto the ground. In the tenth century, Islamic scientist and scholar Abu Ali al-Hasan Ibn al-Haytham fully documented the principle based on his own experiments. Leonardo da Vinci documented

FIGURE 28-1 The Violet Bus *by Tesori and Crawley, scenic and projection design by Frank Ludwig, lighting design by Chris Winnemann, Viterbo University, photo by Frank Ludwig*

the device in two notations in his notebooks in the fifteenth century, and Dutch scientist Reinerus Gemma-Frisius would later use them to observe solar eclipses. The image quality of the device was improved in the sixteenth century through the addition of a convex lens in the aperture and later a mirror that reflected the image down onto the desired viewing surface. The camera obscura would develop into two distinct devices: the photographic camera and the camera obscura room. The device itself needed very little modification to accept a photographic plate by the beginning of the nineteenth century. The camera obscura room benefitted from the development of more sophisticated lenses, which allowed for sharper and larger images, turning them into a source of entertainment at resorts, parks, and other locations.

Another early projection device is the **magic lantern**, the forerunner of the modern slide projector. The magic lantern uses a concave mirror behind a light source to direct as much of the light as possible through a rectangular pane of glass. The surface of this glass rectangle contains the desired image to be projected, which could be a painted or photographic image. At the front of the device is a lens that is used to optimally focus the image at the distance to the projection surface, usually a white wall or a screen. No one knows with absolute certainty who invented the magic lantern but it is Danish mathematician Thomas Rasmussen Walgensten who was the first person to use the term

laterna magica. He is not only credited with understanding and realizing the artistic and technical potential of the lantern, but also its economic potential as well. He traveled extensively around Europe demonstrating the magic lantern and selling them to the public. At the time of their invention, light sources were limited to candles and oil lamps. These were very inefficient and produced dull and limited images. Advances in light sources, including the Argand oil lamp in the 1790s, limelight in the 1820s, the electric arc lamp in the 1860s and finally the incandescent lamp all contributed to making the images brighter, not to mention safer to produce. Improvements in lenses also improved the quality of the images that could be produced, making them sharper and at a greater size and distance from the lantern itself.

The magic lantern could be used to project both static and moving images. Moving images could be created through the use of several types of mechanical slides. One way to achieve movement was to use two slides, one that would project the static background and a second placed on top for the moving part of the image, projecting them together. The moving slide could be operated by hand with a lever or by another mechanism. Another, highly spectacular type of moving slide is the chromotope. Much like a kaleidoscope in appearance and effect, a **chromotope slide** produces brilliant displays of ever changing colors and geometric shapes made by rotating a circular glass slide with a crank and pulley wheel inside the lantern. In the

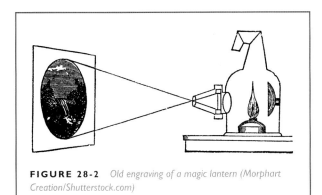

FIGURE 28-2 *Old engraving of a magic lantern (Morphart Creation/Shutterstock.com)*

late eighteenth century, the potential of the magic lantern to create spectacular moving effects was used to create spectacular traveling horror shows called *phantasmagoria*. Here the lantern was often hidden behind a translucent screen, out of sight from the audience in order to add to the effect and mystery of the performance. Ghosts and other scary images could be projected on smoke, moving around the audience to frighten them. One of the most famous of these phantasmagoria artists was Étienne-Gaspard Robert, who used a lantern mounted on wheels, which he referred to as a "Phantascope." By moving the lantern back and forth, he was quickly able to adjust the size of the image being projected, much like a modern zoom lens. Clever adaptations to the device allowed him to maintain the brightness and focus of the image.

The phantasmagoria shows gave way in the early nineteenth century to the Galantee showmen who traveled around the country giving lantern shows in the places they visited. More often than not, the subject of these shows would be the Bible or current events, or shows specifically for children. As the magic lantern became less expensive, it was possible for individuals to purchase one themselves and create slide shows in their own homes. The Galantee showmen gave way to the "Professors,'" who had access to better and more expensive equipment as well as slides that could generate animated effects. Some of the most elaborate and complicated lantern shows were given at the Royal Polytechnic Institution in London. Founded in 1838, the Polytechnic had 25-foot screens and there were often as many as six projectors used to create their complex shows with dissolving images. Accompanied by musicians and a full team of sound effects technicians behind the projection screen, their performances were designed to be complete theatrical experiences. By the end of the nineteenth century, there were as many as 28 companies in London alone producing lantern shows. They were finally put out of business by the invention of the cinematograph in the 1890's. The cinematograph was a camera that captured moving pictures on film that also served as a projector.

In the early twentieth century, projections became a tool for the theatre with the invention of the **Linnebach projector**. Developed by German lighting expert Adolf Linnebach, the projector serves as a theatrical lighting device, capable of projecting broad outlines, colors, and silhouettes that can be incorporated into the background and scenery. Initially created with no lens, the projector consisted of a large enclosed black box and utilized a large transparent glass or mica side with a hand-painted image. A high intensity lamp is located inside the box to serve as a light source. Because there is no lens, the resulting projected image is soft and diffuse. The projector has been refined to include a lens, which prevents image distortion, but is rarely in use due to the size of the slides and the limited number of manufacturers. They are, however, simple to make. German director and producer Erwin Piscator began using them in his productions as early as 1925 and projections were used in the West End productions of *Waltzes from Vienna* and *Tobias* in 1931. Scenic and lighting designer Jo Mielziner is known to have experimented with projections, most notably in the 1947 production of Rodgers and Hammerstein's musical *Allegro*.

Modern theatrical projection design began in the 1950s in the hands of director Alfréd Radok and legendary scenographer Josef Svoboda. At the 1958 World's Fair in Brussels, the two collaborators presented two distinct multimedia performances where actors, scenery and projections were combined to form visual montages. *Laterna Magika* utilized two slide and three film projectors controlled synchronously along with a device that could deflect one projection beam and guide it to any location. In a rectilinear stage space, eight mobile screens with highly reflective surfaces were placed that could be moved in multiple directions to follow the movement of the actors in a precise rhythm. One of the screens could also alter its size and shape through the use of a diaphragmatic aperture. Multi-speaker stereo sound enhanced the production. The production explored the interdependence of the performers and film. Performers appeared both onstage and in the projected images. Svoboda said that the actors could not exist without the film, or the film without the actors and the performance illustrated this connection. In it, projections and actors became one thing, fusing together to form something new, where the film served a dramatic function. This performance would be the foundation of the Laterna Magika theatre in Prague, which still exists today as part of the National Theatre of Prague.

The second performance, *Polyekran*, was a exploration of projection as pure form. Consisting of seven projection screens, all of different size and shape, suspended at different angles from horizontal steel wires in front of a black velvet backdrop, the performance used seven synchronously controlled film projectors and seven slide projectors to project images on the screens. The presence of the projection screens was deliberately emphasized. Film and images were projected simultaneously and allowed to interact with each other in an organic exploration of visual composition. Creation was open and unlimited. Images of real objects and people were part of the projections, but they were combined in surrealistic ways. Their interaction created new relationships and meaning and in Svoboda's mind, a new and different reality.

In the 1960s, lighting designer Richard Pilbrow employed projections in a number of productions, including *A Funny Thing Happened on the Way to the Forum*, *Baal*, *Golden Boy* and *Blitz!* Many of these projections used large format slides that were printed in a single tint and then hand-colored to achieve the desired effect. The projections in these productions were used not only as backdrops, but also to establish locale and set the location of individual scenes; in effect, they served as scenic pieces.

Projections have experienced a resurgence in the past 15 years and it is becoming difficult to find a major production that does not utilize them to some degree. In 2007, United Scenic Artists Local 829 officially recognized projection design by adding it as a category to the union. Modern projectors are certainly more sophisticated in their ability to project images, with greater image quality and over a longer distance, and there are definitely more options for the creation of projections, but the principle remains the same as their earlier counterparts. Increased control and more sophisticated image creation and editing options offer the projection designer more options when developing a projection design and the ways in which projections are utilized is expanding considerably. Projected images, whether moving or stationary, can add another dimension to the performance and enhance the audience's experience of the play when they are carefully integrated with the other design elements.

THE FIVE MAIN COMPONENTS OF PROJECTIONS

In order to project an image in a space, five basic components are required.

1. Images or artwork that you want to project.

2. An output device. Typically a projector of some type.

FIGURE 28-3   Censored on Final Approach *by Phylis Ravel, scenic and projection design by Jeff Entwistle, costume design by Kaoime E. Malloy, lighting design by R. Michael Ingraham, University of Wisconsin Green Bay*

3. A playback device. This is used to transmit the images or artwork to the output device. This is typically a computer.

4. A surface to project the imagery onto. This may be a screen designed for projection, a scrim, the stage floor, or the set itself.

5. A way to control both the output and playback.

Once your images are selected, a playback device is required that can send the imagery to the projector in the form of a digital signal. Once the signal is received by the projector, it will turn the signal into a beam of light that can be projected and focused onto a surface. The projection surface must be able to reflect light back to the audience in order for them to be able to see the image. A control system is also required to manage the functions of the playback and output devices. All three can be connected by lengths of cable to a Web interface or through a wireless connection so that they can communicate with one another.

THE CONTROLLABLE QUALITIES OF PROJECTIONS

There are many aspects of a projected image that the designer can control. Some of them relate to the creation of the image itself and others relate to how the image will be projected in the space. Both aspects of the projection are important and will have an effect on your work. Because there is such an overlap between projection design, scenery, and lighting, it is also important to work closely with the scenic and lighting designer when developing your **content**, delivery system, positions of projection devices, and brightness. Careful collaboration with these colleagues will ensure that each of these design areas work together seamlessly.

Relating to the Image

Content

Content refers to the images in each projection and it is probably the most important aspect of projection design. Here is where images are found, designed, created, selected, edited, and manipulated to produce the desired effect.

Image Creation and Editing

Image creation and editing constitutes the bulk of the creative design work when it comes to projection design. No matter what images are used, whether they are static or moving, individual images or video, the designer has full control of all aspects of each one. The full range of the elements and principles of design are at their disposal: line, shape, value, color, texture, balance, unity and variety, emphasis and subordination, repetition and pattern, and scale and proportion. Image editing programs such as Adobe® Photoshop® and Adobe® After Effects® offer a wide range of tools for creating highly detailed and sophisticated compositions, giving the designer incredible freedom to create evocative images for the production that serve the needs of the play.

Image Resolution

Resolution refers to the quality of the image. As the resolution of an image increases, the clearer it becomes. An image becomes sharper, more detailed, and more defined when the resolution is higher. Computers, digital cameras, and smartphones all have image resolution. It basically refers to the number of dots per inch, or **DPI**, which are placed on the screen. The more dots, or pixels, that are crammed into the height and width of the screen, the higher the resolution. Image resolution is important to the projection designer because the image will likely be projected over a large distance or at an increased size. A low resolution image will look blurry and diffuse in this situation, or "pixelated," meaning that you can see the individual pixels that make up the image. Images for projection need to be high-quality, high-resolution images in order to be clear and sharp when projected onstage. Image resolution is also affected by the resolution of the projector you choose to use; a high-resolution image also requires a projector with a high resolution.

Image Size

Image size refers to two things: the height and width of the image, either in pixels or a unit of measurement, i.e., inches

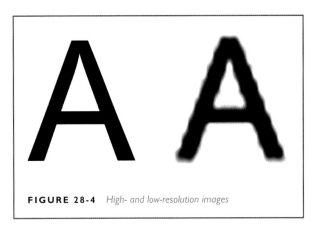

FIGURE 28-4 *High- and low-resolution images*

or centimeters; and the desired size of the image on the projection surface. Your image may be 10 × 12 inches in an image editing program, but needs to be 20 × 24 feet onstage. Image size is an important consideration in projection design and will be affected by several factors, including the distance between the projector and the viewing surface, the desired size of the image onstage, the projector being used, its throw ratio, its lens, and the amount of detail in the image. A large image with a high resolution may be necessary in order to cover a large stage space. Multiple projectors with the same images may need to be stacked together and tiled in order to provide full stage coverage. But a smaller image size may be suitable for a tightly controlled projection or a smaller projection surface.

There will be instances where you have to calculate the size of a projected image. Sometimes, you have an image and a set projection distance and you want the image to be a certain size on the stage, requiring that you determine what lens to use in order to create that size image; other times you have a set lens and screen size for the projected image and you need to figure out where to place the projector to make the image match the screen size. Or, you may need to determine how many projectors are required to create the desired image size onstage.

Movement

When creating an image or series of images for projection onto the stage space, the projection designer has total control over whether the image will be static or mobile. Image movement can be as simple as a slideshow moving from one image to the next, a simple **looping** of a moving image, editing the image seamlessly back onto itself in order to create a longer sequence, or a prolonged video segment shot specifically for the production or broadcast from another location outside the stage space and projected onto the stage. Movement may also be used to animate an image, from a simple fade in and out to create a gentle introduction and exit of an image, to complex layering of images to produce dynamic visual effects.

Projection Mapping

Also referred to as video mapping or spatial augmented reality, video mapping is a projection technology that allows an uneven surface or irregularly shaped object to be turned into a projection surface through the use of specialized software. Two- and three-dimensional objects are mapped by the program, which then creates a virtual environment that mimics

the real stage space or object that the images will be projected on. The software is able to interact with the selected projector or projectors to fit the image or images onto the uneven surface of the object in any size and without distortion. It can also create animation sequences as desired. Projection mapping makes it possible to fit images precisely to scenic elements, even folds of fabric suspended over the stage, allowing for incredible visual effects.

Length

A projection designer has direct control over the duration of any given projection cue. If the image is static, it may be a simple case of turning the projector on and off as required. In the case of moving images or video projections, the designer will need to determine the required length of each projection element and tailor each to fit the desired running length for the performance.

Timing

Timing refers to when the projection takes place, when it begins and when it ends. Close collaboration with the director can help to establish when a projection is needed and desired, but only careful observation of the blocking and action of the play in rehearsal can determine the exact moment the projection should begin and when it should end.

Relating to the Projection Method

Projection Device

The projection device is the mechanical tool you will use to project your image. The choice of projector depends largely on the size of the space, the projection distance, the desired image size, the intended projection surface, and whether the image is static or moving. All of these factors will influence the selection of one projector over another. One concern when selecting a projector has to do with the width of the projected image, which is directly related to image resolution and the aspect ratio of the projector.

Aspect Ratio

The **aspect ratio** of a projector refers to the relationship between the height and width of its maximum projected image size. The aspect ratio not only gives you information about the size of the projected image, but also its shape and resolution. For example, a projector with a ratio of 4:3 will produce a projected image that is close to a square in shape, while one with a ratio of 16:9 produces a more rectangular image. Projecting a 4:3 image using a projector that has a 16:9 aspect ratio will produce an image with black bars on the side. In general, it is best to match the aspect ratio of your projector with the aspect ratio of your source image. Common aspect ratios are listed and described in Table 28.1.

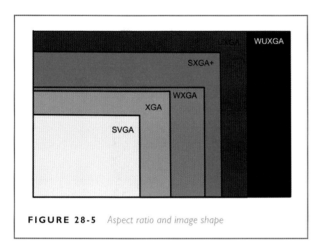

FIGURE 28-5   *Aspect ratio and image shape*

Placement

In some projection designs for the stage, the designer will be working with a projection surface that is integrated into the set and therefore have little influence over the placement of the images or video components they select. In other instances, the projections will be so thoroughly integrated into the design of the stage space that the designer has considerable input regarding their location. It all depends largely on the desired purpose that they will serve in any given production and how the director wishes to use them in the performance.

Projection Surface

If the primary projection surface is the set, an actor in costume, or a small carried prop, then the projection designer may not have a great deal of control over the material selected for the projection surface. However, there will be instances where the projection designer has a great deal of control over the projection surface, such as the use of LED walls, screens, or video monitors. The direction and throw distance of the projected image will influence the choice of surface as well. Rear projections, for example, require a material with a degree of transparency in order for the image to be seen. Given that

TABLE 28-1   *Projector Aspect Ratios and Native Resolution*

Aspect Ratio and Native Resolution			
Resolution Type	**Name**	**Native Resolution**	**Description**
SVGA	Super Video Graphics Array	800 x 600	A low-priced projector that can be a good option for applications that are not dependent on high amounts of detail, such as text.
XGA	Extended Graphics Array	1024 × 768	The native resolution output for many laptops. Matching an XGA laptop to an XGA projector ensures no loss of detail.
WXGA	Wide Extended Graphics Array	1280 × 800	Targeted for use with mid-range widescreen laptops, with a native 1280 × 800 resolution.
SXGA+	Super Extended Graphics Array+	1400 × 1050	Useful for detailed photography and data graphics; overkill for text-based applications.
UXGA	Ultra Extended Graphics Array	1600 × 1200	Used for very high-resolution applications and workstations which demand high levels of detail.
WUXGA	Wide Ultra Extended Graphics Array	1920 × 1200	The widescreen 16:10 version of UXGA. A taller version of 1080p. They can also display native HD 1080 signals.

the projection surface will always have an effect on the image being projected onto it, the projection designer should always give input regarding these choices during the design process. Projections are essentially light and the rules of physics apply to them. Once a projected image hits a surface, it is reflected back to the viewer as much as the material allows. A white painted surface has a great deal of reflective potential; a black velvet drape will absorb far more light than it reflects. In order to create the illusion of depth in a projected image, the surface and source image must be selected carefully.

Direction

Direction refers to the position of the projector in relation to the stage and the projection surface. Projectors can be placed in multiple positions: to the far front in order to provide coverage of the stage, projecting images onto actors and set pieces; above the stage to provide top coverage and project images onto the floor; rear or back projection to project images on scrims or other transparent surfaces from behind the playing space; and to the side or as needed to provide fill or image projection on special scenic units such as canopies. Projectors can be placed on the floor to cast images up into the space, or mounted high in the air side by side with lighting instruments based on need and the desired effect.

Angle

Through the use of an integrated yoke mounting system it is possible to change the position at which a projector is mounted, thereby altering the **angle** of the projected image. This makes it possible to project an image onto a variety of surfaces. Many yoke mounting systems can also be controlled and moved remotely, allowing for the positions to change throughout a performance, creating dynamic effects.

Contrast

Contrast is the difference between the darkest and the lightest parts of a projected image. The greater the range of value between the two, the higher the level of contrast. Contrast is a quality that is easily adjusted when creating an image with image-editing software, but it is also an important consideration when choosing a projector. A projector with high contrast produces an image with clearly defined shadow detail and deep black levels. It makes it possible for the viewer to see the subtle differences in the colors of an image or video. Contrast, in essence, gives images depth. This is particularly important for video images. A high-contrast projector can

almost make a two-dimensional video image look three-dimensional. The contrast of a projector is determined by measuring the reflected light produced by it on both a white and black surface. The measurement is represented by two numbers, such as 3,000:1 or 10,000:1. This means that the white image is 3,000 times brighter than the black image, or 10,000 times brighter, and so on. Ambient light is the enemy of contrast. Even a small amount of ambient light in the stage space can reduce contrast in a projected image. To increase apparent contrast, a projection designer can choose to eliminate or reduce spill or ambient light, darken the audience space, or choose a different projection surface. A projector with high brightness can also reduce the effect of ambient light, so be sure that you have a projector with enough lumens for your needs

Brightness

Brightness refers to the amount of light that an image appears to radiate or reflect. In terms of projections, brightness refers not only to the amount of illumination within a source image, but also the amount of light that can be perceived by the eye from that image on a projected surface. Brightness of the source image can be adjusted with image-editing software. Brightness of the projected image depends on the reflective qualities of the projection surface and the light output of the projector. A projector's brightness is measured in **lumens**, which is a unit measurement that describes the total amount of visible light emitted by the lamp. The American National Standards Institute has developed a rating system for the lumen output of projectors, which is determined by measuring the lumen output of the projector in different positions and averaging the numbers. The final brightness level is quoted in ANSI lumens. The higher the ANSI lumen number, the brighter the resulting projected image will be and, usually, the greater the cost of the projector. A brighter projector does not necessarily mean a better projector. It is important to determine which device is the best for your needs and application. Carefully consider your source images and the levels of light onstage in order to match the projector's brightness to your requirements. Ideally, you want an optimal image that is not too dark or too bright for your specific intent, desired effect and production.

Computer Compatibility

If your projections will be controlled via a computer software program it is important to make sure that your projectors are compatible with your computer and that your control systems are compatible with your projector. Projection control software has certain hardware requirements, particularly with regards to the graphics card, memory, and hard drive. Some require adjunct programs to function properly. If the hardware requirements are not met, some tools available in the **controller** may not be accessible. When using a laptop to control your projections, it is best to match the resolution of your computer to the native resolution of your projector in order to get the cleanest and sharpest image. If you are using a desktop computer that has multiple resolution options, choose the one that is most suited for the content you want to display, whether images, data, or video and then pick a projector that matches that resolution.

Control Systems

A projector control system allows the operator to manage single or multiple projectors through a Web interface connected to one network. Using the network connection, all the devices can be controlled and accessed. Often individual projector menus can be viewed and image programs can be edited without disrupting a performance. Some control systems even offer virtual remote functionality, allowing access to the projector from a long distance. Others allow for multiple device control, offering control over projections, video, and audio playback from one unit. There are several different projection control systems and software programs available, many of which are customizable for the particular needs of theatre.

Distance to the Projection Surface

To a large extent, the distance between the projector and the projection surface is determined by the **throw ratio** of the projector itself. The throw ratio is the distance from the center of a projector's **lens** to the projection surface divided by the width of the image being projected. Projectors usually have a range of throw ratios because they have zoom lenses. Placing the projector within the optimal throw distance for the image size will produce the best quality image on the projection surface.

Keystone Correction

When a projector is not aligned perpendicularly to the projection surface, or if the projection surface is angled, an effect called **keystoning** can occur. A keystoned image appears trapezoidal rather than square or rectilinear, with associated distortion that affects perspective, scale, proportion, size, and other visual aspects of the image. Keystoning can occur both horizontally and vertically. Distortion creates undesirable distraction and can make images difficult to decipher and understand. Early projectors had no ability to correct this effect.

Now, there are two ways to correct keystoning: manual and digital.

Manual keystone correction can be made by physically adjusting the lens of the projector. A simple adjustment sets the device to project at a higher or lower angle than if it were on a flat surface. Although it works well on vertical keystone distortion, this method cannot eliminate horizontal keystoning. To eliminate it manually, the projector needs to be moved farther away from the projection surface. Some projectors are capable of making a digital keystone correction in the process of sending a file or image from the controller to the projector through the addition of a selectable algorithm that is applied as part of the digital file conversion and scaling process. By doing so, a vertical keystone correction between 12 and 35 degrees can be applied, depending on the projector model, and some offer horizontal correction as well. In a long term installation, a better keystone correction may be achieved through the application of a **lens shift**, moving the lens up and down or left and right within the projector housing to reposition the lens and adjust the quality of the projected image.

One Projector? Or Multiple Projectors?

One of the most important considerations in a projection design is how many projection devices will be required to accomplish the design onstage. Multiple simultaneous projections will require multiple devices and it may be necessary to stack several projectors together in order to completely cover a large area with one image. In this instance, the image must be **tiled**, divided into equal parts that will then be projected by the separate projectors. This requires careful overlapping and **edge blending** of the individual projections in order to achieve a seamless image.

THE FUNCTION OF PROJECTIONS

Projections are poised at a unique place in theatrical design. Projections have always hovered at the periphery of lighting, but now they are also overlapping into scenery. They are amorphous, malleable, and adaptable to the needs of the production in unique ways that lend themselves to multiple interpretations and uses. As such, their functions are flexible and dynamic, changing with the needs of the individual production and can therefore be hard to identify with any certainty. What follows are some of the functions that projections can and have played in productions.

- *Imparting information*: Projections have often been used to impart visual and textual information to the audience.

FIGURE 28-6 These Shining Lives by Melanie Marnich, scenic design by Jeff Entwistle, lighting and projection design by R. Michael Ingraham, costume design by Kaoime E. Malloy

Text may indicate the location, time, and date of a scene or provide other key information relating to the action onstage. Images may serve to enhance the physical location or provide a background for the scene. Images and text help to give context, support the action of the play, create emotional connection for the audience, and expand the meaning and understanding of any given moment in a performance.

• *Creating visual compositions*: Composition is the arrangement of visual elements into a harmonious picture. In terms of projection design, the visual elements in question may include three things: the selections made by the projection designer in each individual projection, whether they have created the images or video themselves or used stock content; the contributions of all of the designers, which the projections may affect as part of the performance; and the actors moving on the stage as blocked by the director. When projections stand alone and are projected into the performance space in a way that does not affect the scenery or the performers, then the designer is only responsible for the internal composition of the projections themselves, tailoring them for the individual

production. When they are projected onto the set and the actors, then the designer also has to consider what kinds of compositions are being created as their work interacts with that of the other designers. Like lighting, projections have the ability to reveal or conceal parts of the stage space or the actors in this situation, and the designer must be aware of how their choices affect the overall picture. Projections have the potential to be a unifying or divisive element, and careful adjustments in image placement, color, value, texture, duration, timing, and other qualities may be necessary in order to achieve a unified look.

• *Setting the scene*: In theatre, projections can assist in the communication of important information about the play and the environment that is being created onstage to the audience. This includes critical material such as geographical location, time of day, and season. Combined with all the other elements, projections present a cohesive, unified picture to the audience, often adding an additional, dynamic element to the stage picture. In lighting design, this is referred to as *setting the scene*, but the term is also applicable here. Setting the scene often leads the projection designer to ask a number of questions in order to create or select the most appropriate image or images for any given moment. For example, if the director wants a projection of waves on a beach on part of the scenery to support the action of a scene, the projection designer needs to know a number of different things: What kind of waves? Whitecaps or gentle crests? Tall waves or small? Long, continuous waves or short broken ones? Should the image be moving or static? If a moving image is desired, how much pace and rhythm is desired for the breaking of the waves? Should they crest and break rapidly, implying a restless sea and emotional feel, or should they break slowly and gently, suggesting a more calm tide and emotional state? What time of day should the image present? What season? Should the day be cloudy or sunny? Should the sea be stormy and rough, or relatively calm? How long an animation sequence is required? Can the sequence loop, or does the director prefer one long clip? Asking these kinds of detailed questions for every projection helps you as a designer to refine the image and tailor it precisely to the needs of the specific moment.

- *Serving as scenery*: Increasingly the boundaries of what can be done with projections are being pushed beyond their previous uses into the realm of scenery. Large format projectors are capable of projecting very large images across entire backdrops and stacking projectors makes it possible to fill an entire cyclorama with an image. Video and LED walls, panels, and curtains can create interactive scenic units that can rapidly change their appearance, providing unlimited flexibility for in-house and touring productions alike. Image mapping makes it possible to rapidly transform the surface texture and appearance of static scenic units with the touch of a button. If projections are going to serve as a primary scenic element, the designer needs to give serious consideration to how the actors will interact with the projected elements and how they will be incorporated into any other existing scenic units.

- *Establishing mood and atmosphere*: Creating mood is an important function of projections and has a considerable effect on the audience. Light is an inherent part of projections, and light is also is an incredibly influential design element when it comes to establishing mood and creating an emotional response. The mood and emotional quality of the projections may change several times over the course of a performance, adjusting to the requirements of each individual scene in order to support the dramatic action and following the rhythmic pace set by the script and the staging. Projections can be dark,

oppressive, foreboding, heavy, static, depressing, or passive, or they can be energetic, uplifting, light, carefree, romantic, comfortable, and inviting. Their potential is unlimited. The changes between emotional qualities may be so refined and understated that the audience is entirely unaware of them or they may be painted with quick, broad strokes that are easily recognizable and meant to be noticed.

- *Creating focus*: As with any design element, focus in projection design is the practice of creating emphasis by directing the audience's attention to a particular area, element, person, or group. Projections can be used to direct the attention of the audience where it is desired at any given moment. Because projections are such a dynamic design element, they can naturally take focus, so part of the designer's job is often to integrate them into the stage environment in such a way that they accomplish the desired effect without taking attention away from the actors or the production as a whole. There are a lot of bells, whistles, and fun technological toys available to the projection designer; the challenge is not to become caught up in them to the detriment of the performance.

- *Creating rhythm*: In projection design, rhythm relates to both the staging of movements and transitions from one projection to the next as well as the movement within a projection itself. How these are developed and planned can be very challenging. Transitions can be understated and gentle or they can be dramatic and bold. The animation of a projection can be smooth and calming, or it can be choppy and jarring. The rhythm of the projections may relate directly to the logistical needs of the play or the staging of the story, which may be the best choice for supporting the production. For another play, it may be more appropriate for the projection transitions to follow the dramatic tensions and changes in the script itself. It all depends on the play and the style of the production. It is always important to determine which approach will best support the flow of the action rather than being disruptive.

- *Adding visual texture and modeling form*: Projections have the potential to add a dynamic element of texture to the stage space, scenery, and actors in a way similar to lighting gobos. Image mapping makes it possible to mold projected images to any uneven surface, creating custom textures that appear to be a part of the object rather than sitting on top of it. Texture adds visual interest to a stage environment, creates mood and atmosphere, helps to establish location, and can add dimension to actors and scenic elements by modeling form. Images can be static or moving, sharp or diffuse, full color or in monochrome as needed to provide the desired effect.

- *Supporting the visual style of the production*: As with all of the other design areas, style in projection design refers to a guiding principle or aesthetic convention of representation that serves to inform and unify the overall visual look of the design as a whole. Style can refer to a specific historical, literary, or artistic aesthetic, or an overall pervasive quality that is used to influence the visual elements of a production. The style of the production should be developed collaboratively between the director and the members of the design team in order for them to share an understanding of the common idea and so that they will be able to realize a final product that is unified and consistent, with all elements working together in harmony.

TYPES OF PROJECTIONS AND COMMON PROJECTORS

Projection Types

- *Front*: **Front projections** are those images and video components that are projected from the front of the stage onto the playing space. Front projections have the advantage of a longer throwing distance, especially when combined with a longer throw lens, which makes it possible for them to project larger images onto scenery, backdrops, cycloramas, or stage floors. There are more positions available with a front projection than with a rear projection. Projectors can be mounted on the floor, above the audience or the stage, rigged at various heights or stacked to create a large, continuous image. They may be used to project distinct visuals that serve as scenic backdrops, impart information, to establish mood and atmosphere, or simply to provide texture on the scenery or floor. The viewing angle of a front projection is usually wider, making it possible for more of the audience to see the projected image without distortion. If the projectors used for front projection have enough lumens they can carry their image through the stage lighting surrounding them without adjustment to the surrounding lighting, beyond the use of barn doors and top hats to control spill. The image will be bright and visible on the projection surface with good contrast and sharpness.

- *Rear*: **Rear projections** are those images and videos that are projected from behind the stage space, usually onto a scrim or other semitransparent surface specifically made for rear projections. The material for the projection surface is critical; it must be diffuse or hotspots can be evident in the image on the axis of the projector. The use of a wide angle lens can contribute to the development of hotspots. Rear projections tend to have a shorter throwing distance. A narrower viewing angle can lead to image distortion for members of the audience seated outside the prime viewing area as well as a loss of sharpness and contrast.

- *Top*: **Top projections** are those images and videos that are projected onto the floor from positions directly above the stage. Projectors in these positions can be used to add texture and depth to the stage floor, create special effects and quickly and dramatically change the implied surface texture of the stage floor.

- *Video*: **Video projections** are moving images created with digital, video, or film cameras that are projected into the stage space. Video projections can also be set up as a live feed from other locations across a networked Web interface. Video projections can be a dynamic visual element that adds evocative and interactive components to the stage space.

- *Moving images*: **Moving images** can be created for the purpose of projection through multiple software programs that allow the designer to layer several images together and loop them back onto each other, creating seamless repeating movement. For example, one layer in a moving image could be a background; another, a door opening on a building; a third, a flock of birds flying overhead. Looping these three images together would create a new moving image that contained the qualities of all three. Moving images may also be a simple as a series of images that move forward in a timed sequence or rhythm for effect, perhaps matched to the movement of the actors onstage or timed to match a piece of incidental music.

Projectors

- *Large format slides*: Although standard slides have been replaced in projection technology by digital projections, there is still a place for large format slides in the projection designer's toolbox. Originally called *Son et Lumiere*, nighttime performances conducted with these projectors involved projecting huge images onto buildings of historical significance. Large format slide projectors have existed since the 1950s and have not evolved much past their humble beginnings in terms of technology. Basically, they consist of a large light bulb inside a casing with a lens. Technological advances have made these projectors more powerful and there are several companies which make this technique spectacular. **Pani projectors** are almost synonymous with large format projections. In business since the middle of the twentieth century, they are known for extremely powerful, high-quality projectors that can use slides up to 24 square centimeters/9.4 square inches. They can also employ a **scroller**, a device that changes slides within the housing, allowing for beautiful cross fades between images. Other large format projectors include the Pigi projector(pronounced *pee-gee*), which has a color fader and is dimmable and has dual slide scrollers that can change slides at a rate of one millimeter per minute to one meter per second, and the hardware Xenon projector, which can also use a single or double slide scroller.

Digital Display Devices

- *LCD*: A liquid crystal display projector uses three separate glass LCD panels to process the image signal sent to the projector, one each for the red, green, and blue components. Light passes through these LCD panels and is modulated by individual **pixels**, which is shorthand for "picture elements." The individual pixels open or close, allowing light to pass through the LCD or to block the light, like a tiny shutter. Historically, **LCD projectors** have offered better color saturation and they also tend to offer a sharper image than their DLP counterparts at any resolution. LCD projectors are also more light-efficient because they produce much higher ANSI lumen output than a DLP projector with the same wattage lamp. However, there are some drawbacks to LCD technology. LCD projectors do not produce the best quality black level and contrast, which is important in video projection. There

can also be significant pixilation in a projected image, making it appear as though the viewer is looking through a screen door. Advancements in LCD technology include increased resolution, reduction in the gaps between pixels, and the introduction of the micro lens array (MLA), which reduces the level of pixilation in XGA projectors by increasing light transmission.

- *LCD panels*: Liquid crystal display technology is also available in individual panels of varying sizes. These panels can be used individually as a single projection surface or joined together to create **video walls** of various sizes that can be used to present dynamic, movable scenery that can be changed at the touch of a button. Some LCD panel manufacturers offer near seamless tiling of the individual panels, making it possible to present clear, uninterrupted images that offer fully interactive, multi-touch capabilities. With this technology, the actors can interact directly with

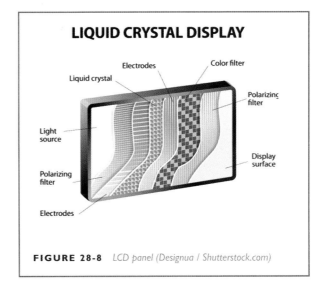

FIGURE 28-8   *LCD panel (Designua / Shutterstock.com)*

FIGURE 28-7   *LCD Projector*

FIGURE 28-9   *Video walls at a concert (Reeed / Shutterstock.com)*

the projected image through finger based gestures like scrolling, swiping, pinching, rotating, and flicking. With one simple touch, multiple users can **zoom** in or out, scroll through a series of images, and start or stop video.

- *DLP*: Digital light processing projectors utilize a proprietary technology first developed by Texas Instruments. They operate very differently than an LCD projector. Instead of glass panels, a **DLP** projector possesses one or three reflective DLP chips. These chips are made of tiny mirrors, each of which represents an individual pixel. When light is projected onto the chips, it causes them to move back and forth, directing light towards the path of the lens to activate the pixel, or away from the lens to deactivate it. In a single-chip DLP projector, colors are defined through the use of a color wheel that is composed of individual red, blue, and green filters. This wheel spins between the light source and the chip, alternating the color of the light that strikes it. The mirrors on the chip tilt toward or away from the lens path based on how much of each color is needed for each pixel at any individual moment. These mirrors move up to 10,000 times per second to control the light emitted by the projector and produce the image on the projection surface. In high-end DLP projectors, there is an individual chip for each of the three color channels and no color wheel. There are several advantages to using a DLP projector. In general, they tend to be smaller and more compact than an LCD projector, because most use one chip compared to three glass panels, making them lighter and more portable. DLPs also have fewer issues with pixilation, eliminating the "screen door effect" in projected images. This is especially important for smooth video playback. They have a higher contrast than LCD units, allowing for deeper blacks and a greater range of subtleties in color difference. Their optic components are sealed within the projector, making them suitable for use in dusty locations and they tend to be more reliable because

they have fewer moving parts—and they can be cheaper to repair. Disadvantages of DLP technology, such as light leakage and a brief flash of rainbow colors around brighter objects in an image when quickly looking away from the projection surface tend to only occur on older projectors and have been eliminated by advances in the technology itself.

- *LED walls, screens, curtains, and panels*: A light emitting diode display is a flat panel digital display unit that uses an array of light emitting diodes to display images and video. An **LED** panel is a smaller display, which may be part of a larger LED unit. Because of their small size, it is possible to manufacture LED displays in several different configurations, including rigid walls, panels and screens of various sizes, as well as flexible curtains. Because they are made up of individual lights, LED displays can appear somewhat diffuse, even at a high resolution. But, they have

FIGURE 28-11   *LED panel (Kristina Postnikova/Shutterstock.com)*

FIGURE 28-10   *DLP projector (image courtesy of Christie)*

FIGURE 28-12   *Holographic projection (Tillicum Village, Washington State, courtesy of Christie)*

the advantage of being lightweight and portable and LED curtains are flexible in all directions, allowing actors to make entrances through the projection surface.

- *Holographic projection system*: Holographic projection or holography is a digital projection technique that makes it possible to project three-dimensional images. High definition **holographic projection systems** make it possible to project life-sized three-dimensional moving images within a live theatrical setting. These can range from interactive holographic projections to fully immersive virtual reality environments.

CONTENT GENERATION

Content generation and creation is one of the most important aspects of projection design. This is where the bulk of your work as a designer takes place. Here is where you make most of the decisions regarding the visual look not only for each individual projection component, but for the entire design as a whole. Content is the end result of translating the elements of the script and the input received from the director and the other design collaborators into a realized visual product. Of key importance in the process is the question "who determines the content of the projections?"

In some cases, the director may have a very strong idea of what images or types of images they want to use in each scene, or the scene designer might want to use a projection to add visual texture to part of the set. A lighting designer may argue that there really is not any difference between a custom glass gobo and a projection, and it could be possible that a gobo is a better solution to a particular design problem than a projection. It could be possible that the content will come from several different colleagues in the design team. In any case, it is important to establish this upfront in order to know what your responsibilities are as the projection designer. It is entirely possible that the projection designer will be responsible for finding or creating all of the projection content. It is also possible that all the content will be provided and that the designer will handle the image editing and control sequencing for the projection design, determining projection length, timing, and placement. The projection designer's duties may also fall somewhere in between these two ends of the scale.

Finding Images versus Creating Images

Where does the image content come from? The simple answer is many places. The larger answer is more complex. It is certainly possible to find stock video clips and images on the Web for download and purchase, both moving and static. There are advantages and disadvantages to using stock images. One advantage is that content has already been created and if it suits your purpose it can be downloaded quickly and then added to your design without much effort. Some stock image providers also allow editing as part of the license to use their images, which makes it possible to customize the files to suit your individual production needs, but not all stock licenses offer this option. The main disadvantage of stock images is that it can be hard to find an image or clip that is exactly what you are looking for and even when you find something close, it has not been created with your production and intent specifically in mind. If there is no option for editing the stock image, then you cannot tailor the media to suit your purpose. While stock images are convenient, it is often easier to create the content you need yourself.

The main advantage of creating your own content is that it is tailored specifically for your production, taking all of the visual and aesthetic concerns into consideration. Self-generated content can be produced in the same artistic style as the rest of the design elements, utilizing the same artistic conventions, color palette, and design approach. It allows you as the designer to develop your own visual language for the production. Self-created projection images have the potential to complement and enhance the other design elements in a way that a stock component simply cannot. They can be endlessly manipulated and edited without concern for copyright or other licensing concerns because they are your work. In short, by generating your own content, you get exactly what you want without making any compromises along the way. Doing so may require more work and more effort, and it certainly may mean that the projection designer must be familiar with a variety of ways to generate images, from hand-drawing to digital image creation, photography, and video technology, but the end result will produce a finished design that is likely more satisfying on an artistic and intellectual level.

THE ART OF THE PROJECTION DESIGNER

Like all designers, a projection designer must possess a wide variety of skills in order to be able to design effectively. They need to understand the rules of visual composition and how they relate to images, video, and projections in order to apply them to their designs in order to create compelling and engaging compositions. As projection designers, we are not simply concerned with what kinds of fantastical things we can do with the technology. Admittedly, there are a lot of toys and tricks involved in projections, but if all we are doing is using projections because we *can*, then we are not really using them

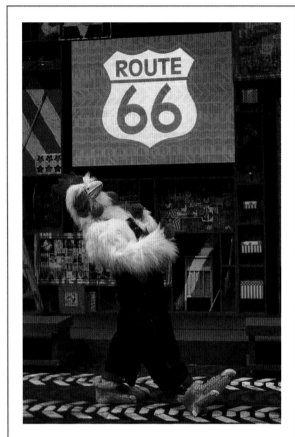

FIGURE 28-13 bobrauschenbergamerica by Charles Mee, set design by Jeff Entwistle, lighting and projection design by R. Michael Ingraham, costume design by Kaoime E. Malloy

to their full potential. We must be concerned with the quality of each projection element, whether it is an image or a video, with how it is perceived, how the audience relates to it, and how they react. We must think about not only what needs to be seen, what image needs to displayed but also how it should be revealed, how it should be used, and how the actors should interact with it, if at all. And because projections use light as their vehicle of transmission, like lighting designers, a projection designer should have an understanding of the psychology of light, including our perceptions of it and how it affects us as human beings.

A projection designer must be a good listener, able to both hear and to understand what the director is asking for in terms of projection in order to translate them into a workable design and also to be able to make adjustments during the rehearsal process. They must also be able to communicate with their colleagues in order to express their ideas and exchange information. He or she must to be able to do detailed script analysis in order to understand the projection requirements of the play in both practical and

artistic terms. They also need to know how to do effective research and locate inspirational images that can be shared with their collaborators and inform their design choices. The designer should be familiar with the history of projection technology, including the differences between devices and the various light qualities produced by each, so that those characteristics may be recreated onstage with modern instruments when necessary. They must understand the principles of stage blocking and how to notate it in a concise and effective manner in the event that the actors will be interacting directly with the projected elements onstage. They must also be organized and able to keep track of multiple images and projections.

Like lighting and sound design, projection design is an incredibly technology-driven design area. There is no way that a projection designer can do what they need to without understanding the technology behind the art form. They must be computer literate and need to possess good skills with at least one image-editing software program in order to create and edit digital images. Gone are the days when a projection consisted of simply throwing up a single static image into the performance space. Now, in order to be current, a projection designer needs to understand how to layer images to create moving projections and animated images. They should have a working knowledge of video creation, editing, and playback. They should have a working knowledge of photography in order to capture their own images. They need to be familiar with the different projector technologies in order to determine which device is best suited for the needs of each production and be aware of the advantages and limitations of each. A projection designer must be aware of the considerations of image resolution and not only how that affects the choice of projector but also how to adjust it for different devices and desired projection size within the stage space. A designer needs to know how to use at least one projection control program or system with a high degree of skill in order to realize their designs. A basic understanding of math is helpful to be able to make the simple calculations associated with throw ratios, projection location, lens selection, projection size, and resolution. They must be part electrician, with a basic understanding of electricity, electrical theory and safety, power distribution, and the ability to make basic electrical calculations for each theatrical venue. They must understand the science and physics of light as well as the art in order to create effective images onstage.

A projection designer is also a visual artist, communicating ideas through selective research images, sketches, storyboarding, digital renderings, images, and animated mockups. Like all designers, a projections designer must constantly learn about new equipment and technologies in order to create better, more evocative work and to stay current in a field that is changing constantly.

FIGURE 28-14   *Songs for a New World by Jason Robert Brown, set design by Jeff Entwistle, lighting design by R. Michael Ingraham, photo by R. Michael Ingraham*

SCRIPT ANALYSIS—GENERAL QUESTIONS TO ASK OF THE PLAY

- What is the genre of the play?

- What is the overall style of the play?

- What type of dramatic structure does the play possess?

- In what time period does the play take place? Are there multiple time periods that might influence the projection design and the choice of images?

- How does the action of the play move through time? Does the action take place over a few hours? Days? Weeks? Months? Or years? Are projections required to help indicate this movement of the action?

- Where is the action of the play located? Are there multiple locations that will affect the design?

- Is the location an interior or an exterior?

- What are the sources of light? Are they natural or artificial?

- Are there any practical lighting instruments installed on the set? Will they affect the quality of any projections?

- What is the season or seasons?

- What is the overall mood of the play?

- What is the overall theme or message of the play?

- What images come to mind as you read the play?

- Are you able to visualize any of the images suggested by the play in terms of light?

- What part do projections play in the dramatic action?

- Are projections ever asked to take the place of scenery?

- What kinds of transitions are required between scenes? Will projections be required to facilitate these changes?

- Has the use of projections been written into the script? If so, how are they integrated into the action of the play? What is their purpose? How have they been used by the playwright to support or tell the story?

- Which character is the protagonist? Whose story is being told?

- What are the major conflicts in the play? What or who is preventing the protagonist from getting what she or he wants?

- How are the characters utilized by the playwright?

- Which characters play the major roles in the story?

- Which characters are secondary or supporting?

ADDITIONAL CONCERNS FOR THE PROJECTION DESIGNER

In addition to the questions that will form the basis of the analysis of the play, the projection designer also needs to take a few other relevant bits of information into consideration in order to create an effective design.

- *Who is generating the content?* Is the projection designer responsible for selecting the content, or will the content be selected by another designer on the production team? Will the director be selecting the content? Or, will the content be selected collaboratively between all the members of the design team?

- *Where is the content coming from?* Will the designer be creating content, or can stock images and video clips be used?

- *Will the images be static or animated?*

- *What kinds of transitions are required between each projection?* How should the projection appear within the stage space? Does the director want the audience to immediately be aware of the projection, or should that awareness be gradual? Should they fade in and out imperceptibly, or should they appear quickly and boldly?

- *When do the projections move?* Timing and duration of each projected image or video clip is important. How will each sequence align with the action taking place on the stage?

- *How do the projections move?*

- *Why do the projections move?* This question is related to the motivation and purpose behind each projection. There should be a reason for their beginning and end just as there is a reason for their inclusion in the production in the first place. What stimulates their arrival and what is the impetus for their departure?

- *What kind of continuity or progression does the projection design need?* It is important to determine if the projection elements need to be linked or tied together in some way and to what extent this requirement will influence your design choices before you make them. In some instances, the projections for a production will serve as standalone images that are primarily unified by the production itself. Or, they may be unified conceptually, thematically, visually,

or stylistically and that may be enough to provide continuity throughout the design. Other productions may require the projections to progress over the course of the play, reacting to the rising tensions of the dramatic action or building on one another to reach a climax and resolution.

- *Will the actors be interacting with the projections?* If so, what is the director's desired expectation in this regard? Knowing just how the director wants the actors to interact with the projections can help the designer select the type of projection, and subsequently the device and the projection surface, and influence the determination of projection length, timing, and visual design.

- *Is video required?* If so, who is responsible for selecting, shooting and editing the video content?

- *Do the projections need to be aligned with any other design element?* Projections are often integrated into the scenery, either by means of the projection surface or as a scenic element in and of themselves. Projections may also need to be linked with sound or lighting content. When this is the desired outcome, a complete discussion of how all the various design elements are expected to work together in the final performance is an important part of the design and collaboration process.

- *Become familiar with the set, costume, lighting design, and sound design.* Projection design does not occur in a vacuum. The projection designer must become acquainted with the work of their colleagues in order to integrate their work with that of the other designers. Look at the set drawings, renderings, and paint elevations. If there is a model, taking a digital photograph of each scene can assist you during the design process, especially if you need to tailor your projections to fit individual parts of the scenery or use image mapping to mold them to the set. Look at the costume sketches, renderings, and fabric swatches. Visit the costume shop to see the actual costumes in order to know how the projections will affect them. Discuss how the projections will be integrated with the lighting designer's choices and if they will affect them so that adjustments can be made. If your work is intended to be integrated with the sound design in any capacity, ask the sound designer for a sample disk of their sound cues in order to assist you with timing and length of projections. This is especially important if the control system used for the production will be running projections and sound together. Pay attention to the color schemes used by the other designers, how the elements and principles of design have been employed and how style has been applied to their designs. These are all things that can inform your work as you proceed.

- *Become acquainted with the venue.* What kind of stage space is the production taking place in? Proscenium, thrust, arena, black box, or outdoor theatre? The projection designer needs to know the theatre and the rigging positions in order to make their design decisions. They will need access to the structural plans in order to select their projection positions. The designer needs to know what projection equipment is in the inventory and detailed information about any available control systems as these will all have an influence on what can or cannot be accomplished in the space.

- *Attend rehearsals.* In order to create effective projections that meet the needs of the production, fit the action and are suitable for each moment, the projection designer needs to know the show, and there is no better way to do that than by attending rehearsals. If projections are being used as scenery, or will have a pronounced effect on the stage environment, or if the actors will be required to interact with the projections in any way, then it will be important to see the blocking created by the director, noting important aspects of the movement and how it affects your work. Although a projection designer should learn to take blocking notations on paper for their own use, they are not a complete substitution for watching the actors go through the action of the play onstage. Adjustments may need to be made to projector placement to fit the blocking and change is inevitable throughout the rehearsal process. Attending several run-through rehearsals not only allows a projection designer to get a sense of the blocking, but also to get a feel for the pacing of the show. Even if the projections are an element that is separate from the actors, attending rehearsals can still provide key information, such as projection placement, length, timing, and desired transition quality.

THE LANGUAGE OF PROJECTION DESIGN

Angle: The orientation of the projector to the projection surface.

Aspect ratio: the relationship between the height and width of its maximum projected image size.

Camera obscura: A black box with a convex lens or aperture used to project the image of an external scene or object onto a screen or wall inside a room.

Chromotope slide: A rotating circular glass slide used with a magic lantern to create changing colors and geometric shapes.

Content: The images in the projections.

Contrast: The difference between the darkest and the lightest parts of a projected image.

Controller: A system that controls the projection devices and the input sent to them.

DLP: Digital light processing.

DPI: Dots per inch. A measure of digital dot or pixel density.

Edge blending: Carefully blending the edges of a projection to overlap and merge seamlessly with another.

Front projection: Images and video components that are projected from in front of the stage space.

Holographic projection system: A device capable of projecting a three-dimensional image.

Keystoning: Distortion of a projected image along the horizontal or vertical axis that occurs when the projector is not perpendicular to the projection surface.

LCD projector: Liquid crystal display projector.

LED: Light emitting diodes.

Lens: A shaped piece of glass or other transparent material with curved sides used to focus, concentrate or disperse rays of light inside a projector.

Lens shift: Moving the lens of the projector up and down or left and right within the projector housing.

Linnebach projector: A lens-free projector consisting of a large enclosed black box that utilizes a large transparent glass or mica side with a hand-painted image.

Looping: Editing a moving image seamlessly back onto itself in order to create a longer sequence.

Lumen: A unit of luminous flux, which measures the amount of visible light emitted by a light source.

Magic lantern: An early type of slide projector that uses a concave mirror behind a light source to direct as much of the light as possible through a rectangular pane of glass that contains a painted or photographic image.

Pani projector: A large format slide projector consisting of a powerful lamp housed in a casing that uses a large slide as the source image. Pani is a brand name.

Pixels: Picture elements. The smallest components in a digital image.

Projection: The display of an image by a device, such as a projector.

Projector: A device that projects an image onto a viewing surface.

Rear projection: Images and video components that are projected from behind the stage space onto a projection surface.

Resolution: The quality of an image.

> **Scroller:** A device that changes slides on a large format projector.
>
> **Throw ratio:** The distance from the center of a projector's lens to the projection surface divided by the width of the image being projected. The ratio itself is dimensionless.
>
> **Tiling:** Using multiple projectors to build a large image by arranging parts of the image in a tiled formation on the projection surface.
>
> **Video wall:** A wall made up of video display units, such as LCD panels.
>
> **Zoom:** To smoothly change from a long shot to a close up or vice versa.

PROJECTION DESIGN EXERCISE

Materials

- Paper
- Pencils
- Color media
- Image editing program, if desired
- Digital camera, if desired.

Description

This is an exercise in generating content, either finding or creating projection images that are visually and emotionally engaging, that communicate information to the audience, and that match the stylistic and aesthetic conventions presented by the play. In this exercise, you will create a series of three images that represent the progression of an activity or state of being, in three different stylistic conventions: realism, stylization, and abstraction. The progression may be sequential, presented in a direct linear format representing a beginning, middle, and end; or it may be episodic, illustrating distinct three points in the experience of the activity or state.

Method

Choose three words/concepts from the following list to use as a basis for content creation:

- Freedom
- Transition
- Searching
- Frustration
- Isolation
- Spirituality
- Enlightenment
- Rebirth
- Assimilation
- Fear

Using these words as your starting point, begin your process of creating content to illustrate and represent them visually by:

- Researching their definition. What do they mean in different parts of the world?
- How have they been represented in art and literature in the past?
- What do they mean to you personally?
- What are the most important aspects of each of the three concepts you selected? How will they translate into visual terms?
- What will your conceptual approach be to the presented design problem?
- What structural format will the sequence of your images take?
- What kinds of images are associated with the ideas you have chosen?
- How will the three artistic styles affect your choices? What do you think are the key aspects of each style and how will you apply them to your designs?
- Where on the stage do you envision your images will be projected? Will they be part of the scenery, projected onto the actors in addition to the set, or will they be separate from the actors onstage? What is the reason for your choice?

Create three images for each concept in a storyboard format, either with traditional art materials or digital image-editing software. Take style into consideration when selecting your media. The media does not have to be the same for each stylistic approach. One might benefit from the advantages that a computer has to offer in image creation while another style might be better suited to collage or another traditional medium.

GLOSSARY

Abstract texture: Actual or implied texture that has been simplified, rearranged, or distorted in order to fulfill the visual needs of a design.

Abstraction: Design that relies on the visual language of line, form, color and so on to create a design that may have no references to the world around us.

Absurdism: Based on the philosophy of existentialism, which calls for the use of the will rather than reason in order to deal with the problems that arise in an increasingly antagonistic world. In absurdist plays life has no meaning and existence is useless. There is no conventional sense of time, place, or structure.

Accessories: Items that enhance the overall look of a costume, but do not take the place of the costume itself.

Acoustics: The generation, transmission, and reception of sound.

Actual line: A line that is real, complete, and unbroken.

Actual texture: Changes in surfaces that are real and three-dimensional. Also known as real texture.

Additive mixing: A model that explains the mixing of colors using light. Each color of light is added together to create white light, which contains all colors.

Airbrush colors: Acrylics with the thinnest viscosity, similar to ink.

Airbushing: Applying paint with an airbrush, which atomizes the paint and produces a fine mist.

Alignment: The arrangement of objects along a straight line or lines.

All-over pattern: Pattern created by repeating design elements with equal visual weight throughout the entire surface of a composition. There is no strong focal point; the visual weight is even and uniform. Also known as crystallographic balance.

Alternating rhythm: Visual rhythm created when an element or motif is repeated and the position, spacing, or content is changed with each repetition.

Ambient sound: Sound that serves as background, creating mood and atmosphere, and enhancing the overall environment.

Analogous: A color scheme that uses only colors that share a primary hue, including all of their tints, shades, and tones.

Analysis: The process of determining what the individual visual elements suggest and deciding *why* the designer used those features to convey specific ideas. It answers the questions "how did the designer do it?", "what elements did the designer choose?" and "how did they arrange them?"

Angle: The orientation of the projector to the projection surface.

Antagonist: The character that directly opposes the protagonist and attempts to keep him or her from reaching their goals.

Area lighting: A lighting system that divides the stage into smaller, individual areas and lights them separately.

Arena theatre: A theatre where the audience entirely surrounds the performance space. Also known as theatre in the round.

Art sticks: Wax colored pencils in stick form.

Artists' chalk: Calcium carbonate mixed with mineral pigments.

Artistic style: A design style based on the aesthetic conventions of an individual artist.

Aspect ratio: The relationship between the height and width of its maximum projected image size.

Assemblage: An artwork created by joining three-dimensional objects together to form a three-dimensional shape.

Asymmetrical balance: A composition that has two sides that do not match; but the composition appears to be balanced because the visual weights in the two sides are very similar.

Atmospheric perspective: A method of conveying depth based on the observation that objects become bluer and less distinct as they move into the distance.

Axis: A line that divides an object into two equal halves.

Backdrop: A painted cloth, often encompassing the entire width of the stage, which is used as part of the scenery.

Background: The area of a composition that surrounds the subject.

Backlight: A light source striking the object in a drawing from behind. Also refers to light that comes from fixtures mounted behind a subject.

Balance: The equal distribution of visual weight to either side of a perceived or implied center of gravity. Also refers to an even distribution of power between forces in the play: the status quo.

Bilateral symmetry: Symmetry where both halves of a design are exactly identical.

Biographical dramas: Dramas that focus on the life of one individual or group, and attempt to present truthful or compelling pictures of the subject and the events surrounding their lives.

Biomorphic shape: Abstract shapes that resemble living forms.

Black box theatre: A flexible theatre space made to provide multiple stage configurations.

Blackout: A transition to complete darkness onstage.

Blacks: The stage drapes used to mask the offstage areas.

Blending: The technique of moving from one degree of value to another in a smooth fashion.

Borders: Short, narrow drapes that run the entire length of the stage and are used to conceal stage lights and battens from view.

Boundary: The perceived border or edges of a shape, which indicates its limits.

Branching: A series of forked, three-way joints of lines or linear shapes that mimic the paths formed by the natural growth of plants or of the system of blood vessels in the body.

Brightness: The visual effect created when a light source interacts with an object, and how that effect is perceived by the eye.

Bronzing powder: A metallic powder that can be mixed with a paint medium to create a metallic paint or placed on top of paint to add texture.

Burnishing: Using a wax pencil with heavy pressure to both blend layers of color together and polish the wax surface, making it shine.

Camera obscura: A black box with a convex lens or aperture used to project the image of an external scene or object onto a screen or wall inside a room.

Candela: The unit of measurement that describes the power emitted by a light source in any particular direction.

Cast shadow: A darker area of value that is created by an object placed between a surface and a light source.

Center of gravity: The average center of the weight of an object. In design, this usually refers to the center of the composition, both horizontally and vertically.

Character analysis: A list of the overall qualities related to the character, such as social status, general mood, notes from the script, and design thoughts—such as line, colors, and texture—to help the costume designer understand them as individuals and to discover the things that motivate them.

Charcoal: Charred wood or vine in sticks of varying widths and hardness.

Characters: The individuals in the play.

Chiaroscuro: "Light and dark." The technique of blending values to show the bending of light around a form in order to represent the illusion of three dimensions on a two-dimensional surface.

Children's theatre: A blanket term used to describe several dramatic genres specifically aimed at younger audiences, including theatre for children, theatre for youth, and theatre for young audiences, each relating to a specific age group.

Chroma: The Greek word for color, which is used to refer to the saturation or purity of a hue.

Chromatic gray: A gray created by mixing two complementary colors, or by mixing a neutral gray with a color, thereby producing a hue that possesses some aspects of color.

Chromotope slide: A rotating circular glass slide used with a magic lantern to create changing colors and geometric shapes.

Circular stroke: Overlapping pencil or brush marks applied in a circular motion.

Circulation: Another name for branching patterns.

Classicism: A style characterized by a return to the formal order that was found in the art and theatrical forms of ancient Greece.

Climax: The culmination of the all the events and action that came before and has led up to that moment. The highest levels of suspense and tension in the plot.

Closed line: A line that connects to form a shape or joins with other lines for visual effect.

Closed value compositions: An image where the values are confined within shapes.

Closed/restricted palette: A color scheme that limits the number of hues used in a work.

Closure: The effect that occurs when enough visual information is presented to allow the viewer to complete an unfinished image by mentally filling in the missing details.

Collaboration: The act of working with another or others on a joint project. Also refers to something created by working jointly with another or other.

Collage: A composition created by gluing three-dimensional objects on a flat surface to alter the visual and tactile quality of the work.

Color: The hue of light, determined by its wavelengths. Also may be used to refer to a color medium.

Color scheme: The selection of colors used in a composition.

Color wheel: A diagram that shows the relationships between colors laid out in the format of a circle.

Colored pencils: Pencils that contain an inner core made of pigment mixed with wax and other fillers, surrounded by wood or plastic.

Colorless blender: A colored pencil or marker with no pigment, used to blend colors together on the surface of a rendering.

Combing: Drawing combs of various sizes and shapes through wet paint on a surface to create pattern and texture.

Comedy: A genre that emphasizes triumph over adversity, a light and humorous tone, ridiculous events or actions and happy endings to thematic conflict.

Complementary: A color scheme that uses complementary colors, including all of their tints, shades, and tones.

Complements: Colors that sit directly opposite each other on the color wheel.

Composer: An individual that writes music.

Composition: The arrangement of shapes or sounds.

Compound rake: A rake that is angled in more than one direction.

Conceptual unity: A design whose elements are related and unified by ideas and subject matter rather than by similarity in visual elements.

Conceptualization: Something formed in the mind; a thought or notion.

Conflict: When a character is prevented from getting what he or she wants.

Constructivism: Plays that build a story through the action they present, rather than telling a story.

Conte crayons: A finely textured, grease-free stick made of powdered graphite and clay to which red ochre, soot, or blackstone is added to give it a red, black, or brown color.

Content: The meaning of the artwork. Also refers to the images in projections.

Context: The external, cultural, and environmental factors that influence the creation of an artwork.

Contextualism: The practice of using context as a basis for analyzing and understanding art.

Continuation: The effect of each object in a design leading to the next, creating a sense of movement and leading the viewer's eye.

Contour hatching/cross contour: Lines of hatching or crosshatching that follow the shape of an object, moving around it, thereby creating the illusion of three dimensions along with value.

Contour line: A line that defines the shape of an object, but which varies in weight and thickness, contributing to the illusion of mass and volume.

Contrast: The differences between light and dark in a composition. Also refers to visual differences within a design, or the difference between the darkest and the lightest parts of a projected image.

Controller: A system that controls the projection devices and the input sent to them.

Convergence: The merging of visual elements, such as the meeting of perspective lines at a vanishing point.

Cool colors: Hues that are perceived to be cool in temperature.

Core shadow: The location on an object where the reflected light ends and the shadow begins.

Costume designer: The artist that is responsible for the visual realization of the characters through clothing.

Costume plot: A chart that lists the changes required for each character in each scene and over the course of the play.

Costume properties: Costume items carried by the actor, such as watches and glasses.

Courtroom dramas: Dramas that use the setting of the justice system as a main component to explore thematic ideas, with all the associated elements present.

Courtyard theatre: A theatre space that combines the qualities of several different theatre types, modeled after a traditional Elizabethan stage.

Crosshatching: Layers of hatched lines that move in different directions, resulting in darker values.

Cross-section drawing: A technical drawing that shows the theatre and lighting positions from a side view.

Crystallographic balance: Balance that is created by repeating design elements with equal visual weight throughout the entire surface of a composition.

Cue: A static lighting composition or look created by a combination of lights, their angles, and mixing.

Curved deck: A rake built with a steep incline and a curved surface, similar to a skateboard park.

Curvilinear shape: Shapes that are dominated by curved edges and lines.

Cyclorama: A large, continuous curtain made of white or neutral fabric that is tightly stretched and hung at the back of the stage.

Dadaism: A revolutionary approach towards both drama and art, where nothing is sacred and expectations are contradicted at every turn.

Decorative notions: Trims, buttons, ribbons, sequins, feathers, and other decorative items that are used to enhance the costume's overall look.

Decorative style: Design that is meant to be purely beautiful from an aesthetic or formalist point of view.

Decorative value: Value that emphasizes the two-dimensional nature and flatness of a composition and uses dark and light tones for ornamental effect.

Denouement: The resolution or conclusion of the plot.

Depth: A measurement of dimension, inward, downward, or backward.

Description: Discussing the visual aspects of the design without value judgments, analysis, or interpretation. It answers the question "what do you see?"

Descriptive line: A type of contour line that communicates mood and feelings through variations in line quality.

Design: Another word for composition.

Design concept: An idea, series of ideas, themes, or aesthetic guidelines that serve as a framework to guide a designer throughout the design process.

Detail drawings: Comprehensive drawings, usually in scale, that provide additional information about the appearance of the design.

Detailed model: A scale model of the set that is fully painted, showing all the details and textures.

Diagonal backlight: Light that comes from a fixture both behind and at an angle from a subject.

Dialogue: Conversation between characters or between characters and the audience. The primary component of a play.

Didacticism/epic theatre: A working-class style of theatre characterized by an attempt to create a sense of distance and alienation by frequently interrupting the action, destroying the theatrical illusion so that the audience will engage with the story on an intellectual rather than an emotional level.

Dimmer: A device that controls the intensity of light.

Distribution: A controllable quality of light, most often considered in terms of angle and quality. Also refers to where the sound comes from onstage and how much coverage there is in the space.

DLP: Digital light processing.

Double complementary: A color scheme that uses two main colors and their complements, including all of their tints, shades, and tones.

Downlight: Light that comes from a fixture directly above a subject.

DPI: Dots per inch. A measure of digital dot or pixel density.

Drama: A genre where the characters represent themselves as ordinary human beings, allowing the audience to analyze the events of the play for themselves and to make their own judgments.

Dramatic action: The events that occur in the play and how they are revealed, including all the dialogue, movement, action, and the development of the plot.

Drawing: The creation of an image, usually on paper, using lines as the primary visual component.

Dripping: Allowing paint to fall on a surface in drops, strings, and ropes to create texture.

Dropping in color: A simple process where thinned paint is dripped onto a wet surface and allowed to spread without interruption.

Dry brushing: Applying paint with a dry brush and allowing the bristles to separate with each stroke to create a textured effect.

Duplication: Creating a replica of an item.

Duration: How long a sound lasts.

Echo: The repetition of a sound over and over.

Edge blending: Carefully blending the edges of a projection to overlap and merge seamlessly with another.

Edges: The perceived outline or boundary of a shape.

Embossing powders: A fine powder available in a variety of colors that is placed over a stamped image and then heated to create a raised impression.

Emphasis: Making one part of an image stand out from its surrounding, which attracts the attention of the viewer.

End stage: A theatre in which the audience and the acting area occupy the same architectural space.

Environmental theatre: A theatrical space that has been completely transformed to create a unique environment for the performance.

Episodic structure: A plot that focuses on multiple scenes, characters, and viewpoints.

Evaluation and judgment: Deciding if the design is effective for the given play. Judgment answers the question "is it a good design?"

Exact duplication: Objects that are replicated exactly, with no variations.

Exaggerated scale: Manipulating the proportions of an object for visual or thematic effect.

Experimental structure: Nontraditional play structure; any plot that does not fit into the classification of traditional structure.

Exposition: The introduction to the plot of the play that gives important aspects of the story.

Expressionism: An artistic style developed in the early twentieth century that is concerned with the communication of emotion, rather than focusing entirely on artistic technique.

Faceting: Removing one of more parts of a polygon, which reveals new faces of the polygon or any polyhedron it is a part of.

Falling action: The point in the play after the climax where the levels of stress and tension begin to dissipate as conflicts begin to be resolved.

Farce: A subgenre of comedy containing exaggerated characters, extremely improbable plots and situations, mistaken identity or disguises, and elements of slapstick and physical comedy.

Feminist theatre: Theatre that is by, for, and about women, presenting their voice, attitudes, beliefs, hopes, and desires.

Figure: The positive space in a composition. It can also be used to refer to the main subject in an image.

Figure/ground: The relationship between the subject of a composition (the figure) and the area it occupies (the background).

Figure/ground reversal: A two-dimensional composition where the figure and the background appear to reverse positions.

Fill light: Ambient light in a theatrical space, or additional light used on a subject to soften high contrast and shadows.

Filter: Color or diffusion medium for a lighting instrument, which alters the appearance of the beam of light.

Final drawings: Drawings that are an artistic presentation of the designs in a completed form without color, including all the final details.

Fixative: An agent that seals the surface of a piece, "fixing" the media in place.

Fixture: A lighting instrument.

Flats: A framed scenic unit used to form walls.

Flexible set: A set that is nonspecific, allowing for multiple scenes to be played out without slowing down the action with multiple realistic set changes.

Floorplan: A layout of the stage space that provides a variety of acting areas for the director to use to stage the action. Also called a groundplan.

Flowing rhythm: Smooth, gliding movement from one repeated form to another.

Fluid acrylics: Acrylics that are thin enough to be poured but contain the same pigment load as heavy body acrylics.

Focal point: A relatively small, clearly defined area of emphasis.

Focus: In lighting, the practice of creating emphasis by directing the audience's attention to a particular area, element, person, or group. Also refers to the sharpness of an image or, in sound, creating emphasis with a cue.

Foil and gesso: Imbedding aluminum foil in gesso to create a heavy textured painting surface.

Foils: Synthetic and precious metal metallic foils that can be applied with adhesives to painted surfaces to create texture.

Followspot: A spotlight that is used to follow actors as they move onstage.

Footcandles: A measure of illuminance based on the amount of light found one foot from a candle.

Foreground: The area of a composition occupied by the subject.

Foreshortening: The distortion that occurs in the dimensions of forms in linear perspective on both the horizontal and vertical axes.

Form: A synthesis of all the visual aspects of a design or a synonymous term for shape. Form may also be used to refer to the type of artwork, i.e., sculpture, painting, or be used to describe a three-dimensional object.

Formal balance: Another name for symmetry.

Format: The size and shape of the work surface. Also refers to the physical qualities of an artwork; the size and form it takes.

Found space: A nontheatrical building or location that is adapted and used for a performance.

Fractals: A shape that, when divided, consists of parts that are exact replicas of the entire image.

Framed units: A scenic unit that possesses a frame on all four sides for support, which can be made of wood or metal.

French scene chart: A diagram that shows the entrances and exits of each character in each scene, making it possible to keep track of who is on stage at any given moment.

Frequency: How many times a pattern of sound repeats in a given time period, usually one second.

Front elevations: Scenic drawings that show the full details of the entire set, properties, or scenic elements from the front, along with measurements.

Front projection: Images and video components that are projected from in front of the stage space.

Frontlight: Light that comes from fixtures mounted in front of a subject.

Frottage: Capturing the texture of a surface by placing a piece of paper over it and rubbing a pencil or other drawing medium against the surface to transfer the texture.

Futurism: A style where the past is rejected, progress is glorified, and technology is embraced as the harbinger of a new and great industrial future.

Gel medium: A thick gel that increases the viscosity of acrylic paint.

Gels: Transparent plastic colored lighting filters.

General illumination: A lighting system that provides basic illumination across the stage as a whole.

Genre: The literary form of the play.

Gesso: An acrylic paint mixture consisting of emulsion mixed with gypsum, chalk, pigment, or any combination of the three, usually used for preparing a ground prior to painting.

Gestalt theory: A psychological theory of visual perception that deals with both the whole artistic image and its individual parts and their relationship to one another.

Gestural line: Quick, freely drawn lines that imply past, present, or future movement or the gesture of a subject. With gesture line, delineating shape is less important than capturing the dynamics of movement.

Glazing: Using layers of thin, transparent washes of paint on top of a painted surface to enhance the underlying color.

Gloss medium: An acrylic additive that increases the sheen of the paint.

Gobo: A metal frame cut with a pattern that is inserted into the lighting instrument that filters the beam as it is cast, changing its shape.

Golden mean: A mathematical ratio developed by the ancient Greeks that expressed the ideal standards for balance and proportion in both life and in art.

Golden rectangle: An ideally proportioned rectangle created from a square through the application of the golden mean.

Granulation: A visual texture produced when paint settles into the grooves of the surface, creating a pattern mimicking the appearance of grains of sand or rice.

Graphite pencils: Thin rods of graphite mixed with clay and baked in a kiln before being encased in wood or some other form of holder

Greek tragedy: The form of tragedy that was developed in ancient Greece, where the disastrous consequences that come to pass at the end of the play are the result of erroneous or misguided actions on the part of the protagonist and the interference of outside sources.

Groundrow: A framed scenic unit placed upstage in front of a cyclorama or a backdrop to hide the bottom and to provide a horizon line, further enhancing the illusion of depth with the sky beyond.

Halftone: A value halfway between the highlight and shadow.

Hand props: Items that are used by the actors in stage business.

Hard edge: A crisp line between a bright highlight and a deep shadow.

Harmony: A pleasing, orderly, or consistent arrangement of parts.

Hatching: Closely spaced, usually parallel lines that are used to create value.

Heavy body acrylics: Thick acrylic paint with a high viscosity.

Helix: A three-dimensional spiral whose path lies along the shape of a cone or cylinder.

Hierarchical scale: Making objects or figures in an image larger in order to visually underscore their rank, status, political, religious, military, or social significance.

High comedy: A subgenre of comedy that relies on intellectual humor, satire, irony, sarcasm, and ridicule to expose and denounce the failings of genteel society.

High key: The range of values from middle gray to white.

Highlight : The area of an object or composition that receives the greatest amount of direct light, or the brightest area of an image related to shadow. Also refers to the brightest amount of reflected light striking an object.

Historical dramas: Dramatic plays that seek to examine a particular time in history or a specific group of people.

Historical style: The aesthetic conventions of a particular time period in history.

Holographic projection system: A device capable of projecting a three-dimensional image.

Horizon line: The point in the distance where the sky and the ground appear to meet.

Hue: The actual name of the color, usually referring to the name of the pigment that is used to create it.

Idealized: Creating a composite version of an object, model, or form based on the idea of perfect mathematical proportions.

Illumination: The amount of light falling on any particular object or surface. Also called illuminance.

Impasto: A very thick, highly textured application of paint to a surface where the marks of the brushes, individual strokes, or painting knives remain visible.

Implied light: The perception of light as it moves around an object.

Implied line: A line that fades, diminishes, or is otherwise deliberately broken as it moves across a composition, positioned in such a way that the viewer's eye automatically connects the individual marks to form a line.

Implied space: Suggesting three-dimensional space on a two-dimensional surface.

Implied texture: Changes in surface textures that are simulated and two-dimensional, which create a convincing visual copy of an actual surface. Also known as visual texture.

Impressionism: As in the art movement of the same name, theatre seeks to capture the impression of a particular moment in time using mood, atmosphere, and feeling.

Inciting incident: The first increase in tension or the point at which the story is taken up.

Informal balance: Another name for asymmetry.

Inherent rhythm: The visual rhythm set up by pattern in a composition.

Inspiration: The source of creativity and innovation.

Instrument: A lighting instrument. Also fixture.

Intarsia: A form of inlaid marquetry that allows for the creation of intricate patterns and textures in wood.

Intensity: The dullness or brightness of a color. Intensity is decreased through neutralizing the color by adding its complement or a neutral gray. Also refers to the strength of a light.

Interference colors: Paint that possesses components that refract light, allowing them to appear differently on various surfaces.

Interpretation: Establishes the broader context for the design you are critiquing. It answers the questions "why did the designer make these choices?" and "what does it mean or express?"

Invented texture: Changes in implied or tactile texture that are created by an individual artist that usually have no relation to a recognizable, real textured surface.

Irregular rhythm: Visual rhythms with unevenly spaced intervals and varied repetitions.

Isolation: Setting an object off by itself.

Isometric perspective: A method of drawing where the goal is to show all measurements of an object to scale no matter how far or close they are to the viewer.

Joists: A series of ladder-like rungs spanning the length of the frame of a platform at regular intervals.

Key light: The main light for an area.

Keystoning: Distortion of a projected image along the horizontal or vertical axis that occurs when the projector is not perpendicular to the projection surface.

Lattice: A pattern created by a fixed arrangement of overlapping or intersecting lines (positive space) combined with open areas (negative space) to produce a basket-weave effect.

Law of prägnanz: A fundamental part of gestalt perception that states that any complex or ambiguous object will be reduced by the viewer's eye into a simple and complete shape.

Layering: Placing colors or media on top of one another for effect, or using multiple sounds to build a new sound or effect.

LCD projector: Liquid crystal display projector.

LED: Light emitting diodes.

Legs: Tall narrow drapes that are hung on either side of the stage, parallel to the proscenium, to mask the offstage areas. Also the name commonly used to refer to the supports for platforms.

Lens: A shaped piece of glass or other transparent material with curved sides used to focus, concentrate or disperse rays of light inside a projector.

Lens shift: Moving the lens of the projector up and down or left and right within the projector housing.

Light board: An electronic device used to program cues and control multiple lighting instruments at once.

Light plot: A technical drawing that conveys all of the information that a lighting crew will need to hang, focus, and circuit the instruments.

Light renderings: Renderings that specifically show the desired effect of the lighting design on the set, costumes, and actors.

Light source: Where the illumination hitting the subject is coming from, such as a lamp or a lighting instrument, ambient or diffuse light from a window, or direct light from the sun.

Lighting designer: The artist that is responsible for illuminating the stage space so that the actors and the environment may be seen.

Line: The path of a moving point traced by an instrument, medium, or tool.

Line quality: The physical characteristics of a line.

Linear fill strokes: Pencil or brushstrokes applied all in the same direction, overlapping, and layered on top of each other to fill in an area with color.

Linear perspective: A drawing method of rendering objects as perceived by the human eye, based on the observations that objects appear to get smaller as they move farther away, and that parallel lines appear to converge in the distance.

Linear rhythm: The movement created by the flow of an individual line or groups of lines in relation to one another.

Linnebach projector: A lens-free projector consisting of a large enclosed black box that utilizes a large transparent glass or mica side with a hand-painted image.

Local value: The relative lightness or darkness of a surface without light falling on it.

Looks: Changes in the overall visual appearance of the design from one static composition to the next.

Looping: Editing a moving image seamlessly back onto itself in order to create a longer sequence.

Low comedy: A subgenre of comedy that emphasizes the use of slapstick and physical humor to elicit laughter.

Low key: The range of values from middle gray to black.

Lumen: A unit of luminous flux, which measures the amount of visible light emitted by a light source.

Luminaire: A lighting instrument or fixture.

Lux: The metric measure of illuminance equal to one lumen per square meter.

Magic lantern: An early type of slide projector that uses a concave mirror behind a light source to direct as much of the light as possible through a rectangular pane of glass that contains a painted or photographic image.

Main garments: The bulk of the character's costume.

Masking: Pieces of hard or soft scenery that are used to hide areas of the theatrical space from the audience's view.

Mass: In three-dimensional artwork, an object that occupies a volume of space. In two-dimensional artwork, mass refers to an object that appears to be three-dimensional, creating the illusion of volume with various techniques.

Matte medium: An acrylic additive that dulls the natural shine of the paint.

Meander: A pattern that follows a winding and turning path.

Media: The plural form of medium.

Medium: The material the artist uses to create a piece or work.

Melodrama: A genre where plot and characters are exaggerated in order to appeal to the emotions of the audience.

Middle ground: The area of a composition between the subject and the background.

MIDI: Musical instrument digital interface.

Midtones: The transitional values between the highlight and the core shadow.

Millinery: The design and making of hats.

Mixed media: Images created using multiple media.

Mixing: Manipulating the various qualities of sound and blending them together to form a balanced finished product. Also refers to the process of fine-tuning a lighting cue, adjusting levels of light, intensity, duration, and movement.

Modeling: Using light to enhance the three-dimensional qualities of the objects that are onstage. Also called sculpting.

Modeling paste: A heavy paste that can be used to create a textured ground for a painting, add texture to a model, as glue for collage, or to create a sculpture.

Modern drama: Realistic drama that focuses on ideas, actual life, emotions, issues of morality, social institutions, and contemporary social problems.

Modern tragedy: Focuses on the ordinary man in extraordinary, tragic circumstances.

Moments: Changes in the overall visual appearance of the design from one static composition to the next.

Monochromatic: A color scheme that is based on one color alone, including the hue and all of its tints, shades, and tones. A monochromatic color scheme may also utilize the color's complement to create vibrant neutral tones.

Monoprint: A printing technique that allows for only one print of the created image by transferring a wet painted image from a smooth surface to a piece of paper.

Motif: Any recurrent visual element.

Motivational light: Light that appears to be coming from realistic or practical sources.

Movement: The changes in light from scene to scene or moment to moment. Also refers to how sound travels through space.

Multidirectional fill strokes: Small overlapping linear marks that move in multiple directions.

Music: Songs or underscoring in a musical format.

Musical comedy: A subgenre of musical theatre characterized by songs, dialogue, and dancing, connected by a light or romantic plot.

Musical plays: A subgenre of musical theatre that focuses on the play itself and everything is subservient to the script.

Musical theatre: A dramatic genre that combines music and songs with spoken dialogue and dance.

Narrative style: Design that tells a story.

Near duplication: When an item is duplicated but details are altered slightly.

Negative space: The space that surrounds the subject in a work and/or the shapes that are defined by the spaces between objects.

Neutral gray: A gray with no chroma, created by mixing only black and white pigments.

Neutral values: Lights and darks created with black and white only, without color. These are also called achromatic values.

Neutralize: Reducing the intensity of a hue by adding gray or its complement, to dull out or cancel the color.

Non-motivational light: Light that focuses on the use of angles, instruments, and color, seeking to create a sense of emotion, a mood, or a particular response to themes presented in the script.

Nonspecific set: A set that provides multiple levels, stairs, doors, ramps, or other scenic elements that permit the playing space to be flexible, allowing for the various scenes to be played out without interrupting the continuity, rhythm, and pace of the dramatic action, which might be adversely affected by the demand for realistic scene changes.

Occult balance: Balance that is created by allowing the background to dominate an image, using a variety of sizes and shapes and creating circular or diagonal movement.

Offstage: Those areas of the theatrical space, usually hidden from the audience, which are not used as acting areas.

Oil-based pencils: Pencils made by combining pigments with oil as a binder.

Onstage: Those areas of the theatrical space, visible to the audience, which will be used for the dramatic action of the play.

Open line: A line or lines that are not connected.

Open palette: A color scheme that uses a large range of colors, often the full range of hues available without restriction.

Open value compositions: An image where the values bleed over the boundaries of shapes into surrounding areas.

Opera: A genre where a script, in the form of a libretto, is combined with a musical score that is performed by musicians and singers in a theatrical setting.

Operetta: A short opera, usually with light, romantic or humorous plot and typically containing some spoken dialogue.

Optical mixing: A visual effect that takes advantage of the eye's ability to combine flecks of closely spaced individual colors, blending them into other colors as if the pigments were actually mixed together.

Organic shape: Shapes that appear as if they were derived from a living process or organism. Also referred to as biomorphic.

Outerwear: Garments worn over the main costume layers often meant to add warmth or protection to the wearer from the elements when outdoors.

Outline: The edge of a two-dimensional object or shape defined by a line of even thickness and weight, which separates it from the surrounding area. Outline does not imply volume or mass, it simply defines shape.

Overlap: Laying one object over another. Overlap provides a visual clue for perceiving depth.

Paint additives: Textural elements that can be added to paint to change its quality, such as sand, glass beads, and gravel.

Paint elevations: Flat renderings of each scenic unit showing the details of the desired paint treatment.

Paint quality: The visual and tactile impression of the surface of paint in a work of art. Paint quality includes both real and implied textures.

Paint skinning: Creating a flexible "skin" of paint that can be cut up and used as a design element by applying a layer of paint to a smooth surface, allowing it to dry, and then peeling it off in one piece.

Painting knives: Metal and plastic hand held knives in various sizes and shapes that can be used in place of brushes to apply paint to a surface.

Pani projector: A large format slide projector consisting of a powerful lamp housed in a casing that uses a large slide as the source image. Pani is a brand name.

Paper collé: A technique whereby papers with different textures are glued on a composition to change the visual and tactile surface quality. It is an artistic precursor of collage.

Pastels: Pigment mixed with filler that is bound together with a small amount of gum or resin.

Pattern: A decorative design often created through repetition.

Pattern drafting: A method of creating a pattern on a flat piece of paper by using measurements to determine the shape, cut, and fit of the garment.

Personal visual library: A combination of a physical library—full of books, magazines, and other items that stimulate your creativity—and an abstract library, creating and nourishing a reservoir of visual information inside your head that you can draw from when needed.

Perspective grid: A network of horizontal and vertical lines drawn on a floorplan in order to approximate the location of planes and points on a drawing.

Picture plane: The flat surface of a two-dimensional work of art.

Pigment: The material that provides the color in paint. Pigments can be made of natural or synthetic materials.

Pitch: The highness or lowness of a tone or sound.

Pixels: Picture elements. The smallest components in a digital image.

Placement: Where individual visual components are located within an image.

Planar shape: A two-dimensional shape that possesses the qualities of a plane.

Plane: A defined area that is two-dimensional, possessing only height and width. Also a compositional format that can be used to create the illusion of three dimensions with advancing and receding elements or techniques.

Plastic value: Value used to create the illusion of mass, space, and volume.

Plastic wrap wash: Using plastic wrap over a wet wash of paint, letting it dry, and then peeling it off to alter the surface texture.

Platform: A rigid frame constructed of wood or metal, mounted on top of a series of supports that add height, and covered with a rigid surface on the top.

Plot: The action that takes place on the stage in front of the audience. A selection and arrangement of scenes from the story to be presented in a theatrical format.

Point symmetry: In this type of symmetry, every point or part of a design has a matching part and the end result is that a pattern or image looks the same right side up as it does upside down.

Pointillism: A technique used to create a range of value by building up layers of dots, points, or dashes.

Polygon: A flat, enclosed shape that is formed by three or more straight lines.

Polyhedron: A three-dimensional object made up of polygons, which serves as the boundary for an interior volume.

Position: Where an object is located within a composition. Position provides a visual clue for perceiving depth.

Positive space: The space occupied by the subject in a composition.

Postmodernism: A style of theatre that removes the idea of make-believe from performance and rejects the idea that universal truths can be accessed or achieved through an artistic representation of life.

Pouncing: Using a balled up cloth or paper to apply paint to the painting surface by pressing it against the paper over and over to create texture.

Power eraser: An electrical eraser.

Practicals: Light fixtures that are included in the set that must turn on and off as part of the action. Also refers to motivated sound cues that emanate from an object on the set.

Preliminary drawings: Drawings made in order to work out the composition of a set, costume, or lighting composition before they actually begin to do a final drawing and render it in another medium. Also called rough sketches or thumbnails.

Preliminary groundplan: An initial groundplan used to map out the locations of the various scenic components.

Preliminary sketches: Initial rough drawings that are used to sketch out your initial design ideas.

Preshow: Music and sound that occurs before the action of the play begins.

Primaries: Colors that are true hues, created from single pigments that have no other colors in them. There are three primary colors in both pigment and light, although they are different.

Primary focus: Creating emphasis on the most important part of the stage picture, making it more prominent.

Primary research sources: Research taken directly from actual historical sources.

Printing: Creating multiple copies of the same image on the painting surface through various means.

Production team: The creative team working on the design of the production, including the designers and the director. Sometimes referred to as the design team.

Progression: The natural movement of cues throughout the design.

Progressive rhythm: When the interchange and variation between one element and the next moves in an identifiable sequence, continuing from one motif to the next.

Projection: The display of an image by a device, such as a projector.

Projections designer: The artist that is responsible for the design and creation of all images, moving and still, that will be projected onto the stage or into the theatrical space. Also known as the multimedia designer.

Projector: A device that projects an image onto a viewing surface.

Proportion: The size relationships between parts of a whole, or between two or more items perceived as a unit.

Proscenium theatre: A theatre space whose main feature is an arch that frames the stage near the front.

Protagonist: The main character in a play.

Proximity: Where objects are placed in relation to one another.

Psychic line: An imaginary line that connects two or more objects in an image and suggests a connection between them, real or implied.

Pure linear strokes: Linear pencil or brush marks that retain their shape, creating visual texture.

Quality: The characteristics or features of sound.

Radial balance: A type of balance that is focused around a central point in an image where the components of the design radiate out from a central axis

Radial design: A design with a central focus, where all other elements lead in or out from the center.

Rake: Angling the stage floor so that it rises in height as it moves away from the audience.

Ramp: A gradual incline leading from one level to another.

Ratio: A quantifiable measurement that explains the relationship between two similar things with respect to how many times the first contains the second.

Realism: The style that seeks to present a truthful representation of real life onstage.

Rear projection: Images and video components that are projected from behind the stage space onto a projection surface.

Rectilinear shape: Shapes that are defined by hard edges, lines, or boundaries that form angles, suggesting the idea of a rectangle.

Reflected highlight: Highlights that are reflected back onto an object from the surface underneath it.

Reflected light: The light that is reflected off the surface underneath an object which then strikes the form underneath the core shadow.

Reflection: When repeated elements are flipped in orientation as if a mirror had been held up to them either horizontally or vertically. Also called flipping.

Regular repetition: When duplicated objects of the same size are arranged in an order with equal spacing.

Regular rhythm: Visual rhythms with evenly spaced intervals and equal repetitions.

Reification: The human tendency to look for pattern and shape to help us see relationships between the individual elements in a composition.

Relative intensity: The comparative relationship between the intensity of two light sources.

Relative value: The lightness or darkness of a color in relation to other colors, compared to the value scale. Also referred to as chromatic value.

Rendering: A final drawing of a theatrical design including all major and minor details, in full color.

Repetition: Repeating one of more of the visual elements in a composition for visual or thematic effect.

Representational: A design that is composed of recognizable images, however distorted or stylized.

Required effects: Those sound effects that are required by the script.

Required music: Music that is required by the script.

Research or response collage: A collection of images, words, and textures collaged together in a digital or two-dimensional format as a response to the play, its story, thematic content, or the ideas it presents.

Resists: Materials that prevent paint from penetrating the painting surface.

Resolution: Another term for denouement. Also refers to the quality of an image.

Retarders: Additives used to extend the drying and working time of acrylics.

Reverberation: An effect created when sound is reflected off of a hard surface, such as floors or walls, and then blends together. It can also be produced through mechanical means.

Rhythm: A connected series of objects that guide the viewer through the image or a succession of marks and motifs that establish a pattern. Also refers to the element of time in sound, and the staging of light movement and transitions from one look to the next.

Rising action: The point of a play where plot, tension, and conflict increase as secondary obstacles are introduced to further complicate the main internal conflict.

Romanticism: A style characterized by the idea that imagination is supreme to reason.

Rotation: Rotating an image around a central axis two or more times. Also called turning or spinning.

Rough sketches: Sketches made in order to work out the composition of a set, costume, or lighting composition before they actually begin to do a final drawing and render it in another medium. Also called preliminary drawings or thumbnails.

Roughs: Another name for preliminary sketches.

Rubbings: Capturing the texture of a surface by placing a piece of paper over it and rubbing a pencil or other drawing medium against the surface to transfer the texture.

Satire: A subgenre of comedy where gallows humor, irony, sarcasm, and ridicule are used to expose and denounce folly and vice.

Saturation: The amount of pigment present in a color. Saturation is altered by diluting the color in some manner, thereby reducing the purity of a hue.

Scale: Size in relation to a standard or "normal" size.

Scenic designer: The artist that is responsible for the design of the stage environment that the actors inhabit.

Screen: A framed scenic unit that provides a surface for the projection of still or moving images on the set.

Scrim: A drop made from an open-weave fabric that appears opaque when lit from the front, but becomes transparent when lit from behind, or if an actor or object behind it is lit.

Scumbling: Applying a very thin coat of opaque paint over a painted surface to produce a soft or dull effect.

Secondary: Colors that are mixed from equal parts of two primary colors. There are three secondary colors.

Secondary focus: Deliberately subordinating parts of the stage to make other areas stand out.

Secondary research sources: Research taken from an intermediary source, rather than directly from a historical source.

Segue: A sound cue that helps to take the audience from one place in a scene to the next.

Selective visibility: Using light to show only what needs to be revealed to the audience.

Semi-neutral: Colors created by mixing complementary colors together in varying degrees to produce hues between the original color and a neutralized, chromatic gray.

Set decoration: Soft goods such as curtains, pillows, throws, wallpaper, and other items of décor.

Set props: Items that are attached to or are an integral part of the set, such as furniture and light fixtures.

Sfumato: A subtle and gradual blending from light to dark values.

Sgraffito: The process of etching into a wet coat of paint over a dry layer to reveal the color below.

Shade: A color mixed with any amount of black, to darken its value.

Shadow: The area of an object or composition that receives the least amount of direct light or a surface where light is blocked. The absence of light.

Shakespearean tragedy: The form of tragedy developed in sixteenth/seventeenth-century theatre, where the protagonist cannot escape their downfall, but the cause is always the actions of men rather than the application of outside forces.

Shape: A two-dimensional, recognizable form defined by line, a shift in color, value, or texture that allows it to stand out from the surrounding area.

Shinbuster: Low side lights, placed on the floor and typically used in dance lighting.

Sidelight: Light cast from a fixture mounted to the side of an object.

Silhouette: The overall shape or outline of an object or costume.

Similarity: How the visual elements in a composition resemble each other.

Simple repetition: When one visual element is repeated without variation.

Simultaneous contrast: An optical phenomena that occurs when two colors of equal intensity, usually complements, are set side by side in a composition. This positioning makes the two colors appear more vibrant, because of the visual contrast between them.

Single element: Using a distinct visual element as a focal point, usually set in isolation from the rest of a composition for a specific effect.

Sketching: Quick, loose drawing meant to record ideas.

Slipstage: A wagon that moves back and forth in a track and has a limited range of motion.

Soft units: Scenic pieces made from fabric, suspended above the stage and typically unframed.

Solvent: A chemical that can dissolve the binders of various media so they may be thinned or manipulated to effect.

Sound cue: The introduction of any aural element into a production.

Sound designer: The artist that is responsible for the design of all of the audio components for a production.

Sound effect: A sound used to convey information or to support the action.

Sound engineer: A sound technician.

Sound reinforcement: Providing mechanical support for the controllable qualities of the actors' voices or the musicians in a production.

Space: The areas around, between, or within the visual elements in a composition. The areas occupied by shapes in a two-dimensional work.

Spattering: Loading a brush with highly diluted paint and quickly running a finger or palette knife across the bristles to disperse a fine spray of color across the surface of your painting surface, producing speckles of color.

Special: A light focused on a precise mark onstage to create focus for a specific moment.

Special effects: Any special need required of a costume.

Specific cues: Required effects that present information.

Spectacle: Lights, costumes, scenic elements, and other special effects.

Sphere: A three-dimensional, round form whose surface consists of a series of points that are all equidistant from the center.

Spill: Light that "spills" over from an instrument.

Splats: Two-dimensional stretch shapes.

Split complement: An analogous color scheme with two additional contrasting colors, directly adjacent to the true complementary color.

Sponging: Applying paint with a sponge to created texture.

Spot effects: Sound cues that have to happen at specific moments in the play and enhance or facilitate the dramatic action.

Staining: When paint pigment seeps into the painting surface and dyes the material.

Stairs: A set of steps leading from one level to another.

Stamping: Printing multiple images on the painting surface through the use of a premade stamp cut into shapes or patterns.

Stellation: The process of lengthening the faces of a polygon or a polyhedron symmetrically to create a new polygon or polyhedron.

Stenciling: Applying paint through a precut template to create an image or texture.

Stippling: Creating texture with very fine drops of paint with a sponge, airbrush, by spattering, or through other means.

Story: Those actions and important events that have occurred before the action of the plot takes place. A complete retelling or recounting of an event or a series of events from which the plot of a play is derived.

Storyboards: A series of small sketches that show a progression of looks from one scene to another which are useful for scenic, lighting, and projection designers to show their design ideas for each scene or cue.

Stretch shapes: Three-dimensional pieces made by stretching fabric over a frame.

Strongly opposed forces: Forces of equal power working against each other.

Style: An overall pervasive quality of an artwork that makes it possible to identify its aesthetic characteristics and discuss them.

Stylization: A departure from absolute realism that emphasizes design over exact representation. In theatre, it is the process of taking a play beyond reality through distortion, exaggeration, or some other stretch of convention, in terms of both performance and design.

Subject matter: The plot, story, circumstances, characters, and other details of a play.

Subplot: Secondary events, actions, and storylines with minor characters that serve to support and develop the main action of the play.

Subordination: Deliberately making parts of a composition less interesting visually in order to focus attention on the emphasized areas of the image.

Subtractive mixing: A model that explains the mixing of pigments. Each additional color reduces the amount of light that can be reflected back to the viewer.

Support: The material on which paint or other media is applied. Also called a surface.

Surface: The material on which paint or other media is applied. Also called a support.

Symbolism: A style of theatre that focuses on and explores the mysteries of life through the rejection of objective reality. It relies on subjective experience, intuition, dreams, and poetry to create a form of theatre that focuses more on the creation of atmosphere than it does on plot and action.

Symmetrical balance: A form of balance where the two halves of a composition on either side of an implied center of gravity are identical or nearly exact.

Symmetry: The quality of similar or exact visual elements that face each other in a design and the manner in which they repeat around or across an axis.

Tabs: Long, narrow drapes hung side by side and perpendicular to the proscenium to mask the wings.

Tactile: Something that can be perceived through the sense of touch, or invokes the sense of touch.

Teaser: A cloth-covered hard horizontal masking unit placed directly behind the proscenium with a pair of tormentors in order to create a small, false portal, thereby reducing the size of the opening.

Technical drawings: Highly detailed drawings, usually in scale, that serve as blueprints for the construction of the scenery, properties, the hanging and focus of lighting instruments, which may provide costume construction details, rigging specifications, or other information.

Tempo: The speed of a sound cue or music.

Tertiary: Colors that are created by mixing a secondary color with its adjacent primary color. Tertiary colors are also referred to as intermediate colors.

Tessellation: A repetitive pattern that fills a two-dimensional surface with plane figures, shapes, or motifs that do not overlap and also have no gaps between them.

Texture: The tactical and visual quality of a surface.

Theatrical design: The art of creating and composing the visual and aural elements that shape a performance space.

Theatrical designer: An artist who creates and organizes one or more aspects of the aural and visual components of a theatrical production.

Thematic unity: Another term for conceptual unity.

Thought: Thematic content and ideas.

Three unities: Time, place, and action.

Throw ratio: The distance from the center of a projector's lens to the projection surface divided by the width of the image being projected. The ratio itself is dimensionless.

Thrust theatre: A theatre space where the stage extends out into the audience and the seating surrounds the playing area on three sides.

Thumbnails: Another name for preliminary sketches.

Tiling: A tessellation created by a regular, repeating geometric pattern. Also refers to using multiple projectors to build a large image by arranging parts of the image in a tiled formation on the projection surface.

Timbre: The overall tone of a sound, comparable to color, that distinguishes one sound from another.

Timing: The pacing of cues.

Tint: A color mixed with any amount of white, to lighten its value.

Tissue paper and paint: An assemblage technique that combines paint and light paper, embedding it in the paint to create texture.

To scale: When an object is created as an exact replica or model of another and the proportions are reduced in size by a specific ratio.

Tone: A color mixed with a neutral gray or its complement, in order to neutralize the color.

Tormentor: A cloth-covered hard vertical masking unit placed directly behind the proscenium with a teaser in order to create a small, false portal, thereby reducing the size of the opening.

Tortillion: A paper stump used to blend drawing media on a surface.

Traditional structure: A linear plot that focuses on a climax, with a clear beginning, middle, and end.

Tragedy: A type of drama that deals with serious or somber themes.

Tragicomedy: A genre that combines traditional elements of both comedy and tragedy into one play.

Transitional sounds: Sound effects and music that are used to assist the transitions between scenes.

Translation: When visual elements are moved horizontally along an axis in order to repeat. Also called sliding.

Trompe l'oeil: A technique that uses realistic imagery to convincingly paint the illusion of three-dimensional space; where objects are depicted in a highly realistic manner, as if they were photographed.

Undergarments: Costume items generally worn underneath everything else, close to the actor's skin.

Underscoring: The use of music in a scene, playing quietly underneath the dialogue or the visual elements, to establish mood, tone, or theme.

Uniform connectedness: When objects in a design share uniform visual characteristics.

Unity: A sense of oneness or organization that holds a composition together and makes all the elements work together.

Value: The amount of light and dark present in a work, independent of color. Also refers to the lightness or darkness of a color.

Value pattern: Organized areas of light and dark within an image.

Value scale: A visual tool that shows the graduated tonal values between black and white, usually containing nine to 12 steps between them.

Vanishing point: The point where parallel lines appear to converge on the horizon line.

Variety: Visual difference and diversity, which creates interest.

Video wall: A wall made up of video display units, such as LCD panels.

Viscosity: The thickness of the paint emulsion.

Visibility: The principle of revealing an object using light.

Visual rhythm: The movement created by the repetition of objects in an image.

Visual unity: Unity that is created by a harmonious arrangement of the visual elements of a composition.

Visual weight: The apparent heaviness or lightness of the forms arranged in a composition, based on how insistently they draw our eyes.

Voiceovers: Disembodied speech, either live or prerecorded, that is used to convey information or fulfill dramatic action.

Void: A large, open space within a composition that serves as a dynamic design element.

Volume: A defined, measurable amount of three-dimensional space. Also refers to the loudness or softness of sound or music.

Volute: A two-dimensional spiral whose path exists on one flat planar surface.

Vomitories: Aisles that extend from the stage through the seating area of a theatre that can be used as entrances and exits.

Wagon: A platform fitted with casters on the bottom rather than supports so that it might be moved on the stage.

Warm colors: Hues that are perceived to be warm in temperature.

Wash: A thin, even coat of color. Also refers to light that fills a large area of the stage.

Water-based pencils: Pencils made of pigment combined with water and a water soluble gum as a binder.

Wave: In art and design, the path that is generated by a disturbance or vibration through a medium and the form and shape it takes.

Wax-based pencils: Pencils made by combining pigments with wax binders.

Wax bloom: A phenomenon where wax rises to the surface of a colored pencil drawing, where it forms a gray, hazy film that dulls the color.

Wet in wet: Applying thinned paint to a wet surface.

White model: A scale model of the set created in white card stock or foam core that shows the basic silhouette without the painted details of the design.

Wings: The backstage area on either side of a proscenium stage, unseen by audience. Also refers to flat scenery that projects into the stage space from the side.

Zoom: To smoothly change from a long shot to a close up or vice versa.

BIBLIOGRAPHY

Abling, Bina. *Marker Rendering for Fashion, Accessories, and Home Fashions*. New York: Fairchild Publications, 2006.

Adams, Laurie. *The Making and Meaning of Art*. Upper Saddle River, NJ: Pearson, 2006.

Anderson, Barbara, and Cletus Anderson. *Costume Design*, 2nd edition. New York: Holt, Rinehart and Winston, 1998.

Auckland, George, and Mervyn Heard. "A History Of The Magic Lantern." Magic Lantern Society, 2007 (Web, accessed February 2014).

Baird, Cecile. *Painting Light with Colored Pencil*. Cincinnati, OH: North Light, 2005.

Ball, David. *Backwards and Forwards: A Technical Manual for Reading Plays*. Carbondale: Southern Illinois University Press, 1983.

Barbour, David. "The Prevalence of Projections." Theatre Communications Group, December 2011 (Web, accessed February 2014).

Bareiss, Seth, and David Annal. "Tessellations—M. C. Escher and How to Make Your Own Tessellation Art." 30 October 2003 (Web, accessed October 2013).

Bishop, Philip E. *Adventures in the Human Spirit*. Englewood Cliffs, NJ: Prentice Hall, 1994.

Box, Richard. *Drawing for the Terrified! A Complete Course for Beginners*. Newton Abbot, Devon: David & Charles, 1997.

Boyle, Katherine. "Creating a Virtual World Onstage." *The Washington Post*, 13 January 2013 (Web, accessed March 2014).

Brady, Patti. *Rethinking Acrylic: Radical Solutions for Exploiting the World's Most Versatile Medium*. Cincinnati, OH: North Light, 2008.

Brewster, Karen, and Melissa Shafer. *Fundamentals of Theatrical Design*. New York: Allworth, 2011.

Bruck, Victoria. *Exploring the Basics of Drawing*. Australia: Thomson-Delmar Learning, 2005.

"Business Units." Visual Display Solutions, Christie Digital Systems, USA, n.d. (Web, accessed March 2014).

Corson, Richard. *Stage Makeup*, 10th edition. Englewood Cliffs, NJ: Prentice Hall, 1990.

Cunningham, Rebecca. *The Magic Garment: Principles of Costume Design*, 2nd edition. Long Grove: Waveland, 2009.

Delahunt, Michael. "ArtLex Art Dictionary." ArtLex Art Dictionary, August 1996 (Web, accessed July 2013).

Di Benedetto, Stephen. *An Introduction to Theatre Design*. London: Routledge, 2012.

Donnelly, Cormac, Doron Reizes, and Erika Basnicki. "Designing Sound." Miguel Isaza, 2009 (Web, accessed December 2013).

Dorbian, Iris. "Project Yourself: What Does the Predominance of Projections Augur for Set Design?" Studio Live Design, 1 March 2008 (Web, accessed March 2014).

Dunham, Richard. *Stage Lighting: Fundamentals and Applications*. Boston: Allyn & Bacon, 2011.

Ebrahimian, Babak A. *Sculpting Space in the Theater: Conversations with the Top Set, Light and Costume Designers*. Burlington, MA: Focal, 2006.

Eddy, Michael S. "Lucky Guy Projection, Parts 1, 2, and 3." *Live Design Magazine*, 18 April 2013 (Web, accessed February 2014).

Edwards, Betty. *The New Drawing on the Right Side of the Brain*, 4th edition. New York: Jeremy P. Tarcher/Putnam, 2010.

Evans, Poppy, and Mark Thomas. *Exploring the Elements of Design*. Clifton Park, NY: Thomson/Delmar Learning, 2008.

Fleishman, Michael. *Exploring Illustration*. Australia: Thomson-Delmar Learning, 2004.

Frank, Patrick, and Duane Preble. *Prebles' Artforms: An Introduction to the Visual Arts*, 10th edition. Upper Saddle River, NJ: Pearson Prentice Hall, 2010.

Gillette, J. Michael. *Theatrical Design and Production: An Introduction to Scene Design and Construction, Lighting, Sound, Costume, and Makeup*, 7th edition. Dubuque, IA: McGraw-Hill Companies, 2012.

Goodwin, John. *British Theatre Design: The Modern Age*. New York: St. Martin's, 2000.

Grode, Eric. "The World of a Broadway Projection Designer." *TDF Stages: A Theatre Magazine*, n.d. (Web, accessed March 2014).

Hartt, Frederick. *History of Italian Renaissance Art*, 3rd edition. London: Thames & Hudson, 1988.

Hogarth, Burne. *Dynamic Figure Drawing*. New York: Watson-Guptill, 1996.

"In the Wings—Projection Designer—October, 2009." In The Wings Video, American Theatre Wing, n.d. (Web, accessed March 2014).

Ingham, Rosemary. *From Page to Stage: How Theatre Designers Make Connections between Scripts and Images*. Portsmouth, NH: Heinemann, 1998.

Ingham, Rosemary, and Liz Covey. *The Costume Designer's Handbook: A Complete Guide for Amateur and Professional Costume Designers*. Portsmouth, NH: Heinemann, 1992.

Johnson, Cathy. *Creating Textures in Watercolor: Paints & Textures from Glass to Fur*. Cincinnati, OH: North Light, 2003.

"Julie Taymor's *A Midsummer Night's Dream* with Projection Support from WorldStage." *Live Design Magazine*, 31 January 2014 (Web, accessed March 2014).

Kaye, Deena, and James LeBrecht. *Sound and Music for the Theatre: The Art and Technique of Design*, 3rd edition. Amsterdam: Elsevier, 2009.

McDaniel, Richard. *The Drawing Book: Materials and Techniques for Today's Artist*. New York: Watson-Guptill Publications, 1995.

McElroy, Steven. "From Afterthought to Essential." *The New York Times*, 17 May 2008 (Web, accessed March 2014).

Metzger, Philip W. *Perspective without Pain*. Cincinnati, OH: North Light, 1992.

Monahan, Patricia, Patricia Seligman, and Wendy Clouse. *Art School: A Complete Painters Course*. London: Hamlyn, 2000.

Morgan, Harry. *Perspective Drawing for the Theatre*. New York: Drama Book Specialists, 1979.

Ortel, Sven. "Projctn—a Projection Design Resource." (Web, accessed March 2014).

Ostroff, Boyd. "Using Video on the Stage by Boyd Ostroff." The Digital Video Information Network, 28 March 2007 (Web, accessed March 2014).

Pecktal, Lynn. *Designing and Painting for the Theatre*. New York: Holt, Rinehart and Winston, 1975.

Pecktal, Lynn. *Costume Design: Techniques of Modern Masters*. New York: Back Stage, 1993.

Pentak, Stephen, Richard Roth, and David A. Lauer. *Design Basics*, 8th edition. Boston, MA: Wadsworth, Cengage Learning, 2013.

Powell, Brittany. "Non-Rectilinear Projection Design For Live." Thesis, University of Florida, 2011.

"Projecting the Future: Projection is One Word that Sums up the Future of Theatrical Design." Studio Live Design, n.d. (Web, March 2014).

"Projector Brightness." Explaining Brightness and ANSI Lumens, Bamboo AV, n.d. (Web, accessed March 2014).

Quiller, Stephen. *Color Choices*. New York: Watson-Guptill, 2002.

Reyner, Nancy. *Acrylic Revolution: New Tricks & Techniques for Working with the World's Most Versatile Medium*. Cincinnati, OH: North Light, 2007.

Rowe, Clare P. *Drawing & Rendering for Theatre: A Practical Course for Scenic, Costume, and Lighting Designers*. Amsterdam: Focal, 2007.

Saw, James T. "Design Notes." Palomar Community College, 2003 (Web, accessed February 2013).

Sayre, Henry M. *A World of Art*, 4th edition. Upper Saddle River, NJ: Prentice Hall, 2000.

Sheaks, Barclay. *The Acrylics Book: Materials and Techniques for Today's Artist*. New York: Watson-Guptill, 1996.

Shelley, Steven. *A Practical Guide to Stage Lighting*, 3rd edition. New York: Focal, 2013.

Smith, Mike. "Welcome to The Magic Lantern Society." The Magic Lantern Society, n.d. (Web, accessed March 2014).

Sugg, Jeff. "American Theatre Wing—In the Wings—Projection Designer." In the Wings Video, American Theatre Wing, October 2009 (Web, accessed February 2014).

Tan, Huaixiang. *Character Costume Figure Drawing: Step-by-Step Drawing Methods for Theatre Costume Designers*, 2nd edition. Amsterdam: Elsevier/Focal, 2010.

"The Chromotrope or Artificial Fireworks # 1." Dick Balzer's Website: Chromotrope, n.d. (Web, accessed March 2014).

Thomas, James. *Script Analysis for Actors, Directors, and Designers*, 5th edition. Boston: Focal, 2013.

"Throw Ratios and Viewing Distances." ADTECH Systems and the Projector Pros, n.d. (Web, accessed March 2014).

"What is a Camera Obscura?" Bright Bytes Studio, n.d. (Web, accessed February 2014).

Williams, Bill. "Part 1: An Introduction to Stage Lighting, Bill Williams." *Stage Lighting*, 1997. (Web, accessed December 2013).

Wilson, Edwin, and Alvin Goldfarb. *Theatre: The Lively Art*. Boston: McGraw-Hill, 2010.

Wolf, R. Craig., and Dick Block. *Scene Design and Stage Lighting*, 10th edition. Boston: Wadsworth Cengage Learning, 2014.

Wolf, Rachel Rubin. *The Acrylic Painter's Book of Styles & Techniques*. Cincinnati, OH: North Light, 1997.

Woodbridge, Patricia, and Hal Tiné. *Designer Drafting and Visualizing for the Entertainment World*, 2nd edition. Burlington, MA: Focal, 2013.

Woods, Michael. *Drawing Basics: An Artist's Guide to Mastering the Medium*. New York: Watson-Guptill Publications, 2000.

INDEX

Note: page numbers in italics refer to figures; page numbers in bold refer to tables